PLAYS BY RENAISSANCE AND RESTORATION DRAMATISTS
General Editor: Graham Storey

WYCHERLEY

VOLUMES IN THIS SERIES

PUBLISHED

The plays of Cyril Tourneur, edited by George Parfitt: *The Revenger's Tragedy; The Atheist's Tragedy*

The selected plays of Philip Massinger, edited by Colin Gibson: *The Duke of Milan; The Roman Actor; A New Way to Pay Old Debts; The City Madam*

The selected plays of Thomas Middleton, edited by David L. Frost: *A Mad World, My Masters; A Chaste Maid in Cheapside; Women Beware Women; The Changeling* (with William Rowley)

FORTHCOMING

The selected plays of John Webster, edited by Inga-Stina Ewbank and Jonathan Dollimore: *The White Devil; The Devil's Law Case; The Duchess of Malfi*

The plays of George Etherege, edited by Michael Cordner: *The Man of Mode; She Would if She Could; The Comical Revenge*

The selected plays of Ben Jonson, edited by Johanna Procter: *Sejanus; Epicoene*, or *The Silent Woman; Volpone; The Alchemist; Bartholomew Fair*

The selected plays of John Marston, edited by M.D. Jackson and Michael Neil: *Antonio and Mellida; Antonio's Revenge; The Malcontent; The Dutch Courtezan; Sophonisba*

The selected plays of John Ford, edited by Colin Gibson: *'Tis Pity She's a Whore; The Broken Heart; Perkin Warbeck*

THE PLAYS OF WILLIAM WYCHERLEY

Love in a Wood

The Gentleman Dancing-Master

The Country Wife

The Plain-Dealer

EDITED BY
PETER HOLLAND
University Assistant Lecturer in English, and Fellow of Trinity Hall, Cambridge

CAMBRIDGE UNIVERSITY PRESS
CAMBRIDGE
LONDON NEW YORK NEW ROCHELLE
MELBOURNE SYDNEY

Published by the Press Syndicate of the University of Cambridge
The Pitt Building, Trumpington Street, Cambridge CB2 1RP
32 East 57th Street, New York, NY 10022, USA
296 Beaconsfield Parade, Middle Park, Melbourne 3206, Australia

First published 1981

Printed in Great Britain at the University Press, Cambridge

British Library Cataloguing in Publication Data

Wycherley, William
The plays of William Wycherley. – (Plays by Renaissance and Restoration dramatists).
I. Title II. Holland, Peter III. Series
822′.4 PR 3770 80-41199
ISBN 0 521 23250 3 hard covers
ISBN 0 521 29880 6 paperback

PREFACE TO THE SERIES

This series provides the best plays (in some cases, the complete plays) of the major English Renaissance and Restoration dramatists, in fully-annotated, modern-spelling texts, soundly edited by scholars in the field.

The introductory matter in each volume is factual and historical rather than critical: it includes, where appropriate, a brief biography of the playwright, a list of his works with dates of plays' first performances, the reasons for the volume editor's choice of plays, a short critical biography and a note on the texts used. An introductory note to each play then gives the source material, a short stage-history, and details of the individual editions of that play. Facsimiles of the original or early title-pages are given.

Annotation is of three types. Short notes at the foot of the page are designed to gloss the text or enlarge on its literary, historical or social allusions. At the end of the volume, in two separate appendices, editors have added more substantial explanatory notes and have commented on textual variants.

The volumes are intended for anyone interested in English drama in two of its richest periods, but they will prove especially useful to students at all levels who want to enjoy and explore the best work of these dramatists.

Graham Storey

CONTENTS

INTRODUCTION

Life

William Wycherley was born in March 1641. He was the eldest son of Daniel Wycherley, a fairly wealthy but obsessively litigious man, adept at making money and keeping it; at this time Daniel was steward to the Marquess of Winchester. William was brought up at Clive Hall, Shropshire, the Wycherley family home for two centuries, and educated at home by his father. When Wycherley was about fifteen, his father sent him to France, where he became part of the circle at Angoulême surrounding the brilliant Julie-Lucine d'Angennes, Madame de Montausier, head of one of the greatest of the *salons*. Intriguingly, her husband has traditionally been held as the source for Alceste, the central character in Molière's *Le Misanthrope*, the source of Wycherley's last play, *The Plain-Dealer*. At this time, as Madame de Montausier's protégé, Wycherley was converted to Catholicism.

Wycherley returned to England in 1659 and entered the Inner Temple in October. His father had done so a year earlier in pursuit of a new career as a barrister and it is more probable that Wycherley was being groomed for a similar career than that he was using the Inns of Court as the usual end of a fashionable gentleman's education. In July 1660, Wycherley entered Queen's College, Oxford as a fellow-commoner. He did not stay in Oxford long and did not matriculate, though he was reconverted to Protestantism by the Provost of Queen's. For the next few years our knowledge of Wycherley is fragmentary. He was in Ireland with the Earl of Arran's regiment of guards in 1662 and he may have been the Wycherley who accompanied Sir Richard Fanshawe, ambassador to the Spanish court, in 1664, reaching Madrid in June and returning to London in February 1665. In a poem Wycherley claimed to have fought in a sea-fight and he probably served in the second Dutch War in 1665, including the defeat of the Dutch fleet at the Battle of Harwich.

In 1669, Wycherley published anonymously his first work, a burlesque parody of the story of Hero and Leander. Two years later, in 1671, with the production of his first play, *Love in a Wood*, Wycherley acquired both a literary reputation and a famous mistress, the Duchess of Cleveland (see additional note, p. 490). He also gained the friendship of another of his mistress's suitors, the Duke of Buckingham. *The Gentleman Dancing-Master*, Wycherley's next play, appeared early in 1672.

By this time he was one of Buckingham's equerries and, in June, was made Captain-Lieutenant in the Duke's own company; he was probably on active service in the winter of 1673 and in February 1674 was appointed Captain, a commission he resigned after one week. In a less military vein, a traditional anecdote recounts how Wycherley tried to use his friendship with Buckingham to help Samuel Butler, who was desperately impoverished; the attempt failed when Buckingham left in pursuit of some passing prostitutes. In 1677, when Buckingham was imprisoned in the Tower, Wycherley, with some courage, wrote a verse-letter of support.

With *The Country Wife* and *The Plain-Dealer*, Wycherley established his position as the foremost satirical playwright of his time, praised by Dryden and others for his power and wit. But the success of *The Plain-Dealer* (1676), a success that he owed to his friends' support for the play, is the highpoint of Wycherley's career. From then on, his life is marked by a succession of illnesses and disastrous mistakes. He did not write another play.

In 1677 Wycherley was seriously ill with a fever which left his health ruined and his memory permanently impaired. He was visited in his lodgings by the King – so highly was he esteemed – and Charles gave him £500 to pay for a recuperative holiday abroad. In addition, in 1679, Charles made Wycherley tutor to one of his bastards, the Duke of Richmond, at a salary of £1500 a year. But, though John Dennis placed the incident a year later, it appears that in the spring of 1678 Wycherley met by chance the Countess of Drogheda while in Tunbridge Wells. They fell in love at once and, when Wycherley left for Montpellier in the summer, the Countess sent her servant after him with a gold ring. In June 1679 the Earl of Drogheda died and by October Wycherley had married his countess. The King was furious at the news of the secret marriage and Wycherley lost all favour at court.

The traditional anecdotal picture, supported by more reliable evidence, shows Wycherley's wife as a passionate and frequently hysterical woman, jealous in the extreme. As John Dennis relates, 'their lodgings were in Bow Street, Covent Garden, over against the Cock, whither if he at any time went with his friends, he was obliged to leave the windows open, that the lady might see there was no woman in company, or she would be immediately in a downright raving condition'. Even more disastrous for the always indebted writer was the revelation that his aristocratic wife was not wealthy: the Earl of Drogheda's will was contested by his family and she was already in debt to a number of people, including her maid. When she died, probably in 1685, her will was contested by her relations, and Wycherley found himself involved in another long and expensive lawsuit and surrounded by ever-increasing debts. Though it was said that Wycherley was in prison for seven years, he seems to have managed to evade arrest until October 1685, when he was committed to the Fleet Prison for non-payment of debts amounting to over £1500. Wycherley wrote for help to his friend, the Earl of Mulgrave, and it was probably at Mulgrave's instigation that *The Plain-Dealer* was performed at court before the new king, James II, on 14 December 1685. James's interest in the author's whereabouts led eventually to Wycherley's release from the Fleet in April 1686 with a present of £500 and an annual pension of £200. But Wycherley failed to declare the full extent of his debts, which were eventually settled by his father.

When James fled in 1688 Wycherley lost his pension and, from then on, spent much of his time at Clive Hall. In 1697 Daniel Wycherley died, leaving his estate tied up in such a way that his son could not ruin it; frightened of Wycherley's careless way with money, Daniel took the normal course of action and limited his son's tenure of the estate to a life tenancy, thereby making it impossible for Wycherley to raise money on the estate.

Eight years after it had been announced for publication, Wycherley's *Miscellany Poems* was published in 1704; a massive folio volume, it was prefaced by a bitter attack on the prejudice of his critics, but the poems themselves are largely mediocre, weak verse, rarely showing his earlier satiric bite. The melancholy frontispiece to the book is an engraving taken from Lely's painting of Wycherley at 28, with a sad Vergilian motto underneath, 'quantum mutatus ab illo' – 'how changed from that'. At about this time Wycherley became friends with the young Alexander Pope. Pope cultivated the friendship with the old man as a means of access to the 'literary scene' of which Wycherley was still part, presiding over the group of wits at Will's coffeehouse. Pope helped Wycherley revise his poems. When Wycherley's *Posthumous Works* were published in 1728, edited by Theobald, Pope instantly produced a rival volume, disguised as volume two, correcting Theobald's errors and publishing for the first time his correspondence with Wycherley.

On 20 December 1715 Wycherley married for the second time and died, eleven days later, on New Year's Eve. If his first marriage had been a faintly comic matter of fortune-hunting thwarted, his second was a black and tragic farce. Ill, feeble, with a weak mind, Wycherley was bullied and victimised, terrorised with the prospect of a pauper's burial, by his cousin, Thomas Shrimpton; eventually he gave in and married a supposed heiress, Elizabeth Jackson, who was in fact Shrimpton's mistress. Wycherley barely knew what was happening to him in the bizarre marriage service. He was buried at St Paul's Church, Covent Garden.

Works

All dates are those of first publication

Hero and Leander in Burlesque	1669
Love in a Wood	1672
The Gentleman Dancing-Master	1673
The Country Wife	1675
The Plain-Dealer	1677
Epistles to the King and Duke	1682
Prologue to Catherine Trotter's *Agnes de Castro*	1696
'The Answer' (verse letter to Shadwell), in *Poems on Affairs of State*, vol. 3	1698
Miscellany Poems	1704
On His Grace the Duke of Marlborough	1707
'To My Friend Mr Pope on his Pastorals', in *Poetical Miscellanies*, part 6	1709
Posthumous Works, vol. 1 (edited by Theobald)	1728
Posthumous Works, 'vol. 2' (edited by Pope)	1729

The text of this edition

The text of Wycherley's plays does not present many problems. In each case the first edition is the only textually significant one and I have relied on it as copy-text for each play. Professor Friedman argues that Q2 of *The Plain-Dealer* contains corrections by Wycherley but I remain unconvinced. I have recorded the very few substantive emendations to the copy-text in the notes; I have not recorded subsequent variations since, given that the later editions have no authority, such details are best left to full-scale old-spelling editions. I must here record my very substantial debt to all previous editors of Wycherley; I have pillaged their work unashamedly and, rather than giving specific attributions in each and every note, I have opted to indicate my gratitude here in the hope that none will feel offended.

In modernising Wycherley, the only significant problem, apart from Monsieur's French (discussed in the Textual Note to *The Gentleman Dancing-Master*), is punctuation. Wycherley writes, and the compositors reflect, enormous free-flowing paragraphs in which the syntax is often vague. It is always easy to speak Wycherley's lines in the theatre but often difficult to read them off the page. In repunctuating I have tried to keep such punctuation as may reflect stage pauses but to convert semi-colons to full stops where the pressures of modern practice seemed to demand it. I do not think I have distorted the meaning of the text by adopting this method. The stage directions are Wycherley's unless enclosed by square brackets.

A select bibliography

Editions

The only complete modern edition of Wycherley is edited by Montague Summers in four volumes (London: Nonesuch Press, 1924). This is less eccentric than some of Summers's other work on Restoration drama but the text is far from reliable. In any case, this is a comparatively rare limited edition. W.C. Ward edited a modernised text of the plays for the Mermaid series in 1888, with a few notes and a clutch of errors. Much more important are the two recent old-spelling editions: Gerald Weales's (New York: Doubleday Anchor, 1966) is a delightful mine of useful and witty annotation; Arthur Friedman's (Oxford: Clarendon Press, 1979) will undoubtedly become the standard text of Wycherley. There is a fine thesis-edition of *Love in a Wood* and *The Gentleman Dancing-Master*, edited by D.S. Rodes (Stanford University, 1968). G.B. Churchill's edition of *The Country Wife* and *The Plain-Dealer* (Boston: D.C. Heath, Belles Lettres Series, 1924) is still useful.

Biography

There is no good modern biography of Wycherley. Willard Connely's attempt, *Brawny Wycherley* (New York: Scribner's, 1930) is flowery and over-extended. In addition to the material in Summers's and Friedman's editions and in K.M. Rogers's book (see below), the following articles explore odd parts of

Wycherley's life: W.G. Hargest and E. Boswell revealed the truth about 'Wycherley and the Countess of Drogheda' (*T.L.S.*, 21 November 1929, p. 960; 28 November 1929, pp. 1001–2); W.R. Chadwick showed how long Wycherley had been in the Fleet Prison in 'Wycherley: the seven lean years' (*Notes and Queries*, 216 (1971), 30–4); H.P. Vincent found the lawsuit that revealed Shrimpton's machinations in 'The death of William Wycherley' (*Harvard Studies and Notes in Philology and Literature*, 15 (1933), 219–42). Since so much of Wycherley's biography is dependent on early anecdotes, it is well worth reading Charles Gildon's *Memoirs of the Life of Wycherley* (1718) and John Dennis's letter containing 'Some Remarkable Passages of Mr Wycherley's Life' (1720, reprinted in J. Dennis, *The Critical Works*, ed. E.N. Hooker (Baltimore: Johns Hopkins Press, 1939–43)).

Criticism

Books

There have been three full-length modern studies of Wycherley's work. K.M. Rogers's *William Wycherley* (New York: Twayne, 1972) tried to cover the biography and all the works in a small space and is plagued by the conviction that *The Plain-Dealer* is a failure. R. Zimbardo's *Wycherley's Drama* (New Haven: Yale University Press, 1965) pushes too hard at the argument that each play derives from formal verse satire and runs into problems in trying to maintain that *Love in a Wood* is an extended commentary on Fletcher's *The Faithful Shepherdess* and *The Country Wife* derived from Juvenal's Sixth Satire. Nonetheless its sustained emphasis on Wycherley's satire is admirable. The best of the three is W.R. Chadwick's *The Four Plays of William Wycherley* (The Hague: Mouton, 1975), closely argued, perceptive and well-written.

Articles

The best introduction to Wycherley's plays is Anne Righter's 'William Wycherley', in *Restoration Theatre* (London: Edward Arnold, Stratford-upon-Avon Studies 6, ed. J.R. Brown and B. Harris, 1965), which sets Wycherley firmly in his context. Norman Holland, in *The First Modern Comedies* (Cambridge, Mass.: Harvard University Press, 1959) concentrates on Wycherley's use of language and imagery in the plays, with excellent results. P.F. Vernon has produced a useful brief survey in *William Wycherley* (London: Longman, British Writers and Their Work, 1965). C.S. Matlack has shown how Wycherley used contemporary casting for one particular end in 'Parody and burlesque of heroic ideals in Wycherley's comedies' (*Papers on Language and Literature*, 8 (1972), 273–86). T.W. Craik studied 'Some aspects of satire in Wycherley's plays' (*English Studies*, 41 (1960), 168–79).

Other studies are most conveniently explored play by play. The two earlier plays have received comparatively little attention, though there is a good study of 'Theme and structure in Wycherley's *Love in a Wood*' by E.S. Rump (*English Studies*, 54 (1973), 326–33) and P.F. Vernon has examined the link to Calderón, first identified by J.U. Rundle, in 'Wycherley's first comedy and its Spanish source' (*Comparative Literature*, 18 (1966), 132–44).

The list of articles on *The Country Wife* is long and rapidly increasing. Ronald Berman has studied 'The ethic of *The Country Wife*' (*Texas Studies in Literature and Language*, 9 (1967), 47–55). Thematic studies are represented by D.M. Vieth's 'Wycherley's *The Country Wife*: an anatomy of masculinity' (*Papers on Language and Literature*, 2 (1966), 335–50) and Vieth's line of approach was taken further by W. Freedman who found 'Impotence and self-destruction in *The Country Wife*' (*English Studies*, 53 (1972), 421–31). There have been the inevitable attempts to find one external model which will somehow provide an instant explanation of the play: A. Kaufman has tried 'Wycherley's *The Country Wife* and the Don Juan character' (*Eighteenth Century Studies*, 9 (1975), 216–31); C.A. Hallett has tried to find 'The Hobbesian substructure of *The Country Wife*' (*Papers on Language and Literature*, 9 (1973), 380–95); G. Beauchamp turned to Machiavelli in 'The amorous Machiavellism of *The Country Wife*' (*Comparative Drama*, 11 (1977), 316–30). More sensibly, P. Malekin started from Wycherley's theatrical technique in 'Wycherley's dramatic skills and the interpretation of *The Country Wife*' (*Durham University Journal*, n.s. 31 (1969), 32–40).

Many of the attempts to cope with *The Plain-Dealer* have tried to place Manly: A.H. Chorney identified him as a humours character in 'Wycherley's Manly reinterpreted' (in *Essays Critical and Historical Dedicated to Lily B. Campbell* (Berkeley: University of California Press, 1950); A.M. Friedson underplays his importance by comparison with Alceste in 'Wycherley and Molière: satirical point of view in *The Plain-Dealer*' (*Modern Philology*, 64 (1967), 189–97); Ian Donaldson has a brilliant approach to the audience's differing responses to Manly as satirist in *The World Upside Down* (Oxford: Clarendon Press, 1970). B.E. McCarthy has pursued Wycherley's changing attitude towards wit, culminating in this play, in 'Wycherley's *The Plain-Dealer* and the limits of wit' (*English Miscellany*, 22 (1971), 47–92). I have approached the disorienting effects of the play by starting from the original production in *The Ornament of Action* (Cambridge University Press, 1979). P.G. Adams has amusingly shown that critics cannot make up their minds about 'What happened in Olivia's bedroom' (in T.A. Kirby ed., *Essays in Honor of Esmond Linworth Marilla* (Baton Rouge: Louisiana State University Press, 1970)).

Last, but by no means least, E.L. Avery has charted the stage history of Wycherley's plays up to the end of the eighteenth century in three articles in *Research Studies*: '*The Country Wife* in the eighteenth century' (10 (1942), 141–72), '*The Plain-Dealer* in the eighteenth century' (11 (1943), 234–56), and 'The reputation of Wycherley's comedies as stage plays in the eighteenth century' (12 (1944), 131–54).

After this introduction was completed, B.E. McCarthy's *William Wycherley: A Biography* (Athens, Ohio: Ohio University Press, 1979) appeared. This is a useful, if solemn, account of the facts of Wycherley's life and I have made two small corrections in the light of its new information. Its only major error is in misdating Wycherley's birth to May 1641; he was baptised at Whitchurch, Hampshire, on 8 April 1641.

Love in a Wood,

OR,

St James's Park.

A

COMEDY,

As it is Acted at the Theatre Royal, by his Majesties Servants.

Written by Mr *WYCHERLEY*.

—*Excludit sanos helicone poetas*
Democritus;— Horat.

LONDON,
Printed by *J. M.* for *H. Herringman*, at the Sign of the *Blew Anchor*, in the Lower-Walk of the New Exchange. 1672.

Title-page of the 1672 Quarto of *Love in a Wood*, reproduced by permission of the University Library, Cambridge.

Motto
Horace, *Ars Poetica*, 296–7:
'Democritus excludes sane poets from Helicon'

Title
'in a wood' means 'confused, perplexed'

INTRODUCTORY NOTE

Wycherley may have adapted his title for his first play from James Shirley's *The Changes or Love in a Maze* (1632), which was frequently performed after the Restoration; 'maze' and 'wood' are similar puns. But the major source is Etherege's *The Comical Revenge or Love in a Tub* (1664), the first great success of the Restoration stage. Wycherley takes from Etherege the form of his play with its multiple plots only loosely interrelated, ranging from a 'love and honour' world of duels to a low world of trickery and cunning. Only the high plot has a direct source; its London setting lightly disguises its Spanish origin in Calderón's *Mañanas de abril y mayo* (1632). Wycherley appears to have used the *tercera parte* of Calderón's comedies, published in 1664.

The reference in Wycherley's dedication to performances in Lent (l. 26) is the only guide to the exact date of the first performance, which is usually placed around March 1671 at the Theatre Royal, Bridges Street, by the King's Company. When it was revived at Drury Lane in August 1718, the bill announced that it had been 'acted but once these thirty years' and, except for a performance of an altered version in 1782, that revival seems to have marked the end of the play's career on the professional stage.

Love in a Wood was first published in 1672. There were further quartos in 1693, 1694 and 1711, and since then the play has only been reprinted as part of complete editions of Wycherley's plays.

TO HER GRACE THE DUCHESS OF CLEVELAND

MADAM,

All authors whatever in their dedications are poets but I am now to write to a lady who stands as little in need of flattery as her beauty of art; otherwise I should prove as ill a poet to her in my dedication as to my reader in my play. I can do your Grace no honour nor make you more admirers than you have already; yet I can do myself the honour to let the world know I am the greatest you have. You will pardon me, madam, for you know 'tis very hard for a new author, and poet too, to govern his ambition, for poets, let them pass in the world never so much for modest, honest men, but begin praise to others, which concludes in themselves and are like rooks who lend people money but to win it back again and so leave them in debt to 'em for nothing; they offer laurel and incense to their heroes but wear it themselves and perfume themselves. This is true, madam, upon the honest word of an author who never yet writ dedication; yet, though I cannot lie like them, I am as vain as they and cannot but publicly give your Grace my humble acknowledgements for the favours I have received from you. This, I say, is the poet's gratitude, which in plain English is only pride and ambition, and that the world might know your Grace did me the honour to see my play twice together; yet perhaps my enviers of your favour will suggest 'twas in Lent and therefore for your mortification. Then, as a jealous author, I am concerned not to have your Grace's favours lessened, or rather my reputation, and to let them know you were pleased, after that, to command a copy from me of this play – the way without beauty and wit to win a poor poet's heart. 'Tis a sign your Grace understands nothing better than obliging all the world after the best and most proper manner. But, madam, to be obliging to that excess as you are (pardon me if I tell you, out of my extreme concern and service for your Grace) is a

---

The Duchess of Cleveland: Barbara Villiers, made Duchess of Cleveland in 1670, was one of Charles II's mistresses and also, after the success of this play, Wycherley's. See Additional Note. The dedication is written in the conventional language of flattery but adds double meanings to words like 'favour' to hint at the real relation between poet and patroness.

13 *rooks*: cheats, con-men.

dangerous quality and may be very incommode to you, for civility makes poets as troublesome as charity makes beggars and your Grace will be hereafter as much pestered with such scurvy offerings as this – poems, panegyrics and the like – as you are now with petitions and, madam, take it from me, no man with papers in's hand is more dreadful than a poet – no, not a lawyer with his declarations. Your Grace, sure, did not well consider what you did in sending for my play; you little thought I would have had the confidence to send you a dedication too. But, madam, you find I am as unreasonable and have as little conscience as if I had driven the poetic trade longer than I have and ne'er consider you had enough of the play. But, having suffered now so severely, I beseech your Grace, have a care for the future, take my counsel and be (if you can possible) as proud and ill-natured as other people of quality, since your quiet is so much concerned and since you have more reason than any to value yourself, for you have that perfection of beauty, without thinking it so, which others of your sex but think they have, that generosity in your actions which others of your quality have only in their promises, that spirit, wit and judgement and all other qualifications which fit heroes to command and would make any but your Grace proud. I begin now, elevated by my subject, to write with the emotion and fury of a poet, yet the integrity of an historian, and I could never be weary – nay, sure, this were my only way to make my readers never weary too, though they were a more impatient generation of people than they are. In fine, speaking thus of your Grace, I should please all the world but you; therefore, I must once observe and obey you against my will and say no more than that I am,

Madam,

Your Grace's

Most obliged and most humble servant,

WILLIAM WYCHERLEY

65–6 *In fine*: in short, to conclude.

PROLOGUE

Custom, which bids the thief from cart harangue
All those that come to make and see him hang,
Wills the damned poet (though he knows he's gone)
To greet you ere his execution.
Not having fear of critic 'fore his eyes
But still rejecting wholesome, good advice,
He e'en is come to suffer here today
For counterfeiting (as you judge) a play,
Which is against dread Phoebus highest treason,
Damned damning judges, therefore you have reason –
You he does mean who for the selfsame fault
That damning privilege of yours have bought
(So the huge bankers when they needs must fail
Send the small brothers of their trade to gaol,
Whilst they by breaking gentlemen are made,
Then more than any scorn, poor men o'th'trade),
You hardened renegado poets, who
Treat rhyming brother worse than Turk would do,
But vent your heathenish rage, hang, draw and quarter,
His muse will die today a fleering martyr;
Since for bald jest, dull libel or lampoon
There are who suffer persecution
With the undaunted briskness of buffoon
And strict professors live of raillery,
Defying Porter's Lodge or pillory.
For those who yet write on our poet's fate
Should as co-sufferers commiserate;
But he in vain their pity now would crave
Who for themselves, alas, no pity have
And their own gasping credit will not save;
And those, much less, our criminal would spare

---

9 *Phoebus*: Apollo, patron of the Muses.
10 *have reason*: are right (Fr. *avez raison*).
11–12 Playwrights were granted free admission to the theatre.
15–16 *Whilst they . . . o'th'trade*: the small-scale bankers are made poor members of their profession by gentlemen who break their bonds rather than by the scorn they receive. Q2 places a comma between *any* and *scorn* making the lines mean 'the big bankers are made rich by ruining gentlemen and scorn the small brothers more than any'.
20 *fleering*: 'smiling flatteringly' and 'mocking'.
21 *lampoon*: scurrilous satire.
25 *Porter's Lodge*: prison in Whitehall Palace.

Who ne'er in rhyme transgress, if such there are.
Well then, who nothing hopes needs nothing fear
And he, before your cruel votes shall do it,
By his despair declares himself no poet.

THE PERSONS

MR RANGER, MR VINCENT, MR VALENTINE — Young gentlemen of the town	
MR RANGER	*Mr Hart*
MR VINCENT	*Mr Bell*
MR VALENTINE	*Mr Kynaston*
ALDERMAN GRIPE, seemingly precise but a covetous, lecherous, old usurer of the City	*Mr Lacy*
SIR SIMON ADDLEPLOT, a coxcomb, always in pursuit of women of great fortunes	*Mr Wintersell*
MR DAPPERWIT, a brisk, conceited, half-witted fellow of the town	*Mr Mohun*
CHRISTINA, Valentine's mistress	*Mrs Boutell*
LYDIA, Ranger's mistress	*Mrs Betty Cox*
MY LADY FLIPPANT, Gripe's sister, an affected widow, in distress for a husband though still declaiming against marriage	*Mrs Knep*
MRS MARTHA, Gripe's daughter	*Mrs Farlow*
MRS JOYNER, a match-maker or precise City bawd	*Mrs Corey*
MRS CROSSBITE, an old, cheating jilt and bawd to her daughter	*Mrs Rutter*
MISS LUCY, her daughter	*Mrs Betty Slade*
ISABEL, Christina's woman	*Mrs James*
LEONORE, servant to Lydia	*Mrs Cartwright*

Crossbite's LANDLORD and his PRENTICES; servants, waiters and other attendants

The Scene: *London*

---

5 *precise*: puritanical.
21 *Crossbite*: deceive, outwit.
22 *jilt*: cheating woman.

LOVE IN A WOOD

ACT I

SCENE I

Gripe's house in the evening.

Enter MY LADY FLIPPANT, MRS JOYNER.

FLIPPANT. Not a husband to be had for money. Come, come, I might have been a better housewife for myself, as the world goes now, if I had dealt for an heir with his guardian, uncle or mother-in-law; and you are no better than a chouse, a cheat.

JOYNER. I a cheat, madam!

FLIPPANT. I am out of my money and my patience too.

JOYNER. Do not run out of your patience whatever you do; 'tis a necessary virtue for a widow without a jointure, in truly.

FLIPPANT. Vile woman, though my fortune be something wasted, my person's in good repair. If I had not depended on you, I had had a husband before this time. When I gave you the last five pound did not you promise I should be married by Christmas?

JOYNER. And had kept my promise if you had co-operated.

FLIPPANT. Co-operated! What should I have done? 'Tis well known no woman breathing could use more industry to get her a husband than I have. Has not my husband's scutcheon walked as much ground as the citizens' signs since the fire, that no quarter of the town might be ignorant of the widow Flippant?

JOYNER. 'Tis well known, madam, indeed.

FLIPPANT. Have I not owned myself (against my stomach) the relict of a citizen, to credit my fortune?

---

4 *mother-in-law*: stepmother.

5 *chouse*: cheat.

10 *jointure*: estate settled on wife or widow for the remainder of her life.

21 *scutcheon*: coat of arms.

21–2 After the Great Fire of London many tradesmen moved their shops further westward into the more fashionable areas.

26 *relict*: widow.

JOYNER. 'Tis confessed, madam.

FLIPPANT. Have I not constantly kept Covent Garden Church, St Martin's, the playhouses, Hyde Park, Mulberry Garden and all other the public marts where widows and maids are exposed?

JOYNER. Far be it from me to think you have an aversion to a husband, but why, madam, have you refused so many good offers?

FLIPPANT. Good offers, Mrs Joyner! I'll be sworn I never had an offer since my late husband's. If I had had an offer, Mrs Joyner – there's the thing, Mrs Joyner.

JOYNER. Then your frequent and public detestation of marriage is thought real and if you have had no offer – there's the thing, madam.

FLIPPANT. I cannot deny but I always rail against marriage, which is the widow's way to it, certainly.

JOYNER. 'Tis the desperate way of the desperate widows, in truly.

FLIPPANT. Would you have us as tractable as the wenches that eat oatmeal, and fooled like them too?

JOYNER. If nobody were wiser than I, I should think, since the widow wants the natural allurement which the virgin has, you ought to give men all other encouragements, in truly.

FLIPPANT. Therefore, on the contrary, because the widow's fortune (whether supposed or real) is her chiefest bait, the more chary she seems of it and the more she withdraws it, the more eagerly the busy gaping fry will bite. With us widows husbands are got like bishoprics, by saying no, and, I tell you, a young heir is as shy of a widow as of a rook, to my knowledge.

JOYNER. I can allege nothing against your practice but your ill success and indeed you must use another method with Sir Simon Addleplot.

28–9 *Covent . . . Martin's*: St Paul's, Covent Garden, and St Martin-in-the-Fields (to the north of what is now Trafalgar Square) were the two most fashionable churches in London.

29–30 *Mulberry Garden*: a park on the site of Buckingham Palace, the setting for the last scene of *Love in a Wood*.

30 *marts*: markets.

47 *wenches that eat oatmeal*: women pining for a lover.

57 *bishoprics . . . no*: the conventional refusal when elected a bishop, 'nolo episcopari'.

FLIPPANT. Will he be at your house at the hour?

JOYNER. He'll be there by ten; 'tis now nine. I warrant you he will not fail.

FLIPPANT. I'll warrant you then I will not fail, for 'tis more than time I were sped.

JOYNER. Mr Dapperwit has not been too busy with you; I hope your experience has taught you to prevent a mischance.

FLIPPANT. No, no, my mischance (as you call it) is greater than that. I have but three months to reckon ere I lie down with my port and equipage and must be delivered of a woman, a footman and a coachman, for my coach must down unless I can get Sir Simon to draw with me.

JOYNER. (*aside*) He will pair with you exactly if you knew all.

FLIPPANT. Ah, Mrs Joyner, nothing grieves me like putting down my coach. For the fine clothes, the fine lodgings, let 'em go, for a lodging is as unnecessary a thing to a widow that has a coach as a hat to a man that has a good peruke, for, as you see about town, she is most properly at home in her coach; she eats and drinks and sleeps in her coach and, for her visits, she receives them in the playhouse.

JOYNER. Ay, ay, let the men keep lodgings (as you say, madam) if they will.

[*Enter*] GRIPE *and* SIR SIMON ADDLEPLOT *following him as his man, in the habit of a clerk, at one door, and* MRS MARTHA *at the other.*

FLIPPANT. Do you think, if things had been with me as they have been, I would ever have housed with this counter-fashion brother of mine (who hates a vest as

---

69–70 As Lady Flippant's reply indicates, Mrs Joyner is hinting at the risk of pregnancy.

72 *port*: retinue.

90 *vest*: this garment was introduced to the court by Charles himself in October 1666 and, not surprisingly, rapidly became *à la mode*. Pepys describes it as 'a long cassock close to the body, of black cloth and pinked with white silk under it' (15 October 1666). Gripe is opposed to court (vest) and church (surplice).

much as a surplice) to have my patches assaulted every day, at dinner my freedom censured, and my visitants shut out of doors? Poor Mr Dapperwit cannot be admitted.

JOYNER. He knows him too well to keep his acquaintance.

FLIPPANT. He is a censorious, rigid fop and knows nothing.

GRIPE. (*behind*) So, so –

JOYNER. (*aside*) Is he here? (*To* MY LADY FLIPPANT) Nay, with your pardon, madam, I must contradict you there. He is a prying Commonwealth's man, an implacable magistrate, a sturdy pillar of his cause and – (*To* GRIPE) But, oh me, is your worship so near then? If I had thought you had heard me –

GRIPE. Why, why, Mrs Joyner, I have said as much of myself ere now and without vanity, I profess.

JOYNER. I know your virtue is proof against vainglory but the truth to your face looks like flattery in your worship's servant.

GRIPE. No, no, say what you will of me in that kind; far be it from me to suspect you of flattery.

JOYNER. In truly, your worship knows yourself and knows me, for I am none of those –

FLIPPANT. (*aside*) Now they are in. – Mrs Joyner, I'll go before to your house; you'll be sure to come after me. *Exit* FLIPPANT.

JOYNER. Immediately. But, as I was saying, I am none of those –

GRIPE. No, Mrs Joyner, you cannot sew pillows under folks' elbows; you cannot hold a candle to the devil; you cannot tickle a trout to take him; you –

JOYNER. Lord, how well you do know me indeed and you shall see I know your worship as well: you cannot backslide from your principles; you cannot be terrified by the laws nor bribed to allegiance by office or preferment; you –

GRIPE. Hold, hold, my praise must not interrupt yours.

---

91 *patches*: small pieces of black silk stuck to the face to add beauty and cover blemishes.

97 *fop*: here *fool*, usually an affected and fashionable one.

102 *prying*: (*a*) diligently inquiring (*b*) snooping.

120–2 All these proverbs describe flattery.

JOYNER. With your worship's pardon, in truly, I must on.
GRIPE. I am full of your praise and it will run over.
JOYNER. Nay, sweet sir, you are –
GRIPE. Nay, sweet Mrs Joyner, you are –
JOYNER. Nay, good your worship, you are –
Stops her mouth with his handkerchief.
GRIPE. I say you are –
JOYNER. I must not be rude with your worship.
GRIPE. You are a nursing-mother to the saints: through you they gather together; through you they fructify and increase and through you the child cries from out of the hand-basket.
JOYNER. Through you virgins are married or provided for as well; through you the reprobate's wife is made a saint and through you the widow is not disconsolate nor misses her husband.
GRIPE. Through you –
JOYNER. Indeed, you will put me to the blush.
GRIPE. Blushes are badges of imperfection; saints have no shame. You are the flower of matrons, Mrs Joyner.
JOYNER. You are the pink of courteous aldermen.
GRIPE. You are the muffler of secrecy.
JOYNER. You are the headband of justice.
GRIPE. Thank you, sweet Mrs Joyner. Do you think so indeed? You are – you are the bonfire of devotion.
JOYNER. You are the bellows of zeal.
GRIPE. You are the cupboard of charity.
JOYNER. You are the fob of liberality.
GRIPE. You are the rivet of sanctified love or wedlock.
JOYNER. You are the picklock and dark lanthorn of policy and, in a word, the conventicle of virtues.
GRIPE. Your servant, your servant, sweet Mrs Joyner; you have stopped my mouth.
JOYNER. Your servant, your servant, sweet alderman; I have nothing to say.
SIR SIMON. The half pullet will be cold, sir.
GRIPE. Mrs Joyner, you shall sup with me.
JOYNER. Indeed, I am engaged to supper with some of your man's friends and I came on purpose to get leave for him too.

---

155 *fob*: (*a*) small pocket (*b*) trick, cheat.
157 *lanthorn*: lantern.
158 *conventicle*: meeting-place, particularly of Puritans.

GRIPE. I cannot deny you anything. But I have forgot to tell you what a kind of fellow my sister's Dapperwit is: before a full table of the coffeehouse sages he had the impudence to hold an argument against me in the defence of vests and protections and therefore I forbid him my house; besides, when he came, I was forced to lock up my daughter for fear of him – nay, I think the poor child herself was afraid of him. Come hither, child. Were you not afraid of Dapperwit?

MARTHA. Yes indeed, sir, he is a terrible man. – (*Aside*) yet I durst meet with him in the Piazzo at midnight.

GRIPE. He shall never come into my doors again.

MARTHA. Shall Mr Dapperwit never come hither again then?

GRIPE. No, child.

MARTHA. I am afraid he will.

GRIPE. I warrant thee.

MARTHA. (*aside*) I warrant you then I'll go to him. – I am glad of that, for I hate him as much as a bishop.

GRIPE. Thou art no child of mine if thou dost not hate bishops and wits. Well, Mrs Joyner, I'll keep you no longer. Jonas, wait on Mrs Joyner.

JOYNER. Goodnight to your worship.

GRIPE. But stay, stay, Mrs Joyner. Have you spoken with the Widow Crossbite about her little daughter, as I desired?

JOYNER. I will tomorrow early. It shall be the first thing I'll do after my prayers.

GRIPE. If Dapperwit should contaminate her – I cannot rest till I have redeemed her from the jaws of that lion. Goodnight.

JOYNER. Good gentleman.

Exeunt GRIPE *and* MARTHA.

Manent SIR SIMON ADDLEPLOT *and* JOYNER.

SIR SIMON. Hah, hah, ha, Mrs Joyner.

JOYNER. What's the matter, Sir Simon?

SIR SIMON. Hah, hah, ha! Let us make haste to your

---

172 *protections*: documents issued by the court guaranteeing immunity from arrest.

178 *Piazzo*: the Piazza was an open arcade on two sides of Covent Garden; Act V Scene iii of *The Country Wife* takes place there.

house or I shall burst. Faith and troth, to see what fools you and I make of these people!

JOYNER. I will not rob you of any of the credit. I am but a feeble instrument; you are the engineer.

SIR SIMON. Remember what you say now when things succeed and do not tell me then I must thank your wit for all.

JOYNER. No, in truly, Sir Simon.

SIR SIMON. Nay, I'm sure Dapperwit and I have been partners in many an intrigue and he uses to serve me so.

JOYNER. He is an ill man to intrigue with, as you call it.

SIR SIMON. Ay, so are all your wits. A pox, if a man's understanding be not so public as theirs he cannot do a wise action but they go away with the honour of it, if he be of their acquaintance.

JOYNER. Why do you keep such acquaintance, then?

SIR SIMON. There is a proverb, Mrs Joyner: you may know him by his company.

JOYNER. No, no, to be thought a man of parts you should always keep company with a man of less wit than yourself.

SIR SIMON. That's the hardest thing in the world for me to do, faith and troth.

JOYNER. What, to find a man of less wit than yourself? Pardon my raillery, Sir Simon.

SIR SIMON. No, no, I cannot keep company with a fool. I wonder how men of parts can do't – there's something in't.

JOYNER. If you could, all your wise actions would be your own and your money would be your own too.

SIR SIMON. Nay, faith and troth, that's true, for your wits are plaguily given to borrow; they'll borrow of their wench, coachman or linkboy their hire. Mrs Joyner, Dapperwit has that trick with a vengeance.

JOYNER. Why will you keep company with him then, I say? For, to be plain with you, you have followed him so long that you are thought but his cully, for every wit has his cully, as every squire his led-captain.

---

227 *raillery*: witty banter.
239 *cully*: dupe, often a cuckold.
240 *led-captain*: parasite, hanger-on.

SIR SIMON. I his cully? I his cully, Mrs Joyner! Lord, that I should be thought a cully to any wit breathing!

JOYNER. Nay, do not take it so to heart, for the best wits of the town are but cullies themselves.

SIR SIMON. To whom, to whom, to whom, Mrs Joyner?

JOYNER. To sem'steresses and bawds.

SIR SIMON. To your knowledge, Mrs Joyner. – [*Aside*] There I was with her.

JOYNER. To tailors and vintners, but especially to the French houses.

SIR SIMON. But Dapperwit is a cully to none of them, for he ticks.

JOYNER. I care not; but I wish you were a cully to none but me – that's all the hurt I wish you.

SIR SIMON. Thank you, Mrs Joyner. Well, I will throw off Dapperwit's acquaintance, when I am married, and will only be a cully to my wife – and that's no more than the wisest husband of 'em all is.

JOYNER. Then you think you shall carry Mrs Martha?

SIR SIMON. Your hundred guineas are as good as in your lap.

JOYNER. But I am afraid this double plot of yours should fail. You would sooner succeed if you only designed upon Mrs Martha or only upon my Lady Flippant.

SIR SIMON. Nay, then you are no woman of intrigue; faith and troth, 'tis good to have two strings to one bow. If Mrs Martha be coy, I tell the widow I put on my disguise for her; but if Mrs Martha be kind to Jonas, Sir Simon Addleplot will be false to the widow – which is no more than widows are used to, for a promise to a widow is as seldom kept as a vow made at sea, as Dapperwit says.

JOYNER. I am afraid they should discover you.

SIR SIMON. You have nothing to fear. You have your twenty guineas in your pocket for helping me into my service and if I get into Mrs Martha's quarters you have a hundred more, if into the widow's, fifty, happy-go-lucky. Will her ladyship be at your house at the hour?

---

250 *French houses*: fashionable eating-houses.
252 *ticks*: runs up bills without paying.

JOYNER. Yes.

SIR SIMON. Then you shall see, when I am Sir Simon Addleplot and myself, I'll look like myself; now I am Jonas I look like an ass. You never thought Sir Simon Addleplot could have looked so like an ass by his ingenuity.

JOYNER. Pardon me, Sir Simon.

SIR SIMON. Nay, do not flatter, faith and troth.

JOYNER. Come, let us go; 'tis time.

SIR SIMON. I will carry the widow to the French house.

JOYNER. If she will go.

SIR SIMON. If she will go! Why, did you ever know a widow refuse a treat? No more than a lawyer a fee, faith and troth; yet I know too.
No treat, sweet words, good mien but sly intrigue,
That must at length the jilting widow feague.

Exeunt.

SCENE II

The scene changes to the French house. A table, wine and candles.

Enter VINCENT, RANGER, DAPPERWIT.

DAPPERWIT. Pray, Mr Ranger, let's have no drinking tonight.

VINCENT. Pray, Mr Ranger, let's have no Dapperwit tonight.

RANGER. Nay, nay, Vincent.

VINCENT. A pox, I hate his impertinent chat more than he does the honest Burgundy.

DAPPERWIT. But why should you force wine upon us? We are not all of your gusto.

VINCENT. But why should you force your chawed jests, your damned ends of your mouldy lampoons and last year's sonnets upon us? We are not all of your gusto.

DAPPERWIT. The wine makes me sick, let me perish.

VINCENT. Thy rhymes make me spew.

---

295 *feague*: get the better of.
9 *gusto*: taste (Fr. *goût*).
10 *chawed*: chewed.

RANGER. At repartee already! Come, Vincent, I know you would rather have him pledge you. Here, Dapperwit. (*Gives him the glass*) But why are you so eager to have him drink always?

VINCENT. Because he is so eager to talk always and there is no other way to silence him.

[*Enter*] WAITER *to them.*

WAITER. Here is a gentleman desires to speak with Mr Vincent.

VINCENT. I come.

[*Exeunt* WAITER *and*] VINCENT.

DAPPERWIT. He may drink because he is obliged to the bottle, for all the wit and courage he has – 'tis not free and natural like yours.

RANGER. He has more courage than wit but wants neither.

DAPPERWIT. As a pump gone dry; if you pour no water down you will get none out, so –

RANGER. Nay, I bar similes too, tonight.

DAPPERWIT. Why, is not the thought new? Don't you apprehend it?

RANGER. Yes, yes, but –

DAPPERWIT. Well, well, will you comply with his sottishness too and hate brisk things in complaisance to the ignorant dull age? I believe shortly 'twill be as hard to find a patient friend to communicate one's wit to as a faithful friend to communicate one's secret to. Wit has as few true judges as painting, I see.

RANGER. All people pretend to be judges of both.

DAPPERWIT. Ay, they pretend – but, set you aside and two more –

RANGER. But why has Vincent neither courage nor wit?

DAPPERWIT. He has no courage because he beat his wench for giving me *les douces yeux* once and no wit because he does not comprehend my thoughts and he is a son of a whore for his ignorance. I take ignorance worse from any man than the lie because it is as much as to say I am no wit.

15–16 *you. Here, Dapperwit*: you here Dapperwit Q1.
40 *as few*: a few Q1.

VINCENT *returns.*

You need not take any notice, though, to him of what I say.

VINCENT. Ranger, there is a woman below in a coach would speak with you.

RANGER. With me? *Exit* RANGER.

DAPPERWIT. This Ranger, Mr Vincent, is as false to his friend as his wench.

VINCENT. You have no reason to say so but because he is absent.

DAPPERWIT. 'Tis disobliging to tell a man of his faults to his face. If he had but your grave parts and manly wit I should adore him but, a pox, he is a mere buffoon, a Jack-pudding, let me perish.

VINCENT. You are an ungrateful fellow. I have heard him maintain you had wit – which was more than e'er you could do for yourself. I thought you had owned him your Maecenas.

DAPPERWIT. A pox, he cannot but esteem me; 'tis for his honour. But I cannot but be just for all that, without favour or affection; yet I confess I love him so well that I wish he had but the hundredth part of your courage.

VINCENT. He has had the courage to save you from many a beating, to my knowledge.

DAPPERWIT. Come, come, I wish the man well and, next to you, better than any man; and I am sorry to say it, he has not courage to snuff a candle with his fingers. When he is drunk indeed, he dares get a clap or so – and swear at a constable.

VINCENT. Detracting fop, when did you see him desert his friend?

DAPPERWIT. You have a rough kind of raillery, Mr Vincent, but since you will have it (though I love the man heartily, I say), he deserted me once in breaking of windows, for fear of the constable.

---

63 *Jack-pudding*: buffoon, clown, fool.
67 *Maecenas*: rich patron.
77 *courage*: a courage Q1.
78 *clap*: dose of syphilis.
84–5 *breaking of windows*: a common night-time activity of rakes.

RANGER *returns.*

But you need not take notice to him of what I tell you; I hate to put a man to the blush.

RANGER. I have had just now a visit from my mistress, who is as jealous of me as a wife of her husband when she lies in – my cousin Lydia, you have heard me speak of her.

VINCENT. But she is more troublesome than a wife that lies in because she follows you to your haunts. Why do you allow her that privilege before her time?

RANGER. Faith, I may allow her any privilege and be too hard for her yet. How do you think I have cheated her tonight? Women are poor credulous creatures, easily deceived.

VINCENT. We are poor credulous creatures when we think 'em so.

RANGER. Intending a ramble to St James's Park tonight, upon some probable hopes of some fresh game I have in chase, I appointed her to stay at home, with a promise to come to her within this hour, that she might not foil the scent and prevent my sport.

VINCENT. She'll be even with you when you are married, I warrant you. In the meantime, here's her health, Dapperwit.

RANGER. Now had he rather be at the window, writing her anagram in the glass with his diamond, or biting his nails in the corner for a fine thought to come and divert us with at the table.

DAPPERWIT. No, a pox, I have no wit tonight; I am as barren and hide-bound as one of your damned scribbling poets, who are sots in company for all their wit, as a miser poor for all his money. How do you like the thought?

VINCENT. Drink, drink.

DAPPERWIT. Well, I can drink this because I shall be reprieved presently.

VINCENT. Who will be so civil to us?

DAPPERWIT. Sir Simon Addleplot. I have bespoke him a supper here, for he treats tonight a new rich mistress.

RANGER. That spark who has his fruitless designs upon

---

93 *lies in*: in the last weeks of pregnancy.

the bedridden rich widow down to the sucking heiresses in her pissing clout. He was once the sport but now the public grievance of all the fortunes in town, for he watches them like a younger brother that is afraid to be mumped of his snip and they cannot steal a marriage nor stay their stomachs but he must know it.

DAPPERWIT. He has now pitched his nets for Gripe's daughter, the rich scrivener, and serves him as a clerk, to get admission to her, which the watchful fop, her father, denies to all others.

RANGER. I thought you had been nibbling at her once, under pretence of love to her aunt.

DAPPERWIT. I confess I have the same design yet and Addleplot is but my agent whilst he thinks me his. He brings me letters constantly from her and carries mine back.

VINCENT. Still betraying your best friends.

DAPPERWIT. I cannot in honour but betray him, let me perish; the poor young wench is taken with my person and would scratch through four walls to come to me.

VINCENT. 'Tis a sign she is kept up close indeed.

DAPPERWIT. Betray him! I'll not be a traitor to love for any man.

[*Enter*] SIR SIMON ADDLEPLOT *to them with the* WAITER.

SIR SIMON. Know 'em! You are a saucy Jack-straw to question me, faith and troth. I know everybody and everybody knows me.

ALL. Sir Simon, Sir Simon, Sir Simon.

RANGER. And you are a welcome man to everybody.

SIR SIMON. Now, son of a whore, do I know the gentlemen? A dog, he would have had a shilling of me before he would let me come to you.

RANGER. The rogue has been bred at court, sure. Get you out, sirrah.

[*Exit* WAITER.]

SIR SIMON. He has been bred at a French house where they are more unreasonable.

---

126 *pissing clout*: nappy.
129 *mumped of his snip*: cheated of his share.
148 *Jack-straw*: worthless man.

VINCENT. Here's to you, Sir Simon.

SIR SIMON. I cannot drink for I have a mistress within, though I would not have the people of the house to know it.

RANGER. You need not be ashamed of your mistresses, for they are commonly rich.

SIR SIMON. And because she is rich I would conceal her, for I never had a rich mistress yet but one or other got her from me presently, faith and troth.

RANGER. But this is an ill place to conceal a mistress in; every waiter is an intelligencer to your rivals.

SIR SIMON. I have trick for that; I let no waiters come into the room – I'll lay the cloth myself rather.

RANGER. But who is your mistress?

SIR SIMON. Your servant, your servant, Mr Ranger.

VINCENT. Come, will you pledge me?

SIR SIMON. No, I'll spare your wine if you will spare me Dapperwit's company; I came for that.

VINCENT. You do us a double favour to take him and leave the wine.

SIR SIMON. Come, come, Dapperwit.

RANGER. (*aside*) Do not go unless he will suffer us to see his mistress too.

SIR SIMON. Come, come, man.

DAPPERWIT. Would you have me so incivil as to leave my company? They'll take it ill.

SIR SIMON. I cannot find her talk without thee. Pray, gentlemen, persuade Mr Dapperwit to go with me.

RANGER. We will not hinder him of better company.

DAPPERWIT. Yours is too good to be left rudely.

SIR SIMON. Nay, gentlemen, I would desire your company too, if you knew the lady.

DAPPERWIT. They know her as well as I; you say I know her not.

SIR SIMON. (*aside*) You are not everybody.

RANGER. Perhaps we do know the lady, Sir Simon.

SIR SIMON. You do not, you do not; none of you ever saw her in your lives. But if you could be secret and civil –

RANGER. We have drunk yet but our bottle apiece.

---

170 *intelligencer*: spy.
199 *bottle*: bottles Q1.

SIR SIMON. But will you be civil, Mr Vincent?

RANGER. He dares not look a woman in the face under three bottles.

SIR SIMON. Come along, then. But can you be civil gentlemen? Will you be civil gentlemen? Pray, be civil if you can and you shall see her.

Exit SIR SIMON.

Returns with MY LADY FLIPPANT *and* MRS JOYNER.

DAPPERWIT. (*aside*) How, has he got his jilt here?

RANGER. (*aside*) The widow Flippant!

VINCENT. (*aside*) Is this the woman we never saw?

FLIPPANT. (*aside*) Does he bring us into company, and Dapperwit one? Though I had married the fool, I thought to have reserved the wit as well as other ladies.

SIR SIMON. Nay, look as long as you will, madam, you will find them civil gentlemen and good company.

FLIPPANT. I am not in doubt of their civility but yours.

JOYNER. (*behind*) You'll never leave snubbing your servants. Did you not promise to use him kindly?

FLIPPANT. (*aside*) 'Tis true. – We wanted no good company, Sir Simon, as long as we had yours.

SIR SIMON. But they wanted good company, therefore I forced them to accept of yours.

FLIPPANT. They will not think the company good they were forced into, certainly.

SIR SIMON. [*aside*] A pox, I must be using the words in fashion, though I never have any luck with 'em. – Mrs Joyner, help me off.

JOYNER. I suppose, madam, he means the gentlemen wanted not inclination to your company but confidence to desire so great an honour, therefore he forced 'em.

DAPPERWIT. What makes this bawd here? Sure, mistress, you bawds should be like the small cards: though at first you make up the pack, yet when the play begins you should be put out as useless.

JOYNER. Well, well, jibing companion, you would have the pimps kept in only? You would so?

VINCENT. What, they are quarrelling?

231–3 Many card games, including picquet and ombre, were played without the low cards in the pack.

234 *jibing*: sneering.

RANGER. Pimp and bawd agree nowadays like doctor and apothecary.

SIR SIMON. Try, madam, if they are not civil gentlemen; talk with 'em while I go lay the cloth – no waiter comes here. (*Aside*) My mother used to tell me I should avoid all occasions of talking before my mistress because silence is a sign of love as well as prudence. (SIR SIMON *laying the cloth*)

FLIPPANT. Methinks you look a little yellow on't, Mr Dapperwit. I hope you do not censure me because you find me passing away a night with this fool; he is not a man to be jealous of, sure.

DAPPERWIT. You are not a lady to be jealous of, sure.

FLIPPANT. No, certainly. But why do you look as if you were jealous then?

DAPPERWIT. If I had met you in Whetstone's Park with a drunken footsoldier I should not have been jealous of you.

FLIPPANT. Fie, fie, now you are jealous certainly, for people always, when they grow jealous, grow rude. But I can pardon it since it proceeds from love, certainly.

DAPPERWIT. (*aside*) I am out of all hopes to be rid of this eternal old acquaintance. When I jeer her, she thinks herself praised; now I call her whore in plain English, she thinks I am jealous.

FLIPPANT. Sweet Mr Dapperwit, be not so censorious. I speak for your sake, not my own, for jealousy is a great torment, but my honour cannot suffer, certainly.

DAPPERWIT. No, certainly, but the greatest torment I have is your love.

FLIPPANT. Alas, sweet Mr Dapperwit, indeed love is a torment but 'tis a sweet torment; but jealousy is a bitter torment. I do not go about to cure you of the torment of my love.

DAPPERWIT. 'Tis a sign so.

FLIPPANT. Come, come, look up, man. Is that a rival to contest with you?

---

236 *and*: an Q1.

244 *yellow*: jealous.

251 *Whetstone's Park*: an area north of Lincoln's Inn Fields and south of Holborn, notorious for its prostitutes.

DAPPERWIT. I will contest with no rival, not with my old rival, your coachman, but they have heartily my resignation; and to do you a favour, but myself a greater, I will help tie the knot you are fumbling for now, betwixt your cully here and you.

FLIPPANT. Go, go, I take that kind of jealousy worst of all, to suspect I would be debauched to beastly matrimony. But who are those gentlemen, pray? – Are they men of fortunes, Mrs Joyner?

JOYNER. I believe so.

FLIPPANT. Do you believe so, indeed? Gentlemen – (*Advancing towards* RANGER *and* VINCENT)

RANGER. If the civility we owe to ladies had not controlled our envy to Mr Dapperwit we had interrupted ere this your private conversation.

FLIPPANT. Your interruption, sir, had been most civil and obliging, for our discourse was of marriage.

RANGER. That is a subject, madam, as grateful as common.

FLIPPANT. O fie, fie, are you of that opinion too? I cannot suffer any to talk of it in my company.

RANGER. Are you married then, madam?

FLIPPANT. No, certainly.

RANGER. I am sure so much beauty cannot despair of it.

FLIPPANT. Despair of it!

RANGER. Only those that are married or cannot be married hate to hear of marriage.

FLIPPANT. Yet you must know, sir, my aversion to marriage is such that you nor no man breathing shall ever persuade me to it.

RANGER. Cursed be the man should do so rude a thing as to persuade you to anything against your inclination. I would not do it for the world, madam.

FLIPPANT. Come, come, though you seem to be a civil gentleman, I think you no better than your neighbours. I do not know a man of you all that will not thrust a woman up into a corner and then talk an hour to her impertinently of marriage.

RANGER. You would find me another man in a corner, I assure you, madam, for you should not have a word of marriage from me, whatsoever you might find in my actions of it. I hate talking as much as you.

FLIPPANT. I hate it extremely.

RANGER. I am your man then, madam, for I find just the

same fault with your sex as you do with ours; I ne'er could have to do with a woman in my life but still she would be impertinently talking of marriage to me.

FLIPPANT. (*aside*) Observe that, Mrs Joyner.

DAPPERWIT. Pray, Mr Ranger, let's go. I had rather drink with Mr Vincent than stay here with you; besides, 'tis Park-time.

RANGER. (*to* DAPPERWIT) I come. – Since you are a lady that hate marriage, I'll do you the service to withdraw the company, for those that hate marriage hate loss of time.

FLIPPANT. Will you go then, sir? But, before you go, sir, pray tell me, is your aversion to marriage real?

RANGER. As real as yours.

FLIPPANT. (*aside*) If it were no more real than mine.

RANGER. Your servant, madam.

FLIPPANT. (*plucks him back*) But do you hate marriage certainly?

RANGER. Certainly.

FLIPPANT. Come, I cannot believe it. You dissemble it only because I pretend it.

RANGER. Do you but pretend it then, madam?

FLIPPANT. (*aside*) I shall discover myself. – I mean, because I hold against it, you do the same in complaisance, for, I have heard say, cunning men think to bring the coy and untractable women to tameness as they do some mad people, by humouring their frenzies.

RANGER. I am none of those cunning men, yet have too much wit to entertain the presumption of designing upon you.

FLIPPANT. 'Twere no such presumption, neither.

DAPPERWIT. Come, away, 'sdeath, don't you see your danger?

RANGER. Those aims are for Sir Simon. Goodnight, madam.

FLIPPANT. Will you needs go then? The gentlemen are a-going, Sir Simon. Will you let 'em?

SIR SIMON. Nay, madam, if you cannot keep 'em, how should I?

FLIPPANT. Stay, sir. Because you hate marriage, I'll sing you a new song against it. (*She sings*)

---

357 s.d. *She sings*: the music by Pelham Humphrey is most

A spouse I do hate,
For either she's false or she's jealous;
But give us a mate
Who nothing will ask us or tell us.

She stands on no terms,
Nor chaffers by way of indenture
Her love for your farms
But takes her kind man at a venture.

If all prove not right,
Without an act, process or warning,
From wife for a night
You may be divorced in the morning.

When parents are slaves
Their brats cannot be any other;
Great wits and great braves
Have always a punk to their mother.

Though it be the fashion for women of quality to sing any song whatever, because the words are not distinguished, yet I should have blushed to have done it now, but for you, sir.

RANGER. The song is edifying, the voice admirable, and once more, I am your servant, madam.

FLIPPANT. What, will you go too, Mr Dapperwit?

SIR SIMON. Pray, Mr Dapperwit, do not you go too.

DAPPERWIT. I am engaged.

SIR SIMON. Well, if we cannot have their company we will not have their room. Ours is a private back room; they have paid their reckoning. Let's go thither again.

FLIPPANT. But, pray, sweet Mr Dapperwit, do not go. Keep him, Sir Simon!

SIR SIMON. I cannot keep him.

Exeunt VINCENT, RANGER, DAPPERWIT.

It is impossible (the world is so):
One cannot keep one's friend and mistress too.

Exeunt omnes.

---

conveniently available in Weales's edition, p. 29. It appeared, with slightly different words, in John Playford's *Choice Airs and Songs* (Book 5, 1684).

363 *chaffers*: barters.

365 *at a venture*: as a commercial speculation, takes a chance.

ACT II

SCENE I

St James's Park at night.

Enter RANGER, VINCENT, DAPPERWIT.

RANGER. Hang me if I am not pleased extremely with the new-fashioned caterwauling, this midnight coursing in the Park.

VINCENT. A man may come after supper with his three bottles in his head, reel himself sober without reproof from his mother, aunt or grave relation.

RANGER. May bring his bashful wench and not have her put out of countenance by the impudent honest women of the town.

DAPPERWIT. And a man of wit may have the better of the dumb show of well-trimmed vest or fair peruke – no man's now is whitest.

RANGER. And now no woman's modest or proud, for her blushes are hid and the rubies on her lips are died and all sleepy and glimmering eyes have lost their attraction.

VINCENT. And now a man may carry a bottle under his arm, instead of his hat, and no observing spruce fop will miss the cravat that lies on one's shoulder or count the pimples on one's face.

DAPPERWIT. And now the brisk repartee ruins the complaisant cringe or wise grimace. Something 'twas, we men of virtue always loved the night.

RANGER. O blessed season.

VINCENT. For good-fellows.

RANGER. For lovers.

DAPPERWIT. And for the muses.

RANGER. When I was a boy I loved the night so well I had a strong vocation to be a bellman's apprentice.

VINCENT. I a drawer.

29 *bellman*: night watchman.
30 *drawer*: barman.

DAPPERWIT. And I to attend the waits of Westminster, let me perish.

RANGER. But why do we not do the duty of this and such other places, walk, censure and speak ill of all we meet?

DAPPERWIT. 'Tis no fault of mine, let me perish.

VINCENT. Fie, fie, satirical gentlemen, this is not your time; you cannot distinguish a friend from a fop.

DAPPERWIT. No matter, no matter. They will deserve amongst 'em the worst we can say.

RANGER. Who comes here, Dapperwit?

People walking slowly over the stage.

DAPPERWIT. By the toss of his head, training of his feet and his elbows playing at bo-peep behind his back, it should be my Lord Easy.

RANGER. And who the woman?

DAPPERWIT. My Lord What-d'ye-call's daughter that had a child by –

VINCENT. Dapperwit, hold your tongue!

RANGER. How are you concerned?

VINCENT. Her brother's an honest fellow and will drink his glass.

RANGER. Prithee, Vincent, Dapperwit did not hinder drinking tonight, though he speak against it; why then should you interrupt his sport? Now let him talk of anybody.

VINCENT. So he will, till you cut his throat.

RANGER. Why should you in all occasions thwart him, contemn him and maliciously look grave at his jests only?

VINCENT. Why does he always rail against my friends then and my best friend, a beer-glass?

RANGER. Dapperwit, be your own advocate; my game, I think, is before me there. *Exit* RANGER.

DAPPERWIT. This Ranger, I think, has all the ill qualities of all your town fops, leaving his company for a spruce lord or a wench.

VINCENT. Nay, if you must rail at your own best friends I may forgive you railing at mine.

---

31 *waits*: wind bands maintained by the city; they often played in the streets at night.

LYDIA *and* MY LADY FLIPPANT *walking across the stage.*

LYDIA. (*aside*) False Ranger, shall I find thee here?

VINCENT. (*to* DAPPERWIT) Those are women, are they not?

DAPPERWIT. (*aside*) The least seems to be my Lucy, sure.

VINCENT. Faith, I think I dare speak to a woman in the dark; let's try.

DAPPERWIT. They are persons of quality of my acquaintance. Hold.

VINCENT. Nay, if they are persons of quality of your acquaintance I may be the bolder with 'em.

The ladies go off; they follow them.

LYDIA *and* FLIPPANT *re-enter.*

LYDIA. I come hither to make a discovery tonight.

FLIPPANT. Of my love to you certainly, for nobody but you could have debauched me to the park, certainly; I would not return another night, if it were to redeem my dear husband from his grave.

LYDIA. I believe you, but to get another, widow.

FLIPPANT. Another husband, another husband, foh!

LYDIA. There does not pass a night here but many a match is made.

FLIPPANT. That a woman of honour should have the word 'match' in her mouth! But I hope, madam, the fellows do not make honourable love here, do they? I abominate honourable love, on my honour.

LYDIA. If they should make honourable love here, I know you would prevent 'em.

VINCENT *and* DAPPERWIT *re-enter and walk slowly towards them.*

But here come two men will inform you what they do.

FLIPPANT. Do they come? Are they men certainly?

LYDIA. Prepare for an assault; they'll put you to't.

FLIPPANT. Will they put us to't certainly? I was never put to't yet. If they should put us to't I should drop down, down certainly.

---

72 *least*: shortest.

LYDIA. I believe, truly, you would not have power to run away.

FLIPPANT. Therefore I will not stay the push. They come, they come, oh, the fellows come!

FLIPPANT *runs away,* LYDIA *follows and* VINCENT *and* DAPPERWIT *after them.* FLIPPANT *re-enters at t'other door alone.*

FLIPPANT. So I am got off clear. I did not run from the men but my companion. For all their brags, men have hardly courage to set upon us when our number is equal. Now they shall see I defy 'em, for we women have always most courage when we are alone. But a pox! The lazy rogues come not or they are drunk and cannot run. Oh drink, abominable drink! Instead of inflaming love, it quenches it and for one lover it encourages it makes a thousand impotent. Curse on all wine, even Rhenish wine and sugar –

Enter ADDLEPLOT *muffled in a cloak.*

But Fortune will not see me want; here comes a single bully – I wish he may stand,
For now anights the jostling nymph is bolder
Than modern satyr with his cloak o'er shoulder.
(*She puts on her mask*) Well met, sir.

SIR SIMON. How shall I know that, forsooth? Who are you? Do you know me?

FLIPPANT. Who are you? Don't you know me?

SIR SIMON. Not I, faith and troth.

FLIPPANT. I am glad on't, for no man e'er liked a woman the better for having known her before.

SIR SIMON. Ay, but then one can't be so free with a new acquaintance as with an old one; she may deny the civility.

FLIPPANT. Not till you ask her.

SIR SIMON. But I am afraid to be denied.

FLIPPANT. Let me tell you, sir, you cannot disoblige us women more than in distrusting us.

---

114 *Rhenish wine and sugar*: often a drink for invalids.
116 *bully*: rake.
118 *satyr*: half-man, half-goat in Greek mythology, drunken, lecherous companion of Bacchus.

SIR SIMON. Pish, what should one ask for when you know one's meaning? But shall I deal freely with you?

FLIPPANT. I love, of my life, men should deal freely with me; there are so few men will deal freely with one –

SIR SIMON. Are you not a fireship, a punk, madam?

FLIPPANT. Well, sir, I love raillery.

SIR SIMON. Faith and troth, I do not rally; I deal freely.

FLIPPANT. This is the time and place for freedom, sir.

SIR SIMON. Are you handsome?

FLIPPANT. Joan's as good as my lady in the dark, certainly. But men that deal freely never ask questions, certainly.

SIR SIMON. How then! I thought to deal freely and put a woman to the question had been all one.

FLIPPANT. But let me tell you, those that deal freely indeed take a woman by –

SIR SIMON. What, what, what, what?

FLIPPANT. By the hand and lead her aside.

SIR SIMON. Now I understand you. Come along then.

Enter torches and music at a distance.

FLIPPANT. What unmannerly rascals are those that bring light into the park? 'Twill not be taken well from 'em by the women certainly. (*Aside*) Still disappointed –

SIR SIMON. Oh the fiddles, the fiddles! I sent for them hither to oblige the women, not offend 'em, for I intend to serenade the whole park tonight. But my frolic is not without an intrigue, faith and troth, for I know the fiddles will call the whole herd of vizard masks together and then shall I discover if a strayed mistress of mine be not amongst 'em, whom I treated tonight at the French house, but as soon as the jilt had eat up my meat and drank her two bottles, she run away from me and left me alone.

FLIPPANT. (*aside*) Is it he? Addleplot! That I could not know him by his 'faith and troth'!

---

138 *fireship, punk*: both are slang words for prostitutes.
152 s.d. *torches*: linkboys carrying torches.
161–2 *vizard masks*: fashionable masks, later the sign of a prostitute.

SIR SIMON. Now I would understand her tricks because I intend to marry her and should be glad to know what I must trust to.

FLIPPANT. (*aside*) So thou shalt, but not yet.

SIR SIMON. Though I can give a great guess already, for, if I have any intrigue or sense in me, she is as arrant a jilt as ever pulled pillow from under husband's head, faith and troth; moreover she is bow-legged, hopper-hipped and, betwixt pomatum and Spanish red, has a complexion like a Holland cheese and no more teeth left than such as give a haust-goust to her breath – but she is rich, faith and troth.

FLIPPANT. (*aside*) Oh rascal! He has heard somebody else say all this of me. But I must not discover myself, lest I should be disappointed of my revenge, for I will marry him.

The torches and music approaching. Exit FLIPPANT.

SIR SIMON. What, gone? Come then, strike up, my lads.

Enter men and women in vizards and dance. ADDLEPLOT *for the most part standing still in a cloak and vizard but sometimes going about, peeping and examining the women's clothes. The dance ended, exeunt dancers, torches, music and* ADDLEPLOT. *Enter* FLIPPANT, LYDIA, *after them* VINCENT, DAPPERWIT.

FLIPPANT. (*to* LYDIA) Nay, if you stay any longer, I must leave you again.

VINCENT. We have overtaken them at last again; these are they.

FLIPPANT *going off.*

They separate too and that's but a challenge to us.

DAPPERWIT. Let me perish, ladies –

LYDIA. Nay, good madam, let's unite, now here's the common enemy upon us.

VINCENT. Damn me, ladies –

DAPPERWIT. Hold; a pox, you are too rough. Let me perish, ladies.

---

174 *or*: on Q1.

176–7 *hopper-hipped*: steatopygous, big-bottomed.

177 *pomatum*: face cream.

177 *Spanish red*: rouge.

178 *Holland cheese*: probably Texel, a green, sheep's milk cheese.

179 *haust-goust*: bad smell (Fr. *haut goût*: highly seasoned).

LYDIA. Not for want of breath, gentlemen; we'll stay rather.

DAPPERWIT. For want of your favour, rather, sweet ladies.

FLIPPANT. [*aside*] That's Dapperwit, false villain, but he must not know I am here. If he should I should lose his thrice agreeable company and he would run from me as fast as from the bailiffs. – What, you will not talk with 'em, I hope?

LYDIA. Yes, but I will.

FLIPPANT. Then you are a park-woman certainly and you will take it kindly if I leave you.

LYDIA. (*apart*) No, you must not leave me.

FLIPPANT. Then you must leave them.

LYDIA. I'll see if they are worse company than you first.

FLIPPANT. Monstrous impudence, will you not come? (*Pulls* LYDIA)

VINCENT. Nay, madam, I never suffer any violence to be used to a woman but what I do myself. She must stay and you must not go.

FLIPPANT. Unhand me, you rude fellow.

VINCENT. Nay, now I am sure you will stay and be kind, for coyness in a woman is as little sign of true modesty as huffing in a man is of true courage.

DAPPERWIT. Use her gently and speak soft things to her.

LYDIA. (*aside*) Now do I guess I know my coxcomb. – Sir, I am extremely glad I am fallen into the hands of a gentleman that can speak soft things and this is so fine a night to hear soft things in – morning, I should have said.

DAPPERWIT. It will not be morning, dear madam, till you pull off your mask. (*Aside*) That I think was brisk!

LYDIA. Indeed, dear sir, my face would frighten back the sun.

DAPPERWIT. With glories more radiant than his own. (*Aside*) I keep up with her, I think.

LYDIA. But why would you put me to the trouble of lighting the world, when I thought to have gone to sleep?

DAPPERWIT. You only can do it, dear madam, let me perish.

---

220 *huffing*: swaggering.

LYDIA. But why would you (of all men) practise treason against your friend Phoebus and depose him for a mere stranger?

DAPPERWIT. (*aside*) I think she knows me.

LYDIA. But he does not do you justice, I believe, and you are so positively cocksure of your wit, you would refer to a mere stranger your plea to the bay-tree.

DAPPERWIT. (*aside*) She jeers me, let me perish.

VINCENT. Dapperwit, a little of your aid, for my lady's invincibly dumb.

DAPPERWIT. (*aside*) Would mine had been so too.

VINCENT. I have used as many arguments to make her speak as are requisite to make other women hold their tongues.

DAPPERWIT. Well, I am ready to change sides. Yet before I go, madam, since the moon consents now I should see your face, let me desire you to pull off your mask, which to a handsome lady is a favour, I'm sure.

LYDIA. Truly, sir, I must not be long in debt to you the obligation. Pray, let me hear you recite some of your verses, which to a wit is a favour, I'm sure.

DAPPERWIT. Madam, it belongs to your sex to be obliged first. Pull off your mask and I'll pull out my paper. (*Aside*) Brisk again of my side.

LYDIA. 'Twould be in vain, for you would want a candle now.

DAPPERWIT. (*aside*) I dare not make use again of the lustre of her face. – I'll wait upon you home then, madam.

LYDIA. Faith no, I believe it will not be much to our advantage to bring my face or your poetry to light, for, I hope, you have yet a pretty good opinion of my face, and so have I of your wit. But if you are for proving your wit, why do not you write a play?

DAPPERWIT. Because 'tis now no more reputation to write a play than it is honour to be a knight; your true wit despises the title of poet as much as your true gentleman the title of knight, for as a man may be a knight and no gentleman, so a man may be a poet and no wit, let me perish.

---

244 *plea to the bay-tree*: claim to poetic laurels.

LYDIA. Pray, sir, how are you dignified or distinguished amongst the rates of wits? And how many rates are there?

DAPPERWIT. There are as many degrees of wits as of lawyers: as there is first your solicitor, then your attorney, then your pleading-counsel, then your chamber-counsel and then your judge; so there is first your court-wit, your coffee-wit, your poll-wit or politic-wit, your chamber-wit or scribble-wit and, last of all, your judge-wit or critic.

LYDIA. But are there as many wits as lawyers? Lord, what will become of us? What employment can they have? How are they known?

DAPPERWIT. First, your court-wit is a fashionable, insinuating, flattering, cringing, grimacing fellow and has wit enough to solicit a suit of love and, if he fail, he has malice enough to ruin the woman with a dull lampoon. But he rails still at the man that is absent, for, you must know, all wits rail, and his wit properly lies in combing perukes, matching ribbons and being severe, as they call it, upon other people's clothes.

LYDIA. Now, what is the coffee-wit?

DAPPERWIT. He is a lying, censorious, gossiping, quibbling wretch and sets people together by the ears over that sober drink, coffee. He is a wit as he is a commentator upon the Gazette and he rails at the pirates of Algiere, the Grand Signior of Constantinople and the Christian Grand Signior.

LYDIA. What kind of man is your poll-wit?

DAPPERWIT. He is a fidgeting, busy, dogmatical, hot-headed fop that speaks always in sentences and proverbs (as others in similitudes) and he rails perpetually against the present government. His wit lies in projects and monopolies and penning speeches for young parliament-men.

LYDIA. But what is your chamber-wit or scribble-wit?

DAPPERWIT. He is a poring, melancholy, modest sot, ashamed of the world. He searches all the records of

---

304 *Gazette*: *The London Gazette*, a semi-official newspaper, mostly with foreign news.

305 *Grand Signior of Constantinople*: the Sultan of Turkey.

306 *Christian Grand Signior*: Louis XIV of France.

wit to compile a breviate of them for the use of players, printers, book-sellers and sometimes cooks and tabacca-men. He employs his railing against the ignorance of the age and all that have more money than he.

LYDIA. Now your last.

DAPPERWIT. Your judge-wit or critic is all these together and yet has the wit to be none of them; he can think, speak, write as well as all the rest but scorns (himself a judge) to be judged by posterity. He rails at all the other classes of wits and his wit lies in damning all but himself; he is your true wit.

LYDIA. Then I suspect you are of his firm.

DAPPERWIT. I cannot deny it, madam.

VINCENT. Dapperwit, you have been all this time on the wrong side, for you love to talk all and here's a lady would not have hindered you.

DAPPERWIT. (*aside*) A pox, I have been talking too long indeed here, for wit is lost upon a silly, weak woman as well as courage.

VINCENT. I have used all common means to move a woman's tongue and mask; I called her ugly, old and old acquaintance and yet she would not disprove me. But here comes Ranger; let him try what he can do, for, since my mistress is dogged, I'll go sleep alone.

Exit.

RANGER *enters.*

LYDIA. (*aside*) Ranger! 'Tis he indeed. I am sorry he is here but glad I discovered him before I went. Yet he must not discover me, lest I should be prevented hereafter in finding him out. False Ranger! – Nay, if they bring fresh force upon us, madam, 'tis time to quit the field.

Exeunt LYDIA, FLIPPANT.

RANGER. What, play with your quarry till it fly from you?

DAPPERWIT. You frightened it away.

RANGER. Ha! Is not one of those ladies in mourning?

DAPPERWIT. All woman are so by this light.

341 *dogged*: stubborn.

RANGER. But you might easily discern it. Don't you know her?

DAPPERWIT. No.

RANGER. Did you talk with her?

DAPPERWIT. Yes, she's one of your brisk, silly baggages.

RANGER. 'Tis she, 'tis she. I was afraid I saw her before. Let us follow 'em. Prithee make haste. (*Aside*) 'Tis Lydia.

Exeunt.

LYDIA, MY LADY FLIPPANT *return at the other door,* RANGER, DAPPERWIT *following them at a distance.*

LYDIA. They follow us yet, I fear.

FLIPPANT. You do not fear it certainly, otherwise you would not have encouraged them.

LYDIA. For heaven's sake, madam, waive your quarrel a little and let us pass by your coach and so on foot to your acquaintance in the Old Pell Mell, for I would not be discovered by the man that came up last to us.

Exeunt.

SCENE II

The scene changes to Christina's lodging.

Enter CHRISTINA, ISABEL.

ISABEL. For heaven's sake, undress yourself, madam; they'll not return tonight – all people have left the park an hour ago.

CHRISTINA. What is't a clock?

ISABEL. 'Tis past one.

CHRISTINA. It cannot be.

ISABEL. I thought that time had only stolen from happy lovers; the disconsolate have nothing to do but to tell the clock.

---

366 *Old Pell Mell*: now Pall Mall, running from St James's Street to the Haymarket, named after the game played there; Act IV Scene ii takes place there.

CHRISTINA. I can only keep account with my misfortunes.

ISABEL. I am glad they are not innumerable.

CHRISTINA. And truly, my undergoing so often your impertinency is not the least of them.

ISABEL. I am then more glad, madam, for then they cannot be great and it is in my power, it seems, to make you in part happy, if I could but hold this villainous tongue of mine. But then let the people of the town hold their tongues if they will, for I cannot but tell you what they say.

CHRISTINA. What do they say?

ISABEL. Faith, madam, I am afraid to tell you, now I think on't.

CHRISTINA. Is it so ill?

ISABEL. Oh, such base unworthy things.

CHRISTINA. Do they say I was really Clerimont's wench as he boasted and that the ground of the quarrel betwixt Valentine and him was not Valentine's vindication of my honour but Clerimont's jealousy of him?

ISABEL. Worse, worse a thousand times. Such villainous things to the utter ruin of your reputation!

CHRISTINA. What are they?

ISABEL. Faith, madam, you'll be angry; 'tis the old trick of lovers to hate their informers after they have made 'em such.

CHRISTINA. I will not be angry.

ISABEL. They say then, since Mr Valentine's flying into France, you are grown mad, have put yourself into mourning, live in a dark room where you'll see nobody nor take any rest day or night but rave and talk to yourself perpetually.

CHRISTINA. Now what else?

ISABEL. But the surest sign of your madness is, they say, because you are desperately resolved (in case my Lord Clerimont should die of his wounds) to transport yourself and fortune into France, to Mr Valentine, a man that has not a groat to return you in exchange.

CHRISTINA. All this hitherto is true; now to the rest.

ISABEL. Indeed, madam, I have no more to tell you. I was sorry, I'm sure, to hear so much of any lady of mine.

CHRISTINA. Insupportable insolence.

ISABEL. (*aside*) This is some revenge for my want of sleep tonight. (*Knocking at the door*) So, I hope my old second is come; 'tis seasonable relief.

Exit ISABEL.

CHRISTINA. Unhappy Valentine, couldst thou but see how soon thy absence and misfortunes have disbanded all thy friends and turned thy slaves all renegades, thou sure wouldst prize my only faithful heart.

Enter MY LADY FLIPPANT, LYDIA, ISABEL *to her.*

FLIPPANT. Hail, faithful shepherdess! But, truly, I had not kept my word with you in coming back tonight, if it had not been for this lady who has her intrigues too with the fellows, as well as you.

LYDIA. Madam, under my Lady Flippant's protection, I am confident to beg yours, being just now pursued out of the park by a relation of mine by whom it imports me extremely not to be discovered. But I fear he is now at the door. (*Knocking at the door. To* ISABEL *going out*) Let me desire you to deny me to him courageously, for he will hardly believe he can be mistaken in me.

CHRISTINA. In such an occasion where impudence is requisite she will serve you as faithfully as you can wish, madam.

FLIPPANT. Come, come, madam, do not upbraid her with her assurance, a qualification that only fits her for a lady's service. A fine woman of the town can be no more without a woman that can make an excuse with an assurance than she can be without a glass, certainly.

CHRISTINA. She needs no advocate.

FLIPPANT. How can anyone alone manage an amorous intrigue? Though the birds are tame, somebody must help draw the net. If 'twere not for a woman that could make an excuse with assurance, how could we

---

55 s.d. *Isabel*: Isabella Q1.

61 *Hail, faithful shepherdess*: a reference to Fletcher's *The Faithful Shepherdess* (1610), a delicate pastoral inquiry into the nature of love, performed as recently as 26 February 1669.

wheedle, jilt, trace, discover, countermine, undermine and blow up the stinking fellows, which is all the pleasure I receive or design by them, for I never admitted a man to my conversation but for his punishment certainly.

CHRISTINA. Nobody will doubt that, certainly.

ISABEL *returns.*

ISABEL. Madam, the gentleman will not be mistaken; he says you are here, he saw you come in, he is your relation, his name's Ranger and is come to wait upon you home. I had much ado to keep him from coming up.

LYDIA. (*to* CHRISTINA) Madam, for heaven's sake, help me; 'tis yet in your power, if but while I retire into your dining room you will please to personate me and own yourself for her he pursued out of the park. You are in mourning too and your stature so much mine it will not contradict you.

CHRISTINA. I am sorry, madam, I must dispute any command of yours. I have made a resolution to see the face of no man till an unfortunate friend of mine, now out of the kingdom, return.

LYDIA. By that friend and by the hopes you have to see him, let me conjure you to keep me from the sight of mine now. Dear madam, let your charity prevail over your superstition.

ISABEL. He comes, he comes, madam.

RANGER *enters.* LYDIA *withdraws and stands unseen at the door.*

RANGER. [*aside*] Ha! This is no Lydia.

CHRISTINA. What unworthy defamer has encouraged you to offer me this insolence?

RANGER. (*aside*) She is liker Lydia in her style than her face. I see I am mistaken but to tell her I followed her for another were an affront rather than an excuse. She's a glorious creature.

---

86 *wheedle*: cheat.

86 *trace*: track, pursue.

CHRISTINA. Tell me sir, whence had you reason for this your rude pursuit of me into my lodging, my chamber? Why should you follow me?

RANGER. Faith, madam, because you run away from me.

CHRISTINA. That was no sign of an acquaintance.

RANGER. You'll pardon me, madam.

CHRISTINA. Then it seems you mistook me for another and the night is your excuse, which blots out all distinctions. But now you are satisfied in your mistake, I hope you will go seek out your woman in another place.

RANGER. Madam, I allow not the excuse you make for me; if I have offended I will rather be condemned for my love than pardoned for my insensibility.

LYDIA. (*behind*) How's that?

CHRISTINA. What do you say?

RANGER. Though the night had been darker my heart would not have suffered me to follow anyone but you; he has been too long acquainted with you to mistake you.

LYDIA. (*behind*) What means this tenderness? He mistook me for her, sure?

CHRISTINA. What says the gentleman? Did you know me then, sir?

RANGER. (*aside*) Not I, the devil take me, but I must on now. – Could you imagine, madam, by the innumerable crowd of your admirers, you had left any man free in the town or ignorant of the power of your beauty?

CHRISTINA. I never saw your face before, that I remember.

RANGER. Ah madam! You would never regard your humblest slave; I was till now a modest lover.

LYDIA. (*behind*) Falsest of men.

CHRISTINA. My woman said you came to seek a relation here, not a mistress.

RANGER. I must confess, madam, I thought you would sooner disprove my dissembled error than admit my visit and I was resolved to see you.

LYDIA. (*behind*) 'Tis clear.

RANGER. Indeed, when I followed you first out of the park, I was afraid you might have been a certain relation of mine, for your statures and habits are the same, but when you entered here I was with joy convinced. Besides, I would not for the world have given her troublesome love so much encouragement to have disturbed my future addresses to you, for the foolish woman does perpetually torment me to make our relation nearer – but never more in vain than since I have seen you, madam.

LYDIA. (*behind*) How shall I suffer this? 'Tis clear he disappointed me tonight for her and made me stay at home that I might not disappoint him of her company in the park.

CHRISTINA. I am amazed! But let me tell you, sir, if the lady were here, I would satisfy her the sight of me should never frustrate her ambitious designs upon her cruel kinsman.

LYDIA. (*behind*) I wish you could satisfy me.

RANGER. If she were here she would satisfy you she were not capable of the honour to be taken for you (though in the dark). Faith, my cousin is but a tolerable woman to a man that had not seen you.

CHRISTINA. Sure, to my plague, this is the first time you ever saw me!

RANGER. Sure, to the plague of my poor heart, 'tis not the hundredth time I have seen you, for since the time I saw you first you have not been at the park, playhouse, Exchange or other public place but I saw you, for it was my business to watch and follow you.

CHRISTINA. Pray, when did you see me last at the park, playhouse or Exchange?

RANGER. Some two, three days or a week ago.

CHRISTINA. I have not been this month out of this chamber.

LYDIA. (*behind*) That is to delude me.

CHRISTINA. I knew you were mistaken.

RANGER. You'll pardon a lover's memory, madam. (*Aside*) A pox, I have hanged myself in my own line. One would think my perpetual ill luck in lying should break me of the quality but, like a losing gamester, I am still for pushing on till none will trust me.

CHRISTINA. Come, sir, you run out of one error into a greater; you would excuse the rudeness of your mis-

---

187 *Exchange*: the New Exchange, an arcade of shops in the Strand.

take and intrusion at this hour into my lodgings with your gallantry to me, more unseasonable and offensive.

RANGER. Nay, I am in love, I see, for I blush and have not a word to say for myself.

CHRISTINA. But, sir, if you will needs play the gallant, pray leave my house before morning, lest you should be seen to go hence, to the scandal of my honour. [. . .] Rather than that should be I'll call up the house and neighbours to bear witness I bid you begone.

RANGER. Since you take a night-visit so ill, madam, I will never wait upon you again but by day. I go that I may hope to return and, for once, I will wish you a good night without me.

CHRISTINA. Goodnight for as long as I live.

Exit RANGER.

LYDIA. (*behind*) And goodnight to my love, I'm sure.

CHRISTINA. Though I have done you an inconsiderable service, I assure, madam, you are not a little obliged to me. (*Aside*) Pardon me, dear Valentine.

LYDIA. I know not yet whether I am more obliged than injured; when I do, I assure you, madam, I shall not be insensible of either.

CHRISTINA. I fear, madam, you are as liable to mistakes as your kinsman.

LYDIA. I fear I am more subject to 'em; it may be for want of sleep, therefore I'll go home.

CHRISTINA. My Lady Flippant, goodnight.

FLIPPANT. Goodnight – or rather good morrow, faithful shepherdess.

CHRISTINA. I'll wait of you down.

LYDIA. Your coach stays yet, I hope.

FLIPPANT. Certainly.

Exeunt omnes.

209–10 *honour. [. . .] Rather*: Q1 repeats the speech-prefix *Christina* before *Rather* and a response from Ranger has probably disappeared.

SCENE III

The scene, the street.

Enter RANGER, DAPPERWIT.

DAPPERWIT. I was a faithful sentinel; nobody came out, let me perish.

RANGER. No no, I hunted upon a wrong scent; I thought I had followed a woman but found her an angel.

DAPPERWIT. What is her name?

RANGER. That you must tell me: what very fine woman is there lies hereabouts?

DAPPERWIT. Faith, I know not any. She is, I warrant you, some fine woman of a term's standing or so in the town, such as seldom appear in public but in their balconies where they stand so constantly one would think they had hired no other part of the house.

RANGER. And look like the pictures which painters expose to draw in customers. But I must know who she is. Vincent's lodging is hard by; I'll go and inquire of him and lie with him tonight. But if he will not let me I'll lie with you, for my lodging is too far off –

DAPPERWIT. Then I will go before and expect you at mine.

Exeunt.

SCENE IV

The scene, Vincent's lodging.

Enter VINCENT, VALENTINE *in a riding habit, as newly from a journey.*

VINCENT. Your mistress, dear Valentine, will not be more glad to see you. But my wonder is no less than my joy that you would return ere you were informed Clerimont were out of danger; his surgeons themselves have not been assured of his recovery till within these two days.

---

9 *term's standing*: one of the four terms of the law-year, hence recently arrived.

VALENTINE. I feared my mistress, not my life; my life I could trust again with my old enemy, Fortune, but not longer my mistress in the hands of my greater enemies, her relations.

VINCENT. Your fear was in the wrong place then, for though my Lord Clerimont live, he and his relations may put you in more danger of your life than your mistress's relations can of losing her.

VALENTINE. Would any could secure me her I would myself secure my life, for I should value it then.

VINCENT. Come, come, her relations can do you no hurt; I dare swear, if her mother should but say your hat did not cock handsomely she would never ask her blessing again.

VALENTINE. Prithee, leave thy fooling and tell me if, since my departure, she has given evidences of her love, to clear those doubts I went away with, for, as absence is the bane of common and bastard love, 'tis the vindication of that which is true and generous.

VINCENT. Nay, if you could ever doubt her love you deserve to doubt on, for there is no punishment great enough for jealousy but jealousy.

VALENTINE. You may remember I told you, before my flight, I had quarrelled with the defamer of my mistress but thought I had killed my rival.

VINCENT. But pray, give me now the answer which the suddenness of your flight denied me: how could Clerimont hope to subdue her heart by the assault of her honour?

VALENTINE. Pish, it might be the stratagem of a rival, to make me desist.

VINCENT. For shame; if 'twere not rather to vindicate her than satisfy you, I would not tell you how like a Penelope she has behaved herself in your absence.

VALENTINE. Let me know.

VINCENT. Then know, the next day you went, she put herself into mourning and –

VALENTINE. That might be for Clerimont, thinking him dead, as all the world besides thought.

VINCENT. Still turning the dagger's point on yourself.

---

13 *than your*: than you Q1.

40 *Penelope*: Odysseus' long-waiting wife.

Hear me out. I say she put herself into mourning for you, locked up herself in her chamber this month for you, shut out her barking relations for you, has not seen the sun or face of man since she saw you, thinks and talks of nothing but you, sends to me daily to hear of you and, in short, I think, is mad for you – all this I can swear, for I am to her so near a neighbour and so inquisitive a friend for you –

[*Enter*] SERVANT *to them.*

SERVANT. Mr Ranger, sir, is coming up.

[*Exit* SERVANT]

VINCENT. What brings him now? He comes to lie with me.

VALENTINE. Who? Ranger?

VINCENT. Yes, pray retire a little till I send him off, unless you have a mind to have your arrival published tomorrow in the coffeehouses.

[*Enter* RANGER.] VALENTINE *retires to the door behind.*

RANGER. What, not yet a-bed? Your man is laying you to sleep with usquebaugh or brandy, is he not so?

VINCENT. What, punk will not be troubled with you tonight, therefore I am – is it not so?

RANGER. I have been turned out of doors indeed just now by a woman – but such a woman, Vincent –

VINCENT. Yes, yes, your women are always such women –

RANGER. A neighbour of yours and, I'm sure, the finest you have.

VINCENT. Prithee, do not asperse my neighbourhood with your acquaintance; 'twould bring a scandal upon an alley.

RANGER. Nay, I do not know her, therefore I come to you.

VINCENT. 'Twas no wonder she turned you out of doors then and, if she had known you, 'twould have been a wonder she had let you stay. But where does she live?

---

63 *usquebaugh*: whisky.

RANGER. Five doors off on the right hand.

VINCENT. Pish, pish –

RANGER. What's the matter?

VINCENT. Does she live there, do you say?

RANGER. Yes, I observed them exactly, that my account from you might be as exact. Do you know who lives there?

VINCENT. Yes, so well that I know you are mistaken.

RANGER. Is she not a young lady of scarce eighteen, of extraordinary beauty, her stature next to low, and in mourning?

VALENTINE. (*behind*) What is this?

VINCENT. She is. But if you saw her you broke in at window.

RANGER. I chased her home from the park, indeed, taking her for another lady who had some claim to my heart, till she show'd a better title to't.

VINCENT. Hah, hah, hah.

VALENTINE. (*behind*) Was she at park then? And have I a new rival?

VINCENT. From the park did you follow her, do you say? I knew you were mistaken.

RANGER. I tell you I am not.

VINCENT. If you are sure it was that house, it might be perhaps her woman stolen to the park unknown to her lady.

RANGER. My acquaintance does usually begin with the maid first but now 'twas with the mistress, I assure you.

VINCENT. The mistress! I tell you she has not been out of her doors since Valentine's flight. She is his mistress, the great heiress Christina.

RANGER. I tell you then again, I followed that Christina from the park home where I talked with her half an hour and intend to see her tomorrow again.

VALENTINE. (*behind*) Would she talk with him too?

VINCENT. It cannot be.

RANGER. Christina, do you call her? Faith, I am sorry she is an heiress, lest it should bring the scandal of interest and design of lucre upon my love.

---

80 *Five . . . hand*: the line comes from Q1's list of errata; the text reads *He whispers.*

VINCENT. No, no, her face and virtues will free you from that censure. But, however, 'tis not fairly done to rival your friend Valentine in his absence and, when he is present, you know 'twill be dangerous, by my Lord Clerimont's example. Faith, if you have seen her, I would not advise you to attempt it again.

RANGER. You may be merry, sir; you are not in love. Your advice I came not for, nor will I for your assistance. Goodnight. *Exit* RANGER.

VALENTINE. Here's your Penelope, the woman that had not seen the sun nor face of man since my departure, for it seems she goes out in the night, when the sun is absent and faces are not distinguished.

VINCENT. Why, do you believe him?

VALENTINE. Should I believe you?

VINCENT. 'Twere more for your interest and you would be less deceived. If you believe him you must doubt the chastity of all the fine women in town and five miles about.

VALENTINE. His reports of them will little invalidate his testimony with me.

VINCENT. He spares not the innocents in bibs and aprons, I'll secure you. He has made, at best, some gross mistake concerning Christina, which tomorrow will discover. In the meantime, let us go sleep.

VALENTINE. I will not hinder you because I cannot enjoy it myself.
Hunger, revenge to sleep are petty foes
But only death the jealous eyes can close.

Exeunt.

ACT III

SCENE I

Crossbite's house.

Enter MRS JOYNER, MRS CROSSBITE.

JOYNER. Good morrow, gossip.

CROSSBITE. Good morrow. But why up so early, good gossip?

JOYNER. My care and passionate concern for you and yours would not let me rest, in truly.

CROSSBITE. For me and mine?

JOYNER. You know we have known one another long. I think it be some nine and thirty years since you were married.

CROSSBITE. Nine and thirty years old, mistress? I'd have you to know I am no far-born child and if the register had not been burned in the last great fire, alas! But my face needs no register, sure. Nine and thirty years old said you, mistress?

JOYNER. I said you had been so long married. But, indeed, you bear your years as well as any she in Pepper Alley.

CROSSBITE. Nine and thirty, mistress.

JOYNER. This it is: a woman nowadays had rather you should find her faulty with a man, I warrant you, than discover her age, I warrant you.

CROSSBITE. Marry, and 'tis the greater secret far. Tell a miser he is rich and a woman she is old, you will get no money of him nor kindness of her. To tell me I was nine and thirty (I say no more), 'twas unneighbourly done of you, mistress.

JOYNER. My memory confesses my age, it seems, as much as my face, for I thought –

CROSSBITE. Pray talk nor think no more of anyone's age. But say, what brought you hither so early?

JOYNER. How does my sweet god-daughter? Poor wretch.

CROSSBITE. Well, very well.

JOYNER. Ah, sweet creature! Alas, alas, I am sorry for her.

CROSSBITE. Why, what has she done to deserve your sorrow or my reprehension?

LUCY *comes to the door.*

LUCY. (*behind*) What, are they talking of me?

---

11 *far-born*: born long ago.

17 *Pepper Alley*: in the notorious suburb of Southwark, across the river from the city.

JOYNER. In short, she was seen going into the meeting-house of the wicked, otherwise called the playhouse, hand-in-hand with that vile fellow Dapperwit.

CROSSBITE. Mr Dapperwit! Let me tell you, if 'twere not for Master Dapperwit we might have lived all this vacation upon green cheese, tripe and ox cheek. If he had it we should not want it. But poor gentleman, it often goes hard with him, for he's a wit.

JOYNER. So then, you are the dog to be fed, while the house is broken up. I say beware, the sweet bits you swallow will make your daughter's belly swell, mistress, and, after all your junkets, there will be a bone for you to pick, mistress.

CROSSBITE. Sure, Master Dapperwit is no such manner of man?

JOYNER. He is a wit, you say, and what are wits but contemners of matrons, seducers or defamers of married women and deflowerers of helpless virgins, even in the streets, upon the very bulks; affronters of midnight magistracy and breakers of windows, in a word.

CROSSBITE. But he is a little-wit, a modest-wit and they do no such outrageous things as your great wits do.

JOYNER. Nay, I dare say he will not say himself he is a little-wit, if you ask him.

LUCY. (*aside*) Nay, I cannot hear this with patience. – With your pardon, mother, you are as much mistaken as my godmother in Mr Dapperwit, for he is as great a wit as any and, in what he speaks or writes, as happy as any. I can assure you he contemns all your tearing wits in comparison of himself.

JOYNER. Alas, poor young wretch, I cannot blame thee so much as thy mother, for thou art not thyself; his bewitching madrigals have charmed thee into some heathenish imp with a hard name.

LUCY. Nymph, you mean, godmother.

JOYNER. But you, gossip, know what's what. Yesterday, as I told you, a fine old alderman of the city, seeing

---

50 *junkets*: treats, pleasure-trips.
57 *bulks*: stalls outside shops.
69 *tearing*: grand, splendid.

your daughter in so ill hands as Dapperwit's, was zealously, and in pure charity, bent upon her redemption and has sent me to tell you he will take her into his care and relieve your necessities, if you think good.

CROSSBITE. Will he relieve all our necessities?

JOYNER. All.

CROSSBITE. Mine as well as my daughter's?

JOYNER. Yes.

CROSSBITE. Well fare his heart. D'ye hear, daughter, Mrs Joyner has satisfied me clearly. Dapperwit is a vile fellow and, in short, you must put an end to that scandalous familiarity between you.

LUCY. Leave sweet Mr Dapperwit! Oh furious ingratitude! Was not he the man that gave me my first farrenden gown, put me out of worsted stockings and plain handkerchiefs, taught me to dress, talk and move well?

CROSSBITE. He has taught you to talk indeed! But, huswife, I will not have my pleasure disputed.

JOYNER. Nay, indeed, you are too tart with her, poor sweet soul.

LUCY. He taught me to rehearse too, would have brought me into the playhouse, where I might have had as good luck as others; I might have had good clothes, plate, jewels and things so well about me that my neighbours, the little gentlemen's wives of fifteen hundred or two thousand pound a year, should have retired into the country, sick with envy of my prosperity and greatness.

JOYNER. If you follow your mother's counsel you are like to enjoy all you talk of sooner than by Dapperwit's assistance, a poor wretch that goes on tick for the paper he writes his lampoons on and the very ale and coffee that inspires him, as they say.

CROSSBITE. I am credibly informed so, indeed, Madam Joyner.

JOYNER. Well, I have discharged my conscience. Good morrow to you both.

Exeunt.

---

92 *farrenden*: farandine, a cloth made out of silk and wool or hair, much more genteel than worsted stockings.

100 *into the playhouse*: as an actress.

SCENE II

Crossbite's dining-room.

Enter DAPPERWIT, RANGER.

DAPPERWIT. This is the cabinet in which I hide my jewel, a small house in an obscure, little, retired street too.

RANGER. Vulgarly an alley.

DAPPERWIT. Nay, I hid my mistress with as much care as a spark of the town does his money from his dun after a good hand at play, and nothing but you could have wrought upon me for a sight of her, let me perish.

RANGER. My obligation to you is great; do not lessen it by delays of the favour you promised.

DAPPERWIT. But do not censure my honour, for if you had not been in a desperate condition – for as one nail must beat out another, one poison expel another, one fire draw out another, one fit of drinking cure the sickness of another, so the surfeit you took last night of Christina's eyes shall be cured by Lucy's this morning, or as –

RANGER. Nay, I bar more similitudes.

DAPPERWIT. What, in my mistress's lodging? That were as hard as to bar a young parson in the pulpit, the fifth of November, railing at the Church of Rome or as hard to put you to bed to Lucy and defend you touching her or as –

RANGER. Or as hard as to make you hold your tongue! I shall not see your mistress, I see!

DAPPERWIT. Miss Lucy, Miss Lucy. (*Knocks at the door and returns*) The devil take me if good men (I say no more) have not been upon their knees to me to see her and you at last must obtain it.

RANGER. I do not believe you.

DAPPERWIT. 'Tis such a she; she is beautiful without affectation, amorous without impertinency, airy and brisk without impudence, frolic without rudeness

---

6 *dun*: creditor.

21 *fifth of November*: anniversary of the Catholic Gunpowder Plot, an unsuccessful attempt to blow up King, Lords and Commons in Parliament.

and, in a word, the justest creature breathing to her assignation.

RANGER. You praise her as if you had a mind to part with her and yet you resolve, I see, to keep her to yourself.

DAPPERWIT. Keep her! Poor creature, she cannot leave me and, rather than leave her, I would leave writing lampoons or sonnets almost.

RANGER. Well, I'll leave you with her then.

DAPPERWIT. What, will you go without seeing her?

RANGER. Rather than stay without seeing her.

DAPPERWIT. Yes, yes, you shall see her. But let me perish if I have not been offered a hundred guineas for a sight of her by – I say no more.

RANGER. (*aside*) I understand you now. – If the favour be to be purchased then I'll bid all I have about me for't.

DAPPERWIT. Fie, fie, Mr Ranger, you are pleasant, i'faith. Do you think I would sell the sight of my rarity? Like those gentlemen who hang out flags at Charing Cross or like –

RANGER. Nay, then I'm gone again.

DAPPERWIT. What, you take it ill I refuse your money? Rather than that should be, give us it. But take notice I will borrow it – now I think on't, Lucy wants a gown and some knacks.

RANGER. Here.

DAPPERWIT. But I must pay it you again; I will not take it unless you engage your honour I shall pay it you again.

RANGER. You must pardon me; I will not engage my honour for such a trifle. Go fetch her out.

DAPPERWIT. Well, she's a ravishing creature; such eyes and lips, Mr Ranger.

RANGER. Prithee go.

DAPPERWIT. Such neck and breasts, Mr Ranger.

RANGER. Again, prithee go.

DAPPERWIT. Such feet, legs and thighs, Mr Ranger.

---

34 *justest*: both 'most suitable, exact' and, ironically, 'most faithful'.

53 *hang out flags*: advertisements for freak shows and other similar entertainments; hardly complimentary.

59 *knacks*: trinkets.

RANGER. Prithee, let me see 'em.

DAPPERWIT. And a mouth no bigger than your ring. I need say no more.

RANGER. Would thou wert never to speak again.

DAPPERWIT. And then so neat, so sweet a creature in bed that to my knowledge she does not change her sheets in half a year.

RANGER. I thank you for that allay to my impatience.

DAPPERWIT. (*knocking at the door*) Miss Lucy, Miss Lucy, Miss.

RANGER. Will she not open?

DAPPERWIT. I am afraid my pretty miss is not stirring and therefore will not admit us. [. . .] Fie, fie, a quibble next your stomach in a morning! What if she should hear us? Would you lose a mistress for a quibble? That's more than I could do, let me perish.

RANGER. Is she not gone her walk to Lamb's Conduit?

DAPPERWIT. She is within; I hear her.

RANGER. But she will not hear you; she's as deaf as if you were a dun or a constable.

DAPPERWIT. Pish, give her but leave to gape, rub her eyes and put on her day-pinner, the long patch under the left eye, awaken the roses on her cheeks with some Spanish wool and warrant her breath with some lemon peel, the door flies off of the hinges and she into my arms. She knows there is as much artifice to keep a victory as to gain it and 'tis a sign she values the conquest of my heart.

RANGER. I thought her beauty had not stood in need of art.

DAPPERWIT. Beauty's a coward still without the help of art and may have the fortune of a conquest but cannot keep it. Beauty and art can no more be asunder than love and honour.

RANGER. Or to speak more like yourself, wit and judgement.

---

84 *admit us. [. . .] Fie*: Q1 repeats the speech-prefix *Dapperwit*, indicating that a speech of Ranger has dropped out.

88 *Lamb's Conduit*: Lamb's Conduit Fields, built in 1577, a popular area to the north of the city.

92 *gape*: yawn.

93 *day-pinner*: a cap with two long flaps fastened at the breast.

95 *Spanish wool*: rouge.

DAPPERWIT. Don't you hear the door wag yet?

RANGER. Not a whit.

DAPPERWIT. Miss, Miss, 'tis your slave that calls. Come, all this tricking for him! Lend me your comb, Mr Ranger.

RANGER. No, I am to be preferred today; you are to set me off. You are in possession; I will not lend you arms to keep me out –

DAPPERWIT. A pox, don't let me be ungrateful; if she has smugged herself up for me, let me prune and flounce my peruke a little for her. There's ne'er a young fellow in the town but will do as much for a mere stranger in the playhouse.

RANGER. A wit's wig has the privilege of being uncombed in the very playhouse or in the presence –

DAPPERWIT. But not in the presence of his mistress; 'tis a greater neglect of her than himself. Pray lend me your comb.

RANGER. I would not have men of wit and courage make use of every fop's mean arts to keep or gain a mistress.

DAPPERWIT. But don't you see every day, though a man have ne'er so much wit and courage, his mistress will revolt to those fops that wear and comb perukes well. I'll break off the bargain and will not receive you my partner.

RANGER. (*combs his peruke*) Therefore, you see, I am setting up for myself.

DAPPERWIT. She comes, she comes; pray, your comb. (*Snatches* RANGER*'s comb*)

Enter MRS CROSSBITE *to them.*

CROSSBITE. Bargain! What are you offering us to sale?

DAPPERWIT. A pox, is't she? Here, take your comb again then. (*Returns the comb*)

CROSSBITE. Would you sell us? 'Tis like you, y'fads.

DAPPERWIT. Sell thee? Where should we find a chapman? Go, prithee, mother, call out my dear Miss Lucy.

---

117 *smugged*: smartened up.
122 *in the presence*: of the King.
140 *y'fads*: in faith.
141–2 *chapman*: trader.

CROSSBITE. Your Miss Lucy! I do not wonder you have the conscience to bargain for us behind our backs, since you have the impudence to claim a propriety in us to my face.

RANGER. How's this, Dapperwit?

DAPPERWIT. Come, come, this gentleman will not think the worse of a woman for my acquaintance with her. He has seen me bring your daughter to the lure with a Chiney orange, from one side of the playhouse to the other.

CROSSBITE. I would have the gentleman and you to know, my daughter is a girl of reputation, though she has been seen in your company, but is now so sensible of her past danger that she is resolved never more to venture her pitcher to the well, as they say.

DAPPERWIT. How's that, widow? I wonder at your new confidence.

CROSSBITE. I wonder at your old impudence, that where you have had so frequent repulses you should provoke another and bring your friend here to witness your disgrace.

DAPPERWIT. Hark you, widow, a little.

CROSSBITE. What, you have mortgaged my daughter to that gentleman and now would offer me a snip to join in the security!

DAPPERWIT. (*aside*) She overheard me talk of a bargain; 'twas unlucky. – Your wrath is grounded upon a mistake; Miss Lucy herself shall be judge. Call her out, pray.

CROSSBITE. She shall not, she will not come to you.

DAPPERWIT. Till I hear it from her own mouth I cannot believe it.

CROSSBITE. You shall hear her say't through the door.

DAPPERWIT. I shall doubt it unless she say it to my face.

CROSSBITE. Shall we be troubled with you no more then?

DAPPERWIT. If she command my death I cannot disobey her.

CROSSBITE. Come out, child.

---

150 *bring . . . the lure*: a hawking term for recalling the bird.
151 *Chiney orange*: the sweet orange (*citrus sinensis*), a delicacy at this time, sold in the theatre.

[*Enter*] LUCY, *holding down her head, to them.*

DAPPERWIT. Your servant, dearest miss, can you have –

CROSSBITE. Let me ask her.

DAPPERWIT. No, I'll ask her.

RANGER. I'll throw up cross or pile who shall ask her.

DAPPERWIT. Can you have the heart to say you will never more break a cheesecake with me at New Spring Garden, the Neat House or Chelsea, never more sit in my lap at a new play, never more wear a suit of knots of my choice and, last of all, never more pass away an afternoon with me again in the green garret? In – Do not forget the green garret.

LUCY. I wish I had never seen the green garret. Dem the green garret!

DAPPERWIT. Dem the green garret! you are strangely altered.

LUCY. 'Tis you are altered.

DAPPERWIT. You have refused Colby's Mulberry Garden and the French houses for the green garret and a little something in the green garret pleased you more than the best treat the other places could yield. And can you of a sudden quit the green garret?

LUCY. Since you have a design to pawn me for the rent, 'tis time to remove my goods.

DAPPERWIT. Thou art extremely mistaken.

LUCY. Besides, I have heard such strange things of you this morning –

DAPPERWIT. What things?

LUCY. I blush to speak 'em.

DAPPERWIT. I know my innocence, therefore take my charge as a favour. What have I done?

LUCY. Then know, vile wit, my mother has confessed

---

185 *cross or pile*: heads or tails.

187–8 *New . . . Chelsea*: New Spring Garden at Vauxhall, gardens for entertainment and refreshment; the Neat Houses at Chelsea were market gardens (Pepys took some friends there in August 1667); Chelsea is probably the Chelsea Bun Shop, another popular place with Londoners.

189 *suit of knots*: bow of ribbons.

193 *Dem*: damn.

198 *Colby*: probably the man who ran the restaurant at Mulberry Garden; see the last scene of *Love in a Wood.*

just now thou wert false to me, to her too certain knowledge, and hast forced even her to be false to me too.

DAPPERWIT. Faults in drink, Lucy, when we are not ourselves, should not condemn us.

LUCY. And now to let me out to hire like hackney. I tell you my own dear mother shall bargain for me no more; there are as little as I can bargain for themselves nowadays, as well as properer women.

CROSSBITE. Whispering all this while! Beware of his snares again. Come away, child.

DAPPERWIT. Sweet, dear Miss.

LUCY. Bargain for me! You have reckoned without your hostess, as they say. Bargain for me, bargain for me!

Exit LUCY.

DAPPERWIT. I must return then to treat with you.

CROSSBITE. Treat me no treatings but take a word for all: you shall no more dishonour my daughter nor molest my lodgings, as you have done at all hours.

DAPPERWIT. Do you intend to change 'em, then, to Bridewell or Long's powdering-tub?

CROSSBITE. No, to a bailiff's house – and then you'll be so civil, I presume, as not to trouble us.

RANGER. Here, will you have my comb again, Dapperwit?

DAPPERWIT. A pox, I think women take inconstancy from me worse than from any man breathing.

CROSSBITE. Pray, sir, forget me before you write your next lampoon. *Exit* CROSSBITE.

[Enter] SIR SIMON ADDLEPLOT *in the dress of a clerk, to* RANGER *and* DAPPERWIT.

SIR SIMON. Have I found you? Have I found you in your by-walks, faith and troth? I am almost out of breath in following you. Gentlemen when they get into an alley walk so fast, as if they had more earnest business there than in the broad streets.

218 *hackney*: a hackney coach.

232 *Bridewell*: a house of correction, for prostitutes in particular, just off Fleet Street.

232 *Long's powdering-tub*: Long is unknown but the powdering-tub is the sweating-tub used in the treatment of venereal diseases.

DAPPERWIT. (*aside*) How came this sot hither? Fortune has sent him to ease my choler. – You impudent rascal, who are you that dares intrude thus on us? (*Strikes him*)

SIR SIMON. (*softly*) Don't you know me, Dapperwit? Sure, you know me.

DAPPERWIT. Wilt thou dishonour me with thy acquaintance too? Thou rascally, insolent pen-and-ink man! (*Strikes him again*)

SIR SIMON. (*speak softly*) Oh, oh, sure you know me, pray know me.

DAPPERWIT. By thy saucy familiarity thou shouldst be a marker at a tennis-court, a barber or a slave that fills coffee.

SIR SIMON. Oh, oh.

DAPPERWIT. What art thou? (*Kicks him*)

SIR SIMON. [*aside*] Nay, I must not discover myself to Ranger for a kick or two. – Oh, pray hold, sir; (*delivers him a letter*) by that you will know me.

DAPPERWIT. How, Sir Simon!

SIR SIMON. Mum, mum, make no excuses, man; I would not Ranger should have known me for five hundred – kicks.

DAPPERWIT. Your disguise is so natural, I protest, it will excuse me.

SIR SIMON. I know that; prithee make no excuses, I say, no ceremony between thee and I, man. Read the letter.

DAPPERWIT. What, you have not opened it?

SIR SIMON. Prithee don't be angry; the seal is a little cracked, for I could not help kissing Mrs Martha's letter. The word is 'now or never'; her father she finds will be abroad all this day and she longs to see your friend, Sir Simon Addleplot – faith, 'tis a pretty jest – while I am with her and praising myself to her at no ordinary rate. Let thee and I alone at an intrigue!

DAPPERWIT. Tell her I will not fail to meet her at the place and time. Have a care of your charge and manage your business like yourself for yourself.

SIR SIMON. I warrant you.

DAPPERWIT. (*aside*) The gaining Gripe's daughter will

---

256 *marker*: scorer.

make me support the loss of this young jilt here.

RANGER. What fellow's that?

DAPPERWIT. A servant to a friend of mine.

RANGER. Methinks he something resembles our acquaintance Sir Simon but it is no compliment to tell him so, for that knight is the most egregious coxcomb that ever played with lady's fan.

SIR SIMON. (*aside*) So; thanks to my disguise, I know my enemies.

RANGER. The most incorrigible ass, beyond the reproof of a kicking rival or a frowning mistress. But, if it be possible, thou dost use him worse than his mistress or rival can: thou dost make such a cully of him.

SIR SIMON. (*aside*) Does he think so too?

DAPPERWIT. Go, friend, about your business.

Exit SIR SIMON.

A pox, you would spoil all, just in the critical time of projection; he brings me here a summons from his mistress to meet her in the evening. Will you come to my wedding?

RANGER. Don't speak so loud – you'll break poor Lucy's heart. Poor creature, she cannot leave you and, rather than leave her, you should leave writing of lampoons or sonnets – almost.

DAPPERWIT. Come, let her go, ungrateful baggage. But, now you talk of sonnets, I am no living wit if her love has not cost me two thousand couplets at least.

RANGER. But what would you give now for a new satire against women ready made; 'twould be as convenient to buy satires against women ready made as to buy cravats ready tied.

DAPPERWIT. Or as –

RANGER. Hey, come away, come away, Mr Or-as –

Exeunt.

Enter MRS JOYNER, GRIPE.

GRIPE. Peace, plenty and pastime be within these walls.

---

301 *projection*: in alchemy, the stage of transmutation of base-metal into gold or silver.

317 Gripe distorts *Luke* 10.5: 'And into whatsoever house ye enter, first say "Peace be to this house" ', adding 'pastime', his special interest.

JOYNER. 'Tis a small house, you see, and mean furniture, for no gallants are suffered to come hither. She might have had ere now as good lodgings as any in town, her Moreclack hangings, great glasses, cabinets, China embroidered beds, Persian carpets, gold plate and the like, if she would have put herself forward but your worship may please to make 'em remove to a place fit to receive one of your worship's quality, for this is a little scandalous, in truly.

GRIPE. No, no, I like it well enough; I am not dainty. Besides, privacy, privacy, Mrs Joyner, I love privacy, in opposition to the wicked who hate it. (*Looks about*)

JOYNER. What do you look for, sir?

GRIPE. Walls have ears, walls have ears, but, besides, I look for a private place to retire to, in time of need. Oh, here's one convenient. (*Turns up a hanging and discovers the slender provisions of the family*)

JOYNER. But you see, poor innocent souls, to what use they put it, not to hide gallants.

GRIPE. Temperance is the nurse of chastity.

JOYNER. But your worship may please to mend their fare and, when you come, may make them entertain you better than, you see, they do themselves.

GRIPE. No, I am not dainty, as I told you. I abominate entertainments; no entertainments, pray, Mrs Joyner.

JOYNER. (*aside*) No.

GRIPE. There can be no entertainment to me more luscious and savoury than the communion with that little gentlewoman. Will you call her out? I fast till I see her.

JOYNER. But, in truly, your worship, we should have brought a bottle or two of Rhenish and some Naples biscuit to have entertained the young gentlewoman; 'tis the mode for lovers to treat their mistresses.

GRIPE. Modes! I tell you, Mrs Joyner, I hate modes and forms.

JOYNER. You must send for something to entertain her with.

---

321 *Moreclack hangings*: tapestries made at the famous works at Mortlake.

348–9 *Naples biscuit*: a crisp biscuit.

GRIPE. Again entertaining! We will be to each other a feast.

JOYNER. I shall be ashamed, in truly, your worship; besides, the young gentlewoman will despise you.

GRIPE. I shall content her, I warrant you; leave it to me.

JOYNER. (*aside*) I am sure you will not content me if you will not content her; 'tis as impossible for a man to love and be a miser as to love and be wise, as they say.

GRIPE. While you talk of treats you starve my eyes; I long to see the fair one. Fetch her hither.

JOYNER. I am so ashamed she should find me so abominable a liar. I have praised you to her and, above all your virtues, your liberality, which is so great a virtue that it often excuses youth, beauty, courage, wit or anything.

GRIPE. Pish, pish, 'tis the virtue of fools; every fool can have it.

JOYNER. And will your worship want it then? I told her –

GRIPE. Why would you tell her anything of me? You know I am a modest man. But come, if you will have me as extravagant as the wicked, take that and fetch us a treat, as you call it.

JOYNER. Upon my life, a groat! What will this purchase?

GRIPE. Two black pots of ale and a cake, at the next cellar. Come, the wine has arsenic in't.

JOYNER. (*aside*) Well, I am mistaken and my hopes are abused. I never knew any man so mortified a miser that he would deny his lechery anything. I must be even with thee then another way. *Goes out.*

GRIPE. These useful old women are more exorbitant and craving in their desires than the young ones in theirs. These prodigals in white perukes spoil 'em both and that's the reason, when the squires come under my clutches, I made 'em pay for their folly and mine – and 'tis but conscience. Oh, here comes the fair one at last.

Enter JOYNER *leading in* LUCY, *who hangs backward as she enters.*

---

380 *black pots*: beer mugs.
388 *white perukes*: powdered in the fashionable mode.

LUCY. Oh Lord, there's a man, godmother!

JOYNER. Come in, child. Thou art so bashful!

LUCY. My mother is from home too; I dare not.

JOYNER. If she were here she'd teach you better manners.

LUCY. I'm afraid she'd be angry.

JOYNER. To see you so much an ass. Come along, I say.

GRIPE. Nay, speak to her gently; if you won't, I will.

LUCY. Thank you, sir.

GRIPE. Pretty innocent, there is, I see, one left yet of her age. What hap have I! Sweet little gentlewoman, come and sit down by me.

LUCY. I am better bred, I hope, sir.

GRIPE. You must sit down by me.

LUCY. I'd rather stand, if you please.

GRIPE. To please me you must sit, sweetest.

LUCY. Not before my godmother, sure.

GRIPE. Wonderment of innocence!

JOYNER. A poor bashful girl, sir. I'm sorry she is not better taught.

GRIPE. I am glad she is not taught – I'll teach her myself.

LUCY. Are you a dancing-master then, sir? But if I should be dull and not move as you would have me, you would not beat me, sir, I hope?

GRIPE. Beat thee, honeysuckle! I'll use thee thus and thus and thus. (*Kisses her*) Ah, Mrs Joyner, prithee go fetch our treat now.

JOYNER. A treat of a groat! I will not wag.

GRIPE. Why don't you go? Here, take more money and fetch what you will. Take here, half a crown.

JOYNER. What will half a crown do?

GRIPE. Take a crown then, an angel, a piece. Be gone.

JOYNER. A treat only will not serve my turn. I must buy the poor wretch there some toys.

GRIPE. What toys? What? Speak quickly.

JOYNER. Pendants, necklaces, fans, ribbons, points, laces, stockings, gloves –

---

421 *wag*: stir.

425 *an angel, a piece*: ten shillings and twenty-two shillings respectively.

429 *points*: lace embroidery.

GRIPE. Hold, hold, before it comes to a gown.

JOYNER. Well remembered, sir! Indeed, she wants a gown, for she has but that one to her back. For your own sake you should give her a new gown, for variety of dresses rouses desire and makes an old mistress seem every day a new one.

GRIPE. For that reason she shall have no new gown, for I am naturally constant and, as I am still the same, I love she should be still the same. But here, take half a piece for the other things.

JOYNER. Half a piece!

GRIPE. Prithee be gone; take t'other piece then, two pieces, three pieces, five – here, 'tis all I have.

JOYNER. I must have the broad-seal ring too or I stir not.

GRIPE. Insatiable woman, will you have that too? Prithee spare me that; 'twas my grandfather's.

JOYNER. (*aside*) That's false; he had ne'er a coat. So now I go. This is but a violent fit and will not hold.

LUCY. Oh, whither do you go, godmother? Will you leave me alone?

JOYNER. The gentleman will not hurt you; you may venture yourself with him alone.

LUCY. I think I may, godmother.

Exit JOYNER.

What, will you lock me in, sir? Don't lock me in, sir!

GRIPE. (*fumbling at the door, locks it*) 'Tis a private lesson I must teach you, fair.

LUCY. I don't see your fiddle, sir. Where is your little kit?

GRIPE. I'll show it thee presently, sweetest. (GRIPE *setting a chair against the door*) Necessity, mother of invention. (*Takes her in his arms*) Come, my dearest.

LUCY. What do you mean, sir? Don't hurt me, sir, will you! (*Cries out*) Oh, oh, you will kill me! Murder, murder, oh, oh! Help, help, oh!

The door broke open, enter CROSSBITE *and two men in aprons, her* LANDLORD *and his* PRENTICE.

---

444 *broad-seal ring*: ring with a coat-of-arms on it for sealing documents.

447 *coat*: of arms, as well as a coat to his back.

458 *kit*: (*a*) dancing-master's small violin (*b*) equipment.

CROSSBITE. What, murder my daughter, villain?

LUCY. I wish he had murdered me, oh, oh!

CROSSBITE. What has he done?

LUCY. Why would you go out and leave me alone? Unfortunate woman that I am.

GRIPE. (*aside*) How now! What will this end in?

CROSSBITE. Who brought him in?

LUCY. That witch, that treacherous false woman, my godmother, who has betrayed me, sold me to his lust. Oh oh!

CROSSBITE. Have you ravished my daughter then, you old goat? Ravished my daughter, ravished my daughter? Speak, villain.

GRIPE. By yea and by nay, no such matter.

CROSSBITE. A canting rogue too. Take notice, landlord, he has ravished my daughter; you see her all in tears and distraction and see there the wicked engine of the filthy execution (*pointing to the chair*). Jeremy, call up my neighbours and the constable. False villain, thou shalt die for't.

GRIPE. Hold, hold. (*Aside*) Nay, I am caught.

CROSSBITE. Go, go, make haste –

LUCY. Oh, oh!

CROSSBITE. Poor wretch. Go quickly.

GRIPE. Hold, hold. Thou young spawn of the old serpent, wicked as I thought thee innocent, wilt thou say I would have ravished thee?

LUCY. I will swear you did ravish me.

GRIPE. (*aside*) I thought so, treacherous Eve. Then I am gone; I must shift as well as I can.

LUCY. Oh, oh!

CROSSBITE. Will none of you call up the neighbours and the authority of the alley?

[*Exit* PRENTICE.]

GRIPE. Hold, I'll give thee twenty mark among you to let me go.

CROSSBITE. Villain, nothing shall buy thy life.

---

478 *By yea and by nay*: Puritans were not allowed to swear but could declare 'by yea and nay'; it was a popular pejorative term for Puritans since it fitted their reputation for equivocation.

479 *canting*: hypocritically pious.

498 *mark*: thirteen shillings and fourpence.

LANDLORD. But, stay, Mrs Crossbite, let me talk with you.

LUCY. Oh, oh!

LANDLORD. Come, sir, I am your friend; in a word, I have appeased her and she shall be contented with a little sum.

GRIPE. What is it? What is it?

LANDLORD. But five hundred pound.

GRIPE. But five hundred pound! Hang me then, hang me rather!

LANDLORD. You will say I have been your friend.

[*Re-enter* PRENTICE.]

PRENTICE. The constable and neighbours are coming.

GRIPE. How, how! (*Kneels to* CROSSBITE) Will you not take a hundred? Pray use conscience in your ways.

CROSSBITE. I scorn your money; I will not take a thousand.

GRIPE. (*aside*) My enemies are many and I shall be a scandal to the faithful as a laughing-stock to the wicked. – Go, prepare your engines for my persecution. I'll give you the best security I can.

LANDLORD. The instruments are drawing in the other room, if you please to go thither.

CROSSBITE. Indeed, now I consider, a portion will do my daughter more good than his death – that would but publish her shame; money will cover it. *Probatum est*, as they say. Let me tell you, sir, 'tis a charitable thing to give a young maid a portion.

Exeunt omnes.

SCENE III

The scene changes to Lydia's lodging.

Enter LYDIA, MY LADY FLIPPANT, [LEONORE].

LYDIA. 'Tis as hard for a woman to conceal her indignation from her apostate lover as to conceal her love from her faithful servant.

525–6 *Probatum est*: It is proved; tried and tested.

FLIPPANT. Or almost as hard as it is for the prating fellows nowadays to conceal the favours of obliging ladies.

LYDIA. If Ranger should come up (I saw him just now in the street), the discovery of my anger to him now would be as mean as the discovery of my love to him before.

FLIPPANT. Though I did so mean a thing as to love a fellow, I would not do so mean a thing as to confess it, certainly, by my trouble to part with him. If I confessed love it should be before they left me.

LYDIA. So you would deserve to be left before you were. But could you ever do so mean a thing as to confess love to any?

FLIPPANT. Yes – but I never did so mean a thing as really to love any.

LYDIA. You had once a husband.

FLIPPANT. Fie, madam, do you think me so ill-bred as to love a husband?

LYDIA. You had a widow's heart before you were a widow, I see.

FLIPPANT. I should rather make an adventure of my honour with a gallant for a gown, a new coach, a necklace, than clap my husband's cheeks for them or sit in his lap. I should be as ashamed to be caught in such a posture with a husband as a brisk, well-bred spark of the town would be to be caught on his knees at prayers, unless to a mistress.

[*Enter*] *to them*, RANGER, DAPPERWIT.

LYDIA. Mr Ranger, 'twas obligingly done of you.

RANGER. Indeed, cousin, I had kept my promise with you last night but this gentleman knows –

LYDIA. You mistake me but you shall not lessen any favour you do me. You are going to excuse your not coming to me last night when I take it as a particular obligation that, though you threatened me with a visit, upon consideration you were so civil as not to trouble me.

DAPPERWIT. (*aside*) This is an unlucky morning with me: here's my eternal persecution, the widow Flippant.

29–30 *well-bred spark*: well-bred Q1 (Q2 supplies the missing word).

FLIPPANT. What, Mr Dapperwit!

RANGER. Indeed, cousin, besides my business, another cause I did not wait on you was my apprehension you were gone to the park, notwithstanding your promise to the contrary.

LYDIA. Therefore you went to the park to visit me there, notwithstanding your promise to the contrary.

RANGER. Who, I at the park, when I had promised to wait upon you at your lodging? But were you at the park, madam?

LYDIA. Who, I at the park, when I had promised to wait for you at home? I was no more at the park than you were. Were you at the park?

RANGER. The park had been a dismal desert to me, notwithstanding all the good company in't, if I had wanted yours.

LYDIA. (*aside*) Because it has been the constant endeavour of men to keep women ignorant, they think us so; but 'tis that increases our inquisitiveness and makes us know them ignorant as false. He is as impudent a dissembler as the widow Flippant who is making her importunate addresses in vain, for ought I see.

FLIPPANT *driving* DAPPERWIT *from one side of the stage to the other.*

FLIPPANT. Dear Mr Dapperwit, merciful Mr Dapperwit.

DAPPERWIT. Unmerciful Lady Flippant.

FLIPPANT. Will you be satisfied?

DAPPERWIT. Won't you be satisfied?

FLIPPANT. (*aside to* DAPPERWIT) That a wit should be jealous! That a wit should be jealous! There's never a brisk young fellow in the town, though no wit, heaven knows, but thinks too well of himself to think ill of his wife or mistress. Now that a wit should lessen his opinion of himself, for shame!

DAPPERWIT. (*softly apart to* RANGER) I promised to bring you off but I find it enough to shift for myself!

LYDIA. What, out of breath, madam?

FLIPPANT. I have been defending our cause, madam. I have beat him out of the pit. I do so mumble these

---

80 *beat him out of the pit*: victory in cock-fighting and in a wit-combat in the pit of the theatre.

80 *mumble*: handle roughly.

prating, censorious fellows they call wits when I meet with them.

DAPPERWIT. Her Ladyship indeed is the only thing in petticoats I dread; 'twas well for me there was company in the room, for I dare no more venture myself with her alone than a cully that has been bit dares venture himself in a tavern with an old rook.

FLIPPANT. I am the revenger of our sex, certainly.

DAPPERWIT. And the most insatiable one I ever knew, madam; I dare not stay your fury longer. Mr Ranger, I will go before and make a new appointment with your friends that expect you at dinner at the French house. 'Tis fit business; still wait on love.

RANGER. Do so – but now I think on't, Sir Thomas goes out of town this afternoon and I shall not see him here again these three months.

LYDIA. Nay, pray take him with you, sir.

FLIPPANT. No, sir, you shall not take the gentleman from his mistress. (*Aside*) Do not go yet, sweet Mr Dapperwit.

LYDIA. Take him with you, sir. I suppose his business may be there to borrow or win money and I ought not to be his hindrance, for when he has none he has his desperate designs upon that little I have, for want of money makes as devout lovers as christians.

DAPPERWIT. I hope, madam, he offers you no less security than his liberty.

LYDIA. His liberty! As poor a pawn to take up money on as honour! He is like the desperate bankrouts of this age, who, if they can get people's fortunes into their hands, care not though they spend them in gaol all their lives.

FLIPPANT. And the poor crediting ladies, when they have parted with their money, must be contented with a pitiful composition or starve for all them.

RANGER. But widows are commonly so wise as to be sure their men are solvable before they trust 'em.

FLIPPANT. Can you blame 'em? I declare I will trust no man; pray do not take it ill, gentlemen. Quacks in

---

109 *bankrouts*: bankrupts.
117 *solvable*: solvent.

their bills and poets in the titles of their plays do not more disappoint us than gallants with their promises. But I trust none.

DAPPERWIT. Nay, she's a very jew in that particular; to my knowledge, she'll know her man over and over again before she trust him.

RANGER. Well, my dearest cousin, good morrow. When I stay from you so long again blame me to purpose and be extremely angry, for nothing can make me amends for the loss of your company but your reprehension of my absence. I'll take such a chiding as kindly as Russian wives do beating.

LYDIA. If you were my husband I could not take your absence more kindly than I do.

RANGER. And if you were my wife I would trust you as much out of my sight as I could, to show my opinion of your virtue.

FLIPPANT. A well-bred gentleman, I warrant. Will you go then, cruel Mr Dapperwit?

Exeunt RANGER *and* DAPPERWIT.

LYDIA. (*apart*) Have I not dissembled well, Leonore?

LEONORE. But, madam, to what purpose? Why do you not put him to his trial and see what he can say for himself?

LYDIA. I am afraid lest my proofs and his guilt should make him desperate and so contemn that pardon which he could not hope for.

LEONORE. 'Tis unjust to condemn him before you hear him.

LYDIA. I will reprieve him till I have more evidence.

LEONORE. How will you get it?

LYDIA. I will write him a letter in Christina's name, desiring to meet him, when I shall soon discover if his love to her be of a longer standing than since last night and, if it be not, I will not longer trust him with the vanity to think she gave him the occasion to follow her home from the park, so will at once disabuse him and myself.

LEONORE. What care the jealous take in making sure of ills which they, but in imagination, cannot undergo.

---

131 *as Russian . . . beating*: a popular belief at the time.

LYDIA. Misfortunes are least dreadful when most near.
'Tis less to undergo the ill than fear.

Exeunt.

ACT IV

SCENE I

Gripe's house.

Enter MRS JOYNER *and* GRIPE *in a blue gown and night-cap.*

JOYNER. What, not well, your worship? This it is, you will be laying out yourself beyond your strength; you have taken a surfeit of the little gentlewoman, I find. Indeed, you should not have been so immoderate in your embraces – your worship is something in years, in truly.

GRIPE. Graceless, perfidious woman, what mak'st thou here? Art thou not afraid to be used like an informer since thou hast made me pay thee for betraying me?

JOYNER. Betray your worship! What do you mean? I an informer! I scorn your words.

GRIPE. Woman, I say again, thou art as treacherous as an informer and more unreasonable, for he lets us have something for our money before he disturbs us.

JOYNER. Your money, I'm sure, was laid out faithfully and I went away because I would not disturb you.

GRIPE. I had not grudged you the money I gave you but the five hundred pound! The five hundred pound, inconscionable, false woman! The five hundred pound! You cheated, trapanned, robbed me of the five hundred pound!

JOYNER. I cheat you, I rob you! Well, remember what you say; you shall answer it before Mr Double-cap, and the best of –

GRIPE. Oh impudent woman, speak softly!

20 *trapanned*: ensnared, beguiled.

JOYNER. I will not speak softly, for innocence is loud as well as bare-faced. Is this your return after you have made me a mere drudge to your filthy lusts?

GRIPE. Speak softly; my sister, daughter and servants will hear.

JOYNER. I would have witnesses to take notice that you blast my good name, which was as white as a tulip and as sweet as the head of your cane before you wrought me to the carrying-on the work of your fleshly carnal seekings.

GRIPE. Softly, softly – they are coming in.

Enter FLIPPANT *and* MARTHA.

FLIPPANT. What's the matter, brother?

GRIPE. Nothing, nothing, sister, only the godly woman is fallen into a fit of zeal against the enormous transgressions of the age. Go, go, you do not love to hear vanity reproved; pray be gone.

JOYNER. Pray stay, madam, that you may know –

GRIPE. (*aside to* JOYNER) Hold, hold, here are five guineas for thee; pray say nothing. – Sister, pray be gone, I say.

Exeunt FLIPPANT *and* MARTHA.

Would you prejudice your own reputation to injure mine?

JOYNER. Would you prejudice your own soul to wrong my repute, in truly? (*She seems to weep*)

GRIPE. Pray, have me in excuse. Indeed, I thought you had a share of the five hundred pound because you took away my seal-ring, which they made me send together with a note to my cash-keeper for five hundred pound. Besides, I thought none but you knew it was my wonted token to send for money by.

JOYNER. 'Twas unlucky I should forget it and leave it on the table. But oh, the harlotry! Did she make that use of it then? 'Twas no wonder you did not stay till I came back.

GRIPE. I stayed till the money released me.

JOYNER. Have they the money then? Five hundred pound!

GRIPE. Too certain.

JOYNER. They told me not a word of it. And have you no way to retrieve it?

GRIPE. Not any.

JOYNER. (*aside*) I am glad of it. – Is there no law but against the saints?

GRIPE. I will not for five hundred pound publish my transgression myself lest I should be thought to glory in't – though, I must confess, 'twould tempt a man to conform to public praying and sinning, since 'tis so chargeable to pray and sin in private.

JOYNER. But are you resolved to give off, a loser?

GRIPE. How shall I help it?

JOYNER. Nay, I'll see you shall have what the young jade has. For your money I'll make 'um use some conscience however. Take a man's money for nothing?

GRIPE. Thou say'st honestly indeed. And shall I have my pennyworths out of the little gentlewoman for all this?

JOYNER. I'll be engaged body for body for her and you shall take the forfeiture on me else.

GRIPE. No, no, I'll rather take your word, Mrs Joyner.

JOYNER. Go in and dress yourself smug and leave the rest to me.

GRIPE. No man breathing would give off a loser, as she says.

Exeunt.

Enter SIR SIMON ADDLEPLOT, *sitting at a desk writing as a clerk,* MY LADY FLIPPANT *jogging him.*

SIR SIMON. 'Tis a lord's mortgage and therefore requires the more haste. Pray do not jog me, madam.

FLIPPANT. (*aside*) Dull rascal.

SIR SIMON. They cannot stay for money as other folks. If you will not let me make an end on't I shall lose my expedition fee.

FLIPPANT. (*aside*) There are some clerks would have understood me before this.

SIR SIMON. Nay, pray be quiet, madam. If you squeeze me so to the wall I cannot write.

FLIPPANT. (*aside*) 'Tis much for the honour of the gentlemen of this age that we persons of quality are forced to descend to the importuning of a clerk, a butler, coachman or footman, while the rogues are as

68 *saints*: the Puritans' term for themselves.

dull of apprehension too as an unfledged country squire amongst his mother's maids. (*Jogs him again*)

SIR SIMON. Again! Let me tell you, madam, familiarity breeds contempt. You'll never leave till you have made me saucy.

FLIPPANT. I would I could see that.

SIR SIMON. I vow and swear then, get you gone, or I'll add a black patch or two to those on your face. (*Aside*) I shall have no time to get Mrs Martha out, for her.

FLIPPANT. (*jogs him again*) Will you, sir? Will you?

SIR SIMON. (*aside*) I must have a plot for her; she is a coy woman. – I vow and swear, if you pass this crevice I'll kiss you, in plain English.

FLIPPANT. I would I could see that. Do you defy me?

Steps to him. He kisses her.

SIR SIMON. (*aside*) How's this? I vow and swear, she kisses as tamely as Mrs Ticklish, and with her mouth open too.

FLIPPANT. I thought you would have been ashamed to have done so to your master's own sister.

SIR SIMON. I hope you'll be quiet now, madam!

FLIPPANT. Nay, I'll be revenged of you, sure.

SIR SIMON. If you come again I shall do more to you than that. (*Aside*) I'll pursue my plot and try if she be honest.

FLIPPANT. You do more to me than that! Nay, if you'll do more to me than that –

She throws down his ink and runs out; he follows her.

Enter JOYNER.

JOYNER. I must visit my young clients in the meantime.

SIR SIMON *returns, holding up his hands.*

What's the matter, Sir Simon?

SIR SIMON. Lord, who would have thought it?

JOYNER. What ails you, Sir Simon?

SIR SIMON. I have made such a discovery, Mrs Joyner.

114–15 Ward suggested that this comes from *Les Cents Nouvelles Nouvelles* (tale 23) and Bandello, *Le Novelle*. I do not think the stage business warrants such esoteric references.

132 *ails*: aile Q1.

JOYNER. What is't?

SIR SIMON. Such an one that makes me at once glad and sorry: I am sorry my Lady Flippant is naught but I'm glad I know it, thanks still to my disguise.

JOYNER. Fie, fie.

SIR SIMON. Nay, this hand can tell!

JOYNER. But how?

SIR SIMON. She threw down my ink-glass and ran away into the next room; I followed her and, in revenge, threw her down upon the bed but, in short, all that I could do to her would not make her squeak.

JOYNER. She was out of breath, man, she was out of breath.

SIR SIMON. Ah, Mrs Joyner, say no more, say no more of that.

Enter FLIPPANT.

FLIPPANT. You rude, unmannerly rascal.

JOYNER. You see she complains now.

SIR SIMON. (*apart*) I know why, Mrs Joyner, I know why.

FLIPPANT. I'll have you turned out of the house; you are not fit for my brother's service.

SIR SIMON. (*aside*) Not for yours, you mean, madam.

FLIPPANT. I'll go and acquaint my brother –

JOYNER. [*aside to* FLIPPANT] Hold, hold, madam, speak not so loud. 'Tis Sir Simon Addleplot, your lover, who has taken this disguise on purpose to be near you, and to watch and supplant his rivals.

FLIPPANT. (*aside to* JOYNER) What a beast was I, I could not discover it! You have undone me. Why would you not tell me sooner of it?

JOYNER. [*aside to* FLIPPANT] I thought he had been discernible enough.

FLIPPANT. [*aside to* JOYNER] I protest I knew him not, for I must confess to you my eyes are none of the best, since I have used the last new wash of Mercury water. What will he think of me?

JOYNER. [*aside to* FLIPPANT] Let me alone with him. – Come, come, did you think you could disguise

---

169 *Mercury water*: a mixture of aqua regia and corrosive sublimate used as a skin-wash – *very* harmful to the eyes.

yourself from my Lady's knowledge? She knew you, man, or else you had ne'er had those liberties. Alas, poor lady, she cannot resist you.

FLIPPANT. 'Tis my weakness.

SIR SIMON. How's this? But here comes my master.

Enter GRIPE *and* MARTHA.

GRIPE. Come, Mrs Joyner, are you ready to go?

JOYNER. I am ever ready when your worship commands.

FLIPPANT. Brother, if you go to t'other end of the town, you'll set me down near the playhouse.

GRIPE. The playhouse! Do you think I will be seen near the playhouse?

FLIPPANT. You shall set me down in Lincoln's Inn Fields then, for I have earnest business there. (*Apart*) When I come home again I'll laugh at you soundly, Sir Simon.

SIR SIMON. (*aside*) Has Joyner betrayed me then? 'Tis time to look to my hits.

GRIPE. Martha, be sure you stay within now. If you go out you shall never come into my doors again.

MARTHA. No, I will not, sir; I'll ne'er come into your doors if once I should go out.

GRIPE. 'Tis well said, girl.

Exeunt GRIPE, JOYNER, FLIPPANT.

SIR SIMON. 'Twas prettily said. I understand you; they are dull and have no intrigue in 'em. But, dear, sweet Mrs Martha, 'tis time we were gone. You have stole away your scarves and hood from your maid, I hope.

MARTHA. Nay, I am ready, but –

SIR SIMON. Come, come, Sir Simon Addleplot, poor gentleman, is an impatient man, to my knowledge.

MARTHA. Well, my venture is great, I'm sure, for a man I know not. But pray, Jonas, do not deceive me. Is he so fine a gentleman as you say he is?

SIR SIMON. Pish, pish, he is the – gentleman of the town, faith and troth.

MARTHA. But may I take your word, Jonas?

183–4 *Lincoln's Inn Fields*: site of the theatre used by the Duke's Company.

188 *to look to my hits*: to have an eye to the main chance.

SIR SIMON. 'Tis not my word; 'tis the word of all the town.

MARTHA. Excuse me, Jonas, for that; I never heard any speak well of him but Mr Dapperwit and you.

SIR SIMON. That's because he has been a rival to all men and a gallant to all ladies; rivals and deserted mistresses never speak well of a man.

MARTHA. Has he been so general in his amours his kindness is not to be valued then?

SIR SIMON. The more by you because 'tis for you he deserts all the rest, faith and troth.

MARTHA. You plead better for him than he could for himself, I believe, for indeed they say he is no better than an idiot.

SIR SIMON. Then believe me, madam, for nobody knows him better than I; he has as much wit, courage and as good a mien to the full as I have. He an idiot?

MARTHA. The common gull, so perspicuous a fop the women find him out, for none of 'em will marry him.

SIR SIMON. You may see now how he and you are abused, for that he is not married is a sign of his wit and, for being perspicuous, 'tis false – he is as mysterious as a new parliament-man or a young statesman, newly taken from a coffeehouse or tennis-court.

MARTHA. But is it a sign of his wit because he is not married?

SIR SIMON. Yes, yes, your women of the town ravish your fops; there's not one about the town unmarried that has anything.

MARTHA. It may be then he has spent his estate.

SIR SIMON. (*aside*) How unluckily guessed! – If he had, he has a head can retrieve it again.

MARTHA. Besides, they say, he has had the modish distemper.

SIR SIMON. He can cure it with the best French chirurgeon in town.

MARTHA. Has his practice on himself been so much?

SIR SIMON. Come, come.

240–1 *modish distemper*: syphilis.
242–3 *French chirurgeon*: surgeon specialising in venereal diseases.

Fame, like deserted jilt, does still belie men.
Who doubts her man must be advised by Hymen,
For he knows best of any how to try men.

Exeunt.

SCENE II

The scene, the Old Pell Mell.

Enter RANGER *and* DAPPERWIT.

RANGER. Now the Lucies have renounced us, hey for the Christinas. She cannot use me worse than your honourable mistress did you.

DAPPERWIT. A pox, some heir or another has promised her marriage. There are so many fools in the world, 'tis impossible for a man of wit to keep his wench from being a lady, let me perish.

RANGER. But have you no other acquaintance that sticks to her vocation in spite of temptations of honour or filthy lucre? I declare, I make honourable love merely out of necessity, as your rooks play on the square rather than not play at all.

[Enter,] to them, LEONORE, LYDIA*'s woman, masked, with a letter in her hand.*

DAPPERWIT. Come, the devil will not lose a gamester. Here's ready money for you; push freely.

RANGER. (*to her*) Thou'rt as well met as if by assignation.

LEONORE. And you are as well met as if you were the man I looked for.

RANGER. Kind rogue!

LEONORE. Sweet sir.

RANGER. Come, I am thy prisoner. Without more words, show but thy warrant. (*Goes to pull off her mask*)

LEONORE. You mistake, sir; here is my pass. (*Gives him the letter*)

RANGER. A letter, and directed to me. (*Reads*) 'I cannot put up the injuries and affronts you did me last

---

247 *Hymen*: god of marriage.
11–12 *on the square*: by the rules, without cheating.

night' – a challenge, upon my life, and by such a messenger! – 'therefore conjure you, by your honour, at eight a'clock precisely this evening to send your man to St James's Gate to wait for me with a chair, to conduct me to what place you shall think most fit for the giving of satisfaction to the injured Christina.' Christina! I am amazed! What is't a'clock, Dapperwit?

DAPPERWIT. It wants not half an hour of eight.

RANGER. (*to the maid*) Go then back, my pretty herald, and tell my fair enemy, the service she designs my man is only fit for my friend here, of whose faith and honour she may be secure of. He shall, immediately, go wait for her at St James's Gate, whilst I go to prepare a place for our rancounter and myself to die at her feet.

Exit LEONORE.

Dapperwit, dear Dapperwit.

DAPPERWIT. What lucky surprisal's this?

RANGER. Prithee ask no questions till I have more leisure and less astonishment. I know you will not deny to be an instrument in my happiness.

DAPPERWIT. No, let me perish, I take as much pleasure to bring lovers together as an old woman that, as a bankrupt gamester loves to look on though he has no advantage by the play, or as a bully that fights not himself yet takes pleasure to set people together by the ears or as –

RANGER. 'Sdeath, is this a time for similitudes?

DAPPERWIT. You have made miscarry of a good thought now, let me perish.

RANGER. Go presently to St James's Gate, where you are to expect the coming of a lady ('tis Christina), accompanied by that woman you saw ev'n now. She will permit you to put her into a chair and then conduct her to my lodging, while I go before to remove some spies and prepare it for her reception.

DAPPERWIT. Your lodging! Had you not better carry her to Vincent's? 'Tis hard by and there a vizard mask has as free egress and regress as at the playhouse.

RANGER. Faith, though it be not very prudent, yet she

38 *St James's Gate*: by St James's Palace, close to Pall Mall.

shall come thither in my vindication, for he would not believe I had seen her last night.

DAPPERWIT. To have a fine woman and not tell on't, as you say, Mr Ranger, –

RANGER. Go and bring her to Vincent's lodging; there I'll expect you.

Exeunt severally.

Enter CHRISTINA, ISABEL, *her woman.*

ISABEL. This is the door, madam; here Mr Vincent lodges.

CHRISTINA. 'Tis no matter; we will pass it by lest the people of our lodging should watch us. But if he should not be here now!

ISABEL. Who, Mr Valentine, madam? I warrant you, my intelligencer dares not fail me.

CHRISTINA. Did he come last night, said he?

ISABEL. Last night late.

CHRISTINA. And not see me yet, nay, not send to me! 'Tis false, he is not come. I wish he were not; I know not which I should take more unkindly from him, exposing his life to his revengeful enemies or being almost four and twenty hours so near me and not let me know't.

ISABEL. A lover's dangers are the only secrets kept from his mistress; he came not to you because he would not purchase his happiness with your fear and apprehensions.

CHRISTINA. Nay, he is come, I see, since you are come about again of his side.

ISABEL. Will you go in, madam, and disprove me if you can; 'tis better than standing in the street.

CHRISTINA. We'll go a little farther first and return.

Exeunt.

SCENE III

Vincent's lodging.

Enter VINCENT *and* VALENTINE.

VINCENT. I told you I had sent my man to Christina's this morning to inquire of her maid (who seldom denies him a secret) if her lady had been at the park last night, which she peremptorily answered to the contrary and assured him she had not stirred out since your departure.

VALENTINE. Will not chambermaids lie, Vincent?

VINCENT. Will not Ranger lie, Valentine?

VALENTINE. The circumstances of his story proved it true.

VINCENT. Do you think so old a master in the faculty as he will want the varnish of probability for his lies?

VALENTINE. Do you think a woman, having the advantage of her sex and education, under such a mistress, will want impudence to disavow a truth that might be prejudicial to that mistress?

VINCENT. But if both testimonies are fallible, why will you needs believe his? We are apter to believe the things we would have than those we would not.

VALENTINE. My ill luck has taught me to credit my misfortune and doubt my happiness.

VINCENT. But Fortune we know inconstant.

VALENTINE. And all of her sex.

VINCENT. Will you judge of Fortune by your experience and not do your mistress the same justice? Go see her and satisfy yourself and her, for, if she be innocent, consider how culpable you are, not only in your censures of her but in not seeing her since your coming.

VALENTINE. If she be innocent I should be afraid to surprise her, for her sake; if false, I should be afraid to surprise her for my own.

VINCENT. To be jealous and not inquisitive is as hard as to love extremely and not be something jealous.

VALENTINE. Inquisitiveness as seldom cures jealousy as drinking in a fever quenches the thirst.

VINCENT. If she were at the park last night 'tis probable she'll not miss this. Go watch her house, see who goes out, who in, while I in the meantime search out Ranger, who, I'll pawn my life, upon more discourse, shall avow his mistake. Here he is; go in. How luckily is he come!

Enter RANGER. VALENTINE *retires to the door behind, overhearing them.*

Ranger, you have prevented me. I was going to look

you out between the scenes at the playhouses, the coffeehouses, tennis-court or Gifford's.

RANGER. Do you want a pretence to go to a bawdy-house? But I have other visits to make.

VINCENT. I forget I should rather have sought you in Christina's lodgings, ha, ha, ha.

RANGER. Well, well, I am just come to tell you that Christina –

VINCENT. Proves not by daylight the kind lady you followed last night out of the park.

RANGER. I have better news for you, to my thinking.

VINCENT. What is't?

RANGER. Not that I have been in Christina's lodging this morning but that she'll be presently here in your lodging with me.

VALENTINE. (*behind*) How!

VINCENT. (*drawing back to the door where* VALENTINE *stood and speaking softly to him*) You see now his report was a jest, a mere jest. (*To* RANGER) Well, must my lodging be your vaulting school still. Thou hast appointed a wench to come hither, I find.

RANGER. A wench! You seemed to have more reverence for Christina last night.

VINCENT. Now you talk of Christina, prithee tell me what was the meaning of thy last night's romance of Christina?

RANGER. You shall know the meaning of all when Christina comes. She'll be here presently.

VINCENT. Who will? Christina?

RANGER. Yes, Christina.

VINCENT. Ha, ha, ha.

RANGER. Incredulous envy! Thou art as envious as an impotent lecher at a wedding.

VINCENT. Thou art either mad or as vain as a Frenchman newly returned home from a campaign or obliging England.

---

45 *Gifford's*: Mother Gifford's famous brothel.

62–3 *vaulting school*: brothel.

79 *obliging England*: either the Frenchman has obliged England (by fulfilling a task) or he has found England, particularly its women, obligingly complaisant and accommodating.

RANGER. Thou art as envious as a rival. But if thou art mine, there's that will make you desist (*gives him the letter*) and if you are not my rival, entrusting you with such a secret will, I know, oblige you to keep it and assist me against all other interests.

VINCENT. Do you think I take your secret as an obligation? Don't I know lovers, travellers and poets will give money to be heard? But what's the paper? A lampoon upon Christina hatched last night betwixt Squire Dapperwit and you, because her maid used you scurvily.

RANGER. No, 'tis only a letter from her to show my company was not disgustful to her last night but that she desires it again today.

VALENTINE. (*behind*) A letter from her.

VINCENT. A letter from Christina. (*Reads*) Ha, ha, ha.

RANGER. Nay, 'tis pleasant.

VINCENT. You mistake; I laugh at you, not the letter.

RANGER. I am like the winning gamester, so pleased with my luck I will not quarrel with any who calls me a fool for't.

VINCENT. Is this the style of a woman of honour?

RANGER. It may be, for ought you know. I'm sure 'tis well if your female correspondents can read.

VINCENT. I must confess I have none of the little letters, half name or title, like your Spanish epistles dedicatory. But that a man so frequent in honourable intrigues as you are should not know the summons of an impudent common woman from that of a person of honour!

RANGER. Christina is so much a person of honour she'll own what she has writ when she comes.

VINCENT. But will she come hither indeed?

RANGER. Immediately. You'll excuse my liberty with you; I could not conceal such a happiness from such a friend as you, lest you should have taken it unkindly.

VINCENT. Faith, you have obliged me indeed, for you and others would often have made me believe your honourable intrigues but never did me the honour to convince me of 'em before.

RANGER. You are merry, I find, yet.

VINCENT. When you are happy, I cannot be otherwise.

RANGER. (*aside*) But I lose time. I should lay a little

person in ambush, that lives hard by, in case Christina should be impatient to be revenged of her friends, as it often happens with a discontented heiress. Women, like old soldiers, more nimbly execute than they resolve. (*Going out*)

VINCENT. What now, you will not disappoint a woman of Christina's quality?

RANGER. I'll be here before she comes, I warrant you.

Exit RANGER.

VINCENT. I do believe you truly. What think you, Valentine?

VALENTINE. I think, since she has the courage to challenge him, she'll have the honour of being first in the field.

VINCENT. Fie, your opinion of her must be as bad as Ranger's of himself is good, to think she would write to him. I long till his *bona roba* comes that you may be both disabused.

VALENTINE. And I have not patience to stay her coming, lest you should be disabused.

Enter CHRISTINA *and* ISABEL.

VINCENT. Here she is, i'faith. I'm glad she's come.

VALENTINE. And I'm sorry. But I will to my post again, lest she should say she came to me.

CHRISTINA *pulls off her mask.*

VINCENT. (*aside*) By heavens, Christina herself, 'tis she!

VALENTINE. (*behind*) 'Tis she. Cursed be these eyes, more cursed than when they first betrayed me to that false bewitching face!

CHRISTINA. You may wonder, sir, to see me here –

VINCENT. I must confess I do.

CHRISTINA. But the confidence your friend has in you is the cause of mine – and yet some blushes it does cost to come to seek a man.

VALENTINE. (*behind*) Modest creature.

VINCENT. (*aside*) How am I deceived!

CHRISTINA. Where is he, sir? Why does he not appear to keep me in countenance? Pray call him, sir; 'tis something hard if he should know I'm here.

---

124 *person*: Ward emends to *parson*, which is what Ranger means.
139 *bona roba*: loose woman.

VINCENT. I hardly can, myself, believe you are here, madam.

CHRISTINA. If my visit be troublesome or unseasonable, 'tis your friend's fault; I designed it not to you, sir. Pray call him out that he may excuse it and take it on himself together with my shame.

VINCENT. (*aside*) How impatient she is!

CHRISTINA. Or do you delay the happiness I ask to make it more welcome? I have stayed too long for it already and cannot more desire it. Dear sir, call him out. Where is he? Above or here within? I'll snatch the favour which you will not give. (*Goes to the door and discovers* VALENTINE) What, do you hide yourself for shame?

VALENTINE. I must confess I do.

CHRISTINA. To see me come hither –

VALENTINE. I acknowledge it.

VALENTINE *offers to go out.*

CHRISTINA. Before you came to me. But whither do you go? Come, I can forgive you.

VALENTINE. But I cannot forgive you.

CHRISTINA. Whither do you go? You need not forge a quarrel to prevent mine to you, nor need you try if I would follow you. You know I will; I have, you see.

VALENTINE. (*aside*) That impudence should look so like innocence.

CHRISTINA. Whither would you go? Why would you go?

VALENTINE. To call your servant to you.

CHRISTINA. She is here. What would you with her?

VALENTINE. I mean your lover, the man you came to meet.

CHRISTINA. Oh heavens! What lover? What man? I came to seek no man but you, whom I had too long lost.

VALENTINE. You could not know that I was here.

CHRISTINA. (*points to* ISABEL) Ask her; 'twas she that told me.

VALENTINE. How could she know?

CHRISTINA. That you shall know hereafter.

VALENTINE. No, you thought me too far out of the way to disturb your assignation and I assure you, madam, 'twas my ill fortune, not my design; and, that it may appear so, I do withdraw (as in all good breeding and civility I am obliged) for, sure, your wished-for lover's coming.

CHRISTINA. What do you mean? Are you aweary of that title?

VALENTINE. I am ashamed of it since it grows common. (*Going out*)

CHRISTINA. Nay, you will not, shall not go.

VALENTINE. My stay might give him jealousy and so do you injury and him the greatest in the world. Heavens forbid! I would not make a man jealous, for though you call a thousand vows and oaths and tears to witness (as you safely may) that you have not the least of love for me, yet, if he ever knew how I have loved you, sure, he would not, could not believe you.

CHRISTINA. I do confess your riddle is too hard for me to solve; therefore you are obliged to do't yourself.

VALENTINE. I wish it were capable of any other interpretation than what you know already.

CHRISTINA. Is this that generous good Valentine who has disguised him so? (*She weeps*)

VINCENT. Nay, I must withhold you then. (*Stops* VALENTINE *going out*) Methinks she should be innocent; her tongue and eyes, together with that flood that swells 'em, do vindicate her heart.

VALENTINE. (*going out*) They show but their long practice of dissimulation.

VINCENT. Come back. I hear Ranger coming up. Stay but till he comes.

VALENTINE. Do you think I have the patience of an alderman?

VINCENT. You may go out this way when you will, by the back-stairs. But stay a little till – oh, here he comes.

RANGER *enters.*

VALENTINE. My revenge will now detain me.

VALENTINE *retires again. Upon* RANGER*'s entrance* CHRISTINA *puts on her mask.*

RANGER. (*aside*) What, come already? Where is Dapperwit? – The blessing's double that comes quickly. I

230–1 the patience of aldermen was proverbial.

did not yet expect you here, otherwise I had not done myself the injury to be absent but I hope, madam, I have not made you stay long for me.

CHRISTINA. I have not stayed at all for you.

RANGER. I am glad of it, madam.

CHRISTINA. (*to* ISABEL *aside; removing from him to t'other side*) Is not this that troublesome stranger who last night followed the lady into my lodgings? 'Tis he.

RANGER. (*aside*) Why does she remove so disdainfully from me? – I find you take it ill I was not at your coming here, madam.

CHRISTINA. Indeed I do not; you are mistaken, sir.

RANGER. Confirm me by a smile then, madam; remove that cloud which makes me apprehend foul weather. (*Goes to take off her mask*) Mr Vincent, pray retire; 'tis you keep on the lady's mask and no displeasure which she has for me – yet, madam, you need not distrust his honour or his faith. But do not keep the lady under constraint; pray leave us a little, Master Vincent.

CHRISTINA. You must not leave us, sir. Would you leave me with a stranger?

VALENTINE. (*behind*) How's that!

RANGER. (*aside*) I've done amiss, I find, to bring her hither. (*Apart to* CHRISTINA) Madam, I understand you –

CHRISTINA. Sir, I do not understand you.

RANGER. You would not be known to Mr Vincent.

CHRISTINA. 'Tis your acquaintance I would avoid.

RANGER. (*aside*) Dull brute that I was to bring her hither! – (*Softly to her*) I have found my error, madam. Give me but a new appointment where I may meet you by and by and straight I will withdraw as if I knew you not.

CHRISTINA. Why, do you know me?

RANGER. (*aside*) I must not own it. (*Offers to whisper*) No, madam, but –

CHRISTINA. Whispering, sir, argues an old acquaintance but I have not the vanity to be thought of yours and resolve you shall never have the disparagement of mine. Mr Vincent, pray let us go in here.

RANGER. [*aside*] How's this! I am undone, I see, but if

I let her go thus I shall be an eternal laughing-stock to Vincent.

VINCENT. Do you not know him, madam? I thought you had come hither on purpose to meet him.

CHRISTINA. To meet him!

VINCENT. By your own appointment.

CHRISTINA. What strange infatuation does delude you all? You know he said he did not know me.

VINCENT. You writ him; he has your letter.

CHRISTINA. Then you know my name sure! Yet you confessed but now you knew me not.

RANGER. I must confess your anger has disguised you more than your mask, for I thought to have met a kinder Christina here.

CHRISTINA. Heavens! How could he know me in this place? He watched me hither, sure, or is there any other of my name? That you may no longer mistake me for your Christina, I'll pull off that which soothes your error. (*Pulls off her mask*)

RANGER. Take but t'other vizard off too, I mean your anger, and I'll swear you are the same and only Christina which I wished and thought to meet here.

CHRISTINA. How could you think to meet me here?

RANGER. By virtue of this your commission (*gives her the letter*) which now, I see, was meant a real challenge, for you look as if you would fight with me.

CHRISTINA. The paper is a stranger to me; I never writ it. You are abused.

VINCENT. Christina is a person of honour and will own what she has written, Ranger.

RANGER. (*aside*) So, the comedy begins. I shall be laughed at sufficiently if I do not justify myself; I must set my impudence to hers. She is resolved to deny all, I see, and I have lost all hope of her.

VINCENT. Come, faith, Ranger –

RANGER. You will deny too, madam, that I followed you last night from the park to your lodging where I stayed with you till morning? You never saw me before, I warrant.

---

297 *soothes*: proves true.

CHRISTINA. That you rudely intruded last night into my lodging I cannot deny but I wonder you have the confidence to brag of it. Sure, you will not of your reception?

RANGER. I never was so ill-bred as to brag of my reception in a lady's chamber, not a word of that, madam.

VALENTINE. [*behind*] How! If he lies I revenge her; if it be true I revenge myself.

VALENTINE *draws his sword which* VINCENT *seeing thrusts him back and shuts the door upon him before he was discovered by* RANGER.

Enter LYDIA *and her woman, stopping at the door.*

LYDIA. [*aside*] What do I see! Christina with him! A counterplot to mine to make me and it ridiculous. 'Tis true, I find, they have been long acquainted and I long abused. But, since she intends a triumph, in spite as well as shame (not emulation) I retire. She deserves no envy who will be shortly in my condition; his natural inconstancy will prove my best revenge on her – on both.

Exeunt LYDIA *with her woman.*

[*Enter*] DAPPERWIT *to them.*

DAPPERWIT. Christina's going away again. What's the matter?

RANGER. What do you mean?

DAPPERWIT. I scarce had paid the chairmen and was coming up after her but I met her on the stairs in as much haste as if she had been frightened.

RANGER. Who do you talk of?

DAPPERWIT. Christina, whom I took up in a chair just now at St James's Gate.

RANGER. Thou art mad. Here she is; this is Christina.

DAPPERWIT. I must confess I did not see her face but I am sure the lady is gone that I brought just now.

RANGER. I tell you again, this is she. Did you bring two?

CHRISTINA. I came in no chair, had no guide but my woman there.

VINCENT. When did you bring your lady, Dapperwit?

DAPPERWIT. Ev'n now, just now.

VINCENT. This lady has been here half an hour.

RANGER. He knows not what he says. He is mad, you are all so, I am so too.

VINCENT. 'Tis the best excuse you can make for yourself and, by owning your mistake, you'll show you are come to yourself. I myself saw your woman at the door, who but looked in and then immediately went down again, as your friend Dapperwit too affirms.

CHRISTINA. You had best follow her that looked for you and I'll go seek out him I came to see, Mr Vincent, pray let me in here.

RANGER. 'Tis very fine, wondrous fine!

CHRISTINA *goes out a little and returns.*

CHRISTINA. Oh, he is gone! Mr Vincent, follow him. He were yet more severe to me in endangering his life than in his censures of me. You know the power of his enemies is great as their malice; just heaven preserve him from them, and me from this ill or unlucky man.

Exeunt CHRISTINA, *her woman and* VINCENT.

RANGER. 'Tis well. Nay, certainly, I shall never be master of my senses more. But why dost thou help to distract me too?

DAPPERWIT. My astonishment was as great as yours, to see her go away again. I would have stayed her if I could.

RANGER. Yet again talking of a woman you met going out, when I talk of Christina.

DAPPERWIT. I talk of Christina too.

RANGER. She went out just now; the woman you found me with was she.

DAPPERWIT. That was not the Christina I brought just now.

RANGER. You brought her almost half an hour ago. 'Sdeath, will you give me the lie?

DAPPERWIT. A lady disappointed by her gallant the night before her journey could not be more touchy with her maid or husband than you are with me now after your disappointment. But if you thank me so I'll go serve myself hereafter. For ought I know I have disappointed Mrs Martha for you and may lose thirty thousand pound by the bargain. Farewell, a raving lover is fit for solitude. *Exit* DAPPERWIT.

RANGER. Lydia, triumph; I now am thine again. Of intrigue, honourable or dishonourable, and all sorts of rambling I take my leave. When we are giddy 'tis time to stand still. Why should we be so fond of the by-paths of love, where we are still waylaid with surprises, trapans, dangers and murdering disappointments?

Just as at Blind-Man's Buff, we run at all,
Whilst those that lead us laugh to see us fall,
And when we think we hold the lady fast
We find it but her scarf or veil at last. *Exit.*

ACT V

SCENE I

St James's Park.

Enter SIR SIMON ADDLEPLOT *leading* MRS MARTHA, DAPPERWIT.

SIR SIMON. At length, you see, I have freed the captive lady for her longing knight. Mr Dapperwit, who brings off a plot cleverly now?

DAPPERWIT. I wish our poets were half so good at it. Mrs Martha, a thousand welcomes – (DAPPERWIT *kisses and embraces* MRS MARTHA)

SIR SIMON. Hold, hold, sir. Your joy is a little too familiar, faith and troth.

DAPPERWIT. Will you not let me salute Mrs Martha?

MARTHA. What, Jonas, do you think I do not know good breeding? Must I be taught by you?

SIR SIMON. I would have kept the maidenhead of your lips for your sweet knight, Mrs Martha, that's all. I dare swear, you never kissed any man before but your father.

MARTHA. My sweet knight, if he will be a knight of mine, must be contented with what he finds as well as other knights.

SIR SIMON. So smart already, faith and troth!

404 s.d. *Exit*: Exeunt Q1.

MARTHA. Dear Mr Dapperwit, I am overjoyed to see you – but I thank honest Jonas for't.

SIR SIMON. (*aside*) How she hugs him!

MARTHA. (*she hugs* DAPPERWIT) Poor Mr Dapperwit, I thought I should never have seen you again – but I thank honest Jonas there.

SIR SIMON. Do not thank me, Mrs Martha, any more than I thank you.

MARTHA. I would not be ungrateful, Jonas.

SIR SIMON. Then reserve your kindness only for your worthy, noble, brave, heroic knight who loves you only and only deserves your kindness.

MARTHA. I will show my kindness to my worthy, brave, heroic knight in being kind to his friend, his dear friend, who helped him to me. (*Hugs* DAPPERWIT *again*)

SIR SIMON. But, Mistress Martha, he is not to help him always; though he helps him to be married, he is not to help him when he is married.

MARTHA. What, Mr Dapperwit, will you love my worthy knight less after marriage than before? That were against the custom, for marriage gets a man friends, instead of losing those he has.

DAPPERWIT. I will ever be his servant and yours; dear madam, do not doubt me.

MARTHA. (*she kisses* DAPPERWIT) I do not, sweet, dear Mr Dapperwit, but I should not have seen you these two days, if it had not been for honest Jonas there.

SIR SIMON. (*apart to* DAPPERWIT) For shame, though she be young and foolish, do not you wrong me to my face.

DAPPERWIT. Would you have me so ill-bred as to repulse her innocent kindness? (*Aside*) What a thing it is to want wit!

SIR SIMON. (*aside*) A pox, I must make haste to discover myself or I shall discover what I would not discover. But if I should discover myself in this habit 'twould not be to my advantage. But I'll go, put on my own clothes and look like a knight. (*To her*) Well, Mrs Martha, I'll go seek out your knight. Are you not impatient to see him?

MARTHA. Wives must be obedient; let him take his own time.

SIR SIMON. Can you trust yourself a turn or two with Master Dapperwit?

MARTHA. Yes, yes, Jonas, as long as you will.

SIR SIMON. (*aside*) But I would not trust you with him if I could help it.

So married wight sees what he dares not blame
And cannot budge for fear, nor stay for shame.

Exit SIR SIMON.

DAPPERWIT. I am glad he is gone that I may laugh. 'Tis such a miracle of fops, that his conversation should be pleasant to me even when it hindered me of yours.

MARTHA. Indeed, I am glad he is gone too, as pleasant as he is.

DAPPERWIT. I know why, I know why, sweet Mrs Martha. I warrant you, you had rather have the parson's company than his! Now you are out of your father's house 'tis time to leave being a hypocrite.

MARTHA. Well, for the jest's sake, to disappoint my knight, I would not care if I disappointed myself of a ladyship.

DAPPERWIT. Come, I will not keep you on the tenters; I know you have a mind to make sure of me. I have a little chaplain – I wish he were a bishop or one of the friars to perfect our revenge upon that zealous jew, your father!

MARTHA. Do not speak ill of my father. He has been your friend, I'm sure.

DAPPERWIT. My friend!

MARTHA. His hard usage of me conspired with your good mien and wit and, to avoid slavery under him, I stoop to your yoke.

DAPPERWIT. I will be obliged to your father for nothing but a portion, nor to you for your love – 'twas due to my merit.

MARTHA. You show yourself Sir Simon's original. If 'twere not for that vanity –

DAPPERWIT. I should be no wit; 'tis the badge of my calling, for you can no more find a man of wit without

82 *on the tenters*: on tenterhooks, in suspense.
85 *jew*: usurer.

vanity than a fine woman without affectation. But let us go before the knight comes again.

MARTHA. Let us go before my father comes; he soon will have the intelligence.

DAPPERWIT. (*pauses*) Stay, let me think a little.

MARTHA. What are you thinking of? You should have thought before this time or I should have thought rather.

DAPPERWIT. Peace, peace.

MARTHA. What are you thinking of?

DAPPERWIT. I am thinking what a wit without vanity is like. He is like –

MARTHA. You do not think we are in a public place and may be surprised and prevented by my father's scouts.

DAPPERWIT. What, would you have me lose my thought?

MARTHA. You would rather lose your mistress, it seems.

DAPPERWIT. He is like – I think I'm a sot tonight, let me perish.

MARTHA. (*offers to go*) Nay, if you are so in love with your thought.

DAPPERWIT. Are you so impatient to be my wife? He is like – he is like – a picture without shadows or, or – a face without patches – or a diamond without a foil; these are new thoughts now, these are new.

MARTHA. You are wedded already to your thoughts, I see. Goodnight.

DAPPERWIT. Madam, do not take it ill.
For loss of happy thought there's no amends;
For his new jest true wit will lose old friends.
That's new again, the thought's new.

Exeunt.

Enter GRIPE, *leading* MRS LUCY; JOYNER, CROSSBITE *following.*

GRIPE. Mrs Joyner, I can conform to this mode of public walking by moonlight because one is not known.

LUCY. Why, are you ashamed of your company?

GRIPE. No, pretty one; because in the dark, or as it were in the dark, there is no envy nor scandal. I would neither lose you nor my reputation.

JOYNER. Your reputation! Indeed, your worship, 'tis

well known there are as grave men as your worship – nay, men in office too – that adjourn their cares and businesses to come and unbend themselves at night here with a little vizard mask.

GRIPE. I do believe it, I do believe it, Mrs Joyner.

LUCY. Ay, godmother, and carries and treats her at Mulberry Garden.

CROSSBITE. Nay, does not only treat her but gives her his whole gleanings of that day.

GRIPE. They may, they may, Mrs Crossbite; they take above six in the hundred.

CROSSBITE. Nay, there are those of so much worth and honour and love that they'll take it from their wives and children to give it to their misses. Now your worship has no wife and but one child.

GRIPE. (*aside*) Still for my edification.

JOYNER. That's true indeed, for I know a great lady that cannot follow her husband abroad to his haunts because her farrendine is so ragged and greasy, whilst his mistress is as fine as fippence in her embroidered satins.

GRIPE. Politicly done of him indeed. If the truth were known, he is a statesman by that, umph!

CROSSBITE. Truly, your women of quality are very troublesome to their husbands. I have heard 'em complain they will allow them no separate maintenance, though the honourable jilts themselves will not marry without it.

JOYNER. Come, come, mistress, sometimes 'tis the craft of those gentlemen to complain of their wives' expenses to excuse their own narrowness to their misses – but your daughter has a gallant can make no excuse.

GRIPE. [*aside*] So, Mrs Joyner! My friend, Mrs Joyner!

CROSSBITE. I hope, indeed, he'll give my daughter no cause to dun him, for, poor wretch, she is as modest as her mother.

GRIPE. I profess, I believe it.

LUCY. But I have the boldness to ask him for a treat.

---

149 *six in the hundred*: 6%, the highest legal rate of interest.
158 *as fine as fippence*: finely dressed, with a hint of pride.

Come, gallant, we must walk towards the Mulberry Garden.

GRIPE. [*aside*] So! – I am afraid, little mistress, the rooms are all taken up by this time.

JOYNER. (*aside to* GRIPE) Will you shame yourself again?

LUCY. If the rooms be full we'll have an arbour.

GRIPE. At this time of night! Besides, the waiters will ne'er come near you.

LUCY. They will be observant of good customers, as we shall be. Come along.

GRIPE. Indeed and verily, little mistress, I would go but that I should be forsworn if I did.

JOYNER. That's so pitiful an excuse –

GRIPE. In truth, I have forsworn the place ever since I was pawned there for a reckoning.

LUCY. You have broken many an oath for the Good Old Cause – and will you boggle at one for your poor little Miss? Come along.

[*Enter*] LADY FLIPPANT *behind.*

FLIPPANT. Unfortunate lady that I am! I have left the herd on purpose to be chased and have wandered this hour here but the park affords not so much as a satyr for me (and that's strange); no Burgundy man or drunken scourer will reel my way. The rag-women and cinder-women have better luck than I – but who are these? If this mongrel light does not deceive me, 'tis my brother. 'Tis he! There's Joyner too and two other women. I'll follow 'em. It must be he, for this world hath nothing like him – I know not what the devil may be in the other.

Exeunt omnes.

Enter SIR SIMON ADDLEPLOT *in fine clothes;* DAPPERWIT *and* MRS MARTHA *unseen by him at the door.*

---

193 *pawned there for a reckoning*: left to pay the bill.
194–5 *Good Old Cause*: the Puritan rebellion.
200 *Burgundy man*: drunk.
201 *scourer*: rowdy rakes who roistered in the streets at night.
202 *cinder-women*: women whose job was to rake the ashes and carry out the cinders.

SIR SIMON. Well, after all my seeking, I can find those I would not find. I'm sure 'twas old Gripe and Joyner with him and the widow followed. He would not have been here but to have sought his daughter, sure; but vigilant Dapperwit has spied him too and has, no doubt, secured her from him.

DAPPERWIT. (*behind*) And you.

SIR SIMON. The rogue is as good at hiding as I am at stealing a mistress. 'Tis a vain, conceited fellow yet I think 'tis an honest fellow. But again, he is a damnable, whoring fellow and what opportunity this air and darkness may incline 'em to, heaven knows! For I have heard the rogue say himself a lady will no more show her modesty in the dark than a Spaniard his courage.

DAPPERWIT. Ha, ha, ha!

SIR SIMON. Nay, if you are there, my true friend, I'll forgive your hearkening, if you'll forgive my censures! I speak to you, dear Madam Martha, dear, dear! Behold your worthy knight –

MARTHA. That's far from neighbours.

SIR SIMON. Is come to reap the fruit of all his labours.

MARTHA. I cannot see the knight; well, but I'm sure I hear Jonas.

SIR SIMON. I am no Jonas, Mrs Martha.

MARTHA. The night is not so dark nor the peruke so big but I can discern Jonas.

SIR SIMON. Faith and troth, I am the very Sir Simon Addleplot that is to marry you, the same Dapperwit solicited you for – ask him else. My name is not Jonas.

MARTHA. You think my youth and simplicity capable of this cheat. But let me tell you, Jonas, 'tis not your borrowed clothes and title shall make me marry my father's man.

SIR SIMON. Borrowed title! I'll be sworn I bought it of my laundress, who was a court laundress, but, indeed, my clothes I have not paid for, therefore in that sense they are borrowed.

MARTHA. Prithee, Jonas, let the jest end or I shall be presently in earnest.

---

228 *far from neighbours*: praise of oneself.
229 *Is*: I's Q1.

SIR SIMON. Pray be in earnest and let us go. The parson and supper stay for us and I am a knight in earnest.

MARTHA. You a knight, insolent, saucy fool?

SIR SIMON. The devil take me, Mrs Martha, if I am not a knight now – a knight baronet too. A man ought, I see, to carry his patent in his pocket when he goes to be married; 'tis more necessary than a licence. I am a knight indeed and indeed now, Mrs Martha.

MARTHA. Indeed and indeed, the trick will not pass, Jonas.

SIR SIMON. Poor wretch, she's afraid she shall not be a Lady. Come, come, discover the intrigue, Dapperwit –

MARTHA. You need not discover the intrigue – 'tis apparent already. Unworthy Mr Dapperwit, after my confidence reposed in you, could you be so little generous as to betray me to my father's man? But I'll be even with you.

SIR SIMON. Do not accuse him, poor man, before you hear him. Tell her the intrigue, man.

DAPPERWIT. A pox, she will not believe us.

SIR SIMON. Will you not excuse yourself? But I must not let it rest so. Know then, Mrs Martha –

MARTHA. Come, I forgive thee before thy confession, Jonas. You never had had the confidence to have designed this cheat upon me but from Mr Dapperwit's encouragement – 'twas his plot.

SIR SIMON. Nay, do not do me that wrong, madam.

MARTHA. But since he has trapanned me out of my father's house he is like to keep me as long as I live – and so goodnight, Jonas.

SIR SIMON. Hold, hold, what d'y'mean both? Prithee tell her that I am Sir Simon and no Jonas.

DAPPERWIT. A pox, she will not believe us, I tell you.

SIR SIMON. I have provided a parson and supper at Mulberry Garden and invited all my friends I could meet in the park.

DAPPERWIT. Nay, rather than they shall be disappointed, there shall be a bride and bridegroom to entertain 'em; Mrs Martha and I'll go thither presently.

SIR SIMON. Why, shall she be your bride?

---

248 *in earnest*: (*a*) serious (*b*) money paid as security.
253 *patent*: the document conferring the title.

DAPPERWIT. You see she will have it so.

SIR SIMON. Will you make Dapperwit your husband?

MARTHA. Rather than my father's man.

SIR SIMON. Oh, the devil –

MARTHA. Nay, come along, Jonas, you shall make one at the wedding since you helped contrive it.

SIR SIMON. Will you cheat yourself for fear of being cheated?

MARTHA. I am desperate now.

SIR SIMON. Wilt thou let her do so ill a thing, Dapperwit, as to marry thee? Open her eyes, prithee, and tell her I am a true knight.

DAPPERWIT. 'Twould be in vain, by my life; you have carried yourself so like a natural clerk – and so adieu, good Jonas.

Exeunt MARTHA *and* DAPPERWIT.

SIR SIMON. What, ruined by my own plot like an old Cavalier; yet like him too, I will plot on still, a plot of prevention. So, I have it – her father was here ev'n now, I'm sure. Well – I'll go tell her father of her, that I will,
And punish so her folly and his treachery.
Revenge is sweet and makes amends for lechery. *Exit.*

Enter LYDIA *and her woman,* LEONORE.

LYDIA. I wish I had not come hither tonight, Leonore.

LEONORE. Why did you, madam, if the place be so disagreeable to you?

LYDIA. We cannot help visiting the place often where we have lost anything we value. I lost Ranger here last night.

LEONORE. You thought you had lost him before, a great while ago, and therefore you ought to be the less troubled.

LYDIA. But 'twas here I missed him first, I'm sure.

LEONORE. Come, madam, let not the loss vex you; he is not worth the looking after.

LYDIA. It cannot but vex me yet, if I lost him by my own fault.

LEONORE. You had but too much care to keep him.

LYDIA. It often happens, indeed, that too much care is

---

301 *natural*: (*a*) genuine (*b*) foolish.

as bad as negligence. But I had rather be robbed than lose what I have carelessly.

LEONORE. But, I believe, you would hang the thief if you could.

LYDIA. Not if I could have my own again.

LEONORE. I see, you would be too merciful.

LYDIA. I wish I were tried.

LEONORE. But, madam, if you please, we will waive the discourse, for people seldom, I suppose, talk with pleasure of their real losses.

LYDIA. 'Tis better than to ruminate on them; mine, I'm sure, will not out of my head nor heart.

LEONORE. Grief is so far from retrieving a loss that it makes it greater; but the way to lessen it is by a comparison with others' losses. Here are ladies in the park of your acquaintance, I doubt not, can compare with you; pray, madam, let us walk and find 'em out.

LYDIA. 'Tis the resentment, you say, makes the loss great or little and then, I'm sure, there is none like mine. However, go on.

Exeunt.

Enter VINCENT *and* VALENTINE.

VINCENT. I am glad I have found you, for now I am prepared to lead you out of the dark and all your trouble; I have good news.

VALENTINE. You are as unmerciful as the physician who with new arts keeps his miserable patient alive and in hopes, when he knows the disease is incurable.

VINCENT. And you, like the melancholy patient, mistrust and hate your physician because he will not comply with your despair. But I'll cure your jealousy now.

VALENTINE. You know all diseases grow worse by relapses.

VINCENT. Trust me once more.

VALENTINE. Well, you may try your experiments upon me.

VINCENT. Just as I shut the door upon you, the woman Ranger expected came upstairs but, finding another woman in discourse with him, went down again – I suppose as jealous of him as you of Christina.

VALENTINE. How does it appear she came to Ranger?

VINCENT. Thus: Dapperwit came up after, who had brought her, just then, in a chair from St James's by Ranger's appointment, and it is certain your Christina came to you.

VALENTINE. How can that be, for she knew not I was in the kingdom?

VINCENT. My man confesses, when I sent him to inquire of her woman about her lady's being here in the park last night, he told her you were come and she, it seems, told her mistress.

VALENTINE. (*aside*) That might be. – But did not Christina confess Ranger was in her lodging last night?

VINCENT. By intrusion, which she had more particularly informed me of, if her apprehensions of your danger had not posted me after you, she not having yet (as I suppose) heard of Clerimont's recovery. I left her, poor creature, at home, distracted with a thousand fears for your life and love.

VALENTINE. Her love, I'm sure, has cost me more fears than my life; yet that little danger is not past, as you think, till the great one be over.

VINCENT. Open but your eyes and the fantastic goblin's vanished and all your idle fears will turn to shame, for jealousy is the basest cowardice.

VALENTINE. I had rather, indeed, blush for myself than her.

VINCENT. I'm sure you will have more reason – But is not that Ranger there?

RANGER *enters, followed by* CHRISTINA *and her woman; after them,* LYDIA *and her woman.*

VALENTINE. I think it is.

VINCENT. I suppose his friend Dapperwit is not far off. I will examine them both before you and not leave you so much as the shadow of a doubt; Ranger's astonishment at my lodging confessed his mistake.

VALENTINE. His astonishment might proceed from Christina's unexpected strangeness to him.

VINCENT. He shall satisfy you now himself to the contrary, I warrant you. Have but patience.

VALENTINE. I had rather, indeed, he should satisfy my doubts than my revenge; therefore I can have patience.

VINCENT. But what women are those that follow him?

VALENTINE. Stay a little –

RANGER. Lydia, Lydia! Poor Lydia.

LYDIA. (*to her maid*) If she be my rival 'tis some comfort yet to see her follow him, rather than he her.

LEONORE. But if you follow them a little longer for your comfort you shall see them go hand in hand.

CHRISTINA. (*to* RANGER) Sir, sir!

LEONORE. She calls to him already.

LYDIA. But he does not hear, you see. Let us go a little nearer.

VINCENT. Sure, it is Ranger?

VALENTINE. As sure as the woman that follows him closest is Christina.

VINCENT. For shame, talk not of Christina. I left her just now at home, surrounded with so many fears and griefs she could not stir.

VALENTINE. She is come, it may be, to divert them here in the park. I'm sure 'tis she.

VINCENT. When the moon, at this instant, scarce affords light enough to distinguish a man from a tree, how can you know her?

VALENTINE. How can you know Ranger then?

VINCENT. I heard him speak.

VALENTINE. So you may her too. I'll secure you if you will draw but a little nearer. She came, doubtless, to no other end but to speak with him; observe.

CHRISTINA. (*to* RANGER) Sir, I have followed you hitherto but now I must desire you to follow me out of the company, for I would not be overheard nor disturbed.

RANGER. [*aside*] Ha! Is not this Christina's voice? It is, I am sure; I cannot be deceived now. – Dear Madam –

VINCENT. (*apart to* VALENTINE) It is she indeed.

VALENTINE. Is it so?

CHRISTINA. (*to* RANGER) Come, sir –

VALENTINE. (*aside*) Nay, I'll follow you too, though not invited.

LYDIA. (*aside*) I must not, cannot stay behind.

They all go off together in a huddle hastily. CHRISTINA, *her woman and* VALENTINE *return on the other side.*

CHRISTINA. Come along, sir.

VALENTINE. (*aside*) So I must stick to her when all is done. Her new servant has lost her in the crowd; she has gone too fast for him – so much my revenge is swifter than his love. Now shall I not only have the deserted lover's revenge of disappointing her of her new man but an opportunity infallibly at once to discover her falseness and confront her impudence.

CHRISTINA. Pray come along, sir; I am in haste.

VALENTINE. (*aside*) So eager, indeed! I wish that cloud may yet withhold the moon, that this false woman may not discover me before I do her.

CHRISTINA. Here no one can hear us and I'm sure we cannot see one another.

VALENTINE. (*aside*) 'Sdeath, what have I giddily run myself upon? 'Tis rather a trial of myself than her; I cannot undergo it.

CHRISTINA. Come nearer, sir.

VALENTINE. (*aside*) Hell and vengeance, I cannot suffer it, I cannot.

CHRISTINA. Come, come, yet nearer, pray come nearer.

VALENTINE. [*aside*] It is impossible; I cannot hold. I must discover myself rather than her infamy.

CHRISTINA. (*speaks, walking slowly*) You are conscious, it seems, of the wrong you have done me and are ashamed, though in the dark.

VALENTINE. (*aside*) How's this!

CHRISTINA. I'm glad to find it so, for all my business with you is to show you your late mistakes and force a confession from you of those unmannerly injuries you have done me.

VALENTINE. (*aside*) What! I think she's honest – or does she know me? Sure, she cannot.

CHRISTINA. First, your intrusion last night into my lodging, which, I suppose, has begot your other gross mistakes.

VALENTINE. (*aside*) No, she takes me for Ranger, I see again.

CHRISTINA. You are to know then, since needs you must, it was not me you followed last night to my lodging from the park but some kinswoman of yours, it seems, whose fear of being discovered by you prevailed with me to personate her, while she withdrew – our habits and our statures being much alike – which I did with as much difficulty as she used importunity to make me – and all this my Lady Flippant can witness, who was then with your cousin.

VALENTINE. (*aside*) I am glad to hear this!

CHRISTINA. Now, what your claim to me at Mr Vincent's lodging meant. The letter and promises you unworthily or erroneously laid to my charge you must explain to me and others or –

VALENTINE. (*aside*) How's this! I hope I shall discover no guilt but my own. She would not speak in threats to a lover!

CHRISTINA. Was it because you found me in Mr Vincent's lodgings you took a liberty to use me like one of your common visitants? But know, I came no more to Mr Vincent than to you; yet I confess my visit was intended to a man – a brave man till you made him use a woman ill, worthy the love of a princess till you made him censure mine, good as angels till you made him unjust. Why, in the name of honour, would you do't?

VALENTINE. (*aside*) How happily am I disappointed! Poor injured Christina!

CHRISTINA. He would have sought me out first if you had not made him fly from me. Our mutual love, confirmed by a contract, made our hearts inseparable till you rudely, if not maliciously, thrust in upon us and broke the close and happy knot. I had lost him before for a month, now for ever. (*She weeps*)

VALENTINE. (*aside*) My joy, and pity, makes me as mute as my shame. Yet I must discover myself.

CHRISTINA. Your silence is a confession of your guilt.

VALENTINE. (*aside*) I own it.

CHRISTINA. But that will not serve my turn, for straight you must go clear yourself, and me, to him you have injured in me – if he has not made too much haste from me as to be found again. You must, I say, for he is a man that will have satisfaction and in satisfying him you do me.

VALENTINE. Then he is satisfied.

CHRISTINA. How! Is it you? Then I am not satisfied.

VALENTINE. Will you be worse than your word?

CHRISTINA. I gave it not to you.

VALENTINE. Come, dear Christina, the jealous, like the drunkard, has his punishment with his offence.

[*Enter*] *to them* VINCENT.

VINCENT. Valentine, Mr Valentine.

VALENTINE. Vincent!

VINCENT. Where have you been all this while?

VALENTINE holds CHRISTINA by the hand, who seems to struggle to get from him.

VALENTINE. Here, with my injured Christina.

VINCENT. She's behind with Ranger who is forced to speak all the tender things himself, for she affords him not a word.

VALENTINE. Pish, pish, Vincent, who is blind now? Who deceived now?

VINCENT. You are, for I'm sure Christina is with him. Come back and see.

They go out at one door and return at the other.

[*Enter* RANGER *and* LYDIA]

RANGER. (*to* LYDIA) Still mocked, still abused! Did you not bid me follow you where we might not be disturbed nor overheard? And now not allow me a word?

VINCENT. (*apart to* VALENTINE) Did you hear him?

VALENTINE. (*apart to* VINCENT) Yes, yes, peace –

RANGER. Disowning your letter and me at Vincent's lodging, declaring you came to meet another there and not me, with a great deal of such affronting unkindness might be reasonable enough, because you would not entrust Vincent with our love. But now, when nobody sees us nor hears us, why this unseasonable shyness? –

LYDIA. (*aside*) It seems she did not expect him there but had appointed to meet another. I wish it were so.

RANGER. I have not patience. Do you design thus to revenge my intrusion into your lodging last night? Sure, if you had then been displeased with my company, you would not have invited yourself to't again by a letter. Or is this a punishment for bringing you to a house so near your own, where, it seems, you were known too? I do confess it was a fault but make me suffer any penance but your silence, because it is the certain mark of a mistress's lasting displeasure –

LYDIA. (*aside*) My cue is not yet come.

---

567 *cue*: the word has dropped out of some copies of Q1.

RANGER. Not yet a word? You did not use me so unkindly last night when you chid me out of your house and with indignation bid me begone. Now, you bid me follow you and yet will have nothing to say to me – and I am more deceived this day and night than I was last night, when, I must confess, I followed you for another. –

LYDIA. (*aside*) I'm glad to hear that.

RANGER. One that would have used me better, whose love I have ungratefully abused for yours, yet from no other reason but my natural inconstancy. (*Aside*) Poor Lydia, Lydia –

LYDIA. (*aside*) He muttered my name, sure, and with a sigh.

RANGER. But as last night by following (as I thought) her, I found you, so this night by following you in vain I do resolve, if I can find her again, to keep her for ever.

LYDIA. (*aside*) Now I am obliged and brought in debt to his inconstancy. Faith, now cannot I hold out any longer; I must discover myself.

RANGER. But, madam, because I intend to see you no more, I'll take my leave of you for good and all. Since you will not speak, I'll try if you will squeak!

Goes to throw her down. She squeaks.

LYDIA. Mr Ranger, Mr Ranger!

VINCENT. Fie, fie, you need not ravish Christina, sure, that loves you so.

RANGER. [*aside*] Is it she? Lydia all this while? How am I gulled! And Vincent in the plot too?

LYDIA. Now, false Ranger.

RANGER. Now, false Christina too. You thought I did not know you now, because I offered you such an unusual civility.

LYDIA. You knew me! I warrant you knew too that I was the Christina you followed out of the park last night, that I was the Christina that writ the letter too.

RANGER. Certainly, therefore I would have taken my revenge, you see, for your tricks.

VALENTINE. (*to* CHRISTINA) Is not this the same woman that took refuge in your house last night, madam?

CHRISTINA. The very same.

VALENTINE. What, Mr Ranger, we have chopped and changed and hid our Christinas so long and often that at last we have drawn each of us our own!

RANGER. Mr Valentine in England! The truth on't is you have juggled together and drawn without my knowledge. But since she will have it so, she shall wear me for good and all now. (*Goes to take her by the hand*)

LYDIA. Come not near me.

RANGER. Nay, you need not be afraid I would ravish you, now I know you.

LYDIA. (*apart to* LEONORE; RANGER *listens*) And yet, Leonore, I think 'tis but justice to pardon the fault I made him commit?

RANGER. You consider it right, cousin, for indeed you are but merciful to yourself in it.

LYDIA. Yet, if I would be rigorous, though I made the blot, your oversight has lost the game.

RANGER. But 'twas rash woman's play, cousin, and ought not to be played again, let me tell you.

[*Enter*] DAPPERWIT *to them.*

DAPPERWIT. Who's there? Who's there?

RANGER. Dapperwit.

DAPPERWIT. Mr Ranger, I am glad I have met with you, for I have left my bride just now, in the house at Mulberry Garden, to come and pick up some of my friends in the park here to sup with us.

RANGER. Your bride! Are you married then? Where is your bride?

DAPPERWIT. Here at Mulberry Garden, I say, where you, these ladies and gentlemen shall all be welcome, if you will afford me the honour of your company.

RANGER. With all our hearts. But who have you married? Lucy?

DAPPERWIT. What, do you think I would marry a wench? I have married an heiress worth thirty thousand pound, let me perish.

VINCENT. An heiress worth thirty thousand pound!

DAPPERWIT. Mr Vincent, your servant, you here too?

---

627 *blot*: in backgammon, a piece liable to be taken or forfeit.

RANGER. Nay, we are more of your acquaintance here, I think. Go, we'll follow you, for, if you have not dismissed your parson, perhaps we may make him more work.

Exeunt.

SCENE II

The scene changes to the dining-room in Mulberry Garden House.

Enter SIR SIMON ADDLEPLOT, GRIPE, MRS MARTHA, JOYNER, CROSSBITE, LUCY, [FLIPPANT]

SIR SIMON. 'Tis as I told you, sir, you see.

GRIPE. Oh graceless babe, married to a wit! An idle, loitering, slandering, foul-mouthed, beggarly wit! Oh that my child should ever live to marry a wit!

JOYNER. Indeed, your worship had better seen her fairly buried, as they say.

CROSSBITE. If my daughter there should have done so I would not have gi'n her a groat.

GRIPE. Marry a wit!

SIR SIMON. (*to* JOYNER *aside*) Mrs Joyner, do not let me lose the widow too, for if you do, betwixt friends, I and my small annuity are both blown up; it will follow my estate.

JOYNER. (*aside*) I warrant you.

FLIPPANT. (*to* JOYNER *aside*) Let us make sure of Sir Simon tonight or –

JOYNER. [*to* FLIPPANT *aside*] You need not fear it. (*Aside*) Like the lawyers, while my clients endeavour to cheat one another, I in justice cheat 'em both.

GRIPE. Marry a wit!

Enter DAPPERWIT, RANGER *and* LYDIA, VALENTINE, CHRISTINA *and* VINCENT. DAPPERWIT *stops 'em and they stand all behind.*

DAPPERWIT. (*aside*) What, is he here? Lucy and her mother?

GRIPE. Tell me how thou cam'st to marry a wit.

MARTHA. Pray be not angry, sir, and I'll give you a good reason.

GRIPE. Reason for marrying a wit!

MARTHA. Indeed, I found myself six months gone with child and saw no hopes of your getting me a husband, or else I had not married a wit, sir.

JOYNER. (*aside*) Then you were the wit.

GRIPE. Had you that reason? Nay then – (*Holding up his hands*)

DAPPERWIT. (*aside*) How's that!

RANGER. (*aside*) Who would have thought, Dapperwit, you would have married a wench?

DAPPERWIT. (*to* RANGER) Well, thirty thousand pound will make me amends; I have known my betters wink and fall on for five or six. (*To* GRIPE *and the rest*) What, you are come, sir, to give me joy? You, Mrs Lucy, you and you? Well, unbid guests are doubly welcome. (*To* SIR SIMON) Sir Simon, I made bold to invite these ladies and gentlemen – for you must know, Mr Ranger, this worthy Sir Simon does not only give me my wedding-supper but my mistress too and is, as it were, my father.

SIR SIMON. Then I am, as it were, a grandfather to your new wife's *hans en kelder*, to which you are but as it were a father – there's for you again, sir, ha, ha!

RANGER. (*to* VINCENT) Ha, ha, ha!

DAPPERWIT. Fools sometimes say unhappy things, if we would mind 'em, but – what, melancholy at your daughter's wedding, sir?

GRIPE. (*aside*) How deplorable is my condition!

DAPPERWIT. Nay, if you will rob me of my wench, sir, can you blame me for robbing you of your daughter? I cannot be without a woman.

GRIPE. (*aside*) My daughter, my reputation and my money gone – but the last is dearest to me. Yet at once I may retrieve that and be revenged for the loss of the other and all this by marrying Lucy here. I shall get my five hundred pound again and get heirs to exclude my daughter and frustrate Dapperwit.

30–1 *Holding up his bands*: in horror.
46 *hans en kelder*: Jack in the cellar (Dutch), the unborn child.

Besides, 'tis agreed on all hands, 'tis cheaper keeping a wife than a wench.

DAPPERWIT. If you are so melancholy, sir, we will have the fiddles and a dance to divert you. Come.

A dance.

GRIPE. Indeed, you have put me so upon a merry pin that I resolve to marry too.

FLIPPANT. Nay, if my brother come to marrying once, I may too. I swore I would when he did, little thinking –

SIR SIMON. I take you at your word, madam.

FLIPPANT. Well, but if I had thought you would have been so quick with me –

GRIPE. Where is your parson?

DAPPERWIT. What, you would not revenge yourself upon the parson?

GRIPE. No, I would have the parson revenge upon you; he should marry me.

DAPPERWIT. I am glad you are so frolic sir. But who would you marry?

GRIPE. (*pointing to* LUCY) This innocent lady.

DAPPERWIT. That innocent lady?

GRIPE. Nay, I am impatient. Mrs Joyner, pray fetch him up if he be yet in the house.

DAPPERWIT. We were not married here. But you cannot be in earnest.

GRIPE. You'll find it so. Since you have robbed me of my housekeeper I must get another.

DAPPERWIT. Why? She was my wench.

GRIPE. I'll make her honest then.

CROSSBITE. Upon my repute he never saw her before. But will your worship marry my daughter then?

GRIPE. I promise her, and you, before all this good company, tomorrow I will make her my wife.

DAPPERWIT. How!

RANGER. (*to* VALENTINE) Our ladies, sir, I suppose, expect the same promise from us.

VALENTINE. They may be sure of us without a promise but let us, if we can, obtain theirs, to be sure of them.

DAPPERWIT. (*to* GRIPE) But will you marry her tomorrow?

GRIPE. I will verily.

DAPPERWIT. I am undone then, ruined, let me perish.

SIR SIMON. No, you may hire a little room in Covent Garden and set up a coffeehouse; you and your wife will be sure of the wits' custom.

DAPPERWIT. Abused by him I have abused!
Fortune our foe we cannot over-wit;
By none but thee our projects are cross-bit.

VALENTINE. Come, dear madam. What, yet angry? Jealousy, sure, is much more pardonable before marriage than after it. But tomorrow, by the help of the parson, you will put me out of all my fears.

CHRISTINA. I am afraid then you would give me my revenge and make me jealous of you and I had rather suspect your faith than you should mine.

RANGER. Cousin Lydia, I had rather suspect your faith too, than you should mine. Therefore, let us e'en marry tomorrow, that I may have my turn of watching, dogging, standing under the window, at the door, behind the hanging or –

LYDIA. But if I could be desperate now and give you up my liberty, could you find in your heart to quit all other engagements and voluntarily turn yourself over to one woman and she a wife too? Could you away with the insupportable bondage of matrimony?

RANGER. You talk of matrimony as irreverently as my Lady Flippant. The bondage of matrimony! No –
The end of marriage now is liberty
And two are bound – to set each other free.

EPILOGUE, *spoken by* DAPPERWIT

Now my brisk brothers of the pit, you'll say
I'm come to speak a good word for the play;
But, gallants, let me perish if I do,
For I have wit and judgement, just like you,
Wit never partial, judgement free and bold,
For fear or friendship never bought or sold,
Nor by good nature e'er to be cajoled.
Good nature in a critic were a crime,
Like mercy in a judge, and renders him
Guilty of all those faults he does forgive;

Besides, if thief from gallows you reprieve,
He'll cut your throat – so poet saved from shame
In damned lampoon will murder your good name.
Yet in true spite to him and to his play,
Good faith, you should not rail at 'em today
But, to be more his foe, seem most his friend
And so maliciously the play commend
That he may be betrayed to writing on
And poet let him be, to be undone.

THE

GENTLEMAN Dancing-Maſter.

A

COMEDY,

Acted at the

DUKE'S THEATRE.

By Mr. *Wycherley*.

Horat.—— *Non ſatis eſt riſu diducere rictum*
Auditoris ; & *eſt quædam tamen hic quoq;* *virtus*.

LONDON,

Printed by *J. M.* for *Henry Herringman* and *Thomas Dring* at the Sign of the *Blew Anchor* in the Lower Walk of the *New Exchange*, and at the Sign of the *White Lyon* in *Fleetſtreet* near *Chancery-lane* end. 1673.

Title-page of the 1673 Quarto of *The Gentleman Dancing-Master*, reproduced by permission of the British Library.

Motto

Horace, *Satires*, I x 7–8:

'It is not enough to draw forth a laugh from the spectators; however, there is a certain value even in that'

INTRODUCTORY NOTE

Wycherley owes the device of the lover disguised as a dancing-master to Calderón's *El Maestro de Danzar* but he took little more than the basic idea from this source. More intriguing for source-hunters are the parallels with *Romeo and Juliet*: like Juliet, Wycherley's Hippolita is fourteen, refuses to marry her strict father's choice of a man named Paris and has a nurse-governess; like Romeo, Gerrard finds himself making an entrance through a window, the balcony metamorphosed into a scramble across from the roof of a neighbouring inn. As in Wycherley's later use of Shakespeare in *The Plain-Dealer*, it is the differences as much as the similarities that Wycherley seems to be pointing up. Hippolita's trick to make Gerrard come and rescue her from the imminent marriage, by making Monsieur tell Gerrard not to do so and thus implanting the idea in his mind, is so conventional as to have two equally probable sources: in Jonson's *The Devil is an Ass*, Mrs Fitzdottrell tells Wittipol not to appear at 'the gentleman's chamber-window . . . That opens to my gallery' (II ii 53–4), in order to make sure that he does; in Molière's *L'École des maris*, Isabelle makes Sganarelle reproach Valère for trying to carry her off by force, again with a similar result. The Frenchified fop had appeared in James Howard's *The English Monsieur* (first performed in 1663) and Wycherley may have derived some hints from Howard's Frenchlove. But, since French fops on stage must have derived from French fops in the audience, Wycherley's Monsieur almost certainly owes more to life than to any dramatic predecessor.

The Gentleman Dancing-Master was first performed by the Duke's Company at their new theatre, Dorset Garden; a performance listed for 6 February 1672 may well have been the first. This is Wycherley's only play for the Duke's Company and the reasons for the move are not clear. The traditional explanation is the disastrous fire that destroyed the Bridges Street Theatre on 25 January 1672 but it is most unlikely that the rival company would perform a play less than a fortnight later. It is more probable that Wycherley wanted to capitalise on the talents of Edward Angel and James Nokes who played Don Diego and Monsieur in the first production. In any case, a more farcical play would suit the city audience at Dorset Garden better. As John Downes records, *The Gentleman Dancing-Master* was 'the third new play acted' at Dorset Garden but 'being liked but indifferently, it was laid by to make room for other new ones' after an initial run of six performances (*Roscius Anglicanus* (1708), p. 32). It may have been revived when the play was reprinted but there are no records for performance after 1672 until this century. It was performed at the Maddermarket Theatre, Norwich, in December 1924 and by the Phoenix Society, as part of their programme of revivals of Restoration drama, at the Regent Theatre in December 1925. In May 1930 Tyrone Guthrie directed the play at the Cambridge Festival Theatre, with Robert Donat as Gerrard (and Flora Robson as Flounce). It was seen at the Vanbrugh Theatre, London, in 1960.

The play was first published in 1673 and reprinted in 1693 and 1702; thereafter it has appeared only in collections of Wycherley's plays.

PROLOGUE TO THE CITY,

Newly after the removal of the Duke's Company from Lincoln Inn Fields to their new theatre, near Salisbury Court.

Our author, like us, finding 'twould scarce do
At t'other end o'th'town, is come to you
And, since 'tis his last trial, has that wit
To throw himself on a substantial pit,
Where needy wit or critic dare not come,
Lest neighbour i'the cloak, with looks so grum,
Should prove a dun;
Where punk in vizor dare not rant and tear
To put us out, since Bridewell is so near.
In short, we shall be heard, he understood,
If not, shall be admired – and that's as good,
For you to senseless plays have still been kind,
Nay, where no sense was you a jest would find
And never was it heard of that the city
Did ever take occasion to be witty
Upon dull poet or stiff player's action
But still with claps opposed the hissing faction.
But if you hissed, 'twas at the pit, not stage,
So, with the poet, damned the damning age
And still, we know, are ready to engage
Against the flouting, ticking gentry who
Citizen, player, poet would undo.
The poet – no, unless by commendation,
For on the Change wits have no reputation
And, rather than be branded for a wit,
He with you, able men, would credit get.

---

new theatre: Dorset Garden, which opened on 9 November 1671.

2 *is come to you*: a reference both to Wycherley's switch from the King's Company to the Duke's and to his shift in subject matter to a more mercantile one.

3 *last*: latest.

6 *grum*: sullen.

7 *dun*: creditor.

8 *punk in vizor*: prostitute wearing a mask.

9 *Bridewell*: a house of correction, for prostitutes in particular, just off Fleet Street.

21 *ticking*: running up bills.

24 *Change*: the Royal Exchange, the business centre for merchants and bankers.

THE PERSONS

MR GERRARD, MR MARTIN	Young gentlemen of the town, and friends.
MR PARRIS or MONSIEUR DE PARIS	A vain coxcomb and rich city-heir, newly returned from France and mightily affected with the French language and fashions.
MR JAMES FORMAL or DON DIEGO	An old, rich, Spanish merchant, newly returned home, as much affected with the habit and customs of Spain and uncle to De Paris.
MRS HIPPOLITA	Formal's daughter.
MRS CAUTION	Formal's sister, an impertinent, precise old woman.
PRUE	Hippolita's maid.
MRS FLIRT, MRS FLOUNCE	Two common women of the town.
A little BLACKAMOOR	Lacquey to Formal.

A PARSON, a FRENCH SCULLION, servants, WAITER and attendants.

The Scene: *London*

15 *precise*: puritanical.

THE GENTLEMAN DANCING-MASTER

ACT I

SCENE I

Don Diego's house in the evening.

Enter HIPPOLITA *and* PRUE, *her maid.*

HIPPOLITA. To confine a woman just in her rambling age! Take away her liberty at the very time she should use it! O barbarous aunt! O unnatural father! To shut up a poor girl at fourteen and hinder her budding; all things are ripened by the sun! To shut up a poor girl at fourteen!

PRUE. 'Tis true, miss, two poor young creatures as we are.

HIPPOLITA. Not suffered to see a play in a twelvemonth –

PRUE. Nor to go to Ponchinello nor Paradise –

HIPPOLITA. Nor to take a ramble to the Park nor Mulberry Gar'n –

PRUE. Nor to Tatnam Court nor Islington –

HIPPOLITA. Nor to eat a sillybub in New Spring Gar'n with a cousin –

---

11 *Ponchinello*: the Italian puppet-show run by Anthony Devolto at Charing Cross.

11 *Paradise*: 'we went to see Paradise, a room in Hatton Garden furnished with the representations of all sorts of animals, handsomely painted on boards or cloth and so cut out and made to stand and move, fly, crawl, roar and make their several cries as was not unpretty' (John Evelyn in his *Diary*, 23 September 1673).

12 *Park*: Hyde Park or St James's Park.

12–13 *Mulberry Gar'n*: a garden of mulberry-trees on the site of Buckingham Palace, a very popular London park.

14 *Tatnam Court . . . Islington*: popular places to ramble to; Tottenham Court Road and Islington were both then firmly in the country.

15 *sillybub*: syllabub, made from milk or cream, curdled, usually with wine, and sweetened.

15 *New Spring Gar'n*: pleasure gardens at Vauxhall.

PRUE. Nor to drink a pint of wine with a friend at the Prince in the Sun –

HIPPOLITA. Nor to hear a fiddle in good company –

PRUE. Nor to hear the organs and tongs at the Gun in Moorfields –

HIPPOLITA. Nay, nor suffered to go to church because the men are sometimes there! Little did I think I should ever have longed to go to church!

PRUE. Or I either but between two maids.

HIPPOLITA. Not see a man –

PRUE. Nor come near a man –

HIPPOLITA. Nor hear of a man –

PRUE. No, miss, but to be denied a man and to have no use at all of a man!

HIPPOLITA. Hold, hold. Your resentment is as much greater than mine, as your experience has been greater. But all this while, what do we make of my cousin, my husband-elect (as my aunt says)? We have had his company these three days. Is he no man?

PRUE. No, faith, he's but a Monsieur. But you'll resolve yourself that question within these three days, for by that time he'll be your husband, if your father come tonight –

HIPPOLITA. Or if I provide not myself with another in the meantime! For fathers seldom choose well and I will no more take my father's choice in a husband than I would in a gown or a suit of knots, so that if that cousin of mine were not an ill-contrived, ugly, freakish fool, in being my father's choice I should hate him. Besides, he has almost made me out of love with mirth and good humour, for he debases it as much as a Jack-pudding and civility and good breeding more than a city dancing-master.

PRUE. What, won't you marry him then, madam?

HIPPOLITA. Wouldst thou have me marry a fool? An idiot?

---

18 *Prince in the Sun*: a tavern, probably the one in Shadwell.
20 *organs and tongs*: organs are pipes, not portable organs: ordinary fire-tongs were used to provide a rhythm in rustic music.
25 *two maids*: bridesmaids at her wedding.
43 *suit of knots*: bow of ribbons.
48 *Jack-pudding*: clown, buffoon.

PRUE. Lord, 'tis a sign you have been kept up indeed and know little of the world, to refuse a man for a husband only because he's a fool. Methinks he's a pretty apish kind of gentleman, like other gentlemen, and handsome enough to lie with in the dark, when husbands take their privileges, and, for the daytimes, you may take the privilege of a wife.

HIPPOLITA. Excellent governess, you do understand the world, I see.

PRUE. Then you should be guided by me.

HIPPOLITA. Art thou in earnest then, damned jade? Wouldst thou have me marry him? Well, there are more poor young women undone and married to filthy fellows by the treachery and evil counsel of chambermaids than by the obstinacy and covetousness of parents.

PRUE. Does not your father come on purpose out of Spain to marry you to him? Can you release yourself from your aunt or father any other way? Have you a mind to be shut up as long as you live? For my part, though you can hold out upon the lime from the walls here, salt, old shoes and oatmeal, I cannot live so. I must confess my patience is worn out.

HIPPOLITA. Alas! Alas! Poor Prue! Your stomach lies another way. I will take pity of you and get me a husband very suddenly, who may have a servant at your service. But, rather than marry my cousin, I will be a nun in the new Protestant nunnery they talk of, where, they say, there will be no hopes of coming near a man.

PRUE. But you can marry nobody but your cousin, Miss. Your father you expect tonight and be certain his Spanish policy and wariness which has kept you up so close ever since you came from Hackney School will make sure of you within a day or two at farthest.

---

56 *apish*: affected, foolish.

73–4 *though you . . . oatmeal*: the diet for a woman pining away for a lover – any lover.

80 *the new Protestant nunnery*: much discussed at this time; one was proposed by Edward Chamberlayne in his pamphlet *An Academy or College* (1671).

86 *Hackney School*: Hackney was famous for its fashionable boarding-schools.

HIPPOLITA. Then 'tis time to think how to prevent him. Stay –

PRUE. In vain, vain miss.

HIPPOLITA. If we knew but any man, any man, though he were but a little handsomer than the devil, so that he were a gentleman.

PRUE. What if you did know any man, if you had an opportunity, could you have the confidence to speak to a man first? But if you could, how could you come to him or he to you? Nay, how could you send to him? For, though you could write, which your father in his Spanish prudence would never permit you to learn, who should carry the letter? But we need not be concerned for that, since we know not to whom to send it.

HIPPOLITA. Stay, it must be so. I'll try however.

Enter MONSIEUR DE PARIS.

MONSIEUR. Serviteur, serviteur, la cousine, I come to give the bon soir, as the French say.

HIPPOLITA. O cousin, you know him, the fine gentleman they talk of so much in town.

PRUE. What, will you talk to him of any man else?

MONSIEUR. I know all the beaux monde, cousine.

HIPPOLITA. Mister –

MONSIEUR. Monsieur Taileur, Monsieur Esmit, Monsieur –

HIPPOLITA. These are Frenchmen.

MONSIEUR. Non, non, would you have me say Mr Taylor, Mr Smith? Fie, fie, tête, non!

HIPPOLITA. But don't you know the brave gentleman they talk of so much in town?

MONSIEUR. Who, Monsieur Gerrard?

HIPPOLITA. What kind of man is that Mr Gerrard? And then I'll tell you.

MONSIEUR. Why – he is truly a pretty man, a pretty man, a pretty so-so kind of man – for an Englishman.

HIPPOLITA. How, a pretty man?

MONSIEUR. Why, he is conveniently tall but –

---

115 *tête*: one of Monsieur's favourite expletives, formed by eliminating the name of God, like English *'sdeath* or *'swounds*; so, 'by God's head'.

HIPPOLITA. But what?

MONSIEUR. And not ill-shaped but –

HIPPOLITA. But what?

MONSIEUR. And handsome, as 'tis thought, but –

HIPPOLITA. But what are your exceptions to him?

MONSIEUR. I can't tell you, because they are innumerable, innumerable, mon foy.

HIPPOLITA. Has he wit?

MONSIEUR. Ay, ay, they say he's witty, brave and de bel humeur and well-bred with all that – but –

HIPPOLITA. But what? He wants judgement?

MONSIEUR. Non, non, they say he has good sense and judgement but it is according to the account Englis', for –

HIPPOLITA. For what?

MONSIEUR. For, jarnie – if I think it –

HIPPOLITA. Why?

MONSIEUR. Why? Why, his tailor lives within Ludgate; his valet de chambre is no Frenchman and he has been seen at noonday to go into an English eating-house.

HIPPOLITA. Say you so, cousin?

MONSIEUR. Then, for being well-bred you shall judge. First, he can't dance a step nor sing a French song nor swear a French oate nor use the polite French word in his conversation and, in fine, can't play at hombré but speaks base good Englis' with the commune home-bred pronunciation and, in fine, to say no more, he ne'er carries a snuffbox about with him.

HIPPOLITA. Indeed!

MONSIEUR. And yet this man has been abroad as much as any man and does not make the least show of it, but a little in his mien, not at all in his discour, jernie. He never talks so much as of St Peter's church and Rome, the Escurial or Madrid, nay, not so much as of

---

140 *jarnie*: a corruption of *je renie dieu*, 'I swear'.
150 *in fine*: to conclude.
150 *hombré*: ombre, a card game.
153 *snuffbox*: much more popular in France than England at this time.

Henry IV of Pont Neuf, Paris and the new Louvre, nor of the Grand Roy.

HIPPOLITA. 'Tis for his commendation if he does not talk of his travels.

MONSIEUR. Auh, auh, cousine, he is conscious himself of his wants, because he is very envious, for he cannot endure me –

HIPPOLITA. (*aside*) He shall be my man then for that. – Ay, ay, 'tis the same, Prue. No, I know he can't endure you, cousin.

MONSIEUR. How do you know it, who never stir out? Tête non!

HIPPOLITA. Well, dear cousin, if you will promise me never to tell my aunt, I'll tell you.

MONSIEUR. I won't, I won't, jarnie.

HIPPOLITA. Nor to be concerned yourself so as to make a quarrel of it.

MONSIEUR. Non, non.

HIPPOLITA. Upon the word of a gentleman.

MONSIEUR. Foy de chevalier, I will not quarrel.

PRUE. Lord, Miss, I wonder you won't believe him without more ado.

HIPPOLITA. Then, he has the hatred of a rival for you.

MONSIEUR. Mal à peste.

HIPPOLITA. You know my chamber is backward and has a door into the gallery which looks into the backyard of a tavern, whence Mr Gerrard, once spying me at the window, has often since attempted to come in at that window by the help of the leads of a low building adjoining and indeed 'twas as much as my maid and I could do to keep him out.

MONSIEUR. Au, le coquin!

HIPPOLITA. But nothing is stronger than aversion, for I hate him perfectly, even as much as I love you.

---

160 *Henry IV of Pont Neuf*: the statue of Henri IV on the new bridge over the Seine was a present from the King of Denmark.

160 *new Louvre*: the colonnade on the east façade was added between 1666 and 1670.

161 *Grand Roy*: Louis XIV.

183 *Mal à peste*: a plague on him.

188 *leads*: used for roofing.

191 *coquin*: rogue, rascal.

PRUE. (*aside*) I believe so, faith. But what design have we now on foot?

HIPPOLITA. This discovery is an argument, sure, of my love to you.

MONSIEUR. Ay, ay, say no more, cousin, I doubt not your amoure for me, because I doubt not your judgement. But what's to be done with this fanfaron? I know where he eats tonight; I'll go find him out, ventre bleu.

HIPPOLITA. Oh my dear cousin, you will not make a quarrel of it? I thought what your promise would come to!

MONSIEUR. Would you have a man of honour –

HIPPOLITA. Keep his promise?

MONSIEUR. And lose his mistress. That were not for my honour, ma foy.

HIPPOLITA. Cousin, though you do me the injury to think I could be false, do not do yourself the injury to think anyone could be false to you. Will you be afraid of losing your mistress? To show such a fear to your rival were for his honour and not for yours, sure.

MONSIEUR. Nay, cousin, I'd have you know I was never afraid of losing my mistress in earnest. Let me see the man can get my mistress from me, jarnie; but he that loves must seem a little jealous.

HIPPOLITA. Not to his rival. Those that have jealousy hide it from their rivals.

MONSIEUR. But there are some who say jealousy is no more to be hid than a cough. But it should never be discovered in me, if I had it, because it is not French, it is not French at all, ventre bleu.

HIPPOLITA. No, you should rally your rival and rather make a jest of your quarrel to him, and that, I suppose, is French too.

MONSIEUR. 'Tis so, 'tis so, cousin, 'tis the veritable French method, for your Englis', for want of wit, drive everything to a serious, grum quarrel and then would make a jest on't, when 'tis too late, when they can't laugh, jarnie!

---

200 *fanfaron*: swaggerer, rake.
202 *ventre bleu*: *bleu* is a euphemism for *Dieu*; 'by God's belly'.
225 *rally*: banter wittily.

HIPPOLITA. Yes, yes, I would have you rally him soundly. Do not spare him a jot. But shall you see him tonight?

MONSIEUR. Ay, ay.

HIPPOLITA. Yes, pray be sure to see him for the jest's sake.

MONSIEUR. I will, for I love a jeste as well as any bel esprit of 'em all, da.

HIPPOLITA. Ay, and rally him soundly, be sure you rally him soundly and tell him just thus: that the Lady he has so long courted from the great window of the Ship tavern is to be your wife tomorrow unless he come at his wonted hour of six in the morning to her window to forbid the banns, for 'tis the first and last time of asking, and, if he come not, let him for ever hereafter stay away and hold his tongue.

MONSIEUR. Ha, ha, ha, a ver good jeste, tête bleu.

HIPPOLITA. And if the fool should come again I would tell him his own, I warrant you, cousin. My gentleman should be satisfied for good and all, I'd secure him.

MONSIEUR. Bon, bon.

PRUE. (*aside*) Well, well, young mistress, you were not at Hackney School for nothing, I see, nor taken away for nothing. A woman may soon be too old but is never too young to shift for herself!

MONSIEUR. Hah, ah, ah, cousin, dou art a merry grig, ma foy. I long to be with Gerrard and I am the best at improving a jeste. I shall have such divertissement tonight, tête bleu.

HIPPOLITA. He'll deny, 'may be, at first that he never courted any such lady.

MONSIEUR. Nay, I am sure he'll be ashamed of it. I shall make him look so sillily, tête non. I long to find him out. Adieu, adieu, la cousine.

HIPPOLITA. Shall you be sure to find him?

MONSIEUR. Indubitablement. I'll search the town over but I'll find, hah, ha, ha. (*Exit* MONSIEUR *and returns*) But I'm afrait, cousine, if I should tell him you are to be my wife tomorrow he would not come;

---

244 *Ship tavern*: since it is in 'What-d'ee-call't' street (I ii 24), no particular tavern seems to be intended.

258 *merry grig*: madcap girl.

now I am for having him come, for the jest's sake, ventre.

HIPPOLITA. So am I, cousin, for having him come too, for the jest's sake.

MONSIEUR. Well, well, leave it to me! Ha, ha, ha.

Enter MRS CAUTION.

CAUTION. What's all this giggling here?

MONSIEUR. Hay, do you tinke we'll tell you? No, fait, I warrant you, tête non. Ha, ha, ha –

HIPPOLITA. My cousin is overjoyed, I suppose, that my father is to come tonight.

CAUTION. I am afraid he will not come tonight – but you'll stay and see, nephew.

MONSIEUR. Non, non, I am to sup at t'other end of the town tonight. La, la, la, la – ra, ra, ra –

Exit MONSIEUR *singing.*

CAUTION. I wish the French levity of this young man may agree with your father's Spanish gravity.

HIPPOLITA. Just as your crabbed old age and my youth agree.

CAUTION. Well, malapert! I know you hate me because I have been the guardian of your reputation. But your husband may thank me one day.

HIPPOLITA. If he be not a fool, he would rather be obliged to me for my virtue than to you since, at long run, he must whether he will or no.

CAUTION. So, so!

HIPPOLITA. Nay, now I think on't, I'd have you to know the poor man, whosoe'er he is, will have little cause to thank you.

CAUTION. No?

HIPPOLITA. No. For I never lived so wicked a life as I have done this twelvemonth since I have not seen a man.

CAUTION. How! How! If you have not seen a man how could you be wicked? How could you do any ill?

HIPPOLITA. No, I have done no ill but I have paid it with thinking.

CAUTION. O, that's no hurt; to think is no hurt. The ancient, grave and godly cannot help thoughts.

---

290 *malapert*: saucy.

HIPPOLITA. I warrant you have had 'em yourself, aunt.

CAUTION. Yes, yes! When I cannot sleep.

HIPPOLITA. Ha, ha, I believe it. But know I have had those thoughts sleeping and waking, for I have dreamt of a man.

CAUTION. No matter, no matter, so that it was but a dream. I have dreamt myself, for you must know widows are mightily given to dream, insomuch that a dream is waggishly called 'the widow's comfort'.

HIPPOLITA. But I did not only dream. Ih! (*Sighs*)

CAUTION. How, how! Did you more than dream? Speak, young harlotry, confess, did you more than dream? How could you do more than dream in this house? Speak, confess!

HIPPOLITA. Well, I will then. Indeed, aunt, I did not only dream but I was pleased with my dream when I waked.

CAUTION. Oh, is that all? Nay, if a dream only will please you you are a modest young woman still. But have a care of a vision.

HIPPOLITA. Ay. But to be delighted when we wake with a naughty dream is a sin, aunt, and I am so very scrupulous that I would as soon consent to a naughty man as to a naughty dream.

CAUTION. I do believe you.

HIPPOLITA. I am for going into the throng of temptations.

CAUTION. There I believe you again.

HIPPOLITA. And making myself so familiar with them that I would not be concerned for 'em a whit.

CAUTION. There I do not believe you.

HIPPOLITA. And would take all the innocent liberty of the town to tattle to your men under a vizard in the playhouses and meet 'em at night in masquerade.

CAUTION. There I do believe you again. I know you would be masquerading. But worse would come on't, as it has done to others who have been in a masquerade and are now virgins but in masquerade and will not be their own women again as long as they live. The children of this age must be wise children indeed

---

342 *tattle*: gossip.

if they know their fathers, since their mothers themselves cannot inform 'em! O, the fatal liberty of this masquerading age! When I was a young woman –

HIPPOLITA. Come, come, do not blaspheme this masquerading age like an ill-bred city dame whose husband is half broke by living in Covent Garden or who has been turned out of the Temple or Lincoln's Inn upon a masquerading night. By what I've heard 'tis a pleasant, well-bred, complacent, free, frolic, good-natured, pretty age and if you do not like it, leave it to us that do.

CAUTION. Lord, how impudently you talk, niece. I'm sure I remember when I was a maid –

HIPPOLITA. Can you remember it, reverend aunt?

CAUTION. Yes, modest niece – that a raw young thing though almost at woman's estate, that was then at thirty or thirty-five years of age, would not so much as have looked upon a man.

HIPPOLITA. Above her father's butler or coachman.

CAUTION. Still taking me up! Well, thou art a mad girl and so goodnight. We may go to bed for I suppose now your father will not come tonight.

HIPPOLITA. I am sorry for it, for I long to see him.

Exit CAUTION.

But I lie. I had rather see Gerrard here and yet I know not how I shall like him. If he has wit he will come and if he has none he would not be welcome.

Exeunt HIPPOLITA *and* PRUE.

SCENE II

Scene changes to the French house. A table, bottles and candles.

Enter MR GERRARD, MARTIN *and* MONSIEUR DE PARIS.

MONSIEUR. 'Tis ver veritable, jarnie, what the French

---

356 *Temple or Lincoln's Inn*: the Inns of Court, places for the study of law.

372 s.d. *Exit CAUTION*: after line 371 Q1.

s.d. *French house*: French restaurant.

say of you English; you use the debauch so much it cannot have with you the French operation – you are never enjoyé. But come, let us for once be enfinement galliard and sing a French sonnet. (*Sings*) La boutelle, la boutelle, glou, glou.

MARTIN. (*to* GERRARD) What a melodious fop it is!

MONSIEUR. Auh, you have no complaisance.

GERRARD. No, we can't sing but we'll drink to you the lady's health whom, you say, I have so long courted at her window.

MONSIEUR. Ay, there is your complaisance; all your English complaisance is pledging complaisance, ventre. But if I do you reason here (*takes the glass*) will you do me reason to a little French chanson à boire? I shall begin to you. (*Sings*) La boutelle, la boutelle –

MARTIN. (*to* GERRARD) I had rather keep company with a set of wide-mouthed, drunken cathedral choristers.

GERRARD. Come, sir, drink and he shall do you reason to your French song since you stand upon't. [*To* MARTIN] Sing him 'Arthur of Bradley' or 'I am the Duke of Norfolk'.

MONSIEUR. Auh, tête bleu, an English catch! Fie, fie, ventre.

GERRARD. He can sing no damned French song.

MONSIEUR. Nor can I drink the damned Englis' wine. (*Sets down the glass*)

GERRARD. Yes, to that lady's health who has commanded me to wait upon her tomorrow at her window which looks, you say, into the inward yard of the Ship tavern near the end of what-d'ee-call't street.

MONSIEUR. Ay, ay, do you not know her? Not you, vert et bleu.

---

5 *galliard*: the galliard is a quick French dance but Monsieur seems only to mean 'gay' ('gaillard').
5 (*Sings*): set as part of speech Q1.
14 *do you reason*: do you justice.
15 *chanson à boire*: drinking-song.
16 *shall*: shall shall Q1.
22–3 *'Arthur of Bradley' . . . 'I am the Duke of Norfolk'*: both were popular, traditional and very English ballads; the former is about a rural wedding; the latter's alternative title is 'Paul's Steeple' but its subject is unknown.
33 *vert et bleu*: corruption of *vertu Dieu*.

GERRARD. But, pray repeat again what she said.

MONSIEUR. Why, she said she is to be married tomorrow to a person of honour, a brave gentleman, that shall be nameless, and so and so forth. (*Aside*) Little does he think who 'tis.

GERRARD. And what else?

MONSIEUR. That if you make not your appearance before her window tomorrow at your wonted hour of six in the morning to forbid the banns, you must for ever hereafter stay away and hold your tongue, for 'tis the first and last time of asking, ha, ha, ha.

GERRARD. (*aside*) 'Tis all a riddle to me. I should be unwilling to be fooled by this coxcomb.

MONSIEUR. (*aside*) I won't tell him all she said, lest he should not go. I would fain have him go for the jest's sake. Ha, ha, ha.

GERRARD. Her name is, you say, Hippolita, daughter to a rich Spanish merchant.

MONSIEUR. Ay, ay. You don't know her – not you; à d'autre, à d'autre, ma foy. Ha, ha, ha.

GERRARD. Well, I will be an easy fool for once.

MARTIN. By all means go.

MONSIEUR. Ay, ay, by all means go. Hah, ha, ha.

GERRARD. (*aside*) To be caught in a fool's trap. – I'll venture it. (*Drinks to him*) Come, 'tis her health.

MONSIEUR. And to your good reception, tête bleu, ha, ha, ha.

GERRARD. Well, Monsieur, I'll say this for thee, thou hast made the best use of three months at Paris as ever English squire did.

MONSIEUR. Considering I was in a dam' Englis' pension too.

MARTIN. Yet you have conversed with some French, I see – footmen, I suppose, at the fencing-school. I judge it by your oaths.

MONSIEUR. French footmen! Well, well, I had rather have the conversation of a French footman than of an English squire. There's for you, da.

MARTIN. I beg your pardon, Monsieur, I did not think the French footmen had been so much your friends.

GERRARD. Yes, yes, I warrant they have obliged him at Paris much more than any of their masters did. Well, there shall be no more said against the French footmen.

MONSIEUR. Non, de grâce. You are always turning the nation françez into ridicule, dat nation so accompli, dat nation which you imitate so dat, in the conclusion, you butte turn yourself into redicule, ma foy. If you are for de raillery, abuse the Duch. Why not abuse the Duch, les grosse villains, pandars, insolents? But here in your England, ma foy, you have more honneur, respecte and estimation for de Dushe swabber who come to cheat your nation den for de Franch footman who come to oblige your nation.

MARTIN. Our nation! Then you disown it for yours, it seems.

MONSIEUR. Well, wat of dat? Are you the disobligé by date?

GERRARD. No, Monsieur, far from it. You could not oblige us nor your country any other way than by disowning it.

MONSIEUR. It is de brutale country which abuse de France an' reverence de Dushe. I vill maintain, sustain and justify dat one little Franch footman have more honneur, courage and generosity, more good blood in his veine an' mush more good manners an' civility den al de State General togeder, jarnie. Dey are only wise and valiant wen dey are drunke.

GERRARD. That is always.

MONSIEUR. But dey are never honeste wen dey are drunke. Dey are de only rogue in de varlde who are not honeste wen dey are drunk, ma foy.

GERRARD. I find you are well acquainted with them, Monsieur.

MONSIEUR. Ay, ay, I have made the toure of Holland but it was en poste – dere was no staying for me, tête non, for de gentleman can no more live dere den de toad in Irland, ma foy, for I did not see on' chevalier in de whole cuntré. Alway, you know, de rebel hate

---

81 With the Dutch War imminent, anti-Dutch jokes were only too easy to make, even to a city audience that might have more pro-Dutch than pro-French sentiments.

84 *swabber*: boorish fool.

99 *State General*: Holland; in line 115 it indicates the ruling representative assembly.

110 *toad in Irland*: toads had all been expelled by St Patrick, according to tradition.

de gens de quality. Besides, I had make sufficient observation of the canaille barbare de first nighte of my arrival at Amsterdame. I did visit, you must know, one of de principal of de Stat General, to whom I had recommendation from England and did find his excellence weighing soap, jarnie. Ha, ha, ha.

GERRARD. Weighing soap!

MONSIEUR. Weighing soape, ma foy, for he was a wholesale chandleer, and his lady was taking the tale of chandels wid her own witer hands, ma foy, and de young lady, his excellence' daughter, stringing harring. Stringing harring, jarnie!

GERRARD. So-h. And what were his sons doing?

MONSIEUR. Auh, his son, for he had but one, was making de tour of France, Espagne, Italy an' Germany in a coach and six – or rader, now I think on't, gone of an embassy hider to dere Master Cromwell whom dey did love and fear because he was sometinge de greater rebel. Bute, now I talk of de rebele, none but de rebel can love de rebele and so mush for you and your friend the Dush. I'll say no more and pray do you say no more of my friend de Franch, not so mush as of my friend the Franch footman, da.

GERRARD. No, no. But, Monsieur, now give me leave to admire thee, that in three months at Paris you could renounce your language, drinking and your country (for which we are not angry with you, as I said) and come home so perfect a Frenchman that the draymen of your father's own brewhouse would be ready to knock thee in the head.

MONSIEUR. Vell, vell, my father was a merchant of his own beer as the noblesse of France of their own wine. But I can forgive you that raillery, that bob, since you say I have the aire françez. But have I the aire françez?

GERRARD. As much as any French footman of 'em all.

MONSIEUR. And do I speak agreeable ill Englis' enough?

---

122 *daughter*: daughters Q1.

128 *Master Cromwell*: Monsieur is associating the rebels together in their Puritan beliefs.

144 *bob*: jest.

GERRARD. Very ill.
MONSIEUR. Veritablement?
GERRARD. Veritablement.
MONSIEUR. For you must know, 'tis as ill-breeding now to speak good Englis' as to write good Englis', good sense or a good hand.
GERRARD. But indeed, methinks, you are not slovenly enough for a Frenchman.
MONSIEUR. Slovenly! You mean negligent?
GERRARD. No, I mean slovenly.
MONSIEUR. Then I will be more slovenly.
GERRARD. You know, to be a perfect Frenchman you must never be silent, never sit still and never be clean.
MARTIN. But you have forgot one main qualification of a true Frenchman: he should never be sound, that is, be very pocky too.
MONSIEUR. Oh, if dat be all, I am very pocky, pocky enough, jarnie. That is the only French qualification may be had without going to Paris, mon foy.

Enter a WAITER.

WAITER. Here are a couple of ladies coming up to you, sir.
GERRARD. To us! Did you appoint any to come hither, Martin?
MARTIN. Not I.
GERRARD. Nor you, Monsieur?
MONSIEUR. Nor I.
GERRARD. Sirrah, tell your master, if he cannot protect us from the constable and these midnight coursers 'tis not a house for us.
MARTIN. Tell 'em you have nobody in the house and shut the doors.
WAITER. They'll not be satisfied with that; they'll break open the door. They searched last night all over the house for my Lord Fiske and Sir Jeffrey Janté who were fain to hide themselves in the bar under my mistress's chair and petticoats.
MONSIEUR. Wat, do the women hunt out the men so now?

---

165 *pocky*: having the pox, suffering from syphilis.
183 *Janté*: from French *gentil*.

MARTIN. Ay, ay, things are altered since you went to Paris. There's hardly a young man in town dares be known of his lodging for 'em.

GERRARD. Bailiffs, pursevants or a city constable are modest people in comparison of them.

MARTIN. And we are not so much afraid to be taken up by the watch as by the tearing midnight ramblers or houza women.

MONSIEUR. Jarnie, ha, ha, ha.

GERRARD. Where are they? I hope they are gone again.

WAITER. No, sir, they are below at the stair-foot, only swearing at their coachman.

GERRARD. Come, you rogue, they are in fee with you waiters and no gentleman can come hither but they have the intelligence straight.

WAITER. Intelligence from us, sir? They should never come here if we could help it. I am sure we wish 'em choked when we see them come in, for they bring such good stomachs from St James's Park or rambling about in the streets that we poor waiters have not a bit left. 'Tis well if we can keep our money in our pockets for 'em. I am sure I have paid seventeen and six in half-crowns for coach hire at several times for a little, damned, tearing lady and when I asked her for it again one morning in her chamber she bid me pay myself for she had no money – but I wanted the courage of a gentleman. Besides, the lord that kept her was a good customer to our house and my friend and I made a conscience of wronging him.

GERRARD. A man of honour!

MONSIEUR. Vert et bleu, pleasant, pleasant, mon foy.

GERRARD. Go, go, sirrah, shut the door. I hear 'em coming up.

WAITER. Indeed I dare not; they'll kick me downstairs if I should.

GERRARD. Go, you rascal, I say.

---

191 *pursevants*: deliverers of court summons.

194 *tearing*: roistering.

195 *houza women*: prostitutes; *houza* was used of rakes, especially noisy ones.

The WAITER *shuts the door. 'Tis thrust open again. Enter* FLOUNCE *and* FLIRT *in vizards, striking the* WAITER, *and come up to the table.*

GERRARD. (*aside*) Flounce and Flirt, upon my life. – Ladies, I am sorry you have no volunteers in your service. This is mere pressing and argues a great necessity you have for men.

FLOUNCE. You need not be afraid, sir. We will use no violence to you – you are not fit for our service, we know you.

FLIRT. The hot service you have been in formerly makes you unfit for ours now. Besides, you begin to be something too old for us; we are for the brisk houzas of seventeen or eighteen.

GERRARD. Nay, faith, I am not too old yet. But an old acquaintance will make any man old. Besides, to tell you the truth, you are come a little too early for me, for I am not drunk yet – but there are your brisk young men who are always drunk and perhaps have the happiness not to know you.

FLOUNCE. The happiness not to know us!

FLIRT. The happiness not to know us!

GERRARD. Be not angry, ladies; 'tis rather happiness to have pleasure to come than to have it past and therefore these gentlemen are happy in not knowing you.

MARTIN. I'd have you to know I do know the ladies too and I will not lose the honour of the ladies' acquaintance for anything.

FLOUNCE. Not for the pleasure of beginning the acquaintance with us, as Mr Gerrard says. But it is the general vanity of you town-fops to lay claim to all good acquaintance and persons of honour; you cannot let a woman pass in the Mall at midnight but, damn you, you know her straight, you know her. But you would be damned before you would say so much for one in a mercer's shop.

GERRARD. He has spoken it in a French house, where

226 *pressing*: being conscripted by a press-gang.
253 *Mall*: the new Mall was a walk in St James's Park, built for the game pell-mell.
256 *mercer*: seller, particularly of expensive fabrics.

he has very good credit, and I dare swear you may make him eat his words.

MONSIEUR. (*peeping under her scarf*) She does want a gown indeet. She is in her dishabilié. This dishabilié is a great mode in England; the women love the dishabilié as well as the men, ma foy.

FLIRT. Well, if we should stay and sup with you, I warrant you would be bragging of it tomorrow amongst your comrades that you had the company of two women of quality at the French house and name us.

MARTIN. (*aside*) Pleasant jilts.

GERRARD. No, upon our honours, we would not brag of your company.

FLOUNCE. Upon your honours?

MARTIN. No, faith.

FLOUNCE. Come, we will venture to sit down then. Yet I know the vanity of you men; you could not contain yourselves from bragging.

GERRARD. No, no. You women nowadays have found out the pleasure of bragging and will allow it the men no longer.

MARTIN. Therefore, indeed, we dare not stay to sup with you, for you would be sure to tell on't.

GERRARD. And we are young men who stand upon our reputations.

FLOUNCE. You are very pleasant, gentlemen.

MARTIN. For my part, I am to be married shortly and know 'twould quickly come to my mistress's ear.

GERRARD. And for my part, I must go visit tomorrow morning by times a new city mistress, and you know they are as inquisitive as precise in the city.

FLIRT. Come, come, pray leave this fooling. Sit down again and let us bespeak supper.

GERRARD. No, faith, I dare not.

MARTIN. Besides, we have supped.

FLOUNCE. No matter, we only desire you should look on while we eat and put the glass about or so.

GERRARD and MARTIN offer to go out.

---

288 *by times*: betimes, early.
295 s.d. *offer*: attempt.

FLIRT. Pray stay.

GERRARD. Upon my life I dare not.

FLOUNCE. Upon our honours we will not tell, if you are in earnest.

GERRARD. Pshaw, pshaw, I know the vanity of you women; you could not contain yourselves from bragging.

MONSIEUR. Ma foy, is it certain? Ha, ha, ha. Hark you, madam, can't you fare well but you must cry roast-meat?
You'll spoil your trade by bragging of your gains;
The silent sow, madam, does eat most grains.
Da.

FLIRT. Your servant, Monsieur Fop.

FLOUNCE. Nay, faith, do not go, we will no more tell –

MONSIEUR. Than you would of a clape, if you had it – dat's the only secret you can keep, jarnie.

MARTIN. I am glad we are rid of these jilts.

GERRARD. And we have taken a very ridiculous occasion.

MONSIEUR. Wat, must we leave the lady then? Dis is dam civility Englis', mon foy.

FLIRT. (*pulling him back*) Nay, sir, you have too much of the French air to have so little honour and good breeding.

MONSIEUR. Dé, you tinke so then, sweet madam, I have mush of de French air?

FLIRT. More than any Frenchman breathing.

MONSIEUR. Auh, you are the curtoise dame, mort bleu. I shall stay then, if you think so. Monsieur Gerrard, you will be certain to see the lady tomorrow – pray not forget. Ha, ha, ha.

GERRARD. No, no, sir.

MARTIN. You will go then?

GERRARD. I will go on a fool's errand for once.

Exeunt GERRARD *and* MARTIN.

FLOUNCE. What will you eat, sir?

MONSIEUR. Wat you please, madame.

FLOUNCE. D'ee hear, waiter, then some young partridge.

WAITER. What else, madam?

---

321 *Dé*: Monsieur's stab at pronouncing *Dieu*.

FLIRT. Some ruffs.

WAITER. What else, madam?

FLOUNCE. Some young pheasants.

WAITER. What else, madam?

FLIRT. Some young rabbits. I love rabbits.

WAITER. What else, madam?

FLOUNCE. Stay –

MONSIEUR. (*aside*) Dis Englis' waiter wit his 'Wat else, madam?' will ruin me, tête non.

WAITER. What else, madam?

MONSIEUR. 'Wat else, madam' again! Call up the French waiter.

WAITER. What else, madam?

MONSIEUR. Again! Call up the French waiter or quesinier, mort-tête-ventre. Vite, vite. Auh, madam, the stupidity of the Englis' waiter! I hate the Englis' waiter, mon foy.

Exit WAITER.

FLIRT. Be not in passion, dear Monsieur.

MONSIEUR. I kiss your hand obligeant, madam.

Enter a FRENCH SCULLION.

Chere Pierrot, serviteur, serviteur, or ça à manger. (*Kisses the* SCULLION)

SCULLION. En voulez vous de cram schiquin?

FLOUNCE. Yes.

SCULLION. De partrish, de faisan, de quailles?

MONSIEUR. [*aside*] This bougre vel ruine me too but he speak wit dat bel aire and grâce. I cannot bid him hold his tongue, ventre. – C'est assez, Pierrot, va-t-en.

Exit SCULLION *and returns.*

SCULLION. And de litel plate de –

MONSIEUR. Jarnie, va-t-en.

Exit SCULLION *and returns.*

SCULLION. And de litel plate de –

---

335 *ruffs*: male sandpipers.

349 *quesinier*: *cuisinier*, cook.

354 *Pierrot*: the diminutive of Pierre but also, perhaps, a reference to the character in the Harlequinade. Monsieur studied under Signior Scaramouche, see III i 48–51.

355 *cram schiquin*: crammed chicken, chickens fattened on a diet of raisins and breadcrumbs.

357 *faisan*: pheasant.

MONSIEUR. De grâce, go dy way.

Exit SCULLION *and returns.*

SCULLION. And de litel de –

MONSIEUR. De fourmage, de brie! Va-t-en, go, go.

FLOUNCE. What's that cheese that stinks?

MONSIEUR. Ay, ay, be sure it stinke extremente, Pierrot. Va-t-en – but stay till I drink dy health. Here's to dat pretty fellow's health, madam.

FLIRT. Must we drink the scullion's health?

MONSIEUR. Auh, you will not be disobligeant, madam. He is the cuisinier for a king, nay for a cardinal or French abbot. (*Drinks*)

[*Exit* SCULLION.]

FLOUNCE. But how shall we divertise ourselves till supper be ready?

FLIRT. Can we have better divertisement than this gentleman?

FLOUNCE. But I think we had better carry the gentleman home with us and, because it is already late, sup at home and divertise the gentleman at cards till it be ready. D'ee hear, waiter, let it be brought when 'tis ready to my lodging hard by in Mustard Alley at the sign of the Crooked Billet.

MONSIEUR. At the Crook Billet!

FLIRT. Come, sir, come.

MONSIEUR. Mort bleu, I have take the vow (since my last clap) never to go again to the bourdel.

FLOUNCE. What is the bourdel?

MONSIEUR. How call you the name of your house?

FLIRT. The Crooked Billet.

MONSIEUR. No, no, the – the bawdy-house, vert et bleu.

FLOUNCE. How, our lodging! We'd have you to know –

MONSIEUR. Auh, mort bleu, I would not know it. De Crooke Billet, hah, ha.

FLIRT. Come, sir.

MONSIEUR. Besides, if I go wit you to the bourdel, you will tell, mort bleu.

---

383 *Mustard Alley*: the road referred to remains unidentified but Partridge's listing of a later use of *mustard-pot* to mean *female sex* probably gives the clue to the name's significance here. The innuendo behind *Crooked Billet* is probably phallic.

388 *bourdel*: bordel, brothel.

FLOUNCE. Fie, fie, come along.

MONSIEUR. Beside, I am to be married within these two days. If you should tell now –

FLIRT. Come, come along. We will not tell.

MONSIEUR. But will you promise then to have the care of my honour? Pray, good madam, have de care of my honneur, pray have de care of my honneur. Will you have care of my honneur? Pray have de care of my honneur and do not tell if you can help it. Pray, dear madam, do not tell. (*Kneels to 'em*)

FLIRT. I would not tell for fear of losing you. My love for you will make me secret.

MONSIEUR. Why, do you love me?

FLIRT. Indeed, I cannot help telling you now what my modesty ought to conceal but my eyes would disclose it too. I have a passion for you, sir.

MONSIEUR. A passion for me!

FLIRT. An extreme passion, dear sir. You are so French, so mightily French, so agreeable French – but I'll tell you more of my heart at home. Come along.

MONSIEUR. But is your passion sincere?

FLIRT. The truest in the world.

MONSIEUR. Well then, I'll venture my body wit thee for one night.

FLIRT. For one night! Don't you believe that, and so you would leave me tomorrow. But I love you so I cannot part with you; you must keep me for good and all if you will have me. I can't leave you for my heart.

MONSIEUR. How, keep! Jarnie, de whore Englis' have notinge but 'keepe, keepe' in dere mouths nowadays, tête non. Formerly 'twas enough to keep de shild, ma foy.

FLIRT. Nay, I will be kept, else – but come, we'll talk on't at home.

MONSIEUR. Umh. So, so, ver vel. De amoure of de whore does alway end in 'keep'. Ha, keep, ma foy, keep, ha –

The punk that entertains you wit' her passion
Is like kind host who makes the invitation,
At your own cost, to his fort bon collation.

Exeunt.

ACT II

SCENE I

Don Diego's house in the morning.

Enter DON DIEGO *in the Spanish habit,* MRS CAUTION, *his sister.*

DON DIEGO. Have you had a Spanish care of the honour of my family, that is to say, have you kept up my daughter close in my absence, as I directed?

CAUTION. I have, sir. But it was as much as I could do.

DON DIEGO. I knew that, for 'twas as much as I could do to keep up her mother – I that have been in Spain, look you.

CAUTION. Nay, 'tis a hard task to keep up an English woman.

DON DIEGO. As hard as it is for those who are not kept up to be honest, look you, con licentia, sister.

CAUTION. How now, brother! I am sure my husband never kept me up.

DON DIEGO. I knew that, therefore I cried 'con licentia', sister, as the Spaniards have it.

CAUTION. But you Spaniards are too censorious, brother.

DON DIEGO. You English women, sister, give us too much cause, look you. But you are sure my daughter has not seen a man since my departure?

CAUTION. No, not so much as a churchman.

DON DIEGO. As a churchman, voto! I thank you for that. Not a churchman, not a churchman!

CAUTION. No, not so much as a churchman. But, of any, one would think one might trust a churchman.

DON DIEGO. No, we are bold enough in trusting them with our souls. I'll never trust 'em with the body of my daughter, look you. Guarda, you see what comes

---

s.d. *in the Spanish habit*: see Additional Note.
11 *con licentia*: 'con licencia', with permission.
22 *voto*: I swear.
28 *Guarda*: look out, beware.

of trusting churchmen here in England – and 'tis because the women govern the families that chaplains are so much in fashion. Trust a churchman! Trust a coward with your honour, a fool with your secret, a gamester with your purse as soon as a priest with your wife or daughter, look you, guarda. I am no fool, look you.

CAUTION. Nay, I know you are a wise man, brother.

DON DIEGO. Why, sister, I have been fifteen years in Spain for it, at several times, look you. Now in Spain he is wise enough that is grave, politic enough that says little and honourable enough that is jealous, and, though I say it that should not say it, I am as grave, grum and jealous as any Spaniard breathing.

CAUTION. I know you are, brother.

DON DIEGO. And I will be a Spaniard in everything still and will not conform, not I, to their ill-favoured English customs, for I will wear my Spanish habit still, I will stroke my Spanish whiskers still and I will eat my Spanish olio still and my daughter shall go a maid to her husband's bed, let the English custom be what 'twill. I would fain see any finical, cunning, insinuating monsieur of the age debauch or steal away my daughter. But well, has she seen my cousin? How long has he been in England?

CAUTION. These three days.

DON DIEGO. And she has seen him, has she? I was contented he should see her, intending him for her husband. But she has seen nobody else upon your certain knowledge?

CAUTION. No, no, alas, how should she? 'Tis impossible she should.

DON DIEGO. Where is her chamber? Pray let me see her.

CAUTION. You'll find her, poor creature, asleep, I warrant you, or if awake, thinking no hurt nor of your coming this morning.

---

47 *Spanish whiskers*: English gentlemen at this time preferred to be clean-shaven.

48 *Spanish olio*: the traditional Spanish stew containing meat, poultry and all sorts of vegetables.

50 *finical*: affectedly fastidious.

DON DIEGO. Let us go to her. I long to see her, poor innocent wretch.

Exeunt.

Enter HIPPOLITA, GERRARD, *and* PRUE *at a distance.*

GERRARD. Am I not come upon your own summons, madam? And yet receive me so?

HIPPOLITA. My summons, sir? No, I assure you, and, if you do not like your reception, I cannot help it, for I am not used to receive men, I'd have you to know.

GERRARD. (*aside*) She is beautiful beyond all things I ever saw.

HIPPOLITA. (*aside*) I like him extremely.

GERRARD. Come, fairest, why do you frown?

HIPPOLITA. Because I am angry.

GERRARD. I am come on purpose to please you then; do not receive me so unkindly.

HIPPOLITA. I tell you, I do not use to receive men. There has not been a man in the house before, but my cousin, this twelvemonth, I'd have you to know.

GERRARD. Then you ought to bid me the more welcome, I'd have you to know.

HIPPOLITA. What, do you mock me too? I know I am but a home-bred, simple girl but I thought you gallants of the town had been better bred than to mock a poor girl in her father's own house. I have heard indeed 'tis a part of good breeding to mock people behind their backs, but not to their faces.

GERRARD. (*aside*) Pretty creature! She has not only the beauty but the innocency of an angel. – Mock you, dear miss! No, I only repeated the words because they were yours, sweet miss. What we like we imitate.

HIPPOLITA. Dear miss! Sweet miss! How came you and I so well acquainted? This is one of your confident tricks too, as I have been told; you'll be acquainted with a woman in the time you can help her over a bench in the playhouse or to her coach. But I need not wonder at your confidence since you could come in at the great gallery-window just now. But pray, who shall pay for the glass you have broken?

---

98 *bench*: the only seating in the theatre.

GERRARD. Pretty creature! Your father might have made the window bigger then, since he has so fine a daughter and will not allow people to come in at the door to her.

HIPPOLITA. (*aside*) A pleasant man! Well, 'tis harder playing the hypocrite with him, I see, than with my aunt or father, and, if dissimulation were not very natural to a woman, I'm sure I could not use it at this time. But the mask of simplicity and innocency is as useful to an intriguing woman as the mask of religion to a statesman, they say.

GERRARD. Why do you look away, dearest miss?

HIPPOLITA. Because you quarrelled with me just now for frowning upon you and I cannot help it, if I look upon you.

GERRARD. O, let me see that face at any rate.

HIPPOLITA. Would you have me frown upon you? For I shall be sure to do't.

GERRARD. Come, I'll stand fair; you have done your worst to my heart already.

HIPPOLITA. (*aside*) Now I dare not look upon him lest I should not be able to keep my word.

GERRARD. Come, I am ready – (*Aside*) and yet I am afraid of her frowns. – Come, look. I – h – am ready, I – h – am ready.

HIPPOLITA. (*aside*) But I am not ready.

GERRARD. Turn, dear miss, come, I – h – am ready.

HIPPOLITA. Are you ready then? I'll look. (*Turns upon him. Aside*) No, faith, I can't frown upon him if I should be hanged.

GERRARD. Dear miss, I thank you. That look has no terror in't.

HIPPOLITA. No, I cannot frown for my heart; for, blushing, I don't use to look upon men, you must know.

GERRARD. (*aside*) If it were possible anything could, those blushes would add to her beauty. Well, bashfulness is the only out-of-fashion thing that is agreeable.

HIPPOLITA. (*aside*) I – h – h like this man strangely – I was going to say 'loved him'. Courage then, Hippolita; make use of the only opportunity thou canst have to enfranchise thyself. Women formerly, they say, never knew how to make use of their time till it was past but let it not be said so of a young woman of this age. My damned aunt will be stirring presently. Well, then, courage, I say, Hippolita, thou art full fourteen years old – shift for thyself.

GERRARD. (*aside*) So, I have looked upon her so long till I am grown bashful too. Love and modesty come together like money and covetousness and the more we have the less we can show it. I dare not look her in the face now nor speak a word.

HIPPOLITA. What, sir, methinks you look away now.

GERRARD. Because you would not look upon me, miss.

HIPPOLITA. Nay, I hope you can't look me in the face since you have done so rude a thing as to come in at the window upon me. Come, come, when once we women find the men bashful, then we take heart. Now I can look upon you as long as you will. Let's see if you can frown upon me now!

GERRARD. Lovely innocency! No, you may swear I can't frown upon you, miss.

HIPPOLITA. So, I knew you were ashamed of what you have done. Well, since you are ashamed and because you did not come of your own head but were sent by my cousin, you say –

GERRARD. (*aside*) Which I wonder at.

HIPPOLITA. For all these reasons, I do forgive you.

GERRARD. In token of your forgiveness then, dearest miss, let me have the honour to kiss your hand.

HIPPOLITA. Nay, there 'tis you men are like our little shock-dogs; if we don't keep you off from us but use you a little kindly, you grow so fiddling and so troublesome there is no enduring you.

GERRARD. O dear miss, if I am like your shock-dog, let it be in his privileges.

HIPPOLITA. Why, I'd have you know he does not lie with me.

GERRARD. 'Twas well guessed, miss, for one so innocent.

HIPPOLITA. No, I always kick him off from the bed and never will let him come near it, for of late indeed (I do

177 *shock-dogs*: lap-dogs, often poodles.

not know what's the reason), I don't much care for my shock-dog nor my babies.

GERRARD. O then, miss, I may have hopes, for after the shock-dog and the babies 'tis the man's turn to be beloved.

HIPPOLITA. Why, could you be so good-natured as to come after my shock-dog in my love? It may be indeed, rather than after one of your brother men.

GERRARD. Hah, ha, ha. – [*Aside*] Poor creature, a wonder of innocency.

HIPPOLITA. But I see you are humble because you would kiss my hand.

GERRARD. No, I am ambitious therefore.

HIPPOLITA. (*aside*) Well, all this fooling but loses time; I must make better use of it. – I could let you kiss my hand but then I'm afraid you would take hold of me and carry me away.

GERRARD. Indeed I would not.

HIPPOLITA. Come, I know you would.

GERRARD. Truly I would not.

HIPPOLITA. You would, you would, I know you would.

GERRARD. I'll swear I wo'not. By –

HIPPOLITA. Nay, don't swear, for you'll be the apter to do it then. (*Aside*) I would not have him forswear it neither. He does not like me, sure, well enough to carry me away.

GERRARD. Dear miss, let me kiss your hand.

HIPPOLITA. I am sure you would carry me away if I should.

GERRARD. Be not afraid of it.

HIPPOLITA. (*aside*) Nay, I am afraid of the contrary. Either he dislikes me and therefore will not be troubled with me or, what is as bad, he loves me and is dull or fearful to displease me.

GERRARD. Trust me, sweetest; I can use no violence to you.

HIPPOLITA. Nay, I am sure you would carry me away. What should you come in at the window for, if you did not mean to steal me?

---

185 *babies*: dolls.

GERRARD. If I should endeavour it you might cry out and I should be prevented.

HIPPOLITA. (*aside*) Dull, dull man of the town, are all like thee? He is as dull as a country squire at questions and commands. – No, if I should cry out never so loud; this is quite at the further end of the house and there nobody could hear me.

GERRARD. I will not give you occasion, dearest.

HIPPOLITA. (*aside*) Well, I will quicken thy sense, if it be possible. – Nay, I know you come to steal me away, because I am an heiress and have twelve hundred pound a year, lately left me by my mother's brother, which my father cannot meddle with and which is the chiefest reason, I suppose, why he keeps me up so close.

GERRARD. (*aside*) Ha!

HIPPOLITA. [*aside*] So, this has made him consider. O money, powerful money! How the ugly, old, crooked, straight, handsome young women are beholding to thee!

GERRARD. [*aside*] Twelve hundred pound a year!

HIPPOLITA. Besides, I have been told my fortune and the woman said I should be stolen away because, she says, 'tis the fate of heiresses to be stolen away.

GERRARD. (*aside*) Twelve hundred pound a year!

HIPPOLITA. Nay more, she described the man to me that was to do it and he was as like you as could be! Have you any brothers?

GERRARD. Not any! 'Twas I, I warrant you, sweetest.

HIPPOLITA. So, he understands himself now.

GERRARD. Well, madam, since 'twas foretold you, what do you think on't? 'Tis in vain, you know, to resist fate.

HIPPOLITA. I do know indeed they say 'tis to no purpose. Besides, the woman that told my fortune or you have bewitched me. (*Sighs*) I – h – think.

GERRARD. My soul, my life, 'tis you have charms powerful as numberless, especially those of your

---

226–7 *questions and commands*: an old-fashioned country game involving foolish questions and tasks and often involving kissing.

247 *pound a*: pound Q1.

innocency irresistible, and do surprise the wariest heart. Such mine was while I could call it mine but now 'tis yours for ever.

HIPPOLITA. Well, well, get you gone then. I'll keep it safe for your sake.

GERRARD. Nay, you must go with me, sweetest.

HIPPOLITA. Well, I see you will part with the jewel but you'll have the keeping of the cabinet to which you commit it.

GERRARD. Come, come, my dearest, let us be gone. Fortune as well as women must be taken in the humour.

Enter PRUE *running hastily to stop 'em,* DON DIEGO *and* MRS CAUTION *immediately after.*

PRUE. O miss, miss, your father, it seems, is just now arrived and here is coming in upon you.

HIPPOLITA. My father!

DON DIEGO. My daughter! And a man!

CAUTION. A man! A man in the house!

GERRARD. Ha! What mean these? A Spaniard!

HIPPOLITA. [*aside*] What shall I do? – Stay. Nay, pray stir not from me but lead me about as if you lead me a corant.

[GERRARD] *leads her about.*

DON DIEGO. Is this your government, sister, and this your innocent charge that has not seen the face of a man this twelvemonth? En hora mala!

CAUTION. O, sure, it is not a man, it cannot be a man! (*Puts on her spectacles*)

DON DIEGO. It cannot be a man! If he be not a man he's a devil. He has her lovingly by the hand too. Valga me el cielo.

HIPPOLITA. Do not seem to mind them but dance on or lead me about still.

---

272 s.d. *Enter PRUE . . . stop 'em*: Prue has not been offstage but she has been keeping watch at a distance. She now runs forward to stop them leaving, entering the action for the first time in the scene.

281 *corant*: the courante or coranto was, in spite of the quick music and the running steps, a stately dance.

284 *En hora mala*: in an evil hour, unluckily.

287–8 *Valga me el cielo*: heaven help me.

GERRARD. (*apart to* HIPPOLITA) What d'ee mean by't?

DON DIEGO. Hey! They are frolic, a-dancing.

CAUTION. Indeed they are dancing, I think. Why, niece!

DON DIEGO. Nay, hold a little. I'll make 'em dance in the devil's name – but it shall not be la galliarda.

Draws his sword; CAUTION *holds him.*

CAUTION. O niece! Why, niece!

GERRARD. (*apart to* HIPPOLITA) Do you hear her? What do you mean?

HIPPOLITA. Take no notice of them but walk about still and sing a little. Sing a corant.

GERRARD. I can't sing but I'll hum, if you will.

DON DIEGO. Are you so merry? Well, I'll be with you en hora mala.

CAUTION. Oh niece, niece, why, niece, oh!

DON DIEGO. Why, daughter, my dainty daughter, my shame, my ruin, my plague. (*Struggling, gets from* CAUTION, *goes towards 'em with his sword drawn*)

HIPPOLITA. Mind him not but dance and sing on.

GERRARD. A pretty time to dance and sing indeed when I have a Spaniard with naked Toledo at my tail. No, pray excuse me, miss, from fooling any longer.

HIPPOLITA. (*turning about*) O my father! My father, poor father! You are welcome. Pray give me your blessing.

DON DIEGO. My blessing en hora mala.

HIPPOLITA. What, am I not your daughter, sir?

DON DIEGO. My daughter, mi mal, mi muerte.

HIPPOLITA. My name's Hippolita, sir; I don't own your Spanish names. But pray, father, why do you frighten one so? You know I don't love to see a sword. What do you mean to do with that ugly thing out?

DON DIEGO. I'll show you. Traidor, ladrón, demi honra, thou diest. (*Runs at* GERRARD)

GERRARD. (*draws*) Not if I can help it, good don. But

---

295 *la galliarda*: the galliard, a lively dance.
309 *Toledo*: a sword made from the famous Toledo steel.
316 *mi mal, mi muerte*: my plague, my death.
321–2 *Traidor, ladrón, demi honra*: Traitor, thief, give me back my honour. Q1 reads *houra* and Ward suggested that the *n* was turned. *Honra* is the great principle of *public* honour.

by the names you give me I find you mistake your man. I suppose some Spaniard has affronted you.

DON DIEGO. None but thee, ladrón, and thou diest for't.

Fight.

CAUTION. Oh, oh, oh, help, help, help.

HIPPOLITA. (*kneels*) Oh, what, will you kill my poor dancing-master?

DON DIEGO. A dancing-master! He's a fencing-master rather, I think. But is he your dancing-master? Umph.

GERRARD. (*aside*) So much wit and innocency were never together before.

DON DIEGO. (*pausing*) Is he a dancing-master?

CAUTION. Is he a dancing-master? He does not look like a dancing-master.

HIPPOLITA. Pish, you don't know a dancing-master; you have not seen one these threescore years, I warrant.

CAUTION. No matter. But he does not look like a dancing-master.

DON DIEGO. Nay, nay, dancing-masters look like gentlemen enough, sister. But he's no dancing-master by drawing his sword so briskly. Those tripping outsides of gentlemen are like gentlemen enough in everything but in drawing a sword and, since he is a gentleman, he shall die by mine.

Fight again.

HIPPOLITA. Oh hold, hold.

CAUTION. Hold, hold! Pray, brother, let's talk with him a little first. I warrant you I shall trap him and if he confesses you may kill him, for those that confess, they say, ought to be hanged. Let's see.

GERRARD. (*aside*) Poor Hippolita, I wish I had not had this occasion of admiring thy wit. I have increased my love whilst I have lost my hopes – the common fate of poor lovers.

CAUTION. Come, you are guilty by that hanging down of your head. Speak. Are you a dancing-master? Speak, speak. A dancing-master?

GERRARD. Yes, forsooth, I am a dancing-master, ay, ay.

DON DIEGO. How dost it appear?

HIPPOLITA. Why, there is his fiddle, there upon the table, father.

CAUTION. No, busybody, but it is not. That is my nephew's fiddle.

HIPPOLITA. Why, he lent it to my cousin. I tell you it is his.

CAUTION. Nay, it may be indeed, he might lend it to him for ought I know.

DON DIEGO. Ay, ay, but ask him, sister, if he be a dancing-master, where.

CAUTION. Pray, brother, let me alone with him. I know what to ask him, sure!

DON DIEGO. What, will you be wiser than I? Nay, then stand away. Come, if you are a dancing-master, where's your school? Adonde, adonde?

CAUTION. Why, he'll say, maybe, he has ne'er a one.

DON DIEGO. Who asked you, nimble chaps? So, you have put an excuse in his head.

GERRARD. Indeed, sir, 'tis no excuse; I have no school.

CAUTION. Well, but who sent you? How came you thither?

GERRARD. (*aside*) There I am puzzled indeed.

CAUTION. How came you hither, I say? How?

GERRARD. Why, how, how, how should I come hither?

DON DIEGO. Ay, how should he come hither? Upon his legs.

CAUTION. So, so, now you have put an excuse in his head too, that you have, so you have. But stay –

DON DIEGO. Nay, with your favour, mistress, I'll ask him now.

CAUTION. Yfacks but you shan't. I'll ask him and ask you no favour, that I will.

DON DIEGO. Yfackins but you shan't ask him. If you go thereto, look you, you prattlebox you, I'll ask him.

CAUTION. I will ask him, I say. Come.

DON DIEGO. Where?

CAUTION. What?

DON DIEGO. Mine's a shrewd question.

CAUTION. Mine's as shrewd as yours.

DON DIEGO. Nay then, we shall have it. Come, answer me. Where's your lodging? Come, come, sir.

CAUTION. A shrewd question indeed. At the Surgeon's

---

376 *Adonde*: where.
378 *chaps*: jaws.
392, 394 *Yfacks, Yfackins*: in faith.

Arms, I warrant, in –, for 'tis springtime, you know.

DON DIEGO. Must you make lies for him?

CAUTION. But come, sir, what's your name? Answer me to that, come.

DON DIEGO. His name. Why, 'tis an easy matter to tell you a false name, I hope.

CAUTION. So, must you teach him to cheat us?

DON DIEGO. Why did you say my questions were not shrewd questions then?

CAUTION. And why would you not let me ask him the question then? Brother, brother, ever while you live, for all your Spanish wisdom, let an old woman make discoveries. The young fellows cannot cheat us in anything. I'd have you to know. Set your old woman still to grope out an intrigue, because you know the mother found her daughter in the oven. A word to the wise, brother.

DON DIEGO. Come, come, leave this tattling. He has dishonoured my family, debauched my daughter and what if he could excuse himself? The Spanish proverb says 'Excuses neither satisfy creditors nor the injured; the wounds of honour must have blood and wounds.' St Jago para mi. (*Kisses the cross of his sword and runs at* GERRARD)

HIPPOLITA. Oh hold, dear father, and I'll confess all.

GERRARD. (*aside*) She will not, sure, after all.

HIPPOLITA. My cousin sent him because, as he said, he would have me recover my dancing a little before our wedding, having made a vow he would never marry a wife who could not dance a corant. I am sure I was unwilling but he would have him come, saying I was to be his wife as soon as you came and therefore expected obedience from me.

---

404 *in –*: Q1 leaves a gap for the street name.

418–19 *the mother . . . the oven*: proverbial; the woman would never have looked in the oven for her daughter if she had not been there herself. 'Oven' may well have had the modern innuendo of 'womb', as in 'bun in the oven'.

426 *St Jago para mi*: St James for me. James Formal swears by St James the apostle, just as his chosen Spanish name, Diego, is a Spanish form of James.

426 s.d. *the cross*: formed by the hilt-guards and the blade.

DON DIEGO. Indeed the venture is most his and the shame would be most his, for I know here in England 'tis not the custom for the father to be much concerned what the daughter does – but I will be a Spaniard still.

HIPPOLITA. Did not you hear him say last night he would send me one this morning?

CAUTION. No, not I, sure. If I had, he had never come here.

HIPPOLITA. Indeed, aunt, you grow old, I see; your memory fails you very much. Did not you hear him, Prue, say he would send him to me?

PRUE. Yes, I'll be sworn did I.

HIPPOLITA. Look you there, aunt.

CAUTION. I wonder I should not remember it.

DON DIEGO. Come, come, you are a doting old fool.

CAUTION. So, so, the fault will be mine now. But pray, mistress, how did he come in? I am sure I had the keys of the doors which, till your father came in, were not opened today.

HIPPOLITA. He came in just after my father, I suppose.

CAUTION. It might be indeed while the porters brought in the things and I was talking with you.

DON DIEGO. O might he so, forsooth. You are a brave governante, look you, you a duenna, voto – and not know who comes in and out.

CAUTION. So, 'twas my fault, I know.

DON DIEGO. Your maid was in the room with you, was she not, child?

HIPPOLITA. Yes, indeed and indeed, father, all the while.

DON DIEGO. Well, child, I am satisfied then. But I hope he does not use the dancing-masters' tricks of squeezing your hands, setting your legs and feet by handling your thighs and seeing your legs.

HIPPOLITA. No, indeed, father. I'd give him a box on the ear if he should.

DON DIEGO. Poor innocent! Well, I am contented you should learn to dance since, for ought I know, you shall be married tomorrow or the next day at farthest.

460 *duenna*: governess.

By that time you may recover a corant, a sarabrand, I would say, and since your cousin too will have a dancing wife it shall be so and I'll see you dance myself. You shall be my charge these two days and then I dare venture you in the hand of any dancing-master, even a saucy French dancing-master, look you.

CAUTION. Well, have a care though, for this man is not dressed like a dancing-master.

DON DIEGO. Go, go, you dote. Are they not, for the most part, better dressed and prouder than many a good gentleman? You would be wiser than I, would you? Cuerno!

CAUTION. Well, I say only look to't, look to't.

DON DIEGO. Hey, hey! Come, friend, to your business; teach her her lesson over again. Let's see.

HIPPOLITA. Come, master.

DON DIEGO. Come, come, let's see your English method. I understand something of dancing myself. Come.

HIPPOLITA. Come, master.

GERRARD. (*apart to* HIPPOLITA) I shall betray you yet, dearest miss, for I know not a step. I could never dance.

HIPPOLITA. [*apart to* GERRARD] No!

DON DIEGO. Come, come, child.

HIPPOLITA. Indeed, I'm ashamed, father.

DON DIEGO. You must not be ashamed, child. You'll never dance well if you are ashamed.

HIPPOLITA. Indeed I can't help it, father.

DON DIEGO. Come, come, I say, go to't.

HIPPOLITA. Indeed I can't father, before you. 'Tis my first lesson and I shall do it so ill. Pray, good father, go into the next room for this once and the next time my master comes I shall be confident enough.

DON DIEGO. Poor, foolish, innocent creature. Well, well, I will, child. Who but a Spanish kind of a father could have so innocent a daughter in England? Well,

---

476 *sarabrand*: Don Diego means saraband, a slow and stately Spanish dance, supposedly introduced to Spain by the Moors; though nothing like the courante, the saraband was a reasonable Spanish approximation for the French dance.

487 *Cuerno*: a very mild expletive, damn.

I would fain see anyone steal or debauch my daughter from me.

HIPPOLITA. Nay, won't you go, father?

DON DIEGO. Yes, yes, I go, child. We will all go but your maid. You can dance before your maid.

HIPPOLITA. Yes, yes, father, a maid at most times with her mistress is nobody.

Exeunt DIEGO *and* MRS CAUTION.

GERRARD. He peeps yet at the door.

HIPPOLITA. Nay, father, you peep; indeed you must not see me. When we have done you shall come in. (*She pulls the door to*)

PRUE. [*apart to* HIPPOLITA] Indeed, little mistress, like the young kitten, you see, you played with your prey till you had almost lost it!

HIPPOLITA. [*apart to* PRUE] 'Tis true. A good old mouser like you had taken it up and run away with it presently.

GERRARD. (*going to embrace her*) Let me adore you, dearest miss, and give you –

HIPPOLITA. No, no embracing, good master. That ought to be the last lesson you are to teach me, I have heard.

GERRARD. Though an after game be the more tedious and dangerous, 'tis won, miss, with the more honour and pleasure, for all that I repent we were put to't. The coming-in of your father as he did was the most unlucky thing that ever befell me.

HIPPOLITA. What, then you think I would have gone with you?

GERRARD. Yes, and will go with me, yet, I hope. Courage, miss. We have yet an opportunity and the gallery window is yet open.

HIPPOLITA. No, no, if I went I would go for good and all. But now my father will soon come in again and may quickly overtake us. Besides, now I think on't, you are a stranger to me. I know not where you live nor whither you might carry me. For ought I know, you might be a spirit and carry me to Barbadoes.

---

528 *taken it*: it taken Q1.

534 *after game*: a second game played to reverse or improve the first result.

549 *spirit*: kidnapper; abductions to the Barbadoes were not uncommon.

GERRARD. No, dear miss, I would carry you to Court, the playhouses and Hyde Park –

HIPPOLITA. Nay, I know 'tis the trick of all you that spirit women away to speak 'em mighty fair at first. But, when you have got 'em in your clutches, you carry 'em into Yorkshire, Wales or Cornwall, which is as bad as to Barbadoes, and, rather than be served so, I would be a prisoner in London still as I am.

GERRARD. I see the air of this town without the pleasures of it is enough to infect women with an aversion for the country. Well, miss, since it seems you have some diffidence in me, give me leave to visit you as your dancing-master, now you have honoured me with the character and, under that, I may have your father's permission to see you, till you may better know me and my heart and have a better opportunity to reward it.

HIPPOLITA. I am afraid to know your heart would require a great deal of time and my father intends to marry me very suddenly to my cousin who sent you hither.

GERRARD. Pray, sweet miss, then let us make the better use of our time if it be short. But how shall we do with that cousin of yours in the meantime? We must needs charm him.

HIPPOLITA. Leave that to me.

GERRARD. But, what's worse, how shall I be able to act a dancing-master who ever wanted inclination and patience to learn myself?

HIPPOLITA. A dancing-school in half an hour will furnish you with terms of the art. Besides, love, as I have heard say, supplies his scholars with all sorts of capacities they have need of, in spite of nature. But what has love to do with you?

GERRARD. Love indeed has made a grave, gouty statesman fight duels, the soldier fly from his colours, a pedant a fine gentleman, nay, and the very lawyer a poet and therefore may make me a dancing-master.

HIPPOLITA. If he were your master.

GERRARD. I'm sure, dearest miss, there is nothing else which I cannot do for you already and therefore may hope to succeed in that.

Enter DON DIEGO.

DON DIEGO. Come, have you done?

HIPPOLITA. [*aside*] O! My father again!

DON DIEGO. Come, now let us see you dance.

HIPPOLITA. Indeed, I am not perfect yet. Pray excuse me till the next time my master comes. But when must he come again, father?

DON DIEGO. Let me see. Friend, you must needs come after dinner again and then at night again and so three times tomorrow too. If she be not married tomorrow (which I am to consider of) she will dance a corant in twice or thrice teaching more, will she not? For 'tis but a twelvemonth since she came from Hackney School.

GERRARD. We will lose no time, I warrant you, sir, if she be to be married tomorrow.

DON DIEGO. Truly I think she may be married tomorrow, therefore I would not have you lose any time, look you.

GERRARD. You need not caution me, I warrant you, sir. Sweet scholar, your humble servant, I will not fail you immediately after dinner.

DON DIEGO. No, no, pray do not and I will not fail to satisfy you very well, look you.

HIPPOLITA. He does not doubt his reward, father, for his pains. If you should not I would make that good to him.

DON DIEGO. Come, let us go in to your aunt. I must talk with you both together, child.

HIPPOLITA. I will follow you, sir.

Exeunt GERRARD, DON DIEGO.

PRUE. Here's the gentlewoman o'th'next house come to see you, mistress.

HIPPOLITA. (*aside*) She's come as if she came expressly to sing the new song she sung last night. I must hear it, for 'tis to my purpose now. –

[*Enter* SINGER.]

Madam, your servant. I dreamt last night of the song you sung last, the new song against delays in love; pray let's hear it again.

620 s.d. after line 619 Q1.

[SINGER.] (*sings*)

1.
Since we poor slavish women know
Our men cannot pick and choose,
To him we like why say we no,
And both our time and lover lose?

With feigned repulses and delays
A lover's appetite we pall
And if too long the gallant stays
His stomach's gone for good and all.

2.
Or our impatient am'rous guest,
Unknown to us, away may steal
And, rather than stay for a feast,
Take up with some coarse, ready meal.

When opportunity is kind,
Let prudent woman be so too
And if the man be to your mind,
Till needs you must, ne'er let him go.

3.
The match soon made is happy still,
For only love has there to do.
Let no one marry 'gainst her will
But stand off, when her parents woo,

And only to their suits be coy,
For she whom joynter can obtain
To let a fop her bed enjoy
Is but a lawful wench for gain.

PRUE. (*steps to the door*) Your father calls for you, miss.

HIPPOLITA. I come, I come. I must be obedient as long as I am with him. (*Pausing*)
Our parents who restrain our liberty,
But take the course to make us sooner free,
Though all we gain be but new slavery.
We leave our fathers and to husbands fly.

Exeunt.

---

629 *Song*: the music, by John Bannister, is most conveniently available in Weales's edition, p. 169; it was first published in John Playford, *Choice Songs and Airs* (1673).

650 *joynter*: the jointure was the estate settled on a wife at marriage for the remainder of her life.

ACT III

SCENE I

Don Diego's house.

Enter MONSIEUR, HIPPOLITA *and* PRUE.

MONSIEUR. Serviteur, serviteur, la cousin, your maid told me she watched at the stairfoot for my coming because you had a mind to speak wit me before I saw your fader, it seem.

HIPPOLITA. I would so indeed, cousin.

MONSIEUR. Or ça, or ça, I know your affair; it is to tell me wat recreation you 'ade with Monsieur Gerrard. But did he come? I was afrait he would not come.

HIPPOLITA. Yes, yes, he did come.

MONSIEUR. Ha, ha, ha. And were you not infiniment divertisé and please? Confess.

HIPPOLITA. I was indeed, cousin, I was very well pleased.

MONSIEUR. I do tinke so. I did tinke to come and be divertisé myself this morning with the sight of his reception but I did rancounter last night wit dam company dat keep me up so late I could not rise in de morning. Mal à peste de putains –

HIPPOLITA. Indeed we wanted you here mightily, cousin.

MONSIEUR. To 'elpe you to laugh, for if I 'adde been here I had made such recreation wid dat coxcomb Gerrard.

HIPPOLITA. Indeed, cousin. You need not have any subject or property to make one laugh; you are so pleasant yourself and when you are but alone you would make one burst.

MONSIEUR. Am I so happy, cousin, then in the bon quality of making people laugh?

HIPPOLITA. Mighty happy, cousin.

MONSIEUR. De grâce.

HIPPOLITA. Indeed!

---

17 *Mal à peste de putains*: a plague on whores.

MONSIEUR. Nay, sans vanitié, I observe wheresoe'er I come I make everybody merry, sans vanitié, da.

HIPPOLITA. I do believe you do.

MONSIEUR. Nay, as I marche in de street, I can make de dull apprenti laugh and sneer.

HIPPOLITA. (*aside*) This fool, I see, is as apt as an ill poet to mistake the contempt and scorn of people for applause and admiration.

MONSIEUR. Ah, cousin, you see wat it is to have been in France. Before I went into France I could get nobody to laugh at me, ma foy.

HIPPOLITA. No? Truly, cousin, I think you deserved it before. But you are improved indeed by going into France.

MONSIEUR. Ay, ay, the Franch education make us propre à tout. Beside, cousin, you must know to play the fool is the science in France and I didde go to the Italian Academy at Paris thrice a week to learn to play de fool of Signior Scaramouche, who is the most excellent personage in the world for dat noble science. Angel is a damn English fool to him.

HIPPOLITA. Methinks now Angel is a very good fool.

MONSIEUR. Nauh, nauh, Nokes is a better fool. But indeed the Englis' are not fit to be fools; here are ver few good fools. 'Tis true you have many a young cavalier who go over into France to learn to be the buffoon but, for all dat, dey return but mauvais buffoon, jarnie.

HIPPOLITA. I'm sure, cousin, you have lost no time there.

MONSIEUR. Auh, le brave Scaramouche!

HIPPOLITA. But is it a science in France, cousin? And is there an Academy for fooling? Sure, none go to it but the players.

---

50 *Signior Scaramouche*: Tiberio Fiorillo, the famous actor of Scaramuccia in commedia dell'arte was playing with the Comédie Italienne at the Hôtel de Bourgogne in Paris at this time. He and his troupe visited London for the first time in April 1673 and were a triumphant success.

52–4 It is almost certain that James Nokes played Monsieur and Edward Angel Don Diego in the first production, thereby adding point to the values Monsieur places on their relative merits as actors. See Additional Note.

MONSIEUR. Dey are comedians dat are de matres but all the beaux monde go to learn, as they do here of Angel and Nokes, for if you did go abroad into company you would find the best almost of de nation conning in all places the lessons which dey have learnt of the fools dere matres, Nokes and Angel.

HIPPOLITA. Indeed?

MONSIEUR. Yes, yes, dey are the gens de quality that practise dat science most and the most ambitieux, for fools and buffoons have been always most welcome to courts and desired in all companies. Auh, to be de fool, de buffoon, is to be de greate personage.

HIPPOLITA. Fools have fortune, they say, indeed.

MONSIEUR. So say old Seneque.

HIPPOLITA. Well, cousin, (not to make you proud) you are the greatest fool in England, I am sure.

MONSIEUR. Non, non, de grâce, non. Nokes de comedian is a pretty man, a pretty man for a comedian, da.

HIPPOLITA. You are modest, cousin. But lest my father should come in presently, which he will do as soon as he knows you are here, I must give you a caution, which 'tis fit you should have before you see him.

MONSIEUR. Well, vel, cousin, vat is dat?

HIPPOLITA. You must know then, as commonly the conclusion of all mirth is sad, after I had a good while pleased myself in jesting and leading the poor gentleman you sent into a fool's paradise and almost made him believe I would go away with him, my father, coming home this morning, came in upon us and caught him with me.

MONSIEUR. Mal à peste.

HIPPOLITA. And drew his sword upon him and would have killed him, for you know my father's Spanish fierceness and jealousy.

MONSIEUR. But how did he come off then? Tête non.

HIPPOLITA. In short, I was fain to bring him off by saying he was my dancing-master.

MONSIEUR. Hah, ha, ha, ver good jeste.

---

66 *matres*: maîtres, masters, but probably pronounced by Monsieur rather more like 'matress'.

78–9 'Fools have fortune' is proverbial but I cannot find Seneca's version of it, nor, I suspect, had Monsieur found it there.

HIPPOLITA. I was unwilling to have the poor man killed, you know, for our foolish frolic with him. But then upon my aunt's and father's inquiry how he came in and who sent him I was forced to say you did, desiring I should be able to dance a corant before our wedding.

MONSIEUR. A ver good jest, da, still bettre as bettre.

HIPPOLITA. Now all that I am to desire of you is to own you sent him, that I may not be caught in a lie.

MONSIEUR. Yes, yes, a ver good jest. Gerrard a mastre de danse, hah, ha, ha.

HIPPOLITA. Nay, the jest is like to be better yet, for my father has obliged him now to come and teach me so that now he must take the dancing-master upon him and come three or four times to me before our wedding lest my father, if he should come no more, should be suspicious I had told him a lie and, for ought I know, if he should know or but guess he were not a dancing-master, in his Spanish strictness and punctilios of honour, he might kill me as the shame and stain of his honour and family which he talks of so much. Now you know the jealous, cruel fathers in Spain serve their poor innocent daughters often so and he is more than a Spaniard.

MONSIEUR. Non, non, fear noting. I warrant you he shall come as often as you will to the house and your father shall never know who he is till we are married. But then I'll tell him all for the jest's sake.

HIPPOLITA. But will you keep my counsel, dear cousin, till we are married?

MONSIEUR. Poor, dear fool, I warrant thee, mon foy.

HIPPOLITA. Nay, what a fool am I indeed, for you would not have me killed. You love me too well, sure, to be an instrument of my death.

Enter DON DIEGO *walking gravely, a little* BLACK *behind him,* [*and*] MRS CAUTION.

But here comes my father – remember.

MONSIEUR. I would no more tell him of it than I would tell you if I had been with a wench, jarnie. (*Aside*) She's afraid to be killed, poor wretch, and he's a capricious, jealous fop enough to do't. But here he comes. – I'll keep thy counsel, I warrant thee, my dear soul, mon petit coeur.

HIPPOLITA. Peace, peace, my father's coming this way.

MONSIEUR. Ay, but by his march he won't be near enough to hear us this half hour, hah, ha, ha.

DON DIEGO *walks leisurely round the* MONSIEUR, *surveying him and shrugging his shoulders whilst* MONSIEUR *makes legs and faces.*

DON DIEGO. (*aside*) Is that thing my cousin, sister?

CAUTION. 'Tis he, sir.

DON DIEGO. Cousin, I'm sorry to see you.

MONSIEUR. Is that a Spanish complement?

DON DIEGO. So much disguised, cousin.

MONSIEUR. (*aside*) Oh, is it out at last, ventre? – Serviteur, serviteur, à monseur mon oncle and I am glad to see you here within doors, most Spanish oncle, ha, ha, ha. But I should be sorry to see you in the streets, tête non.

DON DIEGO. Why soh, would you be ashamed of me, hah? Voto a St Jago, would you? Hauh!

MONSIEUR. Ay, it may be you would be ashamed yourself, monseur mon oncle, of the great train you would get to wait upon your Spanish hose, puh. The boys would follow you and hoot at you, vert et bleu, pardone my Franch franchise, monsieur mon oncle.

HIPPOLITA. (*apart to* PRUE) We shall have sport anon betwixt these two contraries.

DON DIEGO. Dost thou call me monseur, voto a St Jago?

MONSIEUR. No, I did not call you Monseur Voto a St Jago, sir. I know you are my uncle, Mr James Formal, da.

DON DIEGO. But I can hardly know you are my cousin, Mr Nathaniel Paris. But call me Sir Don Diego henceforward, look you, and no Monsieur. Call me Monsieur, guarda!

---

147 s.d. *makes legs*: bows.

152 *aside*: after line 000 Q1.

154 *monseur*: I have preserved the original spelling, since it may well have been that Monsieur and Don Diego pronounce it *monsewer* at this point, though it is more likely to have been the compositor's or Wycherley's mistake.

162 *Spanish hose*: breeches which fitted closely down the thighs; Monsieur's pantaloons (line 180) had vast legs and were pleated to the waist, resembling skirts more than breeches.

164 *Franchise*: frankness.

MONSIEUR. I confess my error, sir, for none but a blind man would call you monsieur, ha, ha, ha. But pray do not call me neder Paris but de Paris, de Paris, si vous plaît, Monseur de Paris! Call me Monseur and welcome, da!

DON DIEGO. Monsieur de Pantalloons then, voto!

MONSIEUR. Monsieur de Pantalloons! A pretty name, a pretty name, ma foy, da. Bien trove, de Pantalloons. How much betre den your de la Fountaines, de la Rivières, de la Roches and all the de's in France, da. Well, but have you not the admiration for my pantaloon, Don Diego mon oncle?

DON DIEGO. I am astonished at them verdaderamente; they are wonderfully ridiculous.

MONSIEUR. Redicule, redicule! Ah, 'tis well you are my uncle, da. Redicule, ah! Is dere anyting in de universe so gentil as de pantaloons? Anyting so ravisaunt as de pantaloons? Auh, I could kneel down and varship a pair of gentil pantaloons. Vat, vat, you would have me have de admiration for dis outward skin of your thigh which you call Spanish hose. Fie, fie, fie, ha, ha, ha.

DON DIEGO. Dost thou deride my Spanish hose, young man, hauh?

MONSIEUR. In comparison of pantaloon I do undervalue 'em indeet, Don Diègue mon oncle, ha, ha, ha.

DON DIEGO. Thou art then a gabacho de malo gusto, look you.

MONSIEUR. You may call me vat you vil, oncle Don Diègue, but I must needs say your Spanish hose are scurvy hose, ugly hose, lousy hose and stinking hose.

DON DIEGO. (*puts his hand to his sword*) Do not provoke me, borracho.

MONSIEUR. Indeet for 'lousy' I recant dat epithet, for dere is scarce room in 'em for dat little animal, ha, ha, ha. But for stinking hose, dat epithet may stand, for how can dey choose but stink since dey are so furieusemente close to your Spanish tail, da.

---

187 *verdaderamente*: (Q1 verde deramentè) indeed.
201 *gabacho*: Q1 reads *gavanho* but Ward's emendation is sensible since *gabacho* means 'frenchified'.
201 *de malo gusto*: of bad taste.
207 *borracho*: wildly angry man.

HIPPOLITA. (*aside*) Ha, ha, ridiculous.

DON DIEGO. (*seems to draw*) Do not provoke me, I say, en hora mala.

MONSIEUR. Nay, oncle, I am sorry you are in de passion but I must live and die for de pantaloon against de Spanish hose, da.

DON DIEGO. You are a rash young man and while you wear pantaloons you are beneath my passion, voto. Auh, they make thee look and waddle, with all those gewgaw ribbons, like a great, old, fat, slovenly water-dog.

MONSIEUR. And your Spanish hose and your nose in the air make you look like a great, grizzled, long, Irish greyhound reaching a crust off from a high shelf, ha, ha, ha.

DON DIEGO. Bueno, bueno.

CAUTION. What, have you a mind to ruin yourself and break off the match?

MONSIEUR. Pshaw, wat do you tell me of de matche? D'ee tink I will not vindicate pantaloons, morbleu?

DON DIEGO. (*aside*) Well, he is a lost man, I see, and desperately far gone in the epidemic malady of our nation, the affectation of the worst of French vanities. But I must be wiser than him as I am a Spaniard, look you, Don Diego, and endeavour to reclaim him by art and fair means, look you, Don Diego. If not he shall never marry my daughter, look you, Don Diego, though he be my own sister's son and has two thousand five hundred seventy three pound sterling twelve shillings and twopence a year penny-rent, segouaramente. – Come, young man, since you are so obstinate, we will refer our difference to arbitration. Your mistress, my daughter, shall be umpire betwixt us concerning Spanish hose and pantaloons.

MONSIEUR. Pantaloons and Spanish hose, si vous plaît.

DON DIEGO. Your mistress is the fittest judge of your dress, sure.

MONSIEUR. I know ver vel dat most of the jeunesse of Englant will not change the ribband upon de crevat

---

242 *penny-rent*: income.

242–3 *segouaramente*: *seguramente*, definitely.

widout the consultation of dere matress but I am no Anglois, da, nor shall I make de reference of my dress to any in the universe, da. I judged by any in England, tête non! I would not be judged by an English looking-glass, jarnie.

DON DIEGO. Be not positivo, young man.

CAUTION. Nay, pray refer it, cousin, pray do.

MONSIEUR. Non, non, your servant, your servant, aunt.

DON DIEGO. But pray be not so positive. Come hither, daughter. Tell me which is best.

HIPPOLITA. Indeed, father, you have kept me in universal ignorance; I know nothing.

MONSIEUR. And do you tink I shall refer an affair of dat consequence to a poor young ting who have not see the varld, da? I am wiser than so, voto.

DON DIEGO. Well, in short, if you will not be wiser and leave off your French dress, stammering and tricks, look you, you shall be a fool and go without my daughter, voto.

MONSIEUR. How, must I leave off my gentil Franch accoutrements and speak base Englis' too or not marry my cousin, mon oncle Don Diego? Do not break off the match, do not, for know I will not leave off my pantaloon and Franch pronunciation for n'er a cousin in Englant, da.

DON DIEGO. I tell you again, he that marries my daughter shall at least look like a wise man, for he shall wear the Spanish habit. I am a Spanish positivo.

MONSIEUR. Ver vel, ver vel! And I am a Franch positivo.

DON DIEGO. Then I am definitivo and, if you do not go immediately into your chamber and put on a Spanish habit I have brought over on purpose for your wedding clothes and put off all these French fopperies and vanidades with all your grimaces, agreeables, adorables, ma foys and jernies, I swear you shall never marry my daughter and by an oath by Spaniard never broken – by my whiskers and snuffbox.

---

252 *matress*: *maîtresse*, mistress.

266 *voto*: intentionally or not, Monsieur borrows Don Diego's favourite word.

286 *vanidades*: vanities.

289 *by my whiskers and snuffbox*: see Additional Note.

MONSIEUR. O hold, do not swear, uncle, for I love your daughter furieusement.

DON DIEGO. If you love her you'll obey me.

MONSIEUR. Auh, wat vil become of me! But have the consideration. Must I leave off all the Franch beautés, graces and embellisements, bot' of my person and language?

Exeunt HIPPOLITA, MRS CAUTION *and* PRUE *laughing.*

DON DIEGO. I will have it so.

MONSIEUR. I am ruine den, undone. Have some consideration for me, for dere is not the least ribbon of my garniture but is as dear to me as your daughter, jernie!

DON DIEGO. Then you do not deserve her and for that reason I will be satisfied you love her better or you shall not have her, for I am positivo.

MONSIEUR. Vil you break mine 'arte? Pray, have de consideration for me.

DON DIEGO. I say again, you shall be dressed before night from top to toe in the Spanish habit or you shall never marry my daughter, look you.

MONSIEUR. If you will not have de consideration for me, have de consideration for your daughter, for she have de passionate amour for me and like me in dis habite betre den in yours, da.

DON DIEGO. What I have said I have said and I am uno positivo.

MONSIEUR. Will you not so mush as allow me one little Franch oat'?

DON DIEGO. No, you shall look like a Spaniard but speak and swear like an Englishman, look you.

MONSIEUR. Hélas, hélas, den I shall take my leave, mort, tête, ventre, jernie, tête bleu, ventre bleu, ma foy, certes.

DON DIEGO. (*calls at the door*) Pedro, Sanchez, wait upon this cavaliero into his chamber with those things I ordered you to take out of the trunks. – I would have you a little accustomed to your clothes before your wedding, for if you comply with me you shall marry my daughter tomorrow, look you.

MONSIEUR. Adieu then dear pantaloon, dear belte,

dear sword, dear peruke and dear chappeaux retrousé and dear shoe garni. Adieu, adieu, adieu, hélas, hélas, hélas. Will you have yet no pitié?

DON DIEGO. I am a Spanish positivo, look you.

MONSIEUR. And more cruel than de Spanish Inquisitiono, to compel a man to a habit against his conscience. Hélas, hélas, hélas. *Exit* MONSIEUR.

Enter PRUE *and* GERRARD.

PRUE. Here is the dancing-master. Shall I call my mistress, sir?

DON DIEGO. Yes.

Exit PRUE.

O, you are as punctual as a Spaniard. I love your punctual men. Nay, I think 'tis before your time something.

GERRARD. Nay, I am resolved your daughter, sir, shall lose no time by my fault.

DON DIEGO. So, so, 'tis well.

GERRARD. I were a very unworthy man if I should not be punctual with her, sir.

DON DIEGO. You speak honestly, very honestly, friend, and I believe a very honest man, though a dancing-master.

GERRARD. I am very glad you think me so, sir.

DON DIEGO. What, you are but a young man. Are you married yet?

GERRARD. No, sir, but I hope I shall, sir, very suddenly, if things hit right.

DON DIEGO. What, the old folks, her friends, are wary and cannot agree with you so soon as the daughter can?

GERRARD. Yes, sir, the father hinders it a little at present but the daughter, I hope, is resolved and then we shall do well enough.

DON DIEGO. What! You do not steal her, according to the laudable custom of some of your brother dancing-masters?

---

330 *chappeaux retrousé*: cocked hat.
331 *shoe garni*: shoe decorated with bows or ribbons.
339 s.d. follows line 338 Q1.

GERRARD. No, no, sir, steal her, sir, steal her! You are pleased to be merry, sir, ha, ha, ha. (*Aside*) I cannot but laugh at that question.

DON DIEGO. No, sir, methinks you are pleased to be merry but you say the father does not consent.

GERRARD. Not yet, sir. But 'twill be no matter whether he does or no.

DON DIEGO. Was she one of your scholars? If she were, 'tis a hundred to ten but you steal her.

GERRARD. (*aside, laughs*) I shall not be able to hold laughing.

DON DIEGO. Nay, nay, I find by your laughing you steal her. She was your scholar, was she not?

GERRARD. Yes, sir, she was the first I ever had and may be the last too, for she has a fortune, if I can get her, will keep me from teaching to dance any more.

DON DIEGO. So, so, then she is your scholar still it seems and she has a good portion. I am glad on't. Nay, I knew you stole her.

GERRARD. (*aside*) My laughing may give him suspicions, yet I cannot hold.

DON DIEGO. What, you laugh, I warrant, to think how the young baggage and you will mump the poor old father. But if all her dependence for a fortune be upon the father, he may chance to mump you both and spoil the jest.

GERRARD. I hope it will not be in his power, sir, ha, ha, ha. (*Aside*) I shall laugh too much anon. – Pray, sir, be pleased to call for your daughter. I am impatient till she comes, for time was never more precious with me and with her too. It ought to be so, sure, since you say she is to be married tomorrow.

DON DIEGO. She ought to bestir her, as you say, indeed. (*Calls at the door*) Wuh, daughter, daughter. Prue, Hippolita. Come away, child. Why do you stay so long?

Enter HIPPOLITA, PRUE *and* CAUTION.

HIPPOLITA. Your servant, master! Indeed, I am ashamed you have stayed for me.

GERRARD. O good madam, 'tis my duty. I know you came as soon as you could.

HIPPOLITA. I knew my father was with you, therefore I did not make altogether so much haste as I might.

But if you had been alone, nothing should have kept me from you; I would not have been so rude as to have made you stay a minute for me, I warrant you.

DON DIEGO. Come, fiddle-faddle, what a deal of ceremony there is betwixt your dancing-master and you, cuerno!

HIPPOLITA. Lord, sir, I hope you'll allow me to show my respect to my master, for I have a great respect for my master.

GERRARD. And I am very proud of my scholar and am a very great honourer of my scholar.

DON DIEGO. Come, come, friend, about your business and honour the king. (*To* MRS CAUTION) Your dancing-masters and barbers are such finical, smooth-tongued, tattling fellows and if you set 'em once a-talking they'll ne'er a done, no more than when you set 'em a-fiddling – indeed, all that deal with fiddles are given to impertinency.

CAUTION. Well, well! This is an impertinent fellow without being a dancing-master. He's no more a dancing-master than I am a maid.

DON DIEGO. What, will you still be wiser than I? Voto. – Come, come about with my daughter, man.

PRUE. So he would, I warrant you, if your worship would let him alone.

DON DIEGO. How now, Mrs Nimble-chaps?

GERRARD. (*aside to* HIPPOLITA) Well, though I have got a little canting at the dancing-school since I was here, yet I do all so bunglingly, he'll discover me.

HIPPOLITA. [*aside*] Try. – Come, take my hand, master.

CAUTION. Look you, brother, the impudent harlotry gives him her hand.

DON DIEGO. Can he dance with her without holding her by the hand?

HIPPOLITA. Here, take my hand, master.

GERRARD. (*aside to her*) I wish it were for good and all.

HIPPOLITA. You dancing-masters are always so hasty, so nimble.

DON DIEGO. Voto a St Jago, not that I can see. About, about with her, man.

---

419 *honour the king*: bow and curtsey before a dance.
442 *for*: for for Q1.

GERRARD. Indeed, sir, I cannot go about with her as I would do, unless you will please to go out a little, sir, for I see she is bashful still before you, sir.

DON DIEGO. Hey, hey, more fooling yet. Come, come, about with her.

HIPPOLITA. Nay, indeed, father, I am ashamed and cannot help it.

DON DIEGO. But you shall help it, for I will not stir. Move her, I say. Begin, hussy, move when he'll have you.

PRUE. (*aside*) I cannot but laugh at that, ha, ha, ha.

GERRARD. (*apart to* HIPPOLITA) Come then, madam, since it must be so, let us try. But I shall discover all. – One, two and coupée.

CAUTION. Nay, d'ee see how he squeezes her hand, brother? O the lewd villain!

DON DIEGO. Come, move, I say, and mind her not.

GERRARD. One, two, three, four and turn around.

CAUTION. D'ee see again? He took her by the bare arm.

DON DIEGO. Come, move on. She's mad.

GERRARD. One, two and a coupée.

DON DIEGO. Come. One, two. Turn out your toes.

CAUTION. There, there, he pinched her by the thigh. Will you suffer it?

GERRARD. One, two, three and fall back.

DON DIEGO. Fall back, fall back, back. Some of you are forward enough to fall back.

GERRARD. Back, madam.

DON DIEGO. Fall back when he bids you, hussy.

CAUTION. How, how! Fall back, fall back! Marry but she shall not fall back when he bids her.

DON DIEGO. I say she shall, huswife. Come.

GERRARD. She will, she will, I warrant you, sir, if you won't be angry with her.

CAUTION. Do you know what he means by that now, you a Spaniard?

DON DIEGO. How's that, I not a Spaniard? Say such a word again.

GERRARD. Come forward, madam, three steps again.

---

460 *coupée*: a step in which the dancer rests on one foot passing the other backward and forward, a bow made in advancing.

473 *to fall back*: to back Q1.

CAUTION. See, see, she squeezes his hand now. O the debauched harlotry!

DON DIEGO. So, so, mind her not. She moves forward pretty well but you must move as well backward as forward or you'll never do anything to purpose.

CAUTION. Do you know what you say, brother, yourself? Now are you at your beastliness before your young daughter?

PRUE. Ha, ha, ha.

DON DIEGO. How now, mistress, are you so merry? Is this your staid maid as you call her, sister impertinent?

GERRARD. (*aside to* HIPPOLITA) I have not much to say to you, miss, but I shall not have an opportunity to do it unless we can get your father out.

DON DIEGO. Come about again with her.

CAUTION. Look you, there she squeezes his hand hard again.

HIPPOLITA. Indeed and indeed, father, my aunt puts me quite out. I cannot dance while she looks on, for my heart. She makes me ashamed and afraid together.

GERRARD. Indeed if you would please to take her out, sir, I am sure I should make my scholar do better than when you are present, sir. Pray, sir, be pleased for this time to take her away. For the next time I hope I shall order it so we shall trouble neither of you.

CAUTION. No, no, brother, stir not. They have a mind to be left alone. Come, there's a beastly trick in't. He's no dancing-master, I tell you.

GERRARD. (*aside to* HIPPOLITA) Damned jade, she'll discover us.

DON DIEGO. What, will you teach me? Nay, then, I will go out and you shall go out too, look you.

CAUTION. I will not go out, look you.

DON DIEGO. Come, come, thou art a censorious, wicked woman and you shall disturb them no longer.

CAUTION. What, will you bawd for your daughter?

DON DIEGO. Ay, ay, come. Go out, out, out.

CAUTION. I will not go out, I will not go out. My conscience will not suffer me, for I know by experience what will follow.

GERRARD. I warrant you, sir, we'll make good use of our time when you are gone.

CAUTION. Do you hear him again? Don't you know what he means?

Exit DON DIEGO *thrusting* CAUTION *out.*

HIPPOLITA. 'Tis very well; you are a fine gentleman to abuse my poor father so.

GERRARD. 'Tis but by your example, miss.

HIPPOLITA. Well, I am his daughter and may make the bolder with him, I hope.

GERRARD. And I am his son-in-law that shall be and therefore may claim my privilege too of making bold with him, I hope.

HIPPOLITA. Methinks you should be contented in making bold with his daughter, for you have made very bold with her, sure.

GERRARD. I hope I shall make bolder with her yet.

HIPPOLITA. I do not doubt your confidence, for you are a dancing-master.

GERRARD. Why, miss, I hope you would not have me a fine, senseless, whining, modest lover, for modesty in a man is as ill as the want of it in a woman.

HIPPOLITA. I thank you for that, sir; now you have made bold with me indeed. But if I am such a confident piece I am sure you made me so. If you had not had the confidence to come in at the window, I had not had the confidence to look upon a man. I am sure I could not look upon a man before.

GERRARD. But that I humbly conceive, sweet miss, was your father's fault because you had not a man to look upon. But, dearest miss, I do not think you confident; you are only innocent, for that which would be called confidence, nay impudence, in a woman of years, is called innocency in one of your age and the more impudent you appear the more innocent you are thought.

HIPPOLITA. Say you so? Has youth such privileges? I do not wonder then most women seem impudent, since it is to be thought younger than they are, it seems. But indeed, master, you are as great an encourager of impudence, I see, as if you were a dancing-master in good earnest.

GERRARD. Yes, yes, a young thing may do anything, may leap out of her window and go away with her dancing-master, if she please.

HIPPOLITA. So, so, the use follows the doctrine very suddenly.

GERRARD. Well, dearest, pray let us make the use we should of it, lest your father should make too bold with us and come in before we would have him.

HIPPOLITA. Indeed old relations are apt to take that ill-bred freedom of pressing into young company at unseasonable hours.

GERRARD. Come, dear miss, let me tell you how I have designed matters, for in talking of anything else we lose time and opportunity. People abroad indeed say the English women are the worst in the world in using an opportunity – they love tittle-tattle and ceremony.

HIPPOLITA. 'Tis because, I warrant, opportunities are not so scarce here as abroad; they have more here than they can use. But let people abroad say what they will of English women, because they do not know 'em – but what say people at home?

GERRARD. Pretty innocent, ha, ha, ha. Well, I say you will not make use of your opportunity.

HIPPOLITA. I say you have no reason to say so yet.

GERRARD. Well then, anon at nine of the clock at night I'll try you, for I have already bespoke a parson and have taken up the three back rooms of the tavern which front upon the gallery window, that nobody may see us escape, and I have appointed, precisely between eight and nine of the clock, when it is dark, a coach and six to wait at the tavern-door for us.

HIPPOLITA. A coach and six, a coach and six, do you say? Nay then, I see you are resolved to carry me away, for a coach and six, though there were not a man but the coachman with it, would carry away any young girl of my age in England. A coach and six!

GERRARD. Then you will be sure to be ready to go with me?

HIPPOLITA. What young woman of the town could ever say no to a coach and six, unless it were going into the country? A coach and six! 'Tis not in the power of fourteen-year-old to resist it.

GERRARD. You will be sure to be ready?

HIPPOLITA. You are sure 'tis a coach and six?

GERRARD. I warrant you, miss.

HIPPOLITA. I warrant you then they'll carry us merrily away. A coach and six?

GERRARD. But have you charmed your cousin, the Monsieur, as you said you would, that he in the meantime say nothing to prevent us?

HIPPOLITA. I warrant you.

Enter to 'em DON DIEGO *and* MRS CAUTION *pressing in.*

CAUTION. I will come in.

DON DIEGO. Well, I hope by this time you have given her full instructions, you have told her what and how to do, you have done all.

GERRARD. We have just done indeed, sir.

HIPPOLITA. Ay, sir, we have just done, sir.

CAUTION. And I fear just undone, sir.

GERRARD. (*aside to* HIPPOLITA) D'ee hear that damned witch?

DON DIEGO. Come, leave your censorious prating. Thou hast been a false right woman thyself in thy youth, I warrant you.

CAUTION. I right! I right! I scorn your words, I'd have you to know, and 'tis well known. I right! No, 'tis your dainty minx, that gillflirt, your daughter here, that is right. Do you see how her handkerchief is ruffled and what a heat she's in?

DON DIEGO. She has been dancing.

CAUTION. Ay, ay, Adam and Eve's dance or the beginning of the world. D'ee see how she pants?

DON DIEGO. She has not been used to motion.

CAUTION. Motion, motion! Motion, d'ee call it? No, indeed, I kept her from motion till now. Motion with a vengeance!

DON DIEGO. You put the poor bashful girl to the blush, you see. Hold your peace.

CAUTION. 'Tis her guilt, not her modesty, marry.

DON DIEGO. Come, come, mind her not, child. Come, master, let me see her dance now the whole dance roundly together. Come, sing to her.

GERRARD. (*aside to* HIPPOLITA) Faith, we shall be discovered after all. You know I cannot sing a note, miss.

---

629 *right*: promiscuous.
634 *gillflirt*: giddy wanton.

DON DIEGO. Come, come, man.

HIPPOLITA. Indeed, father, my master's in haste now. Pray let it alone till anon at night when you say he is to come again and then you shall see me dance it to the violin. Pray stay till then, father.

DON DIEGO. I will not be put off so. Come, begin.

HIPPOLITA. Pray, father.

DON DIEGO. Come, sing to her; come, begin.

GERRARD. Pray, sir, excuse me till anon. I am in some haste.

DON DIEGO. I say begin. I will not excuse you. Come, take her by the hand and about with her.

CAUTION. I say he shall not take her by the hand. He shall touch her no more. While I am here there shall be no more squeezing and tickling her palm, good Mr Dancing-master. Stand off. (*Thrusts* GERRARD *away*)

DON DIEGO. Get you out, Mrs Impertinence. Take her by the hand, I say.

CAUTION. Stand off, I say. He shall not touch her. He has touched her too much already.

DON DIEGO. If patience were not a Spanish virtue, I would lay it aside now. I say let 'em dance.

CAUTION. I say they shall not dance.

HIPPOLITA. Pray, father, since you see my aunt's obstinacy, let us alone till anon when you may keep her out.

DON DIEGO. Well then, friend, do not fail to come.

HIPPOLITA. Nay, if he fail me at last –

DON DIEGO. Be sure you come, for she's to be married tomorrow – do you know it?

GERRARD. Yes, yes, sir. Sweet scholar, your humble servant till night and think in the meantime of the instructions I have given you, that you may be the readier when I come.

DON DIEGO. Ay, girl, be sure you do and do you be sure to come.

CAUTION. You need not be so concerned; he'll be sure to come, I warrant you. But if I could help it he should never set foot again in the house.

DON DIEGO. You would frighten the poor dancing-master from the house. But be sure you come for all her.

GERRARD. Yes, sir. (*Aside*) But this jade will pay me when I am gone.

CAUTION. Hold, hold, sir, I must let you out and I wish I could keep you out. He a dancing-master? He's a chouse, a cheat, a mere cheat and that you'll find.

DON DIEGO. I find any man a cheat! I cheated by any man! I scorn your words. I that have so much Spanish care, circumspection and prudence cheated by a man! Do you think I who have been in Spain, look you, and have kept up my daughter a twelvemonth, for fear of being cheated of her, look you? I cheated of her!

CAUTION. Well, say no more.

Exeunt DON DIEGO, HIPPOLITA, CAUTION *and* PRUE.

GERRARD. Well, old formality, if you had not kept up your daughter, I am sure I had never cheated you of her.

The wary fool is by his care betrayed,
As cuckolds by their jealousy are made. *Exit.*

ACT IV

SCENE I

Enter MONSIEUR DE PARIS *without a peruke, with a Spanish hat, a Spanish doublet, stockings and shoes but in pantaloons, a waist-belt and a Spanish dagger in't and a cravat about his neck. Enter* HIPPOLITA *and* PRUE *behind, laughing.*

MONSIEUR. To see wat a fool love do make of one, jernie! It do metamorphose de brave man into de beast, de sotte, de animal.

HIPPOLITA. Ha, ha, ha.

MONSIEUR. Nay, you may laugh. 'Tis ver vel; I am become as redicule for you as can be, mort bleu. I have deform myself into an ugly Spaniard.

710 s.d. *Exit*: *Exeunt* Q1.
s.d. *Spanish hat*: probably the flat-crowned hat, see Additional Note to III i 289.

HIPPOLITA. Why, do you call this disguising yourself like a Spaniard while you wear pantaloons still and the cravat?

MONSIEUR. But is here not the double doublet and the Spanish dagger aussi?

HIPPOLITA. But 'tis as long as the French sword and worn like it. But where's your Spanish beard, the thing of most consequence?

MONSIEUR. Jernie, do you tink beards are as easy to be had as in de playhouses? Non. But if here be no the ugly, long Spanish beard, here are, I am certain, the ugly, long Spanish ear.

HIPPOLITA. That's very true, ha, ha, ha.

MONSIEUR. Auh de ingrate dat de woman is! When we poor men are your gallants you laugh at us yourselves and wen we are your husband you make all the warld laugh at us, jernie. Love, damn love, it make the man more redicule than poverty, poetry or a new title of honneur, jernie.

Enter DON DIEGO *and* CAUTION.

DON DIEGO. What, at your 'jernies' still? Voto.

MONSIEUR. Why, oncle, you are at your 'votos' still.

DON DIEGO. Nay, I'll allow you to be at your votos too but not to make the incongruous match of Spanish doublet and French pantaloons.

MONSIEUR. (*holding his hat before his pantaloons*) Nay, pray, dear oncle, let me unite France and Spain – 'tis the mode of France now, jarnie, voto.

DON DIEGO. Well, I see I must pronounce. I told you if you were not dressed in the Spanish habit tonight you should not marry my daughter tomorrow, look you.

MONSIEUR. Well, am I not habillé in de Spanish habit? My doublet, ear and hat, leg and feet are Spanish, that dey are.

DON DIEGO. I told you I was a Spanish positivo, voto.

---

19 *Spanish ear*: wearing earrings was no longer popular in England and certainly not fashionable in France.

32 s.d. follows line 31 Q1.

32–3 *let me unite . . . now*: war between France and Spain had ended with the Treaty of Aix-la-Chapelle in 1668.

MONSIEUR. Vil you not spare my pantaloon, begar? I will give you one little finger to excuse my pantaloon, da.

DON DIEGO. I have said, look you.

MONSIEUR. Auh, chères pantaloons! Speak for my pantaloons. My poor pantaloons are as dear to me as de scarf to de country capitaine or de new-made officer. Therefore, have de compassion for my pantaloons, Don Diego, mon oncle. Hélas, hélas, hélas. (*Kneels to* DON DIEGO)

DON DIEGO. I have said, look you, your dress must be Spanish and your language English. I am uno positivo.

MONSIEUR. And must speak base good English too? Ah la pitié, hélas!

DON DIEGO. It must be done and I will see this great change ere it be dark, voto. Your time is not long. Look to't, look you.

MONSIEUR. Hélas, hélas, hélas, dat Espagne should conquer la France in England! Hélas, hélas, hélas.

Exit MONSIEUR.

DON DIEGO. You see what pains I take to make him the more agreeable to you, daughter.

HIPPOLITA. But indeed and indeed, father, you wash the blackamoor white in endeavouring to make a Spaniard of a monsieur, nay an English monsieur too – consider that, father. For when once they have taken the French pli, as they call it, they are never to be made so much as Englishmen again, I have heard say.

DON DIEGO. What, I warrant you are like the rest of the young silly baggages of England that like nothing but what is French. You would not have him reformed, you would have a monsieur to your husband, would you? Cuerno.

HIPPOLITA. No, indeed, father, I would not have a monsieur to my husband, not I indeed, and I am sure you'll never make my cousin otherwise.

DON DIEGO. I warrant you.

HIPPOLITA. You can't, you can't, indeed, father, and

---

48 *scarf*: sash worn diagonally to indicate rank.
66 *pli*: from *prendre le pli*, forming unalterable habits, conforming.

you have sworn, you know, he shall never have me if he does not leave off his monsieurship. Now as I told you, 'tis as hard for him to cease being a monsieur as 'tis for you to break a Spanish oath, so that I am not in any great danger of having a monsieur to my husband.

DON DIEGO. Well, but you shall have him for your husband, look you.

HIPPOLITA. Then you will break your Spanish oath.

DON DIEGO. No, I will break him of his French tricks and you shall have him for your husband, cuerno.

HIPPOLITA. Indeed and indeed, father, I shall not have him.

DON DIEGO. Indeed you shall, daughter.

HIPPOLITA. Well, you shall see, father.

CAUTION. No, I warrant you, she will not have him. She'll have her dancing-master rather. I know her meaning, I understand her.

DON DIEGO. Thou malicious, foolish woman, you understand her! But I do understand her. She says I will not break my oath nor he his French customs, so through our difference she thinks she shall not have him. But she shall.

HIPPOLITA. But I shan't.

CAUTION. I know she will not have him, because she hates him.

DON DIEGO. I tell you, if she does hate him, 'tis a sign she will have him for her husband, for 'tis not one of a thousand marries the man she loves, look you. Besides, 'tis all one whether she loves him now or not, for, as soon as she's married, she'd be sure to hate him. That's the reason we wise Spaniards are jealous and only expect, nay, will be sure our wives shall fear us, look you.

HIPPOLITA. Pray, good father and aunt, do not dispute about nothing, for I am sure he will never be my husband to hate.

CAUTION. I am of your opinion indeed. I understand you. I can see as far as another.

DON DIEGO. You, you cannot see so much as through your spectacles! But I understand her. 'Tis her mere desire to marriage makes her say she shall not have him, for your poor young things, when they are once in the teens, think they shall never be married.

HIPPOLITA. Well, father, think what you will but I know what I think.

Enter MONSIEUR *in the Spanish habit entire only with a cravat and followed by the little* BLACKAMOOR *with a golilla in his hand.*

DON DIEGO. Come, did I not tell you you should have him. Look you there; he has complied with me and is a perfect Spaniard.

MONSIEUR. Ay, ay, I am ugly rogue enough now, sure, for my cousin. But 'tis your father's fault, cousin, that you han't the handsomest, best-dressed man in the nation, a man bien mise.

DON DIEGO. Yet again at your French? And a cravat on still, voto a St Jago! Off, off with it.

MONSIEUR. Nay, I will ever hereafter speak clownish good English. Do but spare me my cravat.

DON DIEGO. I am uno positivo, look you.

MONSIEUR. Let me not put on that Spanish yoke but spare me my cravat, for I love cravat furieusement.

DON DIEGO. Again at your 'furieusements'!

MONSIEUR. Indeed I have forgot myself but have some mercy. (*Kneels*)

DON DIEGO. Off, off, off with it, I say. Come, refuse the ornamento principal of the Spanish habit!

Takes him by the cravat, pulls it off and the BLACK *puts on the golilla.*

MONSIEUR. Will you have no mercy, no pity? Alas, alas, alas. Oh, I had rather put on the English pillory than this Spanish golilla, [*takes it off*] for 'twill be all a case, I'm sure, for, when I go abroad, I shall soon have a crowd of boys about me, peppering me with rotten eggs and turnips, hélas, hélas.

DON DIEGO *puts on the golilla.*

DON DIEGO. 'Hélas' again?

MONSIEUR. Alas, alas, alas.

HIPPOLITA. I shall die. } Ha, ha, ha.
PRUE. I shall burst. }

MONSIEUR. Ay, ay, you see what I am come to for your

---

124 s.d. *golilla*: a stiff and restricting collar standing up at the back of the head and shaped with wire, vastly different from Monsieur's loose cravat.

sake, cousin, and, uncle, pray take notice how ridiculous I am grown to my cousin that loves me above all the world. She can no more forbear laughing at me, I vow and swear, than if I were as arrant a Spaniard as yourself.

DON DIEGO. Be a Spaniard like me and ne'er think people laugh at you. There was never a Spaniard that thought anyone laughed at him. But, what, do you laugh at a golilla, baggage? Come, sirrah black, now do you teach him to walk with the verdadero gesto, gracia and gravidad of a true Castilian.

MONSIEUR. Must I have my dancing-master too? Come, little master, then, lead on.

BLACK *struts about the stage. The* MONSIEUR *follows him, imitating awkwardly all he does.*

DON DIEGO. Malo, malo! With your hat on your pole, as if it hung upon a pin! The French and English wear their hats as if their horns would not suffer 'em to come over their foreheads, voto.

MONSIEUR. 'Tis true. There are some well-bred gentlemen have so much reverence for their peruke that they would refuse to be grandees of your Spain, for fear of putting on their hats, I vow and swear.

DON DIEGO. Come, black, teach him now to make a Spanish leg.

MONSIEUR. Ha, ha, ha, your Spanish leg is an English curtsey, I vow and swear, hah, hah, ha.

DON DIEGO. Well, the hood does not make the monk; the ass was an ass still, though he had the lion's skin on. This will be a light French fool in spite of the grave Spanish habit, look you. But, black, do what you can, make the most of him, walk him about.

PRUE *goes to the door and returns.*

PRUE. Here are the people, sir, you sent to speak with about provisions for the wedding and here are your clothes brought home too, mistress.

164–5 *verdadero gesto, gracia and gravidad*: true countenance, grace and seriousness.
168 *pole*: head.
169 *pin*: peg.
170 *horns*: (*a*) the swept-up horns of the wig (*b*) cuckold's horns.

DON DIEGO. Well, I come. Black, do what you can with him; walk him about.

MONSIEUR. Indeed, uncle, if I were as you, I would not have the grave Spanish habit so travestied. I shall disgrace it and my little black master too, I vow and swear.

DON DIEGO. Learn, learn of him, improve yourself by him. And do you walk him, walk him about soundly. Come, sister and daughter, I must have your judgements, though I shall not need 'em, look you. Walk him, see you walk him.

Exeunt DON DIEGO, HIPPOLITA *and* CAUTION.

MONSIEUR. Jernie, he does not only make a Spaniard of me but a Spanish gennet, in giving me to his lackey to walk. But come along, little master.

The BLACK *instructs the* MONSIEUR *on one side of the stage,* PRUE *standing on the other.*

PRUE. (*aside*) O the unfortunate condition of us poor chambermaids, who have all the carking and caring, the watching and sitting up, the trouble and danger of our mistresses' intrigues, whilst they go away with all the pleasure! And if they can get their man in a corner, 'tis well enough; they ne'er think of the poor watchful chambermaid who sits knocking her heels in the cold, for want of better exercise, in some melancholy lobby or entry, when she could employ her time every whit as well as her mistress, for all her quality, if she were but put to't.

BLACK. Hold up your head, hold up your head, sir. A stooping Spaniard, malo!

MONSIEUR. True, a true Spaniard scorns to look upon the ground.

PRUE. (*aside*) We can shift for our mistresses and not for ourselves. Mine has got a handsome proper young man and is just going to make the most of him, whilst I must be left in the lurch here with a couple of ugly little blackamoor boys in bonnets and an old withered Spanish eunuch – not a servant else in the house, nor have I hopes of any comfortable society at all.

BLACK. Now let me see you make your visit-leg thus.

---

203 *carking*: anxious toil.
221 *bonnets*: servants' caps.

MONSIEUR. Auh, tête non, ha, ha, ha.

BLACK. What, a Spaniard and laugh aloud! No, if you laugh, thus only – [*laughs*] so. Now your salutation in the street as you pass by your acquaintance, look you, thus. If to a woman, thus, putting your hat upon your heart. If to a man, thus, with a nod, so – but frown a little more, frown. But if to a woman you would be very ceremonious to, thus – so – your neck nearer your shoulder, so. Now if you would speak contemptibly of any man or thing, do thus with your head – so – and shrug up your shoulders, till they hide your ears.

MONSIEUR *imitating the* BLACK.

Now walk again.

The BLACK *and the* MONSIEUR *walk off the stage.*

PRUE. All my hopes are in that coxcomb there. I must take up with my mistress's leavings, though we chambermaids are wont to be beforehand with them. But he is the dullest, modestest fool – for a Frenchified fool – as ever I saw, for nobody could be more coming to him than I have been (though I say it) and yet I am ne'er the nearer. I have stolen away his handkerchief and told him of it and yet he would never so much as struggle with me to get it again. I have pulled off his peruke, untied his ribbons and have been very bold with him, yet he would never be so with me. Nay, I have pinched him, punched him and tickled him and yet he would never do the like for me.

The BLACK *and* MONSIEUR *return.*

BLACK. Nay, thus, thus, sir.

PRUE. [*aside*] And to make my person more acceptable to him I have used art, as they say, for, every night since he came, I have worn the forehead-piece of beeswax and bog's grease and every morning washed with buttermilk and wild tansy and have put on every day, for his only sake, my Sunday Bow-dye stockings and

---

246 *get it*: get Q1.

255 *forehead-piece*: piece of cloth worn on the face overnight to improve the complexion; Prue's choice of cosmetic substances is by no means the most bizarre.

258 *Bow-dye*: scarlet, from the dye made at Bow.

have new chalked my shoes and's constantly as the morning came. Nay, I have taken an occasion to garter my stockings before him, as if unawares of him, for a good leg and foot with good shoes and stockings are very provoking, as they say. But the devil would he be provoked! But I must think of a way.

BLACK. Thus, thus.

MONSIEUR. What, so? Well, well, I have lessons enow for this time. Little master, I will have no more lest the multiplicity of 'em make me forget 'em, da. Prue, art thou there and so pensive? What art thou thinking of?

PRUE. Indeed I am ashamed to tell your worship.

MONSIEUR. What, ashamed! Wert thou thinking then of my beastliness? Ha, ha, ha.

PRUE. Nay, then, I am forced to tell your worship in my own vindication.

MONSIEUR. Come then.

PRUE. But indeed your worship – I'm ashamed, that I am, though it was nothing but of a dream I had of your sweet worship last night.

MONSIEUR. Of my sweet worship! I warrant it was a sweet dream then. What was it? Ha, ha, ha.

PRUE. Nay, indeed, I have told your worship enough already – you may guess the rest.

MONSIEUR. I cannot guess, ha, ha, ha. What should it be? Prithee, let's know the rest.

PRUE. Would you have me so impudent?

MONSIEUR. Impudent! Ha, ha, ha, nay, prithee tell me, for I can't guess, da.

PRUE. Nay, 'tis always so; for want of the men's guessing the poor women are forced to be impudent. But I am still ashamed.

MONSIEUR. I will know it. Speak.

PRUE. Why, then, methoughts last night you came up into my chamber in your shirt, when I was in bed, and that you might easily do, for I have ne'er a lock to my door. Now I warrant I am as red as my petticoat.

MONSIEUR. No, thou'rt as yellow as e'er thou wert.

PRUE. Yellow, sir!

MONSIEUR. Ay, ay. But let's hear the dream out.

PRUE. Why, can't you guess the rest now?

MONSIEUR. No, not I, I vow and swear. Come, let's hear.

PRUE. But can't you guess in earnest?

MONSIEUR. Not I, the devil eat me.

PRUE. Not guess yet! Why then, methoughts you came to bed to me! Now am I as red as my petticoat again.

MONSIEUR. Ha, ha, ha. Well and what then? Ha, ha, ha.

PRUE. Nay, now I know by your worship's laughing you guess what you did. I'm sure I cried out and waked all in tears with these words in my mouth, 'You have undone me, you have undone me, your worship has undone me!'.

MONSIEUR. Hah, ha, ha. But you waked and found it was but a dream.

PRUE. Indeed it was so lively I know not whether 'twas a dream or no. But if you were not there I'll undertake you may come when you will and do anything to me you will – I sleep so fast.

MONSIEUR. No, no, I don't believe that.

PRUE. Indeed you may, your worship.

MONSIEUR. It cannot be.

PRUE. (*aside*) Insensible beast! He will not understand me yet and one would think I speak plain enough.

MONSIEUR. Well, but Prue, what art thou thinking of?

PRUE. Of the dream, whether it were a dream or no.

MONSIEUR. 'Twas a dream, I warrant thee.

PRUE. Was it? I am hugeous glad it was a dream.

MONSIEUR. Ay, ay, it was a dream and I am hugeous glad it was a dream too.

PRUE. But now I have told your worship my door hath neither lock nor latch to it, if you should be so naughty as to come one night and prove the dream true – I am so afraid on't.

MONSIEUR. Ne'er fear it. Dreams go by the contraries.

PRUE. Then by that I should come into your worship's chamber and come to bed to your worship. Now am I as red as my petticoat again, I warrant.

MONSIEUR. No, thou art no redder than a brick unburnt, Prue.

PRUE. But if I should do such a trick in my sleep, your worship would not censure a poor harmless maid, I hope, for I am apt to walk in my sleep.

MONSIEUR. Well then, Prue, because thou shalt not shame thyself, poor wretch, I'll be sure to lock my door every night fast.

PRUE. [*aside*] So, so, this way I find will not do. I must come roundly and downright to the business, like other women, or –

Enter GERRARD.

MONSIEUR. O, the dancing-master!

PRUE. Dear sir, I have something to say to you in your ear which I am ashamed to speak aloud.

MONSIEUR. Another time, another time, Prue, but now go call your mistress to her dancing-master. Go, go.

PRUE. Nay, pray hear me, sir, first.

MONSIEUR. Another time, another time, Prue. Prithee be gone.

PRUE. Nay, I beseech your worship hear me.

MONSIEUR. No, prithee be gone.

PRUE. [*aside*] Nay, I am e'en well enough served for not speaking my mind when I had an opportunity. Well, I must be playing the modest woman, forsooth. A woman's hypocrisy in this case does only deceive herself. *Exit* PRUE.

MONSIEUR. O, the brave dancing-master, the fine dancing-master, your servant, your servant.

GERRARD. Your servant, sir, I protest I did not know you at first. (*Aside*) I am afraid this fool should spoil all, notwithstanding Hippolita's care and management. Yet I ought to trust her. But a secret is more safe with a treacherous knave than a talkative fool.

MONSIEUR. Come, sir, you must know a little brother dancing-master of yours – walking-master I should have said, for he teaches me to walk and make legs by the by. Pray know him, sir. Salute him, sir. You Christian dancing-masters are so proud.

GERRARD. But, Monsieur, what strange metamorphosis is this? You look like a Spaniard and talk like an Englishman again, which I thought had been impossible.

MONSIEUR. Nothing impossible to love. I must do't or lose my mistress, your pretty scholar, for 'tis I am to have her. You may remember I told you she was to be married to a great man, a man of honour and quality.

GERRARD. But does she enjoin you to this severe penance? Such I am sure it is to you.

MONSIEUR. (*draws him aside*) No, no, 'tis by the compulsion of the starched fop her father, who is so arrant a Spaniard he would kill you and his daughter if he knew who you were, therefore have a special care to dissemble well.

GERRARD. I warrant you.

MONSIEUR. Dear Gerrard. – Go, little master, and call my cousin. Tell her her dancing-master is here.

Exit BLACK.

I say, dear Gerrard, faith, I'm obliged to you for the trouble you have had. When I sent you I intended a jest indeed but did not think it would have been so dangerous a jest. Therefore pray forgive me.

GERRARD. I do, do heartily forgive you.

MONSIEUR. But can you forgive me for sending you, at first, like a fool as I was? 'Twas ill done of me. Can you forgive me?

GERRARD. Yes, yes, I do forgive you.

MONSIEUR. Well, thou art a generous man, I vow and swear, to come and take upon you this trouble, danger and shame, to be thought a paltry dancing-master and all this to preserve a lady's honour and life, who intended to abuse you. But I take the obligation upon me.

GERRARD. Pish, pish, you are not obliged to me at all.

MONSIEUR. Faith but I am strangely obliged to you.

GERRARD. Faith but you are not.

MONSIEUR. I vow and swear but I am.

GERRARD. I swear you are not.

MONSIEUR. Nay, thou art so generous a dancing-master, ha, ha, ha.

Enter DON DIEGO, HIPPOLITA, CAUTION *and* PRUE.

DON DIEGO. You shall not come in, sister.

CAUTION. I will come in.

DON DIEGO. You will not be civil.

CAUTION. I'm sure they will not be civil if I do not come in. I must, I will.

DON DIEGO. Well, honest friend, you are very punctual, which is a rare virtue in a dancing-master. I take notice of it and will remember it. I will, look you.

MONSIEUR. (*aside*) So, silly, damned, politic Spanish uncle, ha, ha, ha.

GERRARD. My fine scholar, sir, there, shall never have reason, as I told you, sir, to say I am not a punctual man, for I am more her servant than to any scholar I ever had.

MONSIEUR. (*aside*) Well said, i'faith, thou dost make a pretty fool of him, I vow and swear. But I wonder people can be made such fools of, ha, ha, ha.

HIPPOLITA. Well, master, I thank you and I hope I shall be a grateful kind scholar to you.

MONSIEUR. (*aside*) Ha, ha, ha, cunning little jilt, what a fool she makes of him too. I wonder people can be made such fools of, I vow and swear, ha, ha, ha.

HIPPOLITA. Indeed it shall go hard but I'll be a grateful kind scholar to you.

CAUTION. As kind as ever your mother was to your father, I warrant.

DON DIEGO. How! Again with your senseless suspicions!

MONSIEUR. Pish, pish, aunt. (*Aside*) Ha, ha, ha, she's a fool another way. She thinks she loves him, ha, ha, ha. Lord, that people should be such fools!

CAUTION. Come, come, I cannot but speak. I tell you beware in time, for he is no dancing-master but some debauched person who will mump you of your daughter.

DON DIEGO. Will you be wiser than I still? Mump me of my daughter! I would I could see anyone mump me of my daughter.

CAUTION. And mump you of your mistress too, young Spaniard.

MONSIEUR. (*to* CAUTION) Ha, ha, ha, will you be wiser than I too, voto? Mump me of my mistress! I would I could see anyone mump me of my mistress. (*Aside to* GERRARD and HIPPOLITA) I am afraid this damned old aunt should discover us, I vow and swear. Be careful and resolute.

CAUTION. He, he does not go about his business like a dancing-master. He'll ne'er teach her to dance but he'll teach her no goodness soon enough, I warrant. He a dancing-master!

MONSIEUR. Ay, the devil eat me if he be not the best dancing-master in England now. (*Aside to* GERRARD *and* HIPPOLITA) Was not that well said, cousin? Was

---

446 *mump*: cheat.

it not? For he's a gentleman dancing-master, you know.

DON DIEGO. You know him, cousin, very well, cousin? You sent him to my daughter?

MONSIEUR. Yes, yes, uncle, know him. (*Aside*) We'll ne'er be discovered, I warrant, ha, ha, ha.

CAUTION. But will you be made a fool of too?

MONSIEUR. Ay, ay, aunt, ne'er trouble yourself.

DON DIEGO. Come, friend, about your business, about with my daughter.

HIPPOLITA. Nay, pray, father, be pleased to go out a little and let us but practise a while and then you shall see me dance the whole dance to the violin.

DON DIEGO. Tittle-tattle, more fooling still! Did not you say when your master was here last I should see you dance to the violin when he came again?

HIPPOLITA. So I did, father, but let me practise a little first before that I may be perfect. Besides, my aunt is here and she will put me out. You know I cannot dance before her.

DON DEIGO. Fiddle-faddle.

MONSIEUR. (*aside*) They're afraid to be discovered by Gerrard's bungling, I see. – Come, come, uncle, turn out. Let 'em practise.

DON DIEGO. I won't, voto a St Jago. What a fooling's here?

MONSIEUR. Come, come, let 'em practise. Turn out, turn out, uncle.

DON DIEGO. Why, can't she practise it before me?

MONSIEUR. Come, dancers and singers are sometimes humoursome. Besides, 'twill be more grateful to you to see it danced all at once to the violin. Come, turn out, turn out, I say.

DON DIEGO. What a fooling's here still amongst you, voto!

MONSIEUR. So there he is with you, voto. Turn out, turn out. I vow and swear you shall turn out. (*Takes him by the shoulder*)

DON DIEGO. Well, shall I see her dance it to the violin at last?

GERRARD. Yes, yes, sir. What do you think I teach her for?

Exit DON DIEGO.

MONSIEUR. Go, go, turn out, and you too, aunt.

CAUTION. Seriously, nephew, I shall not budge. Royally I shall not.

MONSIEUR. Royally you must, aunt. Come.

CAUTION. Pray hear me, nephew.

MONSIEUR. I will not hear you.

CAUTION. 'Tis for your sake I stay. I must not suffer you to be wronged.

MONSIEUR. Come, no wheedling, aunt. Come away.

CAUTION. That slippery fellow will do't.

MONSIEUR. Let him do't.

CAUTION. Indeed he will do't; royally he will.

MONSIEUR. Well let him do't, royally.

CAUTION. He will wrong you.

MONSIEUR. Well, let him, I say. I have a mind to be wronged. What's that to you? I will be wronged, if you go thereto, I vow and swear.

CAUTION. You shall not be wronged.

MONSIEUR. I will.

CAUTION. You shall not.

DON DIEGO *returns.*

DON DIEGO. What's the matter? Won't she be ruled? Come, come away. You shall not disturb 'em.

DON DIEGO *and* MONSIEUR *thrust* CAUTION *out.*

CAUTION. D'ee see how they laugh at you both? Well, go to, the troth-telling Trojan gentlewoman of old was ne'er believed till the town was taken, rummaged and ransacked, even, even so.

MONSIEUR. Hah, hah, ha, turn out.

Exit CAUTION [*and* DON DIEGO].

Lord, that people should be such arrant cuddens, ha, ha, ha. But I may stay, may I not?

HIPPOLITA. No, no, I'd have you go out and hold the door, cousin, or else my father will come in again before his time.

MONSIEUR. I will, I will then, sweet cousin. 'Twas well thought on, that was well thought on indeed for me to hold the door.

---

508 *royally*: positively.

530 *the troth-telling Trojan gentlewoman*: Cassandra, fated to prophesy accurately but never to be believed.

533 s.d. after line 532 Q1.

534 *cuddens*: dolts.

HIPPOLITA. But be sure you keep him out, cousin, till we knock.

MONSIEUR. I warrant you, cousin. Lord, that people should be made such fools of, ha, ha, ha.

Exit MONSIEUR.

GERRARD. So, so, to make him hold the door while I steal his mistress is not unpleasant.

HIPPOLITA. Ay, but would you do so ill a thing, so treacherous a thing? Faith, 'tis not well.

GERRARD. Faith, I can't help it, since 'tis for your sake. Come, sweetest, is not this our way into the gallery?

HIPPOLITA. Yes, but it goes against my conscience to be accessory to so ill a thing. You say you do it for my sake?

GERRARD. Alas, poor miss! 'Tis not against your conscience but against your modesty, you think, to do it frankly.

HIPPOLITA. Nay, if it be against my modesty too, I can't do it indeed.

GERRARD. Come, come, miss, let us make haste. All's ready.

HIPPOLITA. Nay, faith, I can't satisfy my scruple.

GERRARD. Come, dearest, this is not a time for scruples nor modesty. Modesty between lovers is as impertinent as ceremony between friends and modesty is now as unseasonable as on the wedding night. Come away, my dearest.

HIPPOLITA. Whither?

GERRARD. Nay, sure, we have lost too much time already. Is that a proper question now? If you would know come along, for I have all ready.

HIPPOLITA. But I am not ready.

GERRARD. Truly, miss, we shall have your father come in upon us and prevent us again as he did in the morning.

HIPPOLITA. 'Twas well for me he did, for, on my conscience, if he had not come in I had gone clear away with you when I was in the humour.

GERRARD. Come, dearest, you would frighten me as if you were not yet in the same humour. Come, come away. The coach and six is ready.

HIPPOLITA. 'Tis too late to take the air and I am not ready.

GERRARD. You were ready in the morning.

HIPPOLITA. Ay, so I was.

GERRARD. Come, come, miss. Indeed the jest begins to be none.

HIPPOLITA. What, I warrant you think me in jest then?

GERRARD. In jest, certainly, but it begins to be troublesome.

HIPPOLITA. But, sir, you could believe I was in earnest in the morning when I but seemed to be ready to go with you and why won't you believe me now, when I declare to the contrary? I take it unkindly that the longer I am acquainted with you you should have the less confidence in me.

GERRARD. For heaven's sake, miss, lose no more time thus. Your father will come in upon us, as he did –

HIPPOLITA. Let him, if he will.

GERRARD. He'll hinder our design.

HIPPOLITA. No, he will not, for mine is to stay here now.

GERRARD. Are you in earnest?

HIPPOLITA. You'll find it so.

GERRARD. How! Why, you confessed but now you would have gone with me in the morning.

HIPPOLITA. I was in the humour then.

GERRARD. And I hope you are in the same still. You cannot change so soon.

HIPPOLITA. Why, is it not a whole day ago?

GERRARD. What, are you not a day in the same humour?

HIPPOLITA. Lord, that you who know the town, they say, should think any woman could be a whole day together in an humour! Ha, ha, ha.

GERRARD. Hey! This begins to be pleasant. What, won't you go with me then after all?

HIPPOLITA. No, indeed, sir, I desire to be excused.

GERRARD. Then you have abused me all this while?

HIPPOLITA. It may be so.

GERRARD. Could all that so natural innocency be dissembled? Faith, it could not, dearest miss.

HIPPOLITA. Faith, it was, dear master.

GERRARD. Was it, faith?

HIPPOLITA. Methinks you might believe me without an oath. You saw I could dissemble with my father – why should you think I could not with you?

GERRARD. So young a wheedle?

HIPPOLITA. Ay, a mere damned jade I am.
GERRARD. And I have been abused, you say?
HIPPOLITA. 'Tis well you can believe it at last.
GERRARD. And I must never hope for you?
HIPPOLITA. Would you have me abuse you again?
GERRARD. Then you will not go with me?
HIPPOLITA. No, but for your comfort your loss will not be great and, that you may not resent it, for once I'll be ingenuous and disabuse you. I am no heiress, as I told you, to twelve hundred pound a year. I was only a lying jade then. Now you will part with me willingly I doubt not.
GERRARD. (*sighs*) I wish I could.
HIPPOLITA. Come, now I find 'tis your turn to dissemble. But men use to dissemble for money – will you dissemble for nothing?
GERRARD. 'Tis too late for me to dissemble.
HIPPOLITA. Don't you dissemble, faith?
GERRARD. Nay, this is too cruel.
HIPPOLITA. What, would you take me without the twelve hundred pound a year? Would you be such a fool as to steal a woman with nothing?
GERRARD. I'll convince you, for you shall go with me and since you are twelve hundred pound a year the lighter you'll be the easier carried away.

He takes her in his arms; she struggles.

PRUE. What, he takes her away against her will. I find I must knock for my master then. (*She knocks*)

Enter DON DIEGO *and* MRS CAUTION.

HIPPOLITA. My father, my father is here.
GERRARD. Prevented again! (GERRARD *sets her down again*)
DON DIEGO. What, you have done, I hope, now, friend, for good and all?
GERRARD. Yes, yes, we have done for good and all indeed.
DON DIEGO. How now! You seem to be out of humour, friend.
GERRARD. Yes, so I am. I can't help it.
CAUTION. He's a dissembler in his very throat, brother.
HIPPOLITA. (*aside to* GERRARD) Pray do not carry things so as to discover yourself, if it be but for my sake, good master.

GERRARD. (*aside*) She is grown impudent.

CAUTION. See, see, they whisper, brother, to steal a kiss under a whisper! O the harlotry!

DON DIEGO. What's the matter, friend?

HIPPOLITA. (*to* GERRARD) I say, for my sake, be in humour and do not discover yourself but be as patient as a dancing-master still.

DON DIEGO. What, she is whispering to him indeed! What's the matter? I will know it, friend, look you.

GERRARD. Will you know it?

DON DIEGO. Yes, I will know it.

GERRARD. Why, if you will know it, then she would not do as I would have her and whispered me to desire me not to discover it to you.

DON DIEGO. What, hussy, would you not do as he'd have you? I'll make you do as he'd have you.

GERRARD. I wish you would.

CAUTION. 'Tis a lie. She'll do all he'll have her do and more too, to my knowledge.

DON DIEGO. Come, tell me what 'twas then she would not do. Come to it, hussy, or – Come, take her by the hand, friend. Come, begin. Let's see if she will not do anything now I am here.

HIPPOLITA. Come, pray be in humour, master.

GERRARD. I cannot dissemble like you.

DON DIEGO. What, she can't dissemble already, can she?

CAUTION. Yes but she can, but 'tis with you she dissembles, for they are not fallen out, as we think, for I'll be sworn I saw her just now give him the languishing eye, as they call it, that is, the whiting's eye, of old called the sheep's eye. I'll be sworn I saw it with these two eyes, that I did.

HIPPOLITA. (*aside to* GERRARD) You'll betray us. Have a care, good master.

GERRARD. Hold your peace, I say, silly woman.

DON DIEGO. But does she dissemble already? How do you mean?

GERRARD. She pretends she can't do what she should do and that she is not in humour – the common excuse of women for not doing what they should do.

DON DIEGO. Come, I'll put her in humour. Dance, I say. Come, about with her, master.

GERRARD. (*aside*) I am in a pretty humour to dance. (*To* HIPPOLITA) I cannot fool any longer since you have fooled me.

HIPPOLITA. [*aside to* GERRARD] You would not be so ungenerous as to betray the woman that hated you. I do not do that yet. For heaven's sake, for this once be more obedient to my desires than your passion.

DON DIEGO. What, is she humoursome still? But methinks you look yourself as if you were in an ill humour. But about with her.

GERRARD. I am in no good dancing humour indeed.

Enter MONSIEUR.

MONSIEUR. Well, how goes the dancing forward? What, my aunt here to disturb 'em again.

DON DIEGO. Come, come.

GERRARD *leads her about.*

CAUTION. I say stand off. Thou shalt not come near. Avoid, Satan, as they say.

DON DIEGO. Nay then, we shall have it. Nephew, hold her a little, that she may not disturb 'em. Come, now away with her.

GERRARD. One, two and a coupée. (*Aside*) Fooled and abused!

CAUTION. Wilt thou lay violent hands upon thy own natural aunt, wretch?

The MONSIEUR *holding* CAUTION.

DON DIEGO. Come, about with her.

GERRARD. One, two, three, four and turn round. (*Aside*) By such a piece of innocency!

CAUTION. Dost thou see, fool, how he squeezes her hand?

MONSIEUR. That won't do, aunt.

HIPPOLITA. Pray, master, have patience and let's mind our business.

DON DIEGO. Why did you anger him then, hussy, look you?

CAUTION. Do you see how she smiles in his face and squeezes his hand now?

MONSIEUR. Your servant, aunt, that won't do, I say.

HIPPOLITA. Have patience, master.

GERRARD. (*aside*) I am become her sport. – One, two, three, death, hell and the devil.

DON DIEGO. Ay, they are three indeed. But pray have patience.

CAUTION. Do you see how she leers upon him and clings to him? Can you suffer it?

MONSIEUR. Ay, ay.

GERRARD. One, two and a slur. Can you be so unconcerned after all?

DON DIEGO. What, is she unconcerned? Hussy, mind your business.

GERRARD. One, two, three and turn round. One, two, fall back, hell and damnation.

DON DIEGO. Ay, people fall back indeed into hell and damnation, heaven knows.

GERRARD. One, two, three and your honour. I can fool no longer.

CAUTION. Nor will I be withheld any longer like a poor hen in her pen while the kite is carrying away her chicken before her face.

DON DIEGO. What have you done? Well then, let's see her dance it now to the violin.

MONSIEUR. Ay, ay, let's see her dance it to the violin.

GERRARD. Another time, another time.

DON DIEGO. Don't you believe that, friend. These dancing-masters make no bones of breaking their words. Did not you promise just now I should see her dance it to the violin? And that I will too, before I stir.

GERRARD. Let Monsieur play then while I dance with her. She can't dance alone.

MONSIEUR. I can't play at all. I'm but a learner. But if you'll play, I'll dance with her.

GERRARD. I can't play neither.

DON DIEGO. What, a dancing-master and not play!

CAUTION. Ay, you see what a dancing-master he is. 'Tis as I told you, I warrant. A dancing-master and not play upon the fiddle!

DON DIEGO. How!

HIPPOLITA. (*aside to* GERRARD) O you have betrayed us all! If you confess that you undo us for ever.

---

756 *slur*: glide.

GERRARD. [*aside to* HIPPOLITA] I cannot play. What would you have me say?

MONSIEUR. [*aside*] I vow and swear, we are all undone if you cannot play.

DON DIEGO. What, are you a dancing-master and cannot play? Umph!

HIPPOLITA. He is only out of humour, sir. (*She offers* GERRARD *the violin*) Here, master. I know you will play for me yet, for he has an excellent hand.

MONSIEUR. Ay, that he has – (*Aside*) at giving a box on the ear.

DON DIEGO. Why does he not play then?

HIPPOLITA. (*gives* GERRARD *the violin*) Here, master. Pray play for my sake.

GERRARD. [*aside*] What would you have me do with it? I cannot play a stroke.

HIPPOLITA. (*apart to* GERRARD) No, stay then. Seem to tune it and break the strings.

GERRARD. Come then. (*Aside*) Next to the devil's the invention of women. They'll no more want an excuse to cheat a father with than an opportunity to abuse a husband. – But what do you give me such a damned fiddle with rotten strings for? (*Winds up the strings till they break and throws the violin on the ground*)

DON DIEGO. Hey-day, the dancing-master is frantic.

MONSIEUR. [*aside*] Ha, ha, ha, that people should be made such fools of!

CAUTION. He broke the strings on purpose, because he could not play. You are blind, brother.

DON DIEGO. What, will you see further than I, look you?

HIPPOLITA. But pray, master, why in such haste?

GERRARD. Because you have done with me.

DON DIEGO. But don't you intend to come tomorrow again?

GERRARD. Your daughter does not desire it.

DON DIEGO. No matter. I do. I must be your paymaster, I'm sure. I would have you come betimes too, not only to make her perfect but, since you have so good a hand upon the violin, to play your part with half a dozen of musicians more whom I would have you bring with you, for we will have a very merry wedding, though a very private one. You'll be sure to come?

GERRARD. Your daughter does not desire it.

DON DIEGO. Come, come, baggage, you shall desire it of him; he is your master.

HIPPOLITA. My father will have me desire it of you, it seems.

GERRARD. But you'll make a fool of me again if I should come, would you not?

HIPPOLITA. If I should tell you so you'd be sure not to come.

DON DIEGO. Come, come, she shall not make a fool of you, upon my word. I'll secure you, she shall do what you'll have her.

MONSIEUR. (*aside*) Ha, ha, ha, so, so, silly don.

GERRARD. But, madam, will you have me come?

HIPPOLITA. I'd have you to know, for my part, I care not whether you come or no. There are other dancing-masters to be had. It is my father's request to you. All that I have to say to you is a little good advice which, because I will not shame you, I'll give you in private. (*Whispers* GERRARD)

CAUTION. What, will you let her whisper with him too?

DON DIEGO. Nay, if you find fault with it, they shall whisper. Though I did not like it before, I'll ha' nobody wiser than myself. But do you think if 'twere any hurt she would whisper it to him before us?

CAUTION. If it be no hurt, why does she not speak aloud?

DON DIEGO. Because she says she will not put the man out of countenance.

CAUTION. Hey-day, put a dancing-master out of countenance!

DON DIEGO. You say he is no dancing-master.

CAUTION. Yes, for his impudence he may be a dancing-master.

DON DIEGO. Well, well, let her whisper before me as much as she will tonight since she is to be married tomorrow, especially since her husband that shall be stands by consenting too.

MONSIEUR. Ay, ay, let 'em whisper (as you say) as much as they will before we marry. (*Aside*) She's making more sport with him, I warrant. But I wonder how people can be fooled so, ha, ha, ha.

DON DIEGO. Well, a penny for the secret, daughter.

HIPPOLITA. Indeed, father, you shall have it for nothing tomorrow.

DON DIEGO. Well, friend, you will not fail to come?

GERRARD. No, no, sir. (*Aside*) Yet I am a fool if I do.

DON DIEGO. And be sure you bring the fiddlers with you, as I bid you.

HIPPOLITA. Yes, be sure you bring the fiddlers with you, as I bid you.

CAUTION. So, so, he'll fiddle your daughter out of the house. Must you have the fiddles, with a fiddle-faddle?

MONSIEUR. [*aside*] Lord! That people should be made such fools of, hah, hah!

Exeunt DON DIEGO, HIPPOLITA, MONSIEUR, CAUTION *and* PRUE.

GERRARD. Fortune we sooner may than woman trust;
To her confiding gallant she is just,
But falser woman only him deceives
Who to her tongue and eyes most credit gives. *Exit.*

ACT V

SCENE I

Enter MONSIEUR *and* BLACK *stalking over the stage. To them,* MR GERRARD.

MONSIEUR. Good morrow to thee, noble dancing-master, ha, ha, ha. Your little black brother here, my master, I see, is the more diligent man of the two. But why do you come so late? What, you begin to neglect your scholar, do you? Little black master, con licentia, pray get you out of the room.

Exit BLACK.

What, out of humour, man! A dancing-master should be like his fiddle, always in tune. Come, my cousin has made an ass of thee. What then? I know it.

GERRARD. (*aside*) Does he know it?

MONSIEUR. But prithee don't be angry. 'Twas agreed upon betwixt us before I sent you to make a fool of thee, ha, ha, ha.

GERRARD. Was it so?

MONSIEUR. I knew you would be apt to entertain vain hopes from the summons of a lady but, faith, the design was but to make a fool of thee, as you find.

GERRARD. 'Tis very well.

MONSIEUR. But indeed I did not think the jest would have lasted so long and that my cousin would have made a dancing-master of you, ha, ha, ha.

GERRARD. (*aside*) The fool has reason, I find, and I am the coxcomb while I thought him so.

MONSIEUR. Come, I see you are uneasy and the jest of being a dancing-master grows tedious to you. But have a little patience; the parson is sent for and when once my cousin and I are married my uncle may know who you are.

GERRARD. [*aside*] I am certainly abused.

MONSIEUR *listens.*

MONSIEUR. What do you say?

GERRARD. (*aside*) Merely fooled.

MONSIEUR. Why do you doubt it? Ha, ha, ha.

GERRARD. (*aside*) Can it be?

MONSIEUR. Pish, pish, she told me yesterday as soon as you were gone that she had led you into a fool's paradise and made you believe she would go away with you, ha, ha, ha.

GERRARD. (*aside*) Did she so? I am no longer to doubt it then?

MONSIEUR. Ay, ay, she makes a mere fool of thee, I vow and swear. But don't be concerned; there's hardly a man of a thousand but has been made a fool of by some woman or other. I have been made a fool of myself, man, by the women; I have, I vow and swear, I have.

GERRARD. Well, you have, I believe it, for you are a coxcomb.

MONSIEUR. Lord! You need not be so touchy with one. I tell you but the truth for your good, for, though she does, I would not fool you any longer. But prithee don't be troubled at what can't be helped. Women are made on purpose to fool men. When they are children they fool their fathers and when they have taken leave of their hanging-sleeves they fool their gallants or dancing-masters, ha, ha, ha.

GERRARD. Hark you, sir, to be fooled by a woman, you say, is not to be helped but I will not be fooled by a fool.

MONSIEUR. You show your English breeding now. An English rival is so dull and brutish as not to understand raillery. But what is spoken in your passion I'll take no notice of, for I am your friend and would not have you my rival to make yourself ridiculous. Come, prithee, prithee, don't be so concerned, for, as I was saying, women first fool their fathers, then their gallants, and then their husbands, so that it will be my turn to be fooled too (for your comfort) and when they come to be widows they would fool the devil, I vow and swear. Come, come, dear Gerrard, prithee don't be out of humour and look so sillily.

GERRARD. Prithee do not talk so sillily.

MONSIEUR. Nay, faith, I am resolved to beat you out of this ill humour.

GERRARD. Faith, I am afraid I shall first beat you into an ill humour.

MONSIEUR. Ha, ha, ha. That thou shouldst be gulled so by a little gipsy who left off her bib but yesterday. Faith, I can't but laugh at thee.

GERRARD. Faith, then I shall make your mirth (as being too violent) conclude in some little misfortune to you. The fool begins to be tyrannical.

MONSIEUR. Ha, ha, ha, poor angry dancing-master. Prithee match my Spanish pumps and legs with one of your best and newest sarabands. Ha, ha, ha, come.

GERRARD. I will match your Spanish ear thus, sir, and make you dance thus. (*Strikes and kicks him*)

MONSIEUR. How! Sa, sa, sa. Then I'll make you dance thus.

MONSIEUR *draws his sword and runs at him but,* GERRARD *drawing, he retires.*

Hold, hold a little. (*Aside*) A desperate, disappointed lover will cut his own throat; then, sure, he will make nothing of cutting his rival's throat.

---

54 *hanging-sleeves*: loose open sleeves, worn only by children.

GERRARD. Consideration is an enemy to fighting. If you have a mind to revenge yourself your sword's in your hand.

MONSIEUR. Pray, sir, hold your peace. I'll ne'er take my rival's counsel, be't what 'twill. I know what you would be at. You are disappointed of your mistress and could hang yourself and therefore will not fear hanging. But I am a successful lover and need neither hang for you nor my mistress. Nay, if I should kill you I know I should do you a kindness, therefore e'en live to die daily with envy of my happiness. But if you will needs die, kill yourself and be damned for me, I vow and swear.

GERRARD. But won't you fight for your mistress?

MONSIEUR. I tell you, you shall not have the honour to be killed for her. Besides, I will not be hit in the teeth by her as long as I live with the great love you had for her. Women speak well of their dead husbands – what will they do of their dead gallants?

GERRARD. But if you will not fight for her you shall dance for her, since you desired me to teach you to dance too. I'll teach you to dance thus.

Strikes his sword at his legs. MONSIEUR *leaps.*

MONSIEUR. Nay, if it be for the sake of my mistress, there's nothing I will refuse to do.

GERRARD. Nay, you must dance on.

MONSIEUR. Ay, ay, for my mistress and sing too. La, la, la, ra, la.

Enter HIPPOLITA *and* PRUE.

HIPPOLITA. What, swords drawn betwixt you too? What's the matter?

MONSIEUR. (*aside*) Is she here? – Come, put up your sword. You see this is no place for us. But the devil eat me if you shall not eat my sword but –

HIPPOLITA. What's the matter, cousin?

MONSIEUR. Nothing, nothing, cousin. But your presence is a sanctuary for my greatest enemy or else, tête non.

HIPPOLITA. (*to* GERRARD) What, you have not hurt my cousin, sir, I hope?

GERRARD. (*aside*) How she's concerned for him! Nay, then I need not doubt; my fears are true.

MONSIEUR. What was that you said, cousin? Hurt me,

ha, ha, ha, hurt me! If any man hurt me he must do it basely. He shall ne'er do it when my sword's drawn, sa, sa, sa.

HIPPOLITA. Because you will ne'er draw your sword perhaps.

MONSIEUR. (*aside*) Scurvily guessed. – You ladies may say anything. But, cousin, pray do not talk of swords and fighting. Meddle with your guitar and talk of dancing with your dancing-master there, ha, ha, ha.

HIPPOLITA. But I am afraid you have hurt my master, cousin. He says nothing. Can he draw his breath?

MONSIEUR. No, 'tis you have hurt your master, cousin, in the very heart, cousin, and therefore he would hurt me, for love is a disease makes people as malicious as the plague does.

HIPPOLITA. Indeed, poor master, something does ail you.

MONSIEUR. Nay, nay, cousin, faith, don't abuse him any longer. He's an honest gentleman and has been long of my acquaintance and a man of tolerable sense to take him out of his love. But prithee, cousin, don't drive the jest too far for my sake.

GERRARD. He counsels you well, pleasant, cunning, jilting miss for his sake, for, if I am your divertisement, it shall be at his cost, since he's your gallant in favour.

HIPPOLITA. I don't understand you.

MONSIEUR. (*aside*) But I do, a pox take him, and the custom that so orders it, forsooth: that, if a lady abuse or affront a man, presently the gallant must be beaten; nay, what's more unreasonable, if a woman abuse her husband, the poor cuckold must bear the shame as well as the injury.

HIPPOLITA. But what's the matter, master? What was it you said?

GERRARD. I say, pleasant, cunning, jilting lady, though you make him a cuckold it will not be revenge enough for me upon him for marrying you.

HIPPOLITA. How, my surly, huffing, jealous, senseless, saucy master?

MONSIEUR. Nay, nay, faith, give losers leave to speak, losers of mistresses especially, ha, ha, ha. Besides, your anger is too great a favour for him. I scorn to honour him with mine, you see.

HIPPOLITA. I tell you, my saucy master, my cousin shall never be made that monstrous thing you mention by me.

MONSIEUR. Thank you, I vow and swear, cousin. No, no, I never thought I should.

GERRARD. Sure, you marry him by the sage maxim of your sex, which is, 'wittols make the best husbands', that is, cuckolds.

HIPPOLITA. Indeed, master, whatsoever you think, I would sooner choose you for that purpose than him.

MONSIEUR. Ha, ha, ha, there she was with him, i'faith. I thank you for that, cousin, I vow and swear.

HIPPOLITA. Nay, he shall thank me for that too. But how came you two to quarrel? I thought, cousin, you had more wit than to quarrel or more kindness for me than to quarrel here. What if my father, hearing the bustle, should have come in? He would soon have discovered our false dancing-master (for passion unmasks every man) and then the result of your quarrel had been my ruin.

MONSIEUR. Nay, you had both felt his desperate, deadly, daunting dagger. There are your d's for you.

HIPPOLITA. Go, go presently therefore and hinder my father from coming in, whilst I put my master into a better humour, that we may not be discovered, to the prevention of our wedding or worse, when he comes. Go, go.

MONSIEUR. Well, well, I will, cousin.

HIPPOLITA. Be sure you let him not come in this good while.

MONSIEUR. No, no, I warrant you. (MONSIEUR *goes out and returns*) But if he should come before I would have him, I'll come before him and cough and hawk soundly, that you may not be surprised. Won't that do well, cousin?

HIPPOLITA. Very well. Pray be gone.

Exit MONSIEUR.

Well, master, since I find you are quarrelsome and melancholy and would have taken me away without a portion – three infallible signs of a true lover – faith,

209 *hawk*: clear the throat.

here's my hand now in earnest, to lead me a dance as long as I live.

GERRARD. How's this? You surprise me as much as when first I found so much beauty and wit in company with so much innocency. But, dearest, I would be assured of what you say and yet dare not ask the question. You – h – do not abuse me again. You – h – will fool me no more, sure.

HIPPOLITA. Yes but I will, sure.

GERRARD. How! Nay, I was afraid on't.

HIPPOLITA. For I say you are to be my husband and you say husbands must be wittols and some strange things to boot.

GERRARD. Well, I will take my fortune.

HIPPOLITA. But have a care, rash man.

GERRARD. I will venture.

HIPPOLITA. At your peril. Remember I wished you to have a care. Forewarned, forearmed.

PRUE. Indeed now, that's fair, for most men are fore-armed before they are warned.

HIPPOLITA. Plain-dealing is some kind of honesty, how-ever, and few women would have said so much.

GERRARD. None but those who would delight in a husband's jealousy as the proof of his love and her honour.

HIPPOLITA. Hold, sir, let us have a good understanding betwixt one another at first, that we may be long friends. I differ from you in the point, for a husband's jealousy, which cunning men would pass upon their wives for a compliment, is the worst can be made 'em, for, indeed, it is a compliment to their beauty but an affront to their honour.

GERRARD. But, madam –

HIPPOLITA. So that upon the whole matter I conclude, jealousy in a gallant is humble true love and the height of respect and only an undervaluing of himself to overvalue her but in a husband 'tis arrant sauciness, cowardice and ill-breeding and not to be suffered.

GERRARD. I stand corrected, gracious miss.

HIPPOLITA. Well, have you brought the gentlemen fiddlers with you, as I desired?

GERRARD. They are below.

HIPPOLITA. Are they armed well?

GERRARD. Yes, they have instruments too that are not of wood. But what will you do with them?

HIPPOLITA. What did you think I intended to do with them, when I whispered you to bring gentlemen of your acquaintance instead of fiddlers, as my father desired you to bring? Pray, what did you think I intended?

GERRARD. Faith, e'en to make fools of the gentlemen fiddlers as you had done of your gentleman dancing-master.

HIPPOLITA. I intended 'em for our guard and defence against my father's Spanish and Guinea force, when we were to make our retreat from hence, and to help us to take the keys from my aunt, who has been the watchful porter of this house this twelvemonth, and this design (if your heart do not fail you) we will put in execution, as soon as you have given your friends below instructions.

GERRARD. Are you sure your heart will stand right still? You flinched last night, when I little expected it, I am sure.

HIPPOLITA. The time last night was not so proper for us as now for reasons I will give you. But besides that, I confess I had a mind to try whether your interest did not sway you more than your love, whether the twelve hundred pounds a year I told you of had not made a greater impression in your heart than Hippolita. But finding it otherwise – yet hold, perhaps upon consideration you are grown wiser. Can you yet, as I said, be so desperate, so out of fashion, as to steal a woman with nothing?

GERRARD. With you I can want nothing nor can be made by anything more rich or happy.

HIPPOLITA. Think well again. Can you take me without the twelve hundred pounds a year? The twelve hundred pounds a year?

GERRARD. Indeed, miss, now you begin to be unkind again and use me worse than e'er you did.

HIPPOLITA. Well, though you are so modest a gentleman as to suffer a wife to be put upon you with

270 *Guinea*: not only Spanish Guinea but any part of West Africa.

nothing I have more conscience than to do it. I have the twelve hundred pounds a year, out of my father's power, which is yours and I am sorry it is not the Indies to mend your bargain.

GERRARD. Dear miss, you but increase my fears and not my wealth. Pray, let us make haste away. I desire but to be secure of you. Come, what are you thinking of?

HIPPOLITA. I am thinking, if some little, flinching, inquisitive poet should get my story and represent it on the stage, what those ladies who are never precise but at a play would say of me now; that I were a confident, coming piece, I warrant, and they would damn the poor poet for libelling the sex. But sure, though I give myself and fortune away frankly, without the consent of my friends, my confidence is less than theirs who stand off only for separate maintenance.

GERRARD. They would be widows before their time, have a husband and no husband. But let us be gone, lest fortune should recant my happiness. Now you are fixed my dearest miss. (*He kisses her hand*)

Enter MONSIEUR *coughing and* DON DIEGO.

HIPPOLITA. Oh, here's my father!

DON DIEGO. How now, sir! What, kissing her hand? What means that, friend, ha? Daughter, ha! Do you permit this insolence, ha? Voto a mi honra.

GERRARD. [*aside*] We are prevented again.

HIPPOLITA. Ha, ha, ha, you are so full of your Spanish jealousy, father. Why, you must know he's a city dancing-master and they, forsooth, think it fine to kiss the hand at the honour before the corant.

MONSIEUR. Ay, ay, ay, uncle, don't you know that?

DON DIEGO. Go to, go to, you are an easy French fool. There's more in it than so, look you.

MONSIEUR. I vow and swear there's nothing more in't, if you'll believe one. (*Aside to* HIPPOLITA *and* GERRARD) Did not I cough and hawk? A jealous, prudent husband could not cough and hawk louder at the approach of his wife's chamber in visiting-time and yet you would not hear me. He'll make now ado about nothing and you'll be discovered both.

DON DIEGO. Umph, umph, no, no. I see it plain. He is no dancing-master. Now I have found it out and I think I can see as far into matters as another. I have found it now, look you.

GERRARD. [*aside*] My fear was prophetical.

HIPPOLITA. [*aside*] What shall we do?

GERRARD *offers to go out with her.*

Nay, pray, sir, do not stir yet.

Enter MRS CAUTION.

CAUTION. What's the matter, brother? What's the matter?

DON DIEGO. I have found it out, sister, I have found it out. Sister, this villain here is no dancing-master but a dishonourer of my house and daughter. I caught him kissing her hand.

MONSIEUR. Pish, pish, you are a strange Spanish kind of an uncle, that you are. A dishonourer of your daughter because he kissed her hand! Pray, how could he honour her more? He kissed her hand, you see, while he was making his honour to her.

DON DIEGO. You are an unthinking, shallow, French fop, voto. But I tell you, sister, I have thought of it and have found it out: he is no dancing-master, sister. Do you remember the whispering last night? I have found out the meaning of that too and I tell you, sister, he's no dancing-master. I have found it out.

CAUTION. You found it out, marry come up! Did not I tell you always he was no dancing-master?

DON DIEGO. You tell me, you silly woman! What then? What of that? You tell me! D'ee think I heeded what you told me? But I tell you now I have found it out.

CAUTION. I say I found it out.

DON DIEGO. I say 'tis false, gossip. I found him out.

CAUTION. I say I found him out first – say what you will.

DON DIEGO. Sister, mum, Not such a word again, guarda. You found him out!

CAUTION. Nay, I must submit or dissemble like other prudent women or –

DON DIEGO. Come, come, sister, take it from me, he is no dancing-master.

CAUTION. O yes, he is a dancing-master.

DON DIEGO. What, will you be wiser than I every way? Remember the whispering, I say.

CAUTION. (*aside*) So, he thinks I speak in earnest. Then I'll fit him still. – But what do you talk of their whispering? They would not whisper any ill before us, sure.

DON DIEGO. Will you still be an idiot, a dolt and see nothing?

MONSIEUR. Lord! You'll be wiser than all the world, will you? Are we not all against you? Pshaw, pshaw, I ne'er saw such a donissimo as you are, I vow and swear.

DON DIEGO. No, sister, he's no dancing-master, for, now I think on't too, he could not play upon the fiddle.

CAUTION. Pish, pish, what dancing-master can play upon a fiddle without strings?

DON DIEGO. Again, I tell you, he broke 'em on purpose, because he could not play. I have found it out now, sister.

CAUTION. Nay, you see farther than I, brother.

GERRARD *offers to lead* [HIPPOLITA] *out.*

HIPPOLITA. [*aside to* GERRARD] For heaven's sake, stir not yet.

DON DIEGO. Besides, if you remember, they were perpetually putting me out of the room – that was, sister, because they had a mind to be alone. I have found that out too. Now, sister, look you, he is no dancing-master.

CAUTION. But has he not given her a lesson often before you?

DON DIEGO. Ay, but, sister, he did not go about his business like a dancing-master. But go, go down to the door. Somebody rings.

Exit CAUTION.

MONSIEUR. I vow and swear, uncle, he is a dancing-master. Pray be appeased. Lord, d'ee think I'd tell you a lie?

DON DIEGO. If it prove to be a lie and you do not confess it, though you are my next heir after my daughter, I will disown thee as much as I do her, for thy folly and treachery to thyself as well as me. You may have her but never my estate, look you.

MONSIEUR. (*aside*) How! I must look to my hits then.

DON DIEGO. Look to't.

MONSIEUR. (*aside*) Then I had best confess all before he discover all, which he will soon do.

Enter PARSON.

O, here's the parson too! He won't be in choler nor brandish Toledo before the parson, sure? – Well, uncle, I must confess, rather than lose your favour; he is no dancing-master.

DON DIEGO. No.

GERRARD. What, has the fool betrayed us then at last? Nay then, 'tis time to be gone. Come away, miss. (*Going out*)

DON DIEGO. Nay, sir, if you pass this way, my Toledo will pass that way, look you. (*Thrusts at him with his sword*)

HIPPOLITA. O hold, Mr Gerrard! Hold, father!

MONSIEUR. (*stops his uncle*) I tell you uncle, he's an honest gentleman, means no hurt and came hither but upon a frolic of mine and your daughter's.

DON DIEGO. Ladrón, traidor.

MONSIEUR. I tell you, all's but a jest, a mere jest, I vow and swear.

DON DIEGO. A jest! Jest with my honour, voto! Ha! No family to dishonour but the grave, wise, noble, honourable, illustrious, puissant and right worshipful family of the Formals! Nay, I am contented to reprieve you till you know who you have dishonoured and convict you of the greatness of your crime before you die. We are descended, look you –

MONSIEUR. Nay, pray, uncle, hear me.

DON DIEGO. I say, we are descended –

MONSIEUR. 'Tis no matter for that.

DON DIEGO. And my great-great-great-grandfather was –

MONSIEUR. Well, well, I have something to say more to the purpose.

DON DIEGO. My great-great-great-grandfather, I say, was –

MONSIEUR. Well, a pinmaker in –

---

420 *look to my hits*: look to my chances, attend to my business.

DON DIEGO. But he was a gentleman for all that, fop, for he was a sergeant to a company of the train-bands and my great-great-grandfather was –

MONSIEUR. Was his son. What then? Won't you let me clear this gentleman?

DON DIEGO. He was, he was –

MONSIEUR. He was a feltmaker, his son a wine-cooper, your father a vintner, and so you came to be a Canary merchant.

DON DIEGO. But we were still gentlemen, for our coat was, as the heralds say, was –

MONSIEUR. Was – your sign was the three tuns and the field canary. Now let me tell you, this honest gentleman –

DON DIEGO. Now that you should dare to dishonour this family. By the graves of my ancestors in Great St Ellen's Church –

MONSIEUR. Yard.

DON DIEGO. Thou shalt die for't, ladrón. (*Runs at* GERRARD)

MONSIEUR. Hold, hold, uncle. Are you mad?

HIPPOLITA. Oh, oh.

MONSIEUR. Nay then, by your own Spanish rules of honour, though he be my rival, I must help him, since I brought him into danger. (*Draws his sword. Aside*) Sure, he will not show his valour upon his nephew and son-in-law – otherwise I should be afraid of showing mine. – Here, Mr Gerrard, go in here. Nay, you shall go in, Mr Gerrard. I'll secure you all. And, parson, do you go in too with 'em, for I see you are afraid of a sword and the other world, though you talk of it so familiarly and make it so fine a place.

Opens a door and thrusts GERRARD, HIPPOLITA *and* PARSON *in, then shuts it and guards it with his sword.*

---

457 *train-bands*: the citizen militia.

458 Q1 has one *great* too many.

463–4 *Canary merchant*: a merchant involved in a wide range of West African trade, not only the import of Canary wines.

467 *tuns*: wine barrels.

471–2 *Great St Ellen's Church*: Great St Helen's, Bishopsgate. Only the rich were buried inside church, hence Monsieur's gibe.

DON DIEGO. Tu quoque, Brute.

MONSIEUR. Nay, now, uncle, you must understand reason. What, you are not only a don but you are a Don Quixote too, I vow and swear.

DON DIEGO. Thou spot, sploach of my family and blood! I will have his blood, look you.

MONSIEUR. Pray, good Spanish uncle, have but patience to hear me. Suppose – I say, suppose he had done, done, done the feat to your daughter.

DON DIEGO. How! Done the feat, done the feat, done the feat, en hora mala!

MONSIEUR. I say, suppose, suppose –

DON DIEGO. Suppose –

MONSIEUR. I say, suppose he had, for I do but suppose it. Well, I am ready to marry her however. Now marriage is as good a solder for cracked female honour as blood and can't you suffer the shame but for a quarter of an hour till the parson has married us and then, if there be any shame, it becomes mine. For, here in England, the father has nothing to do with the daughter's business, honour, what-d'ee-call't when once she's married, d'ee see?

DON DIEGO. England! What d'ee tell me of England? I'll be a Spaniard still, voto a mi hora, and I will be revenged. (*Calls at the door*) Pedro, Juan, Sanchez.

Enter MRS CAUTION *followed by* FLIRT *and* FLOUNCE *in vizard masks.*

CAUTION. What's the matter, brother?

DON DIEGO. Pedro, Sanchez, Juan! But who are these, sister? Are they not men in women's clothes? What make they here?

CAUTION. They are relations, they say, of my cousin's, who pressed in when I let in the parson. They say my cousin invited 'em to his wedding.

MONSIEUR. Two of my relations, ha! [*Aside*] They are my cousins indeed of the other night, a pox take 'em. But that's no curse for 'em; a plague take 'em then! But how came they here?

---

491 *sploach*: splotch.
510 *hora*: Don Diego – or Wycherley – means *honra*.

DON DIEGO. (*aside*) Now must I have witnesses too of the dishonour of my family. It were Spanish prudence to dispatch 'em away out of the house before I begin my revenge. – What are you? What make you here? Who would you speak with?

FLIRT. With Monsieur.

DON DIEGO. Here he is.

MONSIEUR. [*aside*] Now will these jades discredit me and spoil my match, just in the coupling minute.

DON DIEGO. Do you know 'em?

MONSIEUR. Yes, sir, sure, I know 'em. (*Aside to 'em*) Pray, ladies, say as I say or you will spoil my wedding, for I am just going to be married and if my uncle or mistress should know who you are it might break off the match.

FLOUNCE. We came on purpose to break the match.

MONSIEUR. How!

FLIRT. Why, d'ee think to marry and leave us so in the lurch?

MONSIEUR. (*aside*) What do the jades mean?

DON DIEGO. Come, who are they? What would they have? If they come to the wedding, ladies, I assure you, there will be none today here.

MONSIEUR. They won't trouble you, sir. They are going again. Ladies, you hear what my uncle says. I know you won't trouble him. (*Aside*) I wish I were well rid of 'em.

FLOUNCE. (*aside*) You shall not think to put us off so.

DON DIEGO. Who are they? What are their names?

FLIRT. We are, sir –

MONSIEUR. (*aside to 'em*) Nay, for heaven's sake, don't tell who you are, for you will undo me and spoil my match infallibly.

FLOUNCE. We care not. 'Tis our business to spoil matches.

MONSIEUR. You need not, for, I believe, married men are your best customers, for greedy bachelors take up with their wives.

DON DIEGO. Come, pray, ladies, if you have no business here, be pleased to retire, for few of us are in humour to be so civil to you as you may deserve.

MONSIEUR. Ay, prithee, dear jades, get you gone.

FLIRT. We will not stir.

DON DIEGO. Who are they, I say, fool, and why don't they go?

FLOUNCE. We are, sir –

MONSIEUR. Hold, hold. – They are persons of honour and quality and –

FLIRT. We are no persons of honour and quality, sir. We are –

MONSIEUR. They are modest ladies and being in a kind of disguise will not own their quality.

FLOUNCE. We modest ladies!

MONSIEUR. (*aside to 'em*) Why, sometimes you are in the humour to pass for women of honour and quality. Prithee, dear jades, let your modesty and greatness come upon you now.

FLIRT. Come, sir, not to delude you, as he would have us, we are –

MONSIEUR. Hold, hold –

FLIRT. The other night at the French house –

MONSIEUR. Hold, I say. [*Aside*] 'Tis even true as Gerrard says: the women will tell, I see.

FLOUNCE. [*aside to him*] If you would have her silent, stop her mouth with that ring.

MONSIEUR. Will that do't? Here, here – (*Takes off his ring and gives it her. Aside*) 'Tis worth one hundred and fifty pounds but I must not lose my match, I must not lose a trout for a fly. That men should live to hire women to silence!

Enter GERRARD, HIPPOLITA, PARSON *and* PRUE.

DON DIEGO. Oh, are you come again? (*Draws his sword and runs at 'em*)

MONSIEUR. Oh, hold, hold, uncle! (MONSIEUR *holds him*) What are you mad, Gerrard, to expose yourself to a new danger? Why would you come out yet?

GERRARD. Because our danger now is over, I thank the parson there. And now we must beg –

GERRARD *and* HIPPOLITA *kneel.*

MONSIEUR. Nay, faith, uncle, forgive him now, since he asks you forgiveness upon his knees and my poor cousin too.

---

588 s.d. follows line 587 Q1.

HIPPOLITA. You are mistaken, cousin. We ask him blessing and you forgiveness.

MONSIEUR. How, how, how! What do you talk of blessing? What, do you ask your father blessing and he asks me forgiveness? But why should he ask me forgiveness?

HIPPOLITA. Because he asks my father blessing.

MONSIEUR. Pish, pish, I don't understand you, I vow and swear.

HIPPOLITA. The parson will expound to you, cousin.

MONSIEUR. Hey! What say you to it, parson?

PARSON. They are married, sir.

MONSIEUR. Married!

CAUTION. Married! So, I told you what 'twould come to.

DON DIEGO. You told us!

MONSIEUR. Nay, she is setting up for the reputation of a witch.

DON DIEGO. Married! Juan, Sanchez, Pedro, arm, arm, arm.

CAUTION. A witch, a witch!

HIPPOLITA. Nay, indeed, father, now we are married you had better call the fiddles. Call 'em, Prue, quickly.

Exit PRUE.

MONSIEUR. Who do you say married, man?

PARSON. Was I not sent for on purpose to marry 'em? Why should you wonder at it?

MONSIEUR. No, no, you were to marry me, man, to her. I knew there was a mistake in't somehow. You were merely mistaken, therefore you must do your business over again for me now. The parson was mistaken, uncle, it seems, ha, ha, ha.

CAUTION. I suppose five or six guineas made him make the mistake, which will not be rectified now, nephew. They'll marry all that come near 'em and for a guinea or two care not what mischief they do, nephew.

DON DIEGO. Married! Pedro, Sanchez!

MONSIEUR. How, and must she be his wife then for ever and ever? Have I held the door then for this, like a fool as I was?

CAUTION. Yes, indeed.

619, 648 *Pedro*: Petro Q1

MONSIEUR. Have I worn golilla here for this? Little breeches for this?

CAUTION. Yes, truly.

MONSIEUR. And put on the Spanish honour with the habit, in defending my rival. Nay then, I'll have another turn of honour in revenge. Come, uncle, I'm of your side now. Sa, sa, sa. But let's stay for our force. Sanchez, Juan, Pedro, arm, arm, arm.

Enter two blacks and the Spaniard, followed by PRUE, MARTIN *and five other gentlemen like fiddlers.*

DON DIEGO. Murder the villain, kill him!

Running all upon GERRARD.

MARTIN. Hold, hold, sir.

DON DIEGO. How now! Who sent for you, friends?

MARTIN. We fiddlers, sir, often come unsent for.

DON DIEGO. And you are often kicked downstairs for't too.

MARTIN. No, sir, our company was never kicked, I think.

DON DIEGO. Fiddlers and not kicked? Then, to preserve your virgin honour, get you downstairs quickly, for we are not at present disposed much for mirth, voto.

MONSIEUR. (*peeping*) A pox, is it you, Martin? Nay, uncle, then 'tis in vain, for they won't be kicked downstairs, to my knowledge. They are gentlemen fiddlers, forsooth. A pox on all gentlemen fiddlers and gentlemen dancing-masters, say I!

DON DIEGO. (*pausing*) How! Ha.

MONSIEUR. Well, Flirt, now I am a match for thee, now I may keep you and there's little difference betwixt keeping a wench and marriage – only marriage is a little the cheaper but the other is the more honourable now, vert et bleu. Nay, now I may swear a French oath too. Come, come, I am thine. Let us strike up the bargain, thine according to the honourable institution of keeping, come.

FLIRT. Nay, hold, sir. Two words to the bargain. First, I have ne'er a lawyer here to draw articles and settlements.

MONSIEUR. How! Is the world come to that? A man cannot keep a wench without articles and settlements? Nay then, 'tis e'en as bad as marriage indeed and there's no difference betwixt a wife and a wench.

FLIRT. Only in cohabitation, for the first article shall be against cohabitation. We mistresses suffer no cohabitation.

MONSIEUR. Nor wives neither now.

FLIRT. Then separate maintenance, in case you should take a wife or I a new friend.

MONSIEUR. How! That too? Then you are every whit as bad as a wife.

FLIRT. Then my house in town and yours in the country, if you will.

MONSIEUR. A mere wife.

FLIRT. Then my coach apart, as well as my bed apart.

MONSIEUR. As bad as a wife still.

FLIRT. But take notice I will have no little, dirty, secondhand chariot new-furbished but a large, sociable, well-painted coach, nor will I keep it till it be as well known as myself and it comes to be called Flirt Coach; nor will I have such pitiful horses as cannot carry me every night to the park, for I will not miss a night in the park, I'd have you to know.

MONSIEUR. 'Tis very well. You must have your great, gilt, fine, painted coaches. I'm sure they are grown so common already amongst you that ladies of quality begin to take up with hackneys again, jarnie. But what else?

FLIRT. Then, that you do not think I will be served by a little dirty boy in a bonnet but a couple of handsome, lusty, cleanly footmen, fit to serve ladies of quality and do their business as they should do.

MONSIEUR. What then?

FLIRT. Then, that you never grow jealous of them.

MONSIEUR. Why, will you make so much of them?

FLIRT. I delight to be kind to my servants.

MONSIEUR. Well, is this all?

FLIRT. No. Then, that when you come to my house you never presume to touch a key, lift up a latch or thrust a door without knocking beforehand and that you ask no questions if you see a stray piece of plate, cabinet or looking-glass in my house.

---

694 *chariot*: a light four-wheeled carriage, less grand and splendid than the coach.

703 *hackneys*: hired coaches.

MONSIEUR. Just a wife in everything. But what else?

FLIRT. Then, that you take no acquaintance with me abroad nor bring me home any when you are drunk whom you will not be willing to see there when you are sober.

MONSIEUR. But what allowance? Let's come to the main business, the money.

FLIRT. Stay, let me think. First, for advance-money, five hundred pounds for pins.

MONSIEUR. A very wife.

FLIRT. Then you must take the lease of my house and furnish it as becomes one of my quality, for don't you think we'll take up with your old Queen Elizabeth furniture, as your wives do.

MONSIEUR. Indeed, there she is least like a wife, as she says.

FLIRT. Then, for housekeeping, servant wages, clothes and the rest, I'll be contented with a thousand pound a year present maintenance and but three hundred pound a year separate maintenance for my life, when our love grows cold. But I am contented with a thousand a year because for pendants, necklaces and all sorts of jewels and such trifles, nay, and some plate, I will shift myself as I can, make shifts, which you shall not take any notice of.

MONSIEUR. A thousand pound a year! What will wenching come to? Time was, a man might have fared as well at a much cheaper rate and a lady of one's affections, instead of a house, would have been contented with a little chamber three pair of stairs backward with a little closet or larder to't and, instead of variety of new gowns and rich petticoats, with her dishabillé or flame-colour gown called Indian and slippers of the same would have been contented for a twelvemonth and, instead of visits and gadding to plays, would have entertained herself at home with *St George for England*, *The Knight of the Sun* or *The*

---

731 *old Queen Elizabeth*: old-fashioned, not necessarily Elizabethan.

751 *flame-colour gown called Indian*: informal, undress gowns, worn only at home.

754–6 *St George . . . Piety*: *St George for England* is presumably

Practice of Piety and, instead of sending her wine and meat from the French houses, would have been contented if you had given her, poor wretch, but credit at the next chandler's and chequered cellar and then, instead of a coach, would have been well satisfied to have gone out and taken the air for three or four hours in the evening in the balcony, poor soul. Well, Flirt, however, we'll agree. 'Tis but three hundred pound a year separate maintenance, you say, when I am weary of thee and the charge.

DON DIEGO. [*aside*] Robbed of my honour, my daughter and my revenge too! Oh my dear honour! Nothing vexes me but that the world should say I had not Spanish policy enough to keep my daughter from being debauched from me. But methinks my Spanish policy might help me yet. I have it so; I will cheat 'em all, for I will declare I understood the whole plot and contrivance and connived at it, finding my cousin a fool and not answering my expectation. Well, but then if I approve of the match I must give this mock dancing-master my estate, especially since half he would have in right of my daughter and in spite of me. Well, I am resolved to turn the cheat upon themselves and give them my consent and estate.

MONSIEUR. Come, come, ne'er be troubled, uncle. 'Twas a combination, you see, of all these heads and your daughter's (you know what I mean, uncle) not to be thwarted or governed by all the Spanish policy in Christendom. I'm sure my French policy would not have governed her. So, since I have scaped her, I am glad to have scaped her, jernie.

Richard Johnson's tremendously popular *The Most Famous History of the Seven Champions of Christendom* (1596 and many subsequent editions); Summers suggested that *The Knight of the Sun* must be the hero of Diego Ortuñez de Calahorra's *The Mirrour of Princely Deedes and Knighthood* (translation published in 1580) but I find no evidence for any particular popularity; Lewis Bayly's *The Practice of Piety* was first published around 1610 and reprinted dozens of times in the century.

759 *chequered cellar*: tavern, from the common inn-sign of the chequered board.

CAUTION. Come, brother, you are wiser than I, you see, ay, ay.

DON DIEGO. No, you think you are wiser than I now in earnest. But know, while I was thought a gull, I gulled you all and made them and you think I knew nothing of the contrivance. Confess. Did you not think, verily, that I knew nothing of it and that I was a gull?

CAUTION. Yes, indeed, brother, I did think verily you were a gull.

HIPPOLITA. (*listening*) How's this?

DON DIEGO. Alas, alas, all the sputter I made was but to make this young man, my cousin, believe, when the thing should be effected, that it was not with my connivance or consent. But, since he is so well satisfied, I own it. For, do you think I would ever have suffered her to marry a monsieur? A monsieur, guarda! Besides, it had been but a beastly, incestuous kind of a match, voto.

CAUTION. Nay then, I see, brother, you were wiser than I indeed.

GERRARD. (*aside*) So, so.

CAUTION. Nay, young man, you have danced a fair dance for yourself royally and now you may go jig it together till you are both weary and, though you were so eager to have him, Mrs Minx, you'll soon have your bellyfull of him, let me tell you, mistress.

PRUE. Hah, ha.

MONSIEUR. How, uncle! What was't you said? Nay, if I had your Spanish policy against me, it was no wonder I missed of my aim, mon foy.

DON DIEGO. I was resolved too my daughter should not marry a coward, therefore made the more ado to try you, sir, but I find you are a brisk man of honour, firm, stiff, Spanish honour and that you may see I deceived you all along and you not me, ay, and am able to deceive you still, for I know now you think that I will give you little or nothing with my daughter (like other fathers) since you have married her without my consent but, I say, I'll deceive you now, for you shall have the most part of my estate in present and the rest at my death. There's for you. I think I have deceived you now, look you.

GERRARD. No, indeed, sir, you have not deceived me,

for I never suspected your love to your daughter nor your generosity.

DON DIEGO. How, sir! Have a care of saying I have not deceived you, lest I deceive you another way – guarda! Pray, gentlemen, do not think any man could deceive me, look you, that any man could steal my daughter, look you, without my connivance.
The less we speak the more we think
And he sees most that seems to wink.

HIPPOLITA. So, so, now I could give you my blessing, father, now you are a good complaisant father, indeed.
When children marry, parents should obey,
Since love claims more obedience far than they.

Exeunt omnes.

EPILOGUE, *spoken by* FLIRT

The ladies first I am to compliment,
Whom, if he could, the poet would content,
But to their pleasure then they must consent.
Most spoil their sport still by their modesty
And, when they should be pleased, cry out 'O fie'
And the least smooty jest will ne'er pass by.
But city damsel ne'er had confidence
At smooty play to take the least offence
But mercy shows to show her innocence.
Yet, lest the merchants' daughters should today
Be scandalised – not at our harmless play
But our Hippolita, since she's like one
Of us bold flirts of t'other end o'th'town –
Our poet, sending to you (though unknown)
His best respects by me, does frankly own
The character to be unnatural.
Hippolita is not like you at all.
You, while your lovers court you, still look grum
And, far from wooing, when they woo, cry 'Mum'
And if some of you e'er were stolen away

6 *smooty*: smutty.

Your portion's fault 'twas only, I dare say.
Thus much for him the poet bid me speak.
Now to the men I my own mind will break.
You good men o'th'Exchange, on whom alone
We must depend when sparks to sea are gone,
Into the pit already you are come –
'Tis but a step more to our tiring-room,
Where none of us but will be wondrous sweet
Upon an able love of Lumber Street.
You we had rather see between our scenes
Then spendthrift fops with better clothes and miens;
Instead of laced coats, belts and pantaloons,
Your velvet jumps, gold chains and grave fur gowns;
Instead of periwigs and broad cocked hats,
Your satin caps, small cuffs and vast cravats.
For you are fair and square in all your dealings;
You never cheat your doxies with gilt shillings;
You ne'er will break our windows – then you are
Fit to make love, while our houzas make war,
And, since all gentlemen must pack to sea
Our gallants and our judges must you be.
We therefore and our poet do submit
To all the camlet cloaks now i'the pit.

---

25 With the Dutch war imminent, many gentlemen had already volunteered.
27 *tiring-room*: dressing-room.
29 *Lumber Street*: Lombard Street, famous for its goldsmiths and bankers.
33 *jumps*: short coats.
35 *satin caps*: worn over the natural hair, as opposed to the gentleman's wig.
35 *small cuffs*: the fashion was for vast, open cuffs.
39 *houzas*: rakes.
43 *camlet*: camelhair or, more often, Angora goat hair.

THE

Country-Wife,

A

COMEDY,

Acted at the

THEATRE ROYAL.

Written by Mr. *Wycherley.*

Indignor quicquam reprehendi, non quia crassè
Compositum illepidéve putetur, sed quia nuper:
Nec veniam Antiquis, sed honorem & præmia posci.
Horat.

L O N D O N,

Printed for *Thomas Dring*, at the *Harrow*, at the Corner of *Chancery-Lane* in *Fleet-street*, 1675.

Title-page of the 1675 Quarto of *The Country Wife*, reproduced by permission of the British Library.

Motto

Horace, *Epistles*, II i 76–8:

'I am angry that any work is criticised, not because it is thought dull or inelegantly written but because it is modern, and that for the ancients they demand not indulgence but honour and rewards'

INTRODUCTORY NOTE

The ultimate source of Horner's stratagem in *The Country Wife* is Terence's *Eunuchus*, in which Chaerea disguises himself as a eunuch in order to gain access to Pamphila. But Wycherley owes nothing more than the disguise to Terence. Wycherley's major source for the Pinchwife plot is Molière. In *L'École des femmes* (1662) Wycherley found Arnolphe, a long-time despiser of marriage, who intends to marry Agnès, a girl brought up in the country apparently in total innocence on Arnolphe's instructions. Like Margery, Agnès admits her love, for Horace, to Arnolphe but he is easily convinced by the complete frankness of her declaration that there is nothing to it. In *L'École des maris* (1661), Isabelle makes Sganarelle carry a letter to Valère by pretending that it is a letter from Valère which she is returning unopened (see Margery's trick with her letter to Horner, carried by Pinchwife, in IV ii); later, Isabelle manages to escape to Valère by pretending to Sganarelle that her sister is planning to do so (see Margery's escape disguised as Alithea in V i). Wycherley's dialogue contains other fragmentary reminiscences of Molière but little of significance. Margery's reasons for not writing to Horner (IV ii 77ff) may derive from Furetière's *Le Roman Bourgeois* (Paris, 1666, translated as *Scarron's City Romance* in 1671).

The Country Wife was first performed by the King's Company at the Theatre Royal, Drury Lane, in January 1675; a performance recorded for 12 January was probably the first. Even though records are fragmentary, the play seems to have been a success, revived at various times for the rest of the century. Between 1700 and 1753 we know of 153 performances of the play and it held a regular place in the repertoire. But after 1753 Wycherley's play in its original form disappears from the stage until the 1920s. In 1765, John Lee turned the play into a two-act farce, performed as an after-piece at various times until the 1780s. In 1766 David Garrick completed the emasculation of Horner by turning him into Belville in *The Country Girl*. Garrick's version retains some of Wycherley's comedy but without any of its satiric bite and also without any sexual improprieties. Only in this sterilised form was Wycherley's play to be performed. Garrick's version was revived in 1979 by Cambridge Theatre Company. In February 1924, the Phoenix Society revived Wycherley's original version at the Regent Theatre; once the audience had got over the 'shock' of seeing Wycherley uncensored, the production was a success. Still in an adapted form, the play was performed at the Everyman Theatre, Hampstead, in December

1926. *The Country Wife* only fully re-established its place with the production by Baliol Holloway at the Ambassadors Theatre in 1934. In 1936 it was performed at the Old Vic, with Michael Redgrave as Horner, Edith Evans as Lady Fidget and Ruth Gordon as Margery. Since then there have been major productions at the Theatre Royal, Stratford East, directed by Tony Richardson (1955), at the Royal Court, directed by George Devine with Joan Plowright as Margery (1956), at Chichester Festival Theatre with Maggie Smith as Margery (1969) and at the National Theatre in a disappointing production directed by Peter Hall with Albert Finney as Horner (1977), as well as countless other productions professional and amateur.

The play was first published in 1675 and there were further quarto editions in 1683, 1688 and 1695 (two). In recent years there have been three editions of the play published separately: Thomas H. Fujimura edited the play for the Regents Restoration Drama Series (1965); John Dixon Hunt's edition with some good annotation and a lively introduction appeared in the New Mermaids series in 1973; David Cook and John Swannell edited the play for the Revels Plays in 1975, but their annotation is often excessive and their introduction disappointingly dull. Scolar Press published a facsimile of the first edition in 1970.

PROLOGUE, *spoken by Mr Hart*

Poets, like cudgelled bullies, never do
At first or second blow submit to you;
But will provoke you still, and ne'er have done,
Till you are weary first with laying on.
The late so baffled scribbler of this day,
Though he stands trembling, bids me boldly say,
What we before most plays are used to do,
For poets out of fear first draw on you;
In a fierce prologue the still pit defy
And ere you speak, like Castril, give the lie.
But though our Bayes's battles oft I've fought,
And with bruised knuckles their dear conquests bought;
Nay, never yet feared odds upon the stage,
In prologue dare not hector with the age,
But would take quarter from your saving hands,
Though Bayes within all yielding countermands,
Says you confederate wits no quarter give,
Therefore his play shan't ask your leave to live.
Well, let the vain rash fop, by huffing so,
Think to obtain the better terms of you;
But we the actors humbly will submit,
Now, and at any time, to a full pit;
Nay, often we anticipate your rage,
And murder poets for you on our stage.
We set no guards upon our tiring-room,
But when with flying colours there you come,
We patiently, you see, give up to you
Our poets, virgins, nay, our matrons too.

---

1 *bullies*: ruffians.
5 A comment on the failure of *The Gentleman Dancing-Master*.
10 *Castril*: the 'angry boy' of Ben Jonson's *The Alchemist* (1610).
11 *Bayes*: the name given by George Villiers, Duke of Buckingham, to his parody of Dryden in *The Rehearsal* (1671). Charles Hart usually played the hero in Dryden's tragedies. The name was also used for any poet, as in line 16 for Wycherley.
19 *huffing*: blustering.
25 *tiring-room*: dressing-room.

THE PERSONS

MR HORNER	*Mr Hart*
MR HARCOURT	*Mr Kynaston*
MR DORILANT	*Mr Lydal*
MR PINCHWIFE	*Mr Mohun*
MR SPARKISH	*Mr Haines*
SIR JASPAR FIDGET	*Mr Cartwright*
MRS MARGERY PINCHWIFE	*Mrs Boutell*
MRS ALITHEA	*Mrs James*
MY LADY FIDGET	*Mrs Knep*
MRS DAINTY FIDGET	*Mrs Corbet*
MRS SQUEAMISH	*Mrs Wyatt*
OLD LADY SQUEAMISH	*Mrs Rutter*
Waiters, servants, and attendants	
A BOY	
A QUACK	*Mr Shatterel*
LUCY, Alithea's maid	*Mrs Corey*
[CLASP]	
[A Parson]	

The Scene: *London*

THE COUNTRY WIFE

ACT I

SCENE I

Enter HORNER, *and* QUACK *following him at a distance.*

HORNER. (*aside*) A quack is as fit for a pimp as a midwife for a bawd; they are still but in their way both helpers of nature. – Well, my dear doctor, hast thou done what I desired?

QUACK. I have undone you forever with the women, and reported you throughout the whole town as bad as an eunuch, with as much trouble as if I had made you one in earnest.

HORNER. But have you told all the midwives you know, the orange-wenches at the playhouses, the city husbands, and old fumbling keepers of this end of the town? For they'll be the readiest to report it.

QUACK. I have told all the chambermaids, waiting-women, tire-women and old women of my acquaintance; nay, and whispered it as a secret to 'em, and to the whisperers of Whitehall; so that you need not doubt, 'twill spread, and you will be as odious to the handsome young women as –

HORNER. As the smallpox. Well –

QUACK. And to the married women of this end of the town as –

HORNER. As the great ones; nay, as their own husbands.

QUACK. And to the city dames as aniseed Robin of filthy and contemptible memory; and they will frighten their children with your name, especially their females.

---

10 *orange-wenches*: orange-sellers.
11 *keepers*: men who maintain a mistress.
11–12 *this end of the town*: the fashionable, west, end of London, away from the merchants in the city.
14 *tire-women*: ladies' maids.
16 *Whitehall*: the king's residence and the ideal place for gossip.
22 *great ones*: syphilis.
23 *aniseed Robin*: a famous hermaphrodite; Charles Cotton wrote a burlesque epitaph on him (*Poems*, 1689).

HORNER. And cry, 'Horner's coming to carry you away.' I am only afraid 'twill not be believed. You told 'em 'twas by an English–French disaster and an English–French chirurgeon, who has given me at once, not only a cure, but an antidote for the future against that damned malady, and that worse distemper, love, and all other women's evils.

QUACK. Your late journey into France has made it the more credible and your being here a fortnight before you appeared in public looks as if you apprehended the shame, which I wonder you do not. Well, I have been hired by young gallants to belie 'em t'other way, but you are the first would be thought a man unfit for women.

HORNER. Dear Mr Doctor, let vain rogues be contented only to be thought abler men than they are, generally 'tis all the pleasure they have; but mine lies another way.

QUACK. You take, methinks, a very preposterous way to it and as ridiculous as if we operators in physic should put forth bills to disparage our medicaments, with hopes to gain customers.

HORNER. Doctor, there are quacks in love as well as physic, who get but the fewer and worse patients for their boasting; a good name is seldom got by giving it oneself, and women no more than honour are compassed by bragging. Come, come, doctor, the wisest lawyer never discovers the merits of his cause till the trial; the wealthiest man conceals his riches, and the cunning gamester his play. Shy husbands and keepers, like old rooks, are not to be cheated but by a new unpractised trick; false friendship will pass now no more than false dice upon 'em; no, not in the city.

Enter BOY.

BOY. There are two ladies and a gentleman coming up. *Exit.*

29–30 *English–French . . . chirurgeon*: the French disease, syphilis, caught by an Englishman from an English whore and cured by an English surgeon specialising in venereal diseases. See Additional Note.

57 *rooks*: cheats, sharpers.

HORNER. A pox! Some unbelieving sisters of my former acquaintance, who, I am afraid, expect their sense should be satisfied of the falsity of the report. No – this formal fool and women!

Enter SIR JASPAR FIDGET, LADY FIDGET *and* MRS DAINTY FIDGET

QUACK. His wife and sister.

SIR JASPAR. My coach breaking just now before your door, sir, I look upon as an occasional reprimand to me, sir, for not kissing your hands, sir, since your coming out of France, sir; and so my disaster, sir, has been my good fortune, sir; and this is my wife, and sister, sir.

HORNER. What then, sir?

SIR JASPAR. My lady, and sister, sir. – Wife, this is Master Horner.

LADY FIDGET. Master Horner, husband!

SIR JASPAR. My lady, my Lady Fidget, sir.

HORNER. So, sir.

SIR JASPAR. Won't you be acquainted with her, sir? (*Aside*) So the report is true, I find, by his coldness or aversion to the sex; but I'll play the wag with him. – Pray salute my wife, my lady, sir.

HORNER. I will kiss no man's wife, sir, for him, sir; I have taken my eternal leave, sir, of the sex already, sir.

SIR JASPAR. (*aside*) Hah, hah, hah! I'll plague him yet. – Not know my wife, sir?

HORNER. I do know your wife, sir; she's a woman, sir, and consequently a monster, sir, a greater monster than a husband, sir.

SIR JASPAR. A husband! How, sir?

HORNER. (*makes horns*) So, sir; but I make no more cuckolds, sir.

SIR JASPAR. Hah, hah, hah! Mercury, Mercury!

LADY FIDGET. Pray, Sir Jaspar, let us be gone from this rude fellow.

---

65 *formal*: pompous.

68 *occasional*: timely.

91 s.d. *makes horns*: the sign of a cuckold, indicated with his fore-fingers on his forehead.

93 *Mercury*: used in the treatment of syphilis.

DAINTY. Who, by his breeding, would think he had ever been in France?

LADY FIDGET. Foh, he's but too much a French fellow, such as hate women of quality and virtue for their love to their husbands, Sir Jaspar; a woman is hated by 'em as much for loving her husband as for loving their money. But pray, let's be gone.

HORNER. You do well, madam, for I have nothing that you came for; I have brought over not so much as a bawdy picture, new postures, nor the second part of the *École des Filles*, nor –

QUACK. (*apart to* HORNER) Hold, for shame, sir! What d'ye mean? You'll ruin yourself forever with the sex –

SIR JASPAR. Hah, hah, hah, he hates women perfectly, I find.

DAINTY. What a pity 'tis he should.

LADY FIDGET. Ay, he's a base, rude fellow for't; but affectation makes not a woman more odious to them than virtue.

HORNER. Because your virtue is your greatest affectation madam.

LADY FIDGET. How, you saucy fellow! Would you wrong my honour?

HORNER. If I could.

LADY FIDGET. How d'ye mean, sir?

SIR JASPAR. Hah, hah, hah! No, he can't wrong your ladyship's honour, upon my honour; he, poor man – hark you in your ear – a mere eunuch.

LADY FIDGET. O filthy French beast, foh, foh! Why do we stay? Let's be gone; I can't endure the sight of him.

SIR JASPAR. Stay but till the chairs come; they'll be here presently.

LADY FIDGET. No, no.

---

105 *new postures*: pornographic engravings like those by Giulio Romano published with Pietro Aretino's notorious *Sonnetti lussuriosi* (1523).

106 *École des filles*: (Q1 *de*) Michel Millot's bawdy dialogues, first published and suppressed in Paris in 1655. Pepys guiltily bought a copy on 8 February 1668.

128 *chairs*: sedan chairs.

129 *presently*: at once.

SIR JASPAR. Nor can I stay longer. 'Tis – let me see, a quarter and a half quarter of a minute past eleven; the Council will be sat, I must away. Business must be preferred always before love and ceremony with the wise, Mr Horner.

HORNER. And the impotent, Sir Jaspar.

SIR JASPAR. Ay, ay, the impotent, Master Horner, hah, ha, ha!

LADY FIDGET. What, leave us with a filthy man alone in his lodgings?

SIR JASPAR. He's an innocent man now, you know. Pray stay, I'll hasten the chairs to you. – Mr Horner, your servant; I should be glad to see you at my house. Pray come and dine with me, and play at cards with my wife after dinner; you are fit for women at that game yet, hah, ha! (*Aside*) 'Tis as much a husband's prudence to provide innocent diversion for a wife as to hinder her unlawful pleasures, and he had better employ her than let her employ herself. – Farewell. *Exit* SIR JASPAR.

HORNER. Your servant, Sir Jaspar.

LADY FIDGET. I will not stay with him, foh!

HORNER. Nay, madam, I beseech you stay, if it be but to see I can be as civil to ladies yet as they would desire.

LADY FIDGET. No, no, foh, you cannot be civil to ladies.

DAINTY. You as civil as ladies would desire?

LADY FIDGET. No, no, no, foh, foh, foh!

Exeunt LADY FIDGET *and* DAINTY.

QUACK. Now, I think, I, or you yourself rather, have done your business with the women.

HORNER. Thou art an ass. Don't you see already, upon the report and my carriage, this grave man of business leaves his wife in my lodgings, invites me to his house and wife, who before would not be acquainted with me out of jealousy?

QUACK. Nay, by this means you may be the more acquainted with the husbands, but the less with the wives.

---

133 *Council*: Privy Council.
161 *done your business*: ruined you.
163 *carriage*: behaviour.

HORNER. Let me alone; if I can but abuse the husbands, I'll soon disabuse the wives. Stay – I'll reckon you up the advantages I am like to have by my stratagem: first, I shall be rid of all my old acquaintances, the most insatiable sorts of duns, that invade our lodgings in a morning. And next to the pleasure of making a new mistress is that of being rid of an old one; and of all old debts, love, when it comes to be so, is paid the most unwillingly.

QUACK. Well, you may be so rid of your old acquaintances; but how will you get any new ones?

HORNER. Doctor, thou wilt never make a good chemist, thou art so incredulous and impatient. Ask but all the young fellows of the town if they do not lose more time, like huntsmen, in starting the game than in running it down; one knows not where to find 'em, who will or will not. Women of quality are so civil, you can hardly distinguish love from good breeding and a man is often mistaken; but now I can be sure, she that shows an aversion to me loves the sport, as those women that are gone, whom I warrant to be right. And then the next thing is, your women of honour, as you call 'em, are only chary of their reputations, not their persons, and 'tis scandal they would avoid, not men. Now may I have, by the reputation of an eunuch, the privileges of one and be seen in a lady's chamber in a morning as early as her husband, kiss virgins before their parents or lovers and may be, in short, the *passe partout* of the town. Now, doctor.

QUACK. Nay, now you shall be the doctor; and your process is so new that we do not know but it may succeed.

HORNER. Not so new neither; *probatum est*, doctor.

QUACK. Well, I wish you luck and many patients whilst I go to mine. *Exit* QUACK.

---

174 *duns*: importunate creditors.
181 *chemist*: alchemist.
190 *right*: game, promiscuous.
198 *passe partout*: one permitted to go anywhere.
202 *probatum est*: tried and tested, used of prescriptions. Perhaps a reference to Wycherley's revival of Terence's stratagem.

Enter HARCOURT *and* DORILANT *to* HORNER.

HARCOURT. Come, your appearance at the play yesterday has, I hope, hardened you for the future against the women's contempt and the men's raillery and now you'll abroad as you were wont.

HORNER. Did I not bear it bravely?

DORILANT. With a most theatrical impudence; nay, more than the orange-wenches show there or a drunken vizard-mask or a great-bellied actress; nay, or the most impudent of creatures, an ill poet; or what is yet more impudent, a secondhand critic.

HORNER. But what say the ladies? Have they no pity?

HARCOURT. What ladies? The vizard-masks, you know, never pity a man when all's gone, though in their service.

DORILANT. And for the women in the boxes, you'd never pity them when 'twas in your power.

HARCOURT. They say, 'tis pity, but all that deal with common women should be served so.

DORILANT. Nay, I dare swear, they won't admit you to play at cards with them, go to plays with 'em, or do the little duties which other shadows of men are wont to do for 'em.

HORNER. Who do you call shadows of men?

DORILANT. Half-men.

HORNER. What, boys?

DORILANT. Ay, your old boys, old *beaux garçons*, who, like superannuated stallions, are suffered to run, feed and whinny with the mares as long as they live, though they can do nothing else.

HORNER. Well, a pox on love and wenching! Women serve but to keep a man from better company; though I can't enjoy them, I shall you the more. Good fellowship and friendship are lasting, rational and manly pleasures.

HARCOURT. For all that, give me some of those pleasures you call effeminate too; they help to relish one another.

---

212 *vizard-mask*: a prostitute, so called from the fashionable masks they wore.

230 *beaux garçons*: ageing gallants.

HORNER. They disturb one another.

HARCOURT. No, mistresses are like books. If you pore upon them too much, they doze you and make you unfit for company; but if used discreetly, you are the fitter for conversation by 'em.

DORILANT. A mistress should be like a little country retreat near the town, not to dwell in constantly, but only for a night and away, to taste the town the better when a man returns.

HORNER. I tell you, 'tis as hard to be a good fellow, a good friend and a lover of women, as 'tis to be a good fellow, a good friend and a lover of money. You cannot follow both, then choose your side. Wine gives you liberty, love takes it away.

DORILANT. Gad, he's in the right on't.

HORNER. Wine gives you joy; love, grief and tortures, besides the chirurgeon's. Wine makes us witty; love, only sots. Wine makes us sleep; love breaks it.

DORILANT. By the world, he has reason, Harcourt.

HORNER. Wine makes –

DORILANT. Ay, wine makes us – makes us princes; love makes us beggars, poor rogues, ygad – and wine –

HORNER. So, there's one converted. – No, no, love and wine, oil and vinegar.

HARCOURT. I grant it; love will still be uppermost.

HORNER. Come, for my part I will have only those glorious, manly pleasures of being very drunk and very slovenly.

Enter BOY.

BOY. Mr Sparkish is below, sir. *Exit.*

HARCOURT. What, my dear friend! A rogue that is fond of me only, I think, for abusing him.

DORILANT. No, he can no more think the men laugh at him than that women jilt him, his opinion of himself is so good.

HORNER. Well, there's another pleasure by drinking I thought not of: I shall lose his acquaintance, because

---

244 *doze*: befuddle.
258 *chirurgeon's. Wine*: Chirurgeon's Wine Q1.
260 *has reason*: is right (from French).
274 *jilt*: deceive.

he cannot drink; and you know 'tis a very hard thing to be rid of him, for he's one of those nauseous offerers at wit, who, like the worst fiddlers, run themselves into all companies.

HARCOURT. One that, by being in the company of men of sense, would pass for one.

HORNER. And may so to the short-sighted world, as a false jewel amongst true ones is not discerned at a distance. His company is as troublesome to us as a cuckold's when you have a mind to his wife's.

HARCOURT. No, the rogue will not let us enjoy one another, but ravishes our conversation, though he signifies no more to't than Sir Martin Mar-all's gaping and awkward thrumming upon the lute does to his man's voice and music.

DORILANT. And to pass for a wit in town shows himself a fool every night to us that are guilty of the plot.

HORNER. Such wits as he are, to a company of reasonable men, like rooks to the gamesters, who only fill a room at the table, but are so far from contributing to the play that they only serve to spoil the fancy of those that do.

DORILANT. Nay, they are used like rooks too, snubbed, checked and abused; yet the rogues will hang on.

HORNER. A pox on 'em, and all that force nature and would be still what she forbids 'em! Affectation is her greatest monster.

HARCOURT. Most men are the contraries to that they would seem. Your bully, you see, is a coward with a long sword; the little, humbly fawning physician, with his ebony cane, is he that destroys men.

DORILANT. The usurer, a poor rogue possessed of mouldy bonds and mortgages, and we they call spendthrifts are only wealthy, who lay out his money upon daily new purchases of pleasure.

HORNER. Ay, your arrantest cheat is your trustee or executor; your jealous man, the greatest cuckold;

---

284 *short-sighted*: short-sighed Q1.

290 *Sir Martin Mar-all*: the foolish hero of Dryden's comedy of that name (1667) who serenades his mistress by miming to the performance of his out-of-sight servant. Sir Martin forgets to stop when his servant does and is found out.

296 *rooks*: here, *fools* rather than *cheats*.

your churchman, the greatest atheist; and your noisy, pert rogue of a wit, the greatest fop, dullest ass and worst company, as you shall see: for here he comes.

Enter SPARKISH *to them.*

SPARKISH. How is't, sparks, how is't? Well, faith, Harry, I must rally thee a little, ha, ha, ha, upon the report in town of thee, ha, ha, ha, I can't hold i'faith; shall I speak?

HORNER. Yes, but you'll be so bitter then.

SPARKISH. Honest Dick and Frank here shall answer for me, I will not be extreme bitter, by the universe.

HARCOURT. We will be bound in ten thousand pound bond, he shall not be bitter at all.

DORILANT. Nor sharp, nor sweet.

HORNER. What, not downright insipid?

SPARKISH. Nay then, since you are so brisk and provoke me, take what follows. You must know, I was discoursing and rallying with some ladies yesterday, and they happened to talk of the fine new signs in town.

HORNER. Very fine ladies, I believe.

SPARKISH. Said I, 'I know where the best new sign is.' 'Where?' says one of the ladies. 'In Covent Garden,' I replied. Said another, 'In what street?' 'In Russell Street,' answered I. 'Lord,' says another, 'I'm sure there was ne'er a fine new sign there yesterday.' 'Yes, but there was,' said I again, 'and it came out of France and has been there a fortnight.'

DORILANT. A pox, I can hear no more, prithee.

HORNER. No, hear him out; let him tune his crowd a while.

HARCOURT. The worst music, the greatest preparation.

SPARKISH. Nay, faith, I'll make you laugh. 'It cannot be,' says a third lady. 'Yes, yes,' quoth I again. Says a fourth lady –

HORNER. Look to't, we'll have no more ladies.

SPARKISH. No – then mark, mark, now. Said I to the fourth, 'Did you never see Mr Horner? He lodges in

---

332 *signs*: hung over shops to indicate the trade.
335 *Covent Garden*: then the most fashionable part of London.
342 *crowd*: fiddle, with a pun on Sparkish's audience.

Russell Street, and he's a sign of a man, you know, since he came out of France.' Heh, hah, he!

HORNER. But the devil take me, if thine be the sign of a jest.

SPARKISH. With that they all fell a-laughing, till they bepissed themselves. What, but it does not move you, methinks? Well, I see one had as good go to law without a witness as break a jest without a laugher on one's side. Come, come, sparks, but where do we dine? I have left at Whitehall an earl to dine with you.

DORILANT. Why, I thought thou hadst loved a man with a title better than a suit with a French trimming to't.

HARCOURT. Go, to him again.

SPARKISH. No, sir, a wit to me is the greatest title in the world.

HORNER. But go dine with your earl, sir; he may be exceptious. We are your friends and will not take it ill to be left, I do assure you.

HARCOURT. Nay, faith, he shall go to him.

SPARKISH. Nay, pray, gentlemen.

DORILANT. We'll thrust you out, if you wo'not. What, disappoint anybody for us?

SPARKISH. Nay, dear gentlemen, hear me.

HORNER. No, no, sir, by no means; pray go, sir.

SPARKISH. Why, dear rogues –

DORILANT. No, no.

They all thrust him out of the room.

ALL. Ha, ha, ha!

SPARKISH *returns.*

SPARKISH. But, sparks, pray hear me. What, d'ye think I'll eat then with gay, shallow fops and silent coxcombs? I think wit as necessary at dinner as a glass of good wine, and that's the reason I never have any stomach when I eat alone. – Come, but where do we dine?

HORNER. Even where you will.

---

357 *I*: Q1 omits.
362 *French trimming*: a pun on Horner's 'state'.
364 see Additional Note.
368 *exceptious*: vexed.

SPARKISH. At Chateline's?

DORILANT. Yes, if you will.

SPARKISH. Or at the Cock?

DORILANT. Yes, if you please.

SPARKISH. Or at the Dog and Partridge?

HORNER. Ay, if you have a mind to't, for we shall dine at neither.

SPARKISH. Pshaw, with your fooling we shall lose the new play; and I would no more miss seeing a new play the first day than I would miss setting in the wits' row. Therefore I'll go fetch my mistress and away.

Exit SPARKISH.

Manent HORNER, HARCOURT, DORILANT.

Enter to them MR PINCHWIFE.

HORNER. Who have we here? Pinchwife?

PINCHWIFE. Gentlemen, your humble servant.

HORNER. Well, Jack, by the long absence from the town, the grumness of thy countenance and the slovenliness of thy habit, I should give thee joy, should I not, of marriage?

PINCHWIFE. (*aside*) Death! Does he know I'm married too? I thought to have concealed it from him at least. – My long stay in the country will excuse my dress and I have a suit of law, that brings me up to town, that puts me out of humour; besides, I must give Sparkish tomorrow five thousand pound to lie with my sister.

HORNER. Nay, you country gentlemen, rather than not purchase, will buy anything; and he is a cracked title, if we may quibble. Well, but am I to give thee joy? I heard thou wert married.

PINCHWIFE. What then?

HORNER. Why, the next thing that is to be heard is thou'rt a cuckold.

---

386 *Chateline's*: a famous French restaurant in Covent Garden.

388 *the Cock*: out of many possible taverns, most probably the one in Bow Street; see *The Plain-Dealer*, Act V Scene ii.

390 *the Dog and Partridge*: a tavern in Fleet Street.

391 *a mind*: mind Q1.

400 *grumness*: sullenness.

408 *five thousand pound*: as a dowry.

411 *cracked title*: an unsound right of ownership; *cracked* also means foolish.

PINCHWIFE. (*aside*) Insupportable name!

HORNER. But I did not expect marriage from such a whoremaster as you, one that knew the town so much and women so well.

PINCHWIFE. Why, I have married no London wife.

HORNER. Pshaw, that's all one; that grave circumspection in marrying a country wife is like refusing a deceitful, pampered Smithfield jade to go and be cheated by a friend in the country.

PINCHWIFE. (*aside*) A pox on him and his simile. – At least we are a little surer of the breed there, know what her keeping has been, whether foiled or unsound.

HORNER. Come, come, I have known a clap gotten in Wales; and there are cozens, justices, clerks and chaplains in the country, I won't say coachmen. But she's handsome and young?

PINCHWIFE. (*aside*) I'll answer as I should do. – No, no, she has no beauty but her youth; no attraction but her modesty; wholesome, homely and housewifely; that's all.

DORILANT. He talks as like a grazier as he looks.

PINCHWIFE. She's too awkward, ill-favoured, and silly to bring to town.

HARCOURT. Then methinks you should bring her, to be taught breeding.

PINCHWIFE. To be taught! No, sir! I thank you. Good wives and private soldiers should be ignorant. [*Aside*] I'll keep her from your instructions, I warrant you.

HARCOURT. (*aside*) The rogue is as jealous as if his wife were not ignorant.

HORNER. Why, if she be ill-favoured, there will be less danger here for you than by leaving her in the country; we have such variety of dainties that we are seldom hungry.

---

419 *whoremaster*: a man experienced in whoring.

424 *Smithfield jade*: a worn-out horse bought at Smithfield Market, a place notorious for sharp practice; *jade* also means a disreputable woman.

428 *foiled*: injured, defective (horse); deflowered, diseased (woman)

429 *clap*: syphilis.

430 *cozens*: cheats.

437 *grazier*: grazer of cattle fattened for market.

441 *breeding*: (*a*) gentility (*b*) pregnancy.

DORILANT. But they have always coarse, constant, swingeing stomachs in the country.

HARCOURT. Foul feeders indeed.

DORILANT. And your hospitality is great there.

HARCOURT. Open house, every man's welcome.

PINCHWIFE. So, so, gentlemen.

HORNER. But, prithee, why wouldst thou marry her? If she be ugly, ill-bred and silly, she must be rich then.

PINCHWIFE. As rich as if she brought me twenty thousand pound out of this town, for she'll be as sure not to spend her moderate portion as a London baggage would be to spend hers, let it be what it would; so 'tis all one. Then, because she's ugly, she's the likelier to be my own; and being ill-bred, she'll have conversation; and since silly and innocent, will not know the difference betwixt a man of one-and-twenty and one of forty.

HORNER. Nine – to my knowledge; but if she be silly, she'll expect as much from a man of forty-nine as from him of one-and-twenty. But methinks wit is more necessary than beauty, and I think no young woman ugly that has it, and no handsome woman agreeable without it.

PINCHWIFE. 'Tis my maxim, he's a fool that marries, but he's a greater that does not marry a fool. What is wit in a wife good for, but to make a man a cuckold?

HORNER. Yes, to keep it from his knowledge.

PINCHWIFE. A fool cannot contrive to make her husband a cuckold.

HORNER. No, but she'll club with a man that can; and what is worse, if she cannot make her husband a cuckold, she'll make him jealous and pass for one, and then 'tis all one.

PINCHWIFE. Well, well, I'll take care for one, my wife shall make me no cuckold, though she had your help, Mr Horner; I understand the town, sir.

DORILANT. (*aside*) His help!

HARCOURT. (*aside*) He's come newly to town, it seems, and has not heard how things are with him.

HORNER. But tell me, has marriage cured thee of whoring, which it seldom does?

---

452 *swingeing stomachs*: enormous appetites.
479 *club*: get together with.

HARCOURT. 'Tis more than age can do.

HORNER. No, the word is, I'll marry and live honest; but a marriage vow is like a penitent gamester's oath and entering into bonds and penalties to stint himself to such a particular small sum at play for the future, which makes him but the more eager and, not being able to hold out, loses his money again and his forfeit to boot.

DORILANT. Ay, ay, a gamester will be a gamester whilst his money lasts, and a whoremaster whilst his vigour.

HARCOURT. Nay, I have known 'em, when they are broke and can lose no more, keep a-fumbling with the box in their hands to fool with only and hinder other gamesters.

DORILANT. That had wherewithal to make lusty stakes.

PINCHWIFE. Well, gentlemen, you may laugh at me, but you shall never lie with my wife; I know the town.

HORNER. But prithee, was not the way you were in better? Is not keeping better than marriage?

PINCHWIFE. A pox on't! The jades would jilt me; I could never keep a whore to myself.

HORNER. So, then you only married to keep a whore to yourself. Well, but let me tell you, women, as you say, are like soldiers, made constant and loyal by good pay rather than by oaths and covenants. Therefore I'd advise my friends to keep rather than marry, since too, I find, by your example, it does not serve one's turn, for I saw you yesterday in the eighteen-penny place with a pretty country wench.

PINCHWIFE. (*aside*) How the devil! Did he see my wife then? I sat there that she might not be seen. But she shall never go to a play again.

HORNER. What, dost thou blush at nine-and-forty, for having been seen with a wench?

DORILANT. No, faith, I warrant 'twas his wife, which he seated there out of sight, for he's a cunning rogue and understands the town.

---

503 *box*: for shaking the dice.

518–19 *eighteen-penny place*: the middle gallery of the theatre, frequented by citizens and whores.

HARCOURT. He blushes. Then 'twas his wife, for men are now more ashamed to be seen with them in public than with a wench.

PINCHWIFE. (*aside*) Hell and damnation! I'm undone, since Horner has seen her and they know 'twas she.

HORNER. But prithee, was it thy wife? She was exceedingly pretty; I was in love with her at that distance.

PINCHWIFE. You are like never to be nearer to her. Your servant, gentlemen. (*Offers to go*)

HORNER. Nay, prithee stay.

PINCHWIFE. I cannot, I will not.

HORNER. Come, you shall dine with us.

PINCHWIFE. I have dined already.

HORNER. Come, I know thou hast not. I'll treat thee, dear rogue; thou shalt spend none of thy Hampshire money today.

PINCHWIFE. (*aside*) Treat me! So, he uses me already like his cuckold.

HORNER. Nay, you shall not go.

PINCHWIFE. I must, I have business at home.

Exit PINCHWIFE.

HARCOURT. To beat his wife; he's as jealous of her as a Cheapside husband of a Covent Garden wife.

HORNER. Why, 'tis as hard to find an old whoremaster without jealousy and the gout, as a young one without fear or the pox.

As gout in age from pox in youth proceeds,
So wenching past, then jealousy succeeds,
The worst disease that love and wenching breeds.

[*Exeunt.*]

---

537 s.d. *Offers*: attempts.

550 *Cheapside . . . wife*: a city merchant of a fashionable wife.

ACT II

SCENE I

MRS MARGERY PINCHWIFE *and* ALITHEA. MR PINCHWIFE *peeping behind at the door.*

MRS PINCHWIFE. Pray, sister, where are the best fields and woods to walk in, in London?

ALITHEA. A pretty question! Why, sister, Mulberry Garden and St James's Park and, for close walks, the New Exchange.

MRS PINCHWIFE. Pray, sister, tell me why my husband looks so grum here in town and keeps me up so close and will not let me go a-walking, nor let me wear my best gown yesterday.

ALITHEA. Oh, he's jealous, sister.

MRS PINCHWIFE. Jealous? What's that?

ALITHEA. He's afraid you should love another man.

MRS PINCHWIFE. How should he be afraid of my loving another man, when he will not let me see any but himself?

ALITHEA. Did he not carry you yesterday to a play?

MRS PINCHWIFE. Ay, but we sat amongst ugly people; he would not let me come near the gentry, who sat under us, so that I could not see 'em. He told me none but naughty women sat there, whom they toused and moused. But I would have ventured for all that.

ALITHEA. But how did you like the play?

3–4 *Mulberry Garden*: a garden of mulberry trees, now the site of Buckingham Palace, a fashionable meeting-place. *Love in a Wood*, Act V Scene ii, is set in 'the dining-room in Mulberry Garden House'.

4 *St James's Park*: the park near Whitehall, scene of Act II and part of Act V of *Love in a Wood* – and also its subtitle.

4 *close*: covered.

5 *New Exchange*: an arcade with two galleries of shops, situated south of the Strand; it is the setting for Act III Scene ii of *The Country Wife*.

7 *grum*: sullen.

21 *toused and moused*: rumpled and played with, usually sexily.

MRS PINCHWIFE. Indeed, I was a-weary of the play, but I liked hugeously the actors; they are the goodliest, properest men, sister!

ALITHEA. O, but you must not like the actors, sister.

MRS PINCHWIFE. Ay, how should I help it, sister? Pray, sister, when my husband comes in, will you ask leave for me to go a-walking?

ALITHEA. (*aside*) A-walking, hah, ha! Lord, a country gentlewoman's leisure is the drudgery of a foot-post; and she requires as much airing as her husband's horses.

Enter MR PINCHWIFE *to them.*

But here comes your husband; I'll ask, though I'm sure he'll not grant it.

MRS PINCHWIFE. He says he won't let me go abroad for fear of catching the pox.

ALITHEA. Fie! The smallpox you should say.

MRS PINCHWIFE. O my dear, dear bud, welcome home! Why dost thou look so fropish? Who has nangered thee?

PINCHWIFE. You're a fool.

MRS PINCHWIFE *goes aside and cries.*

ALITHEA. Faith, so she is, for crying for no fault, poor tender creature!

PINCHWIFE. What, you would have her as impudent as yourself, as arrant a jill-flirt, a gadder, a magpie and, to say all, a mere notorious town-woman?

ALITHEA. Brother, you are my only censurer; and the honour of your family shall sooner suffer in your wife there than in me, though I take the innocent liberty of the town.

PINCHWIFE. Hark you, mistress, do not talk so before my wife. The innocent liberty of the town!

ALITHEA. Why, pray, who boasts of any intrigue with me? What lampoon has made my name notorious?

---

32 *foot-post*: letter-carrier on foot.
41 *fropish*: peevish.
41 *nangered*: angered.
47 *jill-flirt, a gadder, a magpie*: a wanton girl, a gadabout, an idle chatterer.
56 *lampoon*: scurrilous satire.

What ill women frequent my lodgings? I keep no company with any women of scandalous reputations.

PINCHWIFE. No, you keep the men of scandalous reputations company.

ALITHEA. Where? Would you not have me civil? Answer 'em in a box at the plays? In the drawing room at Whitehall? In St James's Park? Mulberry Gardens? Or –

PINCHWIFE. Hold, hold! Do not teach my wife where the men are to be found! I believe she's the worse for your town documents already. I bid you keep her in ignorance, as I do.

MRS PINCHWIFE. Indeed, be not angry with her, bud; she will tell me nothing of the town, though I ask her a thousand times a day.

PINCHWIFE. Then you are very inquisitive to know, I find!

MRS PINCHWIFE. Not I, indeed, dear; I hate London. Our place-house in the country is worth a thousand of't; would I were there again!

PINCHWIFE. So you shall, I warrant. But were you not talking of plays and players when I came in? [*To* ALITHEA] You are her encourager in such discourses.

MRS PINCHWIFE. No, indeed, dear; she chid me just now for liking the playermen.

PINCHWIFE. (*aside*) Nay, if she be so innocent as to own to me her liking them, there is no hurt in't. – Come, my poor rogue, but thou lik'st none better than me?

MRS PINCHWIFE. Yes, indeed, but I do; the playermen are finer folks.

PINCHWIFE. But you love none better than me?

MRS PINCHWIFE. You are mine own dear bud, and I know you; I hate a stranger.

PINCHWIFE. Ay, my dear, you must love me only and not be like the naughty town-women, who only hate their husbands and love every man else, love plays, visits, fine coaches, fine clothes, fiddles, balls, treats, and so lead a wicked town-life.

---

67 *documents*: information.
75 *place-house*: chief house on an estate.

MRS PINCHWIFE. Nay, if to enjoy all these things be a town-life, London is not so bad a place, dear.

PINCHWIFE. How! If you love me, you must hate London.

ALITHEA. [*aside*] The fool has forbid me discovering to her the pleasures of the town and he is now setting her agog upon them himself.

MRS PINCHWIFE. But, husband, do the town-women love the playermen too?

PINCHWIFE. Yes, I warrant you.

MRS PINCHWIFE. Ay, I warrant you.

PINCHWIFE. Why, you do not, I hope?

MRS PINCHWIFE. No, no, bud; but why have we no playermen in the country?

PINCHWIFE. Ha – Mrs Minx, ask me no more to go to a play.

MRS PINCHWIFE. Nay, why, love? I did not care for going; but when you forbid me, you make me, as 'twere, desire it.

ALITHEA. (*aside*) So 'twill be in other things, I warrant.

MRS PINCHWIFE. Pray let me go to a play, dear.

PINCHWIFE. Hold your peace, I wo'not.

MRS PINCHWIFE. Why, love?

PINCHWIFE. Why, I'll tell you.

ALITHEA. (*aside*) Nay, if he tell her, she'll give him more cause to forbid her that place.

MRS PINCHWIFE. Pray, why, dear?

PINCHWIFE. First, you like the actors and the gallants may like you.

MRS PINCHWIFE. What, a homely country girl? No, bud, nobody will like me.

PINCHWIFE. I tell you, yes, they may.

MRS PINCHWIFE. No, no, you jest – I won't believe you, I will go.

PINCHWIFE. I tell you then that one of the lewdest fellows in town, who saw you there, told me he was in love with you.

MRS PINCHWIFE. Indeed! Who, who, pray, who was't?

PINCHWIFE. (*aside*) I've gone too far and slipped before I was aware. How overjoyed she is!

MRS PINCHWIFE. Was it any Hampshire gallant, any of our neighbours? I promise you, I am beholding to him.

PINCHWIFE. I promise you, you lie, for he would but ruin you, as he has done hundreds. He has no other love for women but that; such as he look upon women, like basilisks, but to destroy 'em.

MRS PINCHWIFE. Ay, but if he loves me, why should he ruin me? Answer me to that. Methinks he should not; I would do him no harm.

ALITHEA. Hah, ha, ha!

PINCHWIFE. 'Tis very well; but I'll keep him from doing you any harm, or me either.

Enter SPARKISH *and* HARCOURT.

But here comes company; get you in, get you in.

MRS PINCHWIFE. But pray, husband, is he a pretty gentleman that loves me?

PINCHWIFE. In, baggage, in. (*Thrusts her in, shuts the door*) What, all the lewd libertines of the town brought to my lodging by this easy coxcomb! 'Sdeath, I'll not suffer it.

SPARKISH. Here, Harcourt, do you approve my choice? [*To* ALITHEA] Dear little rogue, I told you I'd bring you acquainted with all my friends, the wits, and –

HARCOURT *salutes her.*

PINCHWIFE. [*aside*] Ay, they shall know her, as well as you yourself will, I warrant you.

SPARKISH. This is one of those, my pretty rogue, that are to dance at your wedding tomorrow; and him you must bid welcome ever to what you and I have.

PINCHWIFE. (*aside*) Monstrous!

SPARKISH. Harcourt, how dost thou like her, faith? – Nay, dear, do not look down; I should hate to have a wife of mine out of countenance at anything.

PINCHWIFE. [*aside*] Wonderful!

SPARKISH. Tell me, I say, Harcourt, how dost thou like her? Thou hast stared upon her enough to resolve me.

HARCOURT. So infinitely well that I could wish I had a mistress too, that might differ from her in nothing but her love and engagement to you.

ALITHEA. Sir, Master Sparkish has often told me that his acquaintance were all wits and railleurs and now I find it.

---

140 *basilisks*: mythical serpents whose glance was fatal.
173 *railleurs*: witty banterers.

SPARKISH. No, by the universe, madam, he does not rally now; you may believe him. I do assure you, he is the honestest, worthiest, true-hearted gentleman – a man of such perfect honour, he would say nothing to a lady he does not mean.

PINCHWIFE. [*aside*] Praising another man to his mistress!

HARCOURT. Sir, you are so beyond expectation obliging that –

SPARKISH. Nay, ygad, I am sure you do admire her extremely; I see't in your eyes. – He does admire you, madam. – By the world, don't you?

HARCOURT. Yes, above the world, or the most glorious part of it, her whole sex; and till now I never thought I should have envied you, or any man about to marry, but you have the best excuse for marriage I ever knew.

ALITHEA. Nay, now, sir, I'm satisfied you are of the society of the wits and railleurs, since you cannot spare your friend, even when he is but too civil to you; but the surest sign is since you are an enemy to marriage, for that, I hear, you hate as much as business or bad wine.

HARCOURT. Truly, madam, I never was an enemy to marriage till now, because marriage was never an enemy to me before.

ALITHEA. But why, sir, is marriage an enemy to you now? Because it robs you of your friend here? For you look upon a friend married as one gone into a monastery, that is dead to the world.

HARCOURT. 'Tis indeed because you marry him; I see, madam, you can guess my meaning. I do confess heartily and openly, I wish it were in my power to break the match; by heavens I would.

SPARKISH. Poor Frank!

ALITHEA. Would you be so unkind to me?

HARCOURT. No, no, 'tis not because I would be unkind to you.

SPARKISH. Poor Frank! No, gad, 'tis only his kindness to me.

PINCHWIFE. (*aside*) Great kindness to you indeed! Insensible fop, let a man make love to his wife to his face!

SPARKISH. Come, dear Frank, for all my wife there that shall be, thou shalt enjoy me sometimes, dear rogue. By my honour, we men of wit condole for our deceased brother in marriage as much as for one dead in earnest. I think that was prettily said of me, ha, Harcourt? But come, Frank, be not melancholy for me.

HARCOURT. No, I assure you I am not melancholy for you.

SPARKISH. Prithee, Frank, dost think my wife that shall be there a fine person?

HARCOURT. I could gaze upon her till I became as blind as you are.

SPARKISH. How, as I am? How?

HARCOURT. Because you are a lover and true lovers are blind, stock blind.

SPARKISH. True, true; but by the world, she has wit too, as well as beauty. Go, go with her into a corner and try if she has wit; talk to her anything; she's bashful before me.

HARCOURT. Indeed, if a woman wants wit in a corner, she has it nowhere.

ALITHEA. (*aside to* SPARKISH) Sir, you dispose of me a little before your time –

SPARKISH. Nay, nay, madam, let me have an earnest of your obedience, or – go, go, madam –

HARCOURT *courts* ALITHEA *aside.*

PINCHWIFE. How, sir! If you are not concerned for the honour of a wife, I am for that of a sister; he shall not debauch her. Be a pander to your own wife, bring men to her, let 'em make love before your face, thrust 'em into a corner together, then leave 'em in private! Is this your town wit and conduct?

SPARKISH. Hah, ha, ha, a silly wise rogue would make one laugh more than a stark fool, hah, ha! I shall burst. Nay, you shall not disturb 'em; I'll vex thee, by the world. (*Struggles with* PINCHWIFE *to keep him from* HARCOURT *and* ALITHEA)

ALITHEA. The writings are drawn, sir, settlements made; 'tis too late, sir, and past all revocation.

---

222 *not*: not not Q1.
232 *stock blind*: as blind as a log.
241 *earnest*: foretaste.
251 *vex*: stop.

HARCOURT. Then so is my death.

ALITHEA. I would not be unjust to him.

HARCOURT. Then why to me so?

ALITHEA. I have no obligation to you.

HARCOURT. My love.

ALITHEA. I had his before.

HARCOURT. You never had it; he wants, you see, jealousy, the only infallible sign of it.

ALITHEA. Love proceeds from esteem; he cannot distrust my virtue. Besides, he loves me, or he would not marry me.

HARCOURT. Marrying you is no more sign of his love than bribing your woman, that he may marry you, is a sign of his generosity. Marriage is rather a sign of interest than love, and he that marries a fortune covets a mistress, not loves her. But if you take marriage for a sign of love, take it from me immediately.

ALITHEA. No, now you have put a scruple in my head; but, in short, sir, to end our dispute, I must marry him, my reputation would suffer in the world else.

HARCOURT. No, if you do marry him, with your pardon, madam, your reputation suffers in the world and you would be thought in necessity for a cloak.

ALITHEA. Nay, now you are rude, sir. – Mr Sparkish, pray come hither, your friend here is very troublesome, and very loving.

HARCOURT. (*aside to* ALITHEA) Hold, hold! –

PINCHWIFE. D'ye hear that?

SPARKISH. Why, d'ye think I'll seem to be jealous, like a country bumpkin?

PINCHWIFE. No, rather be a cuckold, like a credulous cit.

HARCOURT. Madam, you would not have been so little generous as to have told him.

ALITHEA. Yes, since you could be so little generous as to wrong him.

HARCOURT. Wrong him! No man can do't, he's beneath an injury; a bubble, a coward, a senseless idiot, a

---

277 *necessity for a cloak*: to hide pregnancy, perhaps, as well as other affairs.

286 *cit*: contemptuous term for a citizen, a merchant not a gentleman.

292 *bubble*: gullible fool.

wretch so contemptible to all the world but you that –

ALITHEA. Hold, do not rail at him, for since he is like to be my husband, I am resolved to like him. Nay, I think I am obliged to tell him you are not his friend. – Master Sparkish, Master Sparkish.

SPARKISH. What, what? – Now, dear rogue, has not she wit?

HARCOURT. (*speaks surlily*) Not so much as I thought and hoped she had.

ALITHEA. Mr Sparkish, do you bring people to rail at you?

HARCOURT. Madam –

SPARKISH. How! No, but if he does rail at me, 'tis but in jest, I warrant; what we wits do for one another and never take any notice of it.

ALITHEA. He spoke so scurrilously of you, I had no patience to hear him; besides, he has been making love to me.

HARCOURT. (*aside*) True, damned, telltale woman!

SPARKISH. Pshaw, to show his parts – we wits rail and make love often but to show our parts; as we have no affections, so we have no malice. We –

ALITHEA. He said you were a wretch, below an injury.

SPARKISH. Pshaw!

HARCOURT. [*aside*] Damned, senseless, impudent, virtuous jade! Well, since she won't let me have her, she'll do as good, she'll make me hate her.

ALITHEA. A common bubble.

SPARKISH. Pshaw!

ALITHEA. A coward.

SPARKISH. Pshaw, pshaw!

ALITHEA. A senseless, drivelling idiot.

SPARKISH. How! Did he disparage my parts? Nay, then my honour's concerned; I can't put up that, sir, by the world. Brother, help me to kill him. (*Aside*) I may draw now, since we have the odds of him. 'Tis a good occasion, too, before my mistress – (*Offers to draw*)

ALITHEA. Hold, hold!

SPARKISH. What, what?

ALITHEA. (*aside*) I must not let 'em kill the gentleman neither, for his kindness to me; I am so far from hating him that I wish my gallant had his person and understanding. – Nay, if my honour –

SPARKISH. I'll be thy death.

ALITHEA. Hold, hold! Indeed, to tell the truth, the gentleman said after all that what he spoke was but out of friendship to you.

SPARKISH. How! say I am, I am a fool, that is, no wit, out of friendship to me?

ALITHEA. Yes, to try whether I was concerned enough for you and made love to me only to be satisfied of my virtue, for your sake.

HARCOURT. (*aside*) Kind, however –

SPARKISH. Nay, if it were so, my dear rogue, I ask thee pardon; but why would not you tell me so, faith?

HARCOURT. Because I did not think on't, faith.

SPARKISH. Come, Horner does not come, Harcourt, let's be gone to the new play. – Come, madam.

ALITHEA. I will not go if you intend to leave me alone in the box and run into the pit, as you use to do.

SPARKISH. Pshaw! I'll leave Harcourt with you in the box to entertain you, and that's as good; if I sat in the box, I should be thought no judge but of trimmings. – Come away, Harcourt, lead her down.

Exeunt SPARKISH, HARCOURT *and* ALITHEA.

PINCHWIFE. Well, go thy ways, for the flower of the true town fops, such as spend their estates before they come to 'em and are cuckolds before they're married. But let me go look to my own freehold. – How! –

Enter MY LADY FIDGET, MRS DAINTY FIDGET *and* MRS SQUEAMISH.

LADY FIDGET. Your servant, sir; where is your lady? We are come to wait upon her to the new play.

PINCHWIFE. New play!

LADY FIDGET. And my husband will wait upon you presently.

PINCHWIFE. (*aside*) Damn your civility. – Madam, by no means; I will not see Sir Jaspar here till I have waited upon him at home; nor shall my wife see you till she has waited upon your ladyship at your lodgings.

LADY FIDGET. Now we are here, sir –

PINCHWIFE. No, madam.

DAINTY. Pray, let us see her.

355–6 *trimmings*: clothes.

SQUEAMISH. We will not stir till we see her.

PINCHWIFE. (*aside*) A pox on you all! (*Goes to the door, and returns*) – She has locked the door and is gone abroad.

LADY FIDGET. No, you have locked the door and she's within.

DAINTY. They told us below she was here.

PINCHWIFE. (*aside*) Will nothing do? – Well, it must out then. To tell you the truth, ladies, which I was afraid to let you know before, lest it might endanger your lives, my wife has just now the smallpox come out upon her. Do not be frightened but pray, be gone, ladies; you shall not stay here in danger of your lives. Pray get you gone, ladies.

LADY FIDGET. No, no, we have all had 'em.

SQUEAMISH. Alack, alack.

DAINTY. Come, come, we must see how it goes with her; I understand the disease.

LADY FIDGET. Come.

PINCHWIFE. (*aside*) Well, there is no being too hard for women at their own weapon, lying; therefore I'll quit the field. *Exit* PINCHWIFE.

SQUEAMISH. Here's an example of jealousy.

LADY FIDGET. Indeed, as the world goes, I wonder there are no more jealous, since wives are so neglected.

DAINTY. Pshaw, as the world goes, to what end should they be jealous?

LADY FIDGET. Foh, 'tis a nasty world.

SQUEAMISH. That men of parts, great acquaintance and quality should take up with and spend themselves and fortunes in keeping little playhouse creatures, foh!

LADY FIDGET. Nay, that women of understanding, great acquaintance and good quality should fall a-keeping too of little creatures, foh!

SQUEAMISH. Why, 'tis the men of quality's fault; they never visit women of honour and reputation, as they used to do and have not so much as common civility for ladies of our rank, but use us with the same indifferency and ill-breeding as if we were all married to 'em.

LADY FIDGET. She says true; 'tis an arrant shame women of quality should be so slighted. Methinks birth, birth should go for something. I have known men admired, courted and followed for their titles only.

SQUEAMISH. Ay, one would think men of honour should not love, no more than marry, out of their own rank.

DAINTY. Fie, fie upon 'em! They are come to think crossbreeding for themselves best, as well as for their dogs and horses.

LADY FIDGET. They are dogs and horses for't.

SQUEAMISH. One would think, if not for love, for vanity a little.

DAINTY. Nay, they do satisfy their vanity upon us sometimes and are kind to us in their report, tell all the world they lie with us.

LADY FIDGET. Damned rascals! That we should be only wronged by 'em! To report a man has had a person, when he has not had a person, is the greatest wrong in the whole world that can be done to a person.

SQUEAMISH. Well, 'tis an arrant shame noble persons should be so wronged and neglected.

LADY FIDGET. But still 'tis an arranter shame for a noble person to neglect her own honour and defame her own noble person with little inconsiderable fellows, foh!

DAINTY. I suppose the crime against our honour is the same with a man of quality as with another.

LADY FIDGET. How! No, sure, the man of quality is likest one's husband and therefore the fault should be the less.

DAINTY. But then the pleasure should be the less.

LADY FIDGET. Fie, fie, fie, for shame, sister! Whither shall we ramble? Be continent in your discourse, or I shall hate you.

DAINTY. Besides, an intrigue is so much the more notorious for the man's quality.

SQUEAMISH. 'Tis true, nobody takes notice of a private man and therefore with him 'tis more secret, and the crime's the less when 'tis not known.

LADY FIDGET. You say true; i'faith, I think you are in the right on't. 'Tis not an injury to a husband till it be an injury to our honours; so that a woman of honour loses no honour with a private person; and to say truth –

DAINTY. (*apart to* SQUEAMISH) So, the little fellow is grown a private person – with her –

LADY FIDGET. But still my dear, dear honour.

Enter SIR JASPAR, HORNER, DORILANT.

SIR JASPAR. Ay, my dear, dear of honour, thou hast still so much honour in thy mouth –

HORNER. (*aside*) That she has none elsewhere.

LADY FIDGET. Oh, what d'ye mean to bring in these upon us?

DAINTY. Foh, these are as bad as wits.

SQUEAMISH. Foh!

LADY FIDGET. Let us leave the room.

SIR JASPAR. Stay, stay; faith, to tell you the naked truth –

LADY FIDGET. Fie, Sir Jaspar, do not use that word 'naked'.

SIR JASPAR. Well, well, in short, I have business at Whitehall and cannot go to the play with you, therefore would have you go –

LADY FIDGET. With those two to a play?

SIR JASPAR. No, not with t'other but with Mr Horner; there can be no more scandal to go with him than with Mr Tattle or Master Limberham.

LADY FIDGET. With that nasty fellow! No – no!

SIR JASPAR. Nay, prithee, dear, hear me. (*Whispers to* LADY FIDGET)

HORNER. Ladies –

HORNER, DORILANT *drawing near* SQUEAMISH *and* DAINTY.

DAINTY. Stand off.

SQUEAMISH. Do not approach us.

DAINTY. You herd with the wits, you are obscenity all over.

SQUEAMISH. And I would as soon look upon a picture of Adam and Eve, without fig leaves, as any of you, if I could help it; therefore keep off and do not make us sick.

---

482 *Mr Tattle or Master Limberham*: the 'old civil gentlemen' of line 557; Tattle was later used by Congreve for the fop in *Love for Love* (1695) and Limberham by Dryden for the title character in *The Kind Keeper* (1678).

DORILANT. What a devil are these?

HORNER. Why, these are pretenders to honour, as critics to wit, only by censuring others; and as every raw, peevish, out-of-humoured, affected, dull, tea-drinking, arithmetical fop sets up for a wit by railing at men of sense, so these for honour by railing at the Court and ladies of as great honour as quality.

SIR JASPAR. Come, Mr Horner, I must desire you to go with these ladies to the play, sir.

HORNER. I, sir!

SIR JASPAR. Ay, ay, come, sir.

HORNER. I must beg your pardon, sir, and theirs; I will not be seen in women's company in public again for the world.

SIR JASPAR. Ha, ha, strange aversion!

SQUEAMISH. No, he's for women's company in private.

SIR JASPAR. He – poor man – he! Hah, ha, ha!

DAINTY. 'Tis a greater shame amongst lewd fellows to be seen in virtuous women's company than for the women to be seen with them.

HORNER. Indeed, madam, the time was I only hated virtuous women, but now I hate the other too; I beg your pardon, ladies.

LADY FIDGET. You are very obliging, sir, because we would not be troubled with you.

SIR JASPAR. In sober sadness, he shall go.

DORILANT. Nay, if he wo'not, I am ready to wait upon the ladies; and I think I am the fitter man.

SIR JASPAR. You, sir, no, I thank you for that – Master Horner is a privileged man amongst the virtuous ladies; 'twill be a great while before you are so; heh, he, he! He's my wife's gallant, heh, he, he! No, pray withdraw, sir, for as I take it, the virtuous ladies have no business with you.

DORILANT. And I am sure he can have none with them. 'Tis strange a man can't come amongst virtuous women now but upon the same terms as men are admitted into the Great Turk's seraglio; but heavens

---

498 *arithmetical*: precise.
531 *the Great Turk's seraglio*: the Turkish Sultan's harem.

keep me from being an ombre player with 'em! But where is Pinchwife? *Exit* DORILANT.

SIR JASPAR. Come, come, man; what, avoid the sweet society of womankind? that sweet, soft, gentle, tame, noble creature, woman, made for man's companion –

HORNER. So is that soft, gentle, tame and more noble creature a spaniel, and has all their tricks: can fawn, lie down, suffer beating and fawn the more; barks at your friends when they come to see you; makes your bed hard; gives you fleas, and the mange sometimes. And all the difference is, the spaniel's the more faithful animal and fawns but upon one master.

SIR JASPAR. Heh, he, he!

SQUEAMISH. Oh, the rude beast!

DAINTY. Insolent brute!

LADY FIDGET. Brute! Stinking, mortified, rotten French wether, to dare –

SIR JASPAR. Hold, an't please your ladyship. – For shame, Master Horner, your mother was a woman. (*Aside*) Now shall I never reconcile 'em. [*Aside to* LADY FIDGET] Hark you, madam, take my advice in your anger. You know you often want one to make up your drolling pack of ombre players; and you may cheat him easily, for he's an ill gamester and consequently loves play. Besides, you know, you have but two old civil gentlemen, with stinking breaths too, to wait upon you abroad; take in the third into your service. The other are but crazy; and a lady should have a supernumerary gentleman-usher, as a supernumerary coach-horse, lest sometimes you should be forced to stay at home.

LADY FIDGET. But are you sure he loves play and has money?

SIR JASPAR. He loves play as much as you and has money as much as I.

LADY FIDGET. Then I am contented to make him pay for his scurrility; money makes up in a measure all

---

532 *ombre*: a card game and a pun on *hombre* (man).
548 *French wether*: castrated ram.
554 *drolling*: ridiculous.
559 *crazy*: decrepit.

other wants in men. (*Aside*) Those whom we cannot make hold for gallants, we make fine.

SIR JASPAR. (*aside*) So, so; now to mollify, to wheedle him. – Master Horner, will you never keep civil company? Methinks 'tis time now, since you are only fit for them. Come, come, man, you must e'en fall to visiting our wives, eating at our tables, drinking tea with our virtuous relations after dinner, dealing cards to 'em, reading plays and gazettes to 'em, picking fleas out of their shocks for 'em, collecting receipts, new songs, women, pages and footmen for 'em.

HORNER. I hope they'll afford me better employment, sir.

SIR JASPAR. Heh, he, he! 'Tis fit you know your work before you come into your place; and since you are unprovided of a lady to flatter and a good house to eat at, pray frequent mine and call my wife mistress and she shall call you gallant, according to the custom.

HORNER. Who, I?

SIR JASPAR. Faith, thou shalt for my sake; come, for my sake only.

HORNER. For your sake –

SIR JASPAR. [*to* LADY FIDGET] Come, come, here's a gamester for you; let him be a little familiar sometimes. Nay, what if a little rude? Gamesters may be rude with ladies, you know.

LADY FIDGET. Yes, losing gamesters have a privilege with women.

HORNER. I always thought the contrary, that the winning gamester had most privilege with women, for when you have lost your money to a man, you'll lose anything you have, all you have, they say, and he may use you as he pleases.

SIR JASPAR. Heh, he, he! Well, win or lose, you shall have your liberty with her.

LADY FIDGET. As he behaves himself; and for your sake I'll give him admittance and freedom.

---

570 *fine*: pay; particularly appropriate here, since the word was used in cases where a man paid to avoid the duties of an office.

578 *shocks*: poodles.

578 *receipts*: recipes.

HORNER. All sorts of freedom, madam?

SIR JASPAR. Ay, ay, ay, all sorts of freedom thou canst take, and so go to her, begin thy new employment; wheedle her, jest with her and be better acquainted one with another.

HORNER. (*aside*) I think I know her already, therefore may venture with her, my secret for hers.

HORNER *and* LADY FIDGET *whisper.*

SIR JASPAR. Sister, cuz, I have provided an innocent playfellow for you there.

DAINTY. Who, he!

SQUEAMISH. There's a playfellow indeed!

SIR JASPAR. Yes, sure; what, he is good enough to play at cards, blindman's buff, or the fool with sometimes.

SQUEAMISH. Foh, we'll have no such playfellows.

DAINTY. No, sir, you shan't choose playfellows for us, we thank you.

SIR JASPAR. Nay, pray hear me. (*Whispering to them*)

LADY FIDGET. [*aside to* HORNER] But, poor gentleman, could you be so generous, so truly a man of honour, as for the sakes of us women of honour, to cause yourself to be reported no man? No man! And to suffer yourself the greatest shame that could fall upon a man, that none might fall upon us women by your conversation? But indeed, sir, as perfectly, perfectly the same man as before your going into France, sir? As perfectly, perfectly, sir?

HORNER. As perfectly, perfectly, madam. Nay, I scorn you should take my word; I desire to be tried only, madam.

LADY FIDGET. Well, that's spoken again like a man of honour; all men of honour desire to come to the test. But, indeed, generally you men report such things of yourselves, one does not know how or whom to believe and it is come to that pass we dare not take your words, no more than your tailors, without some staid servant of yours be bound with you. But I have so strong a faith in your honour, dear, dear, noble sir, that I'd forfeit mine for yours at any time, dear sir.

---

640 *tailors*: tailors could not trust a gentleman's word about payment.

HORNER. No, madam, you should not need to forfeit it for me; I have given you security already to save you harmless, my late reputation being so well known in the world, madam.

LADY FIDGET. But if upon any future falling out or upon a suspicion of my taking the trust out of your hands to employ some other, you yourself should betray your trust, dear sir? I mean, if you'll give me leave to speak obscenely, you might tell, dear sir.

HORNER. If I did, nobody would believe me; the reputation of impotency is as hardly recovered again in the world as that of cowardice, dear madam.

LADY FIDGET. Nay then, as one may say, you may do your worst, dear, dear sir.

SIR JASPAR. Come, is your ladyship reconciled to him yet? Have you agreed on matters? For I must be gone to Whitehall.

LADY FIDGET. Why, indeed, Sir Jaspar, Master Horner is a thousand, thousand times a better man than I thought him. Cousin Squeamish, Sister Dainty, I can name him now; truly, not long ago, you know, I thought his very name obscenity and I would as soon have lain with him as have named him.

SIR JASPAR. Very likely, poor madam.

DAINTY. I believe it.

SQUEAMISH. No doubt on't.

SIR JASPAR. Well, well – that your ladyship is as virtuous as any she, I know, and him all the town knows – heh, he, he! Therefore, now you like him, get you gone to your business together; go, go to your business, I say, pleasure, whilst I go to my pleasure, business.

LADY FIDGET. Come then, dear gallant.

HORNER. Come away, my dearest mistress.

SIR JASPAR. So, so. Why, 'tis as I'd have it.

Exit SIR JASPAR.

HORNER. And as I'd have it.

LADY FIDGET. Who for his business from his wife will run,
Takes the best care to have her business done.

Exeunt omnes.

ACT III

SCENE I

ALITHEA *and* MRS PINCHWIFE.

ALITHEA. Sister, what ails you? You are grown melancholy.

MRS PINCHWIFE. Would it not make anyone melancholy to see you go every day fluttering about abroad, whilst I must stay at home like a poor, lonely, sullen bird in a cage?

ALITHEA. Ay, sister, but you came young and just from the nest to your cage, so that I thought you liked it and could be as cheerful in't as others that took their flight themselves early and are hopping abroad in the open air.

MRS PINCHWIFE. Nay, I confess I was quiet enough till my husband told me what pure lives the London ladies live abroad, with their dancing, meetings and junketings, and dressed every day in their best gowns, and, I warrant you, play at ninepins every day of the week, so they do.

Enter MR PINCHWIFE.

PINCHWIFE. Come, what's here to do? You are putting the town pleasures in her head and setting her a-longing.

ALITHEA. Yes, after ninepins; you suffer none to give her those longings, you mean, but yourself.

PINCHWIFE. I tell her of the vanities of the town like a confessor.

ALITHEA. A confessor! Just such a confessor as he that, by forbidding a silly ostler to grease the horse's teeth, taught him to do't.

PINCHWIFE. Come, Mistress Flippant, good precepts are lost when bad examples are still before us; the liberty

13 *pure*: fine
24–6 unscrupulous ostlers would grease a horse's teeth, which supposedly stopped it eating, but still charge the horse's owner for the uneaten feed; see *King Lear*, II iv 123–4.
25 *silly*: ignorant.

you take abroad makes her hanker after it, and out of humour at home, poor wretch! She desired not to come to London; I would bring her.

ALITHEA. Very well.

PINCHWIFE. She has been this week in town and never desired, till this afternoon, to go abroad.

ALITHEA. Was she not at a play yesterday?

PINCHWIFE. Yes, but she ne'er asked me; I was myself the cause of her going.

ALITHEA. Then, if she ask you again, you are the cause of her asking, and not my example.

PINCHWIFE. Well, tomorrow night I shall be rid of you and the next day, before 'tis light, she and I'll be rid of the town, and my dreadful apprehensions. [*To* MRS PINCHWIFE] Come, be not melancholy, for thou shalt go into the country after tomorrow, dearest.

ALITHEA. Great comfort!

MRS PINCHWIFE. Pish, what d'ye tell me of the country for?

PINCHWIFE. How's this! What, pish at the country!

MRS PINCHWIFE. Let me alone, I am not well.

PINCHWIFE. Oh, if that be all – what ails my dearest?

MRS PINCHWIFE. Truly I don't know; but I have not been well since you told me there was a gallant at the play in love with me.

PINCHWIFE. Ha –

ALITHEA. That's by my example too!

PINCHWIFE. Nay, if you are not well, but are so concerned because a lewd fellow chanced to lie and say he liked you, you'll make me sick too.

MRS PINCHWIFE. Of what sickness?

PINCHWIFE. O, of that which is worse than the plague, jealousy.

MRS PINCHWIFE. Pish, you jeer! I'm sure there's no such disease in our receipt-book at home.

PINCHWIFE. No, thou never met'st with it, poor innocent. (*Aside*) Well, if thou cuckold me, 'twill be my own fault – for cuckolds and bastards are generally makers of their own fortune.

MRS PINCHWIFE. Well, but pray, bud, let's to go a play tonight.

PINCHWIFE. 'Tis just done, she comes from it. But why are you so eager to see a play?

MRS PINCHWIFE. Faith, dear, not that I care one pin for their talk there; but I like to look upon the playermen and would see, if I could, the gallant you say loves me; that's all, dear bud.

PINCHWIFE. Is that all, dear bud?

ALITHEA. This proceeds from my example.

MRS PINCHWIFE. But if the play be done, let's go abroad, however, dear bud.

PINCHWIFE. Come, have a little patience and thou shalt go into the country on Friday.

MRS PINCHWIFE. Therefore I would see first some sights, to tell my neighbours of. Nay, I will go abroad, that's once.

ALITHEA. I'm the cause of this desire too.

PINCHWIFE. But now I think on't, who was the cause of Horner's coming to my lodging today? That was you.

ALITHEA. No, you, because you would not let him see your handsome wife out of your lodging.

MRS PINCHWIFE. Why, O Lord! Did the gentleman come hither to see me indeed?

PINCHWIFE. No, no. – You are not cause of that damned question too, Mistress Alithea? (*Aside*) Well, she's in the right of it. He is in love with my wife – and comes after her – 'tis so – but I'll nip his love in the bud, lest he should follow us into the country and break his chariot-wheel near our house on purpose for an excuse to come to't. But I think I know the town.

MRS PINCHWIFE. Come, pray, bud, let's go abroad before 'tis late, for I will go, that's flat and plain.

PINCHWIFE. (*aside*) So! the obstinacy already of a town-wife, and I must, whilst she's here, humour her like one. – Sister, how shall we do, that she may not be seen or known?

ALITHEA. Let her put on her mask.

PINCHWIFE. Pshaw, a mask makes people but the more inquisitive and is as ridiculous a disguise as a stage-beard; her shape, stature, habit will be known and if we should meet with Horner, he would be sure to take acquaintance with us, must wish her joy, kiss her, talk to her, leer upon her, and the devil and all. No, I'll

---

84 *once*: once and for all.

not use her to a mask, 'tis dangerous, for masks have made more cuckolds than the best faces that ever were known.

ALITHEA. How will you do then?

MRS PINCHWIFE. Nay, shall we go? The Exchange will be shut, and I have a mind to see that.

PINCHWIFE. So – I have it – I'll dress her up in the suit we are to carry down to her brother, little Sir James; nay, I understand the town tricks. Come, let's go dress her. A mask! No – a woman masked, like a covered dish, gives a man curiosity and appetite, when, it may be, uncovered, 'twould turn his stomach; no, no.

ALITHEA. Indeed your comparison is something a greasy one. But I had a gentle gallant used to say, 'A beauty masked, like the sun in eclipse, gathers together more gazers than if it shined out.'

Exeunt.

SCENE II

The scene changes to the New Exchange.

Enter HORNER, HARCOURT, DORILANT.

DORILANT. Engaged to women, and not sup with us?

HORNER. Ay, a pox on 'em all!

HARCOURT. You were much a more reasonable man in the morning and had as noble resolutions against 'em as a widower of a week's liberty.

DORILANT. Did I ever think to see you keep company with women in vain?

HORNER. In vain! No – 'tis, since I can't love 'em, to be revenged on 'em.

HARCOURT. Now your sting is gone, you looked in the box amongst all those women, like a drone in the hive, all upon you, shoved and ill-used by 'em all, and thrust from one side to t'other.

DORILANT. Yet he must be buzzing amongst 'em still,

---

125 *greasy*: filthy, vulgar.
127 *like*: lik'd Q1.

like other old beetle-headed, liquorish drones. Avoid 'em, and hate 'em as they hate you.

HORNER. Because I do hate 'em, and would hate 'em yet more, I'll frequent 'em; you may see by marriage, nothing makes a man hate a woman more than her constant conversation. In short, I converse with 'em, as you do with rich fools, to laugh at 'em and use 'em ill.

DORILANT. But I would no more sup with women, unless I could lie with 'em, than sup with a rich coxcomb, unless I could cheat him.

HORNER. Yes, I have known thee sup with a fool for his drinking; if he could set out your hand that way only, you were satisfied, and if he were a wine-swallowing mouth 'twas enough.

HARCOURT. Yes, a man drinks often with a fool, as he tosses with a marker, only to keep his hand in ure. But do the ladies drink?

HORNER. Yes, sir, and I shall have the pleasure at least of laying 'em flat with a bottle, and bring as much scandal that way upon 'em as formerly t'other.

HARCOURT. Perhaps you may prove as weak a brother amongst 'em that way as t'other.

DORILANT. Foh, drinking with women is as unnatural as scolding with 'em; but 'tis a pleasure of decayed fornicators, and the basest way of quenching love.

HARCOURT. Nay, 'tis drowning love instead of quenching it. But leave us for civil women too!

DORILANT. Ay, when he can't be the better for 'em. We hardly pardon a man that leaves his friend for a wench, and that's a pretty lawful call.

HORNER. Faith, I would not leave you for 'em, if they would not drink.

DORILANT. Who would disappoint his company at Lewis's for a gossiping?

---

15 *beetle-headed*: stupid.
15 *liquorish*: lecherous.
27 *set out your hand*: furnish you with food and drink.
31 *tosses with a marker*: plays dice with a score-keeper.
31 *ure*: practice.
49 *Lewis's*: an unidentified London eating-house, perhaps the one in Bread Street, Cheapside.

HARCOURT. Foh, wine and women, good apart, together as nauseous as sack and sugar. But hark you, sir, before you go, a little of your advice; an old maimed general, when unfit for action, is fittest for counsel. I have other designs upon women than eating and drinking with them. I am in love with Sparkish's mistress, whom he is to marry tomorrow. Now how shall I get her?

Enter SPARKISH, *looking about.*

HORNER. Why, here comes one will help you to her.

HARCOURT. He! He, I tell you, is my rival, and will hinder my love.

HORNER. No, a foolish rival and a jealous husband assist their rival's designs, for they are sure to make their women hate them, which is the first step to their love for another man.

HARCOURT. But I cannot come near his mistress but in his company.

HORNER. Still the better for you, for fools are most easily cheated when they themselves are accessories; and he is to be bubbled of his mistress, as of his money, the common mistress, by keeping him company.

SPARKISH. Who is that, that is to be bubbled? Faith, let me snack, I han't met with a bubble since Christmas. Gad, I think bubbles are like their brother woodcocks, go out with the cold weather.

HARCOURT. (*apart to* HORNER) A pox! He did not hear all, I hope.

SPARKISH. Come, you bubbling rogues you, where do we sup? – Oh, Harcourt, my mistress tells me you have been making fierce love to her all the play long, hah, ha! But I –

---

51 *sack and sugar*: sack was any white wine from Spain or the Canary Islands and was often drunk with sugar at this time (as Falstaff said 'If sack and sugar be a fault, God help the wicked': *1 Henry IV*, II iv 454–5). It was often an invalid's drink, hence perhaps Harcourt's distaste.

69 *bubbled*: cheated, gulled.

73 *snack*: share.

75 *woodcocks*: simpletons.

HARCOURT. I make love to her?

SPARKISH. Nay, I forgive thee, for I think I know thee, and I know her, but I am sure I know myself.

HARCOURT. Did she tell you so? I see all women are like these of the Exchange, who, to enhance the price of their commodities, report to their fond customers offers which were never made 'em.

HORNER. Ay, women are as apt to tell before the intrigue as men after it, and so show themselves the vainer sex. But hast thou a mistress, Sparkish? 'Tis as hard for me to believe it as that thou ever hadst a bubble, as you bragged just now.

SPARKISH. Oh, your servant, sir; are you at your raillery, sir? But we were some of us beforehand with you today at the play. The wits were something bold with you, sir; did you not hear us laugh?

HORNER. Yes, but I thought you had gone to plays to laugh at the poet's wit, not at your own.

SPARKISH. Your servant, sir; no, I thank you. Gad, I go to a play as to a country treat; I carry my own wine to one and my own wit to t'other, or else I'm sure I should not be merry at either. And the reason why we are so often louder than the players is because we think we speak more wit and so become the poet's rivals in his audience. For to tell you the truth, we hate the silly rogues, nay, so much that we find fault even with their bawdy upon the stage, whilst we talk nothing else in the pit as loud.

HORNER. But why shouldst thou hate the silly poets? Thou hast too much wit to be one, and they, like whores, are only hated by each other – and thou dost scorn writing, I'm sure.

SPARKISH. Yes, I'd have you to know I scorn writing; but women, women, that make men do all foolish things, make 'em write songs too. Everybody does it. 'Tis even as common with lovers as playing with fans; and you can no more help rhyming to your Phyllis than drinking to your Phyllis.

HARCOURT. Nay, poetry in love is no more to be avoided than jealousy.

DORILANT. But the poets damned your songs, did they?

SPARKISH. Damn the poets! They turned 'em into burlesque, as they call it. That burlesque is a hocus-pocus trick they have got, which, by virtue of *hictius doctius*, *topsy-turvy*, they make a wise and witty man in the world a fool upon the stage, you know not how; and 'tis therefore I hate 'em too, for I know not but it may be my own case, for they'll put a man into a play for looking asquint. Their predecessors were contented to make serving-men only their stage-fools, but these rogues must have gentlemen, with a pox to 'em, nay, knights; and, indeed, you shall hardly see a fool upon the stage but he's a knight and, to tell you the truth, they have kept me these six years from being a knight in earnest, for fear of being knighted in a play, and dubbed a fool.

DORILANT. Blame 'em not; they must follow their copy, the age.

HARCOURT. But why shouldst thou be afraid of being in a play, who expose yourself every day in the playhouses and as public places?

HORNER. 'Tis but being on the stage, instead of standing on a bench in the pit.

DORILANT. Don't you give money to painters to draw you like? And are you afraid of your pictures at length in a playhouse, where all your mistresses may see you?

SPARKISH. A pox! Painters don't draw the smallpox or pimples in one's face. Come, damn all your silly authors whatever, all books and booksellers, by the world, and all readers, courteous or uncourteous.

HARCOURT. But who comes here, Sparkish?

Enter MR PINCHWIFE *and his wife in man's clothes,* ALITHEA, LUCY *her maid.*

SPARKISH. Oh, hide me! There's my mistress too. (SPARKISH *hides himself behind* HARCOURT)

HARCOURT. She sees you.

SPARKISH. But I will not see her. 'Tis time to go to Whitehall and I must not fail the drawing room.

HARCOURT. Pray, first carry me, and reconcile me to her.

125–6 *hictius doctius*: a piece of jugglers' patter.
142 *as*: equally.

SPARKISH. Another time; faith, the King will have supped.

HARCOURT. Not with the worse stomach for thy absence; thou art one of those fools that think their attendance at the King's meals as necessary as his physicians', when you are more troublesome to him than his doctors, or his dogs.

SPARKISH. Pshaw, I know my interest, sir. Prithee hide me.

HORNER. Your servant, Pinchwife. – What, he knows us not!

PINCHWIFE. (*to his wife aside*) Come along.

MRS PINCHWIFE. Pray, have you any ballads? Give me sixpenny worth.

CLASP. We have no ballads.

MRS PINCHWIFE. Then give me *Covent Garden Drollery*, and a play or two – Oh, here's *Tarugo's Wiles*, and *The Slighted Maiden*; I'll have them.

PINCHWIFE. (*apart to her*) No, plays are not for your reading. Come along; will you discover yourself?

HORNER. Who is that pretty youth with him, Sparkish?

SPARKISH. I believe his wife's brother, because he's something like her, but I never saw her but once.

HORNER. Extremely handsome; I have seen a face like it too. Let us follow 'em.

Exeunt PINCHWIFE, MRS PINCHWIFE, ALITHEA, LUCY; HORNER, DORILANT *following them.*

HARCOURT. Come, Sparkish, your mistress saw you and will be angry you go not to her. Besides, I would fain be reconciled to her, which none but you can do, dear friend.

SPARKISH. Well, that's a better reason, dear friend, I would not go near her now, for hers or my own sake, but I can deny you nothing, for though I have known

---

174 *Covent Garden Drollery*: a miscellany of songs, poems, prologues and epilogues by various writers, including Wycherley, published in 1672.

175–6 *Tarugo's Wiles, and The Slighted Maiden*: *Tarugo's Wiles*, a comedy by Sir Thomas St Serfe (1668), best remembered for its scene of coffeehouse talk; *The Slighted Maiden*, a tragicomedy by Sir Robert Stapylton (1663). Margery's taste in plays is out-of-date.

thee a great while, never go, if I do not love thee as well as a new acquaintance.

HARCOURT. I am obliged to you indeed, dear friend. I would be well with her, only to be well with thee still, for these ties to wives usually dissolve all ties to friends. I would be contented she should enjoy you a-nights, but I would have you to myself a-days, as I have had, dear friend.

SPARKISH. And thou shalt enjoy me a-days, dear, dear friend, never stir, and I'll be divorced from her sooner than from thee. Come along.

HARCOURT. (*aside*) So, we are hard put to't when we make our rival our procurer; but neither she nor her brother would let me come near her now. When all's done, a rival is the best cloak to steal to a mistress under, without suspicion, and when we have once got to her as we desire, we throw him off like other cloaks.

Exit SPARKISH, *and* HARCOURT *following him.*

Re-enter MR PINCHWIFE, MRS PINCHWIFE *in man's clothes.*

PINCHWIFE. (*to* ALITHEA [*off-stage*]) Sister, if you will not go, we must leave you. (*Aside*) The fool her gallant and she will muster up all the young saunterers of this place, and they will leave their dear seamstresses to follow us. What a swarm of cuckolds and cuckold-makers are here! – Come, let's be gone, Mistress Margery.

MRS PINCHWIFE. Don't you believe that; I han't half my bellyful of sights yet.

PINCHWIFE. Then walk this way.

MRS PINCHWIFE. Lord, what a power of brave signs are here! Stay – the Bull's-Head, the Ram's-Head and the Stag's-Head, dear –

PINCHWIFE. Nay, if every husband's proper sign here were visible, they would be all alike.

MRS PINCHWIFE. What d'ye mean by that, bud?

PINCHWIFE. 'Tis no matter – no matter, bud.

MRS PINCHWIFE. Pray tell me; nay, I will know.

---

191 *never go*: like *never stir* (line 200), it means little more than *don't worry*.

221 *proper sign*: a cuckold's horns.

PINCHWIFE. They would be all bulls', stags' and rams' heads.

Exeunt MR PINCHWIFE, MRS PINCHWIFE.

Re-enter SPARKISH, HARCOURT, ALITHEA, LUCY, *at t'other door.*

SPARKISH. Come, dear madam, for my sake you shall be reconciled to him.

ALITHEA. For your sake I hate him.

HARCOURT. That's something too cruel, madam, to hate me for his sake.

SPARKISH. Ay indeed, madam, too, too cruel to me, to hate my friend for my sake.

ALITHEA. I hate him because he is your enemy; and you ought to hate him too, for making love to me, if you love me.

SPARKISH. That's a good one! I hate a man for loving you! If he did love you, 'tis but what he can't help and 'tis your fault, not his, if he admires you. I hate a man for being of my opinion! I'll ne'er do't by the world.

ALITHEA. Is it for your honour or mine, to suffer a man to make love to me, who am to marry you tomorrow?

SPARKISH. Is it for your honour or mine, to have me jealous? That he makes love to you is a sign you are handsome and that I am not jealous is a sign you are virtuous. That, I think, is for your honour.

ALITHEA. But 'tis your honour too I am concerned for.

HARCOURT. But why, dearest madam, will you be more concerned for his honour than he is himself? Let his honour alone, for my sake and his. He, he has no honour –

SPARKISH. How's that?

HARCOURT. But what my dear friend can guard himself.

SPARKISH. O ho – that's right again.

HARCOURT. Your care of his honour argues his neglect of it, which is no honour to my dear friend here;

---

227 s.d. *t'other door*: there were two doors on each side of the forestage; this entrance is through the other door on the same side as the one the Pinchwifes used to leave by.

therefore once more, let his honour go which way it will, dear madam.

SPARKISH. Ay, ay, were it for my honour to marry a woman whose virtue I suspected and could not trust her in a friend's hands?

ALITHEA. Are you not afraid to lose me?

HARCOURT. He afraid to lose you, madam! No, no – you may see how the most estimable and most glorious creature in the world is valued by him. Will you not see it?

SPARKISH. Right, honest Frank, I have that noble value for her that I cannot be jealous of her.

ALITHEA. You mistake him, he means you care not for me, nor who has me.

SPARKISH. Lord, madam, I see you are jealous. Will you wrest a poor man's meaning from his words?

ALITHEA. You astonish me, sir, with your want of jealousy.

SPARKISH. And you make me giddy, madam, with your jealousy and fears and virtue and honour. Gad, I see virtue makes a woman as troublesome as a little reading or learning.

ALITHEA. Monstrous!

LUCY. (*behind*) Well, to see what easy husbands these women of quality can meet with; a poor chambermaid can never have such lady-like luck. Besides, he's thrown away upon her; she'll make no use of her fortune, her blessing. None to a gentleman for a pure cuckold, for it requires good breeding to be a cuckold.

ALITHEA. I tell you then plainly, he pursues me to marry me.

SPARKISH. Pshaw!

HARCOURT. Come, madam, you see you strive in vain to make him jealous of me; my dear friend is the kindest creature in the world to me.

SPARKISH. Poor fellow.

HARCOURT. But his kindness only is not enough for me, without your favour; your good opinion, dear madam, 'tis that must perfect my happiness. Good

---

275 *jealous*: vehement, wrought. Alithea puns on its other meaning, line 278.

288 *None*: there is no one like.

gentleman, he believes all I say – would you would do so. Jealous of me! I would not wrong him nor you for the world.

SPARKISH. Look you there; hear him, hear him, and do not walk away so.

ALITHEA *walks carelessly to and fro.*

HARCOURT. I love you, madam, so –

SPARKISH. How's that! Nay – now you begin to go too far indeed.

HARCOURT. So much, I confess, I say I love you, that I would not have you miserable and cast yourself away upon so unworthy and inconsiderable a thing as what you see here. (*Clapping his hand on his breast, points at* SPARKISH)

SPARKISH. No, faith, I believe thou wouldst not; now his meaning is plain. But I knew before thou wouldst not wrong me nor her.

HARCOURT. No, no, heavens forbid the glory of her sex should fall so low as into the embraces of such a contemptible wretch, the last of mankind – my dear friend here – I injure him! (*Embracing* SPARKISH)

ALITHEA. Very well.

SPARKISH. No, no, dear friend, I knew it. – Madam, you see he will rather wrong himself than me, in giving himself such names.

ALITHEA. Do not you understand him yet?

SPARKISH. Yes, how modestly he speaks of himself, poor fellow.

ALITHEA. Methinks he speaks impudently of yourself, since – before yourself too; insomuch that I can no longer suffer his scurrilous abusiveness to you, no more than his love to me. (*Offers to go*)

SPARKISH. Nay, nay, madam, pray stay – his love to you! Lord, madam, he has not spoke yet plain enough?

ALITHEA. Yes, indeed, I should think so.

SPARKISH. Well then, by the world, a man can't speak civilly to a woman now but presently she says he makes love to her. Nay, madam, you shall stay, with your pardon, since you have not yet understood

---

304 s.d. *carelessly*: unconcernedly.

him, till he has made an éclaircissement of his love to you, that is, what kind of love it is. [*To* HARCOURT] Answer to thy catechism. Friend, do you love my mistress here?

HARCOURT. Yes, I wish she would not doubt it.

SPARKISH. But how do you love her?

HARCOURT. With all my soul.

ALITHEA. I thank him; methinks he speaks plain enough now.

SPARKISH. (*to* ALITHEA) You are out still. – But with what kind of love, Harcourt?

HARCOURT. With the best and truest love in the world.

SPARKISH. Look you there then, that is with no matrimonial love, I'm sure.

ALITHEA. How's that? Do you say matrimonial love is not best?

SPARKISH. Gad, I went too far ere I was aware. But speak for thyself, Harcourt; you said you would not wrong me nor her.

HARCOURT. No, no, madam, e'en take him for heaven's sake –

SPARKISH. Look you there, madam.

HARCOURT. Who should in all justice be yours, he that loves you most. (*Claps his hand on his breast*)

ALITHEA. Look you there, Mr Sparkish, who's that?

SPARKISH. Who should it be? – Go on, Harcourt.

HARCOURT. Who loves you more than women titles or fortune fools. (*Points at* SPARKISH)

SPARKISH. Look you there, he means me still, for he points at me.

ALITHEA. Ridiculous!

HARCOURT. Who can only match your faith and constancy in love.

SPARKISH. Ay.

HARCOURT. Who knows, if it be possible, how to value so much beauty and virtue.

SPARKISH. Ay.

HARCOURT. Whose love can no more be equalled in the world than that heavenly form of yours.

SPARKISH. No.

---

338 *éclaircissement*: full explanation.

HARCOURT. Who could no more suffer a rival than your absence, and yet could no more suspect your virtue than his own constancy in his love to you.

SPARKISH. No.

HARCOURT. Who, in fine, loves you better than his eyes that first made him love you.

SPARKISH. Ay – nay, madam, faith, you shan't go till –

ALITHEA. Have a care, lest you make me stay too long –

SPARKISH. But till he has saluted you, that I may be assured you are friends, after his honest advice and declaration. Come, pray, madam, be friends with him.

Enter MR PINCHWIFE, MRS PINCHWIFE

ALITHEA. You must pardon me, sir, that I am not yet so obedient to you.

PINCHWIFE. What, invite your wife to kiss men? Monstrous! Are you not ashamed? I will never forgive you.

SPARKISH. Are you not ashamed that I should have more confidence in the chastity of your family than you have? You must not teach me. I am a man of honour, sir, though I am frank and free; I am frank, sir –

PINCHWIFE. Very frank, sir, to share your wife with your friends.

SPARKISH. He is an humble, menial friend, such as reconciles the differences of the marriage bed. You know man and wife do not always agree; I design him for that use, therefore would have him well with my wife.

PINCHWIFE. A menial friend! – you will get a great many menial friends by showing your wife as you do.

SPARKISH. What then? It may be I have a pleasure in't, as I have to show fine clothes at a playhouse the first day and count money before poor rogues.

PINCHWIFE. He that shows his wife or money will be in danger of having them borrowed sometimes.

SPARKISH. I love to be envied and would not marry a wife that I alone could love; loving alone is as dull as

---

382 *in fine*: to conclude.
397 *frank*: candid, open, generous.
401 *menial*: domestic.

eating alone. Is it not a frank age? And I am a frank person. And to tell you the truth, it may be I love to have rivals in a wife; they make her seem to a man still but as a kept mistress. And so good night, for I must to Whitehall. – Madam, I hope you are now reconciled to my friend and so I wish you a good night, madam, and sleep if you can, for tomorrow you know I must visit you early with a canonical gentleman. Good night, dear Harcourt. *Exit* SPARKISH.

HARCOURT. Madam, I hope you will not refuse my visit tomorrow, if it should be earlier, with a canonical gentleman, than Mr Sparkish's.

PINCHWIFE. (*coming between* ALITHEA *and* HARCOURT) This gentlewoman is yet under my care; therefore you must yet forbear your freedom with her, sir.

HARCOURT. Must, sir!

PINCHWIFE. Yes, sir, she is my sister.

HARCOURT. 'Tis well she is, sir – for I must be her servant, sir. – Madam –

PINCHWIFE. Come away, sister; we had been gone, if it had not been for you, and so avoided these lewd rake-hells, who seem to haunt us.

Enter HORNER, DORILANT *to them.*

HORNER. How now, Pinchwife?

PINCHWIFE. Your servant.

HORNER. What, I see a little time in the country makes a man turn wild and unsociable and only fit to converse with his horses, dogs and his herds.

PINCHWIFE. I have business, sir, and must mind it; your business is pleasure, therefore you and I must go different ways.

HORNER. Well, you may go on, but this pretty young gentleman – (*Takes hold of* MRS PINCHWIFE)

HARCOURT. The lady –

DORILANT. And the maid –

HORNER. Shall stay with us, for I suppose their business is the same with ours, pleasure.

435–6 *rakehells*: rakes, ruffians.

PINCHWIFE. (*aside*) 'Sdeath, he know her, she carries it so sillily! Yet if he does not, I should be more silly to discover it first.

ALITHEA. Pray, let us go, sir.

PINCHWIFE. Come, come –

HORNER. (*to* MRS PINCHWIFE) Had you not rather stay with us? – Prithee, Pinchwife, who is this pretty young gentleman?

PINCHWIFE. One to whom I'm a guardian. (*Aside*) I wish I could keep her out of your hands.

HORNER. Who is he? I never saw anything so pretty in all my life.

PINCHWIFE. Pshaw, do not look upon him so much. He's a poor bashful youth, you'll put him out of countenance. – Come away, brother. (*Offers to take her away*)

HORNER. Oh, your brother!

PINCHWIFE. Yes, my wife's brother. – Come, come, she'll stay supper for us.

HORNER. I thought so, for he is very like her I saw you at the play with, whom I told you I was in love with.

MRS PINCHWIFE. (*aside*) O jeminy! Is this he that was in love with me? I am glad on't, I vow, for he's a curious fine gentleman, and I love him already too. (*To* MR PINCHWIFE) Is this he, bud?

PINCHWIFE. (*to his wife*) Come away, come away.

HORNER. Why, what haste are you in? Why won't you let me talk with him?

PINCHWIFE. Because you'll debauch him; he's yet young and innocent and I would not have him debauched for anything in the world. (*Aside*) How she gazes on him! The devil!

HORNER. Harcourt, Dorilant, look you here; this is the likeness of that dowdy he told us of, his wife. Did you ever see a lovelier creature? The rogue has reason to be jealous of his wife since she is like him, for she would make all that see her in love with her.

HARCOURT. And as I remember now, she is as like him here as can be.

DORILANT. She is indeed very pretty, if she be like him.

---

483 *dowdy*: a plain, dull woman.

HORNER. Very pretty? A very pretty commendation! She is a glorious creature, beautiful beyond all things I ever beheld.

PINCHWIFE. So, so.

HARCOURT. More beautiful than a poet's first mistress of imagination.

HORNER. Or another man's last mistress of flesh and blood.

MRS PINCHWIFE. Nay, now you jeer, sir; pray don't jeer me.

PINCHWIFE. Come, come. (*Aside*) By heavens, she'll discover herself!

HORNER. I speak of your sister, sir.

PINCHWIFE. Ay, but saying she was handsome, if like him, made him blush. (*Aside*) I am upon a rack!

HORNER. Methinks he is so handsome he should not be a man.

PINCHWIFE. [*aside*] Oh, there 'tis out! He has discovered her! I am not able to suffer any longer. (*To his wife*) Come, come away, I say.

HORNER. Nay, by your leave, sir, he shall not go yet. – (*To them*) Harcourt, Dorilant, let us torment this jealous rogue a little.

HARCOURT.
DORILANT. } How?

HORNER. I'll show you.

PINCHWIFE. Come, pray, let him go, I cannot stay fooling any longer. I tell you his sister stays supper for us.

HORNER. Does she? Come then, we'll all go sup with her and thee.

PINCHWIFE. No, now I think on't, having stayed so long for us, I warrant she's gone to bed. (*Aside*) I wish she and I were well out of their hands. – Come, I must rise early tomorrow, come.

HORNER. Well, then, if she be gone to bed, I wish her and you a good night. But pray, young gentleman, present my humble service to her.

MRS PINCHWIFE. Thank you heartily, sir.

PINCHWIFE. (*aside*) 'Sdeath! she will discover herself yet in spite of me. – He is something more civil to you, for your kindness to his sister, than I am, it seems.

HORNER. Tell her, dear sweet little gentleman, for all

your brother there, that you have revived the love I had for her at first sight in the playhouse.

MRS PINCHWIFE. But did you love her indeed, and indeed?

PINCHWIFE. (*aside*) So, so. – Away, I say.

HORNER. Nay, stay. Yes, indeed, and indeed, pray do you tell her so, and give her this kiss from me. (*Kisses her*)

PINCHWIFE. (*aside*) O heavens! What do I suffer! Now 'tis too plain he knows her, and yet –

HORNER. And this, and this – (*Kisses her again*)

MRS PINCHWIFE. What do you kiss me for? I am no woman.

PINCHWIFE. (*aside*) So – there, 'tis out. – Come, I cannot, nor will stay any longer.

HORNER. Nay, they shall send your lady a kiss too. Here, Harcourt, Dorilant, will you not?

They kiss her.

PINCHWIFE. (*aside*) How! Do I suffer this? Was I not accusing another just now for this rascally patience, in permitting his wife to be kissed before his face? Ten thousand ulcers gnaw away their lips! – Come, come.

HORNER. Good night, dear little gentleman. Madam, good night. Farewell, Pinchwife. (*Apart to* HARCOURT *and* DORILANT) Did not I tell you I would raise his jealous gall?

Exeunt HORNER, HARCOURT *and* DORILANT.

PINCHWIFE. So, they are gone at last; stay, let me see first if the coach be at this door. *Exit.*

HORNER, HARCOURT, DORILANT *return.*

HORNER. What, not gone yet? Will you be sure to do as I desired you, sweet sir?

MRS PINCHWIFE. Sweet sir, but what will you give me then?

HORNER. Anything. Come away into the next walk.

Exit HORNER, *haling away* MRS PINCHWIFE.

ALITHEA. Hold, hold! What d'ye do?

LUCY. Stay, stay, hold –

HARCOURT. Hold, madam, hold! Let him present him,

567 *present*: give a present to.

he'll come presently. Nay, I will never let you go till you answer my question.

LUCY. For God's sake, sir, I must follow 'em.

DORILANT. No, I have something to present you with too; you shan't follow them.

ALITHEA, LUCY struggling with HARCOURT and DORILANT.

PINCHWIFE returns.

PINCHWIFE. Where? – how? – what's become of? – gone! – whither?

LUCY. He's only gone with the gentleman, who will give him something, an't please your worship.

PINCHWIFE. Something – give him something, with a pox! – where are they?

ALITHEA. In the next walk only, brother.

PINCHWIFE. Only, only! Where, where?

Exit PINCHWIFE and returns presently, then goes out again.

HARCOURT. What's the matter with him? Why so much concerned? But dearest madam –

ALITHEA. Pray let me go, sir; I have said and suffered enough already.

HARCOURT. Then you will not look upon nor pity my sufferings?

ALITHEA. To look upon 'em, when I cannot help 'em, were cruelty, not pity; therefore I will never see you more.

HARCOURT. Let me then, madam, have my privilege of a banished lover, complaining or railing, and giving you but a farewell reason why, if you cannot condescend to marry me, you should not take that wretch, my rival.

ALITHEA. He only, not you, since my honour is engaged so far to him, can give me a reason why I should not marry him; but if he be true and what I think him to me, I must be so to him. Your servant, sir.

HARCOURT. Have women only constancy when 'tis a vice and, like fortune, only true to fools?

DORILANT. (*to LUCY, who struggles to get from him*) Thou shalt not stir, thou robust creature; you see I can deal with you, therefore you should stay the rather, and be kind.

Enter PINCHWIFE.

PINCHWIFE. Gone, gone, not to be found! Quite gone! Ten thousand plagues go with 'em! Which way went they?

ALITHEA. But into t'other walk, brother.

LUCY. Their business will be done presently sure, an't please your worship; it can't be long in doing, I'm sure on't.

ALITHEA. Are they not there?

PINCHWIFE. No; you know where they are, you infamous wretch, eternal shame of your family, which you do not dishonour enough yourself, you think, but you must help her to do it too, thou legion of bawds!

ALITHEA. Good brother –

PINCHWIFE. Damned, damned sister!

ALITHEA. Look you here, she's coming.

Enter MRS PINCHWIFE *in man's clothes, running, with her hat under her arm, full of oranges and dried fruit;* HORNER *following.*

MRS PINCHWIFE. O dear bud, look you here what I have got, see!

PINCHWIFE. (*aside, rubbing his forehead*) And what I have got here too, which you can't see.

MRS PINCHWIFE. The fine gentleman has given me better things yet.

PINCHWIFE. Has he so? (*Aside*) Out of breath and coloured! I must hold yet.

HORNER. I have only given your little brother an orange, sir.

PINCHWIFE. (*to* HORNER) Thank you, sir. (*Aside*) You have only squeezed my orange, I suppose, and given it me again; yet I must have a city patience. (*To his wife*) Come, come away.

MRS PINCHWIFE. Stay, till I have put up my fine things, bud.

Enter SIR JASPAR FIDGET.

---

631 *city patience*: the patience of a city husband cuckolded by a gallant.

SIR JASPAR. O Master Horner, come, come, the ladies stay for you; your mistress, my wife, wonders you make not more haste to her.

HORNER. I have stayed this half hour for you here and 'tis your fault I am not now with your wife.

SIR JASPAR. But pray, don't let her know so much; the truth on't is, I was advancing a certain project to his Majesty about – I'll tell you.

HORNER. No, let's go and hear it at your house. – Good night, sweet little gentleman. One kiss more, you'll remember me now, I hope. (*Kisses her*)

DORILANT. What, Sir Jaspar, will you separate friends? He promised to sup with us; and if you take him to your house, you'll be in danger of our company too.

SIR JASPAR. Alas, gentlemen, my house is not fit for you; there are none but civil women there, which are not fit for your turn. He, you know, can bear with the society of civil women now, ha, ha, ha! Besides, he's one of my family – he's – heh, heh, heh!

DORILANT. What is he?

SIR JASPAR. Faith, my eunuch, since you'll have it, heh, he, he!

Exeunt SIR JASPAR FIDGET, *and* HORNER.

DORILANT. I rather wish thou wert his, or my cuckold. Harcourt, what a good cuckold is lost there for want of a man to make him one! Thee and I cannot have Horner's privilege, who can make use of it.

HARCOURT. Ay, to poor Horner 'tis like coming to an estate at threescore, when a man can't be the better for't.

PINCHWIFE. Come.

MRS PINCHWIFE. Presently, bud.

DORILANT. Come, let us go too. (*To* ALITHEA) Madam, your servant. (*To* LUCY) Good night, strapper.

HARCOURT. Madam, though you will not let me have a good day or night, I wish you one; but dare not name the other half of my wish.

---

656 s.d. *Exeunt*: *Exit* Q1.

668 *strapper*: strapping wench, tall and robust.

ALITHEA. Good night, sir, forever.

MRS PINCHWIFE. I don't know where to put this here, dear bud; you shall eat it; nay, you shall have part of the fine gentleman's good things, or treat as you call it, when we come home.

PINCHWIFE. Indeed, I deserve it, since I furnished the best part of it. (*Strikes away the orange*)
The gallant treats, presents, and gives the ball
But 'tis the absent cuckold pays for all.

[*Exeunt.*]

ACT IV

SCENE I

In PINCHWIFE*'s house in the morning.*

LUCY, ALITHEA *dressed in new clothes.*

LUCY. Well – madam, now have I dressed you and set you out with so many ornaments and spent upon you ounces of essence and pulvilio; and all this for no other purpose but as people adorn and perfume a corpse for a stinking secondhand grave – such or as bad I think as Master Sparkish's bed.

ALITHEA. Hold your peace.

LUCY. Nay, madam, I will ask you the reason why you would banish poor Master Harcourt forever from your sight. How could you be so hardhearted?

ALITHEA. 'Twas because I was not hardhearted.

LUCY. No, no, 'twas stark love and kindness, I warrant.

ALITHEA. It was so; I would see him no more because I love him.

LUCY. Hey-day, a very pretty reason!

ALITHEA. You do not understand me.

LUCY. I wish you may yourself.

3 *essence and pulvilio*: scent and perfumed powder.

ALITHEA. I was engaged to marry, you see, another man, whom my justice will not suffer me to deceive or injure.

LUCY. Can there be a greater cheat or wrong done to a man than to give him your person without your heart? I should make a conscience of it.

ALITHEA. I'll retrieve it for him after I am married a while.

LUCY. The woman that marries to love better will be as much mistaken as the wencher that marries to live better. No, madam, marrying to increase love is like gaming to become rich; alas, you only lose what little stock you had before.

ALITHEA. I find by your rhetoric you have been bribed to betray me.

LUCY. Only by his merit, that has bribed your heart, you see, against your word and rigid honour. But what a devil is this honour! 'Tis sure a disease in the head, like the megrim, or falling sickness, that always hurries people away to do themselves mischief. Men lose their lives by it; women what's dearer to 'em, their love, the life of life.

ALITHEA. Come, pray talk you no more of honour, nor Master Harcourt. I wish the other would come to secure my fidelity to him and his right in me.

LUCY. You will marry him then?

ALITHEA. Certainly. I have given him already my word and will my hand too, to make it good when he comes.

LUCY. Well, I wish I may never stick pin more if he be not an arrant natural to t'other fine gentleman.

ALITHEA. I own he wants the wit of Harcourt, which I will dispense withal for another want he has, which is want of jealousy, which men of wit seldom want.

LUCY. Lord, madam, what should you do with a fool to your husband? You intend to be honest, don't you? Then that husbandly virtue, credulity, is thrown away upon you.

ALITHEA. He only that could suspect my virtue should

---

36 *megrim*: migraine.
36 *falling sickness*: epilepsy.
47 *natural*: simpleton.

have cause to do it; 'tis Sparkish's confidence in my truth that obliges me to be so faithful to him.

LUCY. You are not sure his opinion may last.

ALITHEA. I am satisfied 'tis impossible for him to be jealous after the proofs I have had of him. Jealousy in a husband – Heaven defend me from it! It begets a thousand plagues to a poor woman, the loss of her honour, her quiet and her –

LUCY. And her pleasure.

ALITHEA. What d'ye mean, impertinent?

LUCY. Liberty is a great pleasure, madam.

ALITHEA. I say, loss of her honour, her quiet, nay, her life sometimes, and what's as bad almost, the loss of this town; that is, she is sent into the country, which is the last ill usage of a husband to a wife, I think.

LUCY. (*aside*) Oh, does the wind lie there? – Then, of necessity, madam, you think a man must carry his wife into the country, if he be wise. The country is as terrible, I find, to our young English ladies as a monastery to those abroad, and, on my virginity, I think they would rather marry a London gaoler than a high sheriff of a county, since neither can stir from his employment. Formerly women of wit married fools for a great estate, a fine seat, or the like, but now 'tis for a pretty seat only in Lincoln's Inn Fields, St James's Fields or the Pall Mall.

Enter to them SPARKISH *and* HARCOURT *dressed like a parson.*

SPARKISH. Madam, your humble servant, a happy day to you, and to us all.

HARCOURT. Amen.

ALITHEA. Who have we here?

SPARKISH. My chaplain, faith. O madam, poor Harcourt remembers his humble service to you and, in obedience to your last commands, refrains coming into your sight.

80–1 *Lincoln's Inn . . . Pall Mall*: fashionable areas to live in. Lincoln's Inn Fields is a square west of Lincoln's Inn; St James's Fields had been built over and become St James's Square; Pall Mall, the 'Old Pell Mell' in which Act IV Scene ii of *Love in a Wood* is set, is near St James's Palace and was then the home of Nell Gwynn, among others.

ALITHEA. Is not that he?

SPARKISH. No, fie, no; but to show that he ne'er intended to hinder our match, has sent his brother here to join our hands. When I get me a wife, I must get her a chaplain, according to the custom; this is his brother, and my chaplain.

ALITHEA. His brother?

LUCY. (*aside*) And your chaplain, to preach in your pulpit then.

ALITHEA. His brother!

SPARKISH. Nay, I knew you would not believe it. – I told you, sir, she would take you for your brother Frank.

ALITHEA. Believe it!

LUCY. (*aside*) His brother! hah, ha, he! He has a trick left still, it seems.

SPARKISH. Come, my dearest, pray let us go to church before the canonical hour is past.

ALITHEA. For shame, you are abused still.

SPARKISH. By the world, 'tis strange now you are so incredulous.

ALITHEA. 'Tis strange you are so credulous.

SPARKISH. Dearest of my life, hear me. I tell you this is Ned Harcourt of Cambridge; by the world, you see he has a sneaking college look. 'Tis true he's something like his brother Frank and they differ from each other no more than in their age, for they were twins.

LUCY. Hah, ha, he!

ALITHEA. Your servant, sir; I cannot be so deceived, though you are. But come, let's hear; how do you know what you affirm so confidently?

SPARKISH. Why, I'll tell you all. Frank Harcourt coming to me this morning, to wish me joy and present his service to you, I asked him if he could help me to a parson, whereupon he told me he had a brother in town who was in orders and he went straight away and sent him you see there to me.

ALITHEA. Yes, Frank goes and puts on a black coat, then tells you he is Ned; that's all you have for't.

SPARKISH. Pshaw, pshaw, I tell you by the same token,

---

107 *canonical hour*: marriages could only be celebrated in church between 8 a.m. and noon.

the midwife put her garter about Frank's neck to know 'em asunder, they were so like.

ALITHEA. Frank tells you this too.

SPARKISH. Ay, and Ned there too; nay, they are both in a story.

ALITHEA. So, so; very foolish!

SPARKISH. Lord, if you won't believe one, you had best try him by your chambermaid there, for chambermaids must needs know chaplains from other men, they are so used to 'em.

LUCY. Let's see; nay, I'll be sworn he has the canonical smirk and the filthy, clammy palm of a chaplain.

ALITHEA. Well, most reverend doctor, pray let us make an end of this fooling.

HARCOURT. With all my soul, divine, heavenly creature, when you please.

ALITHEA. He speaks like a chaplain indeed.

SPARKISH. Why, was there not 'soul', 'divine', 'heavenly', in what he said?

ALITHEA. Once more, most impertinent black coat, cease your persecution and let us have a conclusion of this ridiculous love.

HARCOURT. (*aside*) I had forgot. I must suit my style to my coat, or I wear it in vain.

ALITHEA. I have no more patience left; let us make once an end of this troublesome love, I say.

HARCOURT. So be it, seraphic lady, when your honour shall think it meet and convenient so to do.

SPARKISH. Gad, I'm sure none but a chaplain could speak so, I think.

ALITHEA. Let me tell you, sir, this dull trick will not serve your turn; though you delay our marriage, you shall not hinder it.

HARCOURT. Far be it from me, munificent patroness, to delay your marriage. I desire nothing more than to marry you presently, which I might do, if you yourself would, for my noble, good-natured and thrice generous patron here would not hinder it.

SPARKISH. No, poor man, not I, faith.

137–9 a standard Restoration joke on the promiscuity of clergymen – and chambermaids.

HARCOURT. And now, madam, let me tell you plainly, nobody else shall marry you; by heavens, I'll die first, for I'm sure I should die after it.

LUCY. [*aside*] How his love has made him forget his function, as I have seen it in real parsons!

ALITHEA. That was spoken like a chaplain too! Now you understand him, I hope.

SPARKISH. Poor man, he takes it heinously to be refused. I can't blame him; 'tis putting an indignity upon him not to be suffered. But you'll pardon me, madam, it shan't be, he shall marry us. Come away, pray, madam.

LUCY. [*aside*] Hah, ha, he! More ado! 'Tis late.

ALITHEA. Invincible stupidity! I tell you he would marry me as your rival, not as your chaplain.

SPARKISH. (*pulling her away*) Come, come, madam.

LUCY. Ay, pray, madam, do not refuse this reverend divine the honour and satisfaction of marrying you, for I dare say he has set his heart upon't, good doctor.

ALITHEA. What can you hope or design by this?

HARCOURT. [*aside*] I could answer her, a reprieve for a day only often revokes a hasty doom; at worst, if she will not take mercy on me and let me marry her, I have at least the lover's second pleasure, hindering my rival's enjoyment, though but for a time.

SPARKISH. Come, madam, 'tis e'en twelve o'clock, and my mother charged me never to be married out of the canonical hours. Come, come. Lord, here's such a deal of modesty, I warrant, the first day.

LUCY. Yes, an't please your worship, married women show all their modesty the first day, because married men show all their love the first day.

Exeunt SPARKISH, ALITHEA, HARCOURT *and* LUCY.

170–1 *die . . . die*: the traditional pun on *orgasm* and *death*.

SCENE II

The scene changes to a bedchamber, where appear PINCHWIFE, MRS PINCHWIFE.

PINCHWIFE. Come, tell me, I say.

MRS PINCHWIFE. Lord, han't I told it an hundred times over?

PINCHWIFE. (*aside*) I would try if, in the repetition of the ungrateful tale, I could find her altering it in the least circumstance, for if her story be false, she is so too. – Come, how was't, baggage?

MRS PINCHWIFE. Lord, what pleasure you take to hear it, sure!

PINCHWIFE. No, you take more in telling it, I find; but speak, how was't?

MRS PINCHWIFE. He carried me up into the house next to the Exchange.

PINCHWIFE. So, and you two were only in the room.

MRS PINCHWIFE. Yes, for he sent away a youth that was there, for some dried fruit and China oranges.

PINCHWIFE. Did he so? Damn him for it – and for –

MRS PINCHWIFE. But presently came up the gentlewoman of the house.

PINCHWIFE. O, 'twas well she did; but what did he do whilst the fruit came?

MRS PINCHWIFE. He kissed me an hundred times and told me he fancied he kissed my fine sister, meaning me, you know, whom he said he loved with all his soul and bid me be sure to tell her so and to desire her to be at her window by eleven of the clock this morning and he would walk under it at that time.

PINCHWIFE. (*aside*) And he was as good as his word, very punctual – a pox reward him for't.

MRS PINCHWIFE. Well, and he said if you were not within, he would come up to her, meaning me, you know, bud, still.

PINCHWIFE. (*aside*) So – he knew her certainly; but for this confession, I am obliged to her simplicity. – But what, you stood very still when he kissed you?

---

16 *China oranges*: the sweet orange, *citrus sinensis*, supposedly from China; a delicacy at this time.

MRS PINCHWIFE. Yes, I warrant you; would you have had me discovered myself?

PINCHWIFE. But you told me he did some beastliness to you, as you called it; what was't?

MRS PINCHWIFE. Why, he put –

PINCHWIFE. What?

MRS PINCHWIFE. Why, he put the tip of his tongue between my lips and so mousled me – and I said, I'd bite it.

PINCHWIFE. An eternal canker seize it, for a dog!

MRS PINCHWIFE. Nay, you need not be so angry with him neither, for to say truth, he has the sweetest breath I ever knew.

PINCHWIFE. The devil! – you were satisfied with it then, and would do it again.

MRS PINCHWIFE. Not unless he should force me.

PINCHWIFE. Force you, changeling! I tell you no woman can be forced.

MRS PINCHWIFE. Yes, but she may, sure, by such a one as he, for he's a proper, goodly strong man; 'tis hard, let me tell you, to resist him.

PINCHWIFE. So, 'tis plain she loves him, yet she has not love enough to make her conceal it from me; but the sight of him will increase her aversion for me and love for him and that love instruct her how to deceive me and satisfy him, all idiot as she is. Love! 'Twas he gave women first their craft, their art of deluding; out of nature's hands they came plain, open, silly and fit for slaves, as she and Heaven intended 'em; but damned love – well – I must strangle that little monster whilst I can deal with him. – Go fetch pen, ink and paper out of the next room.

MRS PINCHWIFE. Yes, bud. *Exit* MRS PINCHWIFE.

PINCHWIFE. (*aside*) Why should women have more invention in love than men? It can only be because they have more desires, more soliciting passions, more lust, and more of the devil.

MRS PINCHWIFE *returns.*

Come, minx, sit down and write.

---

43 *mousled*: rumpled.
65–6 *little monster*: Cupid.

MRS PINCHWIFE. Ay, dear bud, but I can't do't very well.

PINCHWIFE. I wish you could not at all.

MRS PINCHWIFE. But what should I write for?

PINCHWIFE. I'll have you write a letter to your lover.

MRS PINCHWIFE. O Lord, to the fine gentleman a letter!

PINCHWIFE. Yes, to the fine gentleman.

MRS PINCHWIFE. Lord, you do but jeer; sure, you jest.

PINCHWIFE. I am not so merry. Come, write as I bid you.

MRS PINCHWIFE. What, do you think I am a fool?

PINCHWIFE. [*aside*] She's afraid I would not dictate any love to him, therefore she's unwilling. – But you had best begin.

MRS PINCHWIFE. Indeed, and indeed, but I won't, so I won't.

PINCHWIFE. Why?

MRS PINCHWIFE. Because he's in town; you may send for him if you will.

PINCHWIFE. Very well, you would have him brought to you; is it come to this? I say, take the pen and write, or you'll provoke me.

MRS PINCHWIFE. Lord, what d'ye make a fool of me for? Don't I know that letters are never writ but from the country to London and from London into the country? Now he's in town and I am in town too; therefore I can't write to him, you know.

PINCHWIFE. (*aside*) So, I am glad it is no worse; she is innocent enough yet. – Yes, you may, when your husband bids you, write letters to people that are in town.

MRS PINCHWIFE. O, may I so? Then I'm satisfied.

PINCHWIFE. Come, begin. – (*Dictates*) 'Sir' –

MRS PINCHWIFE. Shan't I say, 'Dear Sir'? You know one says always something more than bare 'Sir'.

PINCHWIFE. Write as I bid you, or I will write 'whore' with this penknife in your face.

MRS PINCHWIFE. Nay, good bud – (*She writes*) 'Sir' –

PINCHWIFE. 'Though I suffered last night your nauseous, loathed kisses and embraces' – Write.

MRS PINCHWIFE. Nay, why should I say so? You know I told you he had a sweet breath.

PINCHWIFE. Write.

MRS PINCHWIFE. Let me but put out 'loathed'.

PINCHWIFE. Write, I say.

MRS PINCHWIFE. Well then. (*Writes*)

PINCHWIFE. Let's see, what have you writ? (*Takes the paper and reads*) 'Though I suffered last night your kisses and embraces' – Thou impudent creature, where is 'nauseous' and 'loathed'?

MRS PINCHWIFE. I can't abide to write such filthy words.

PINCHWIFE. Once more write as I'd have you, and question it not, or I will spoil thy writing with this. (*Holds up the penknife*) I will stab out those eyes that cause my mischief.

MRS PINCHWIFE. O Lord, I will!

PINCHWIFE. So – so – let's see now! (*Reads*) 'Though I suffered last night your nauseous, loathed kisses and embraces' – go on – 'yet I would not have you presume that you shall ever repeat them' – So –

She writes.

MRS PINCHWIFE. I have writ it.

PINCHWIFE. On then. – 'I then concealed myself from your knowledge to avoid your insolencies' –

She writes.

MRS PINCHWIFE. So –

PINCHWIFE. 'The same reason, now I am out of your hands' –

She writes.

MRS PINCHWIFE. So –

PINCHWIFE. 'Makes me own to you my unfortunate, though innocent, frolic, of being in man's clothes' –

She writes.

MRS PINCHWIFE. So –

PINCHWIFE. 'That you may for evermore cease to pursue her, who hates and detests you' –

She writes on.

MRS PINCHWIFE. So – h – (*Sighs*)

PINCHWIFE. What, do you sigh? – 'detests you – as much as she loves her husband and her honour'.

MRS PINCHWIFE. I vow, husband, he'll ne'er believe I should write such a letter.

PINCHWIFE. What, he'd expect a kinder from you? Come, now your name only.

MRS PINCHWIFE. What, shan't I say, 'Your most faithful, humble servant till death'?

PINCHWIFE. No, tormenting fiend! (*Aside*) Her style, I find, would be very soft. – Come, wrap it up now, whilst I go fetch wax and a candle, and write on the backside, 'For Mr Horner.' *Exit* PINCHWIFE.

MRS PINCHWIFE. 'For Mr Horner.' – So, I am glad he has told me his name. Dear Mr Horner! But why should I send thee such a letter that will vex thee and make thee angry with me? – Well, I will not send it – Ay, but then my husband will kill me – for I see plainly he won't let me love Mr Horner – but what care I for my husband? – I won't, so I won't send poor Mr Horner such a letter – But then my husband – But oh – What if I writ at bottom, my husband made me write it? – Ay, but then my husband would see't – Can one have no shift? Ah, a London woman would have had a hundred presently. Stay – what if I should write a letter, and wrap it up like this, and write upon't too? Ay, but then my husband would see't – I don't know what to do – But yet y'vads I'll try, so I will – for I will not send this letter to poor Mr Horner, come what will on't. (*She writes, and repeats what she hath writ*)
'Dear, sweet Mr Horner' – so – 'my husband would have me send you a base, rude, unmannerly letter – but I won't' – so – 'and would have me forbid you loving me – but I won't' – so – 'and would have me say to you, I hate you, poor Mr Horner – but I won't tell a lie for him' – there – 'for I'm sure if you and I were in the country at cards together' – so – 'I could not help treading on your toe under the table' – so – 'or rubbing knees with you and staring in your face till you saw me' – very well – 'and then looking down and blushing for an hour together' – so – 'but I must make haste before my husband comes; and now he has taught me to write letters, you shall have longer ones from me, who am,
Dear, dear, poor, dear Mr Horner,
Your most humble friend, and servant
to command till death,
Margery Pinchwife.'

---

171 *shift*: stratagem.
175 *y'vads*: in faith.

Stay, I must give him a hint at bottom – so – now wrap it up just like t'other – so – now write, 'For Mr Horner' – But, oh now, what shall I do with it? For here comes my husband.

Enter PINCHWIFE.

PINCHWIFE. (*aside*) I have been detained by a sparkish coxcomb, who pretended a visit to me; but I fear 'twas to my wife. – What, have you done?

MRS PINCHWIFE. Ay, ay, bud, just now.

PINCHWIFE. Let's see't. What d'ye tremble for? What, you would not have it go?

MRS PINCHWIFE. Here. (*Aside*) No, I must not give him that; so I had been served if I had given him this.

PINCHWIFE. (*He opens, and reads the first letter*) Come, where's the wax and seal?

MRS PINCHWIFE. (*aside*) Lord, what shall I do now? Nay, then, I have it. – Pray let me see't. Lord, you think me so arrant a fool I cannot seal a letter. I will do't, so I will. (*Snatches the letter from him, changes it for the other, seals it and delivers it to him*)

PINCHWIFE. Nay, I believe you will learn that, and other things too, which I would not have you.

MRS PINCHWIFE. So, han't I done it curiously? (*Aside*) I think I have; there's my letter going to Mr Horner, since he'll needs have me send letters to folks.

PINCHWIFE. 'Tis very well; but I warrant you would not have it go now?

MRS PINCHWIFE. Yes, indeed, but I would, bud, now.

PINCHWIFE. Well, you are a good girl then. Come, let me lock you up in your chamber, till I come back, and be sure you come not within three strides of the window when I am gone, for I have a spy in the street.

Exit MRS PINCHWIFE. PINCHWIFE *locks the door.*

At least, 'tis fit she think so. If we do not cheat women, they'll cheat us, and fraud may be justly used with secret enemies, of which a wife is the most dangerous, and he that has a handsome one to keep, and a frontier town, must provide against treachery rather than open force. Now I have secured all within, I'll deal with the foe without with false intelligence.

Holds up the letter. Exit PINCHWIFE.

---

216 *curiously*: skilfully.

SCENE III

The scene changes to HORNER*'s lodging.*

QUACK *and* HORNER.

QUACK. Well, sir, how fadges the new design? Have you not the luck of all your brother projectors, to deceive only yourself at last?

HORNER. No, good domine doctor, I deceive you, it seems, and others too, for the grave matrons and old, rigid husbands think me as unfit for love as they are but their wives, sisters and daughters know some of 'em better things already.

QUACK. Already!

HORNER. Already, I say. Last night I was drunk with half a dozen of your civil persons, as you call 'em, and people of honour, and so was made free of their society and dressing-rooms forever hereafter, and am already come to the privileges of sleeping upon their pallats, warming smocks, tying shoes and garters, and the like, doctor, already, already, doctor.

QUACK. You have made use of your time, sir.

HORNER. I tell thee, I am now no more interruption to 'em when they sing or talk bawdy than a little squab French page who speaks no English.

QUACK. But do civil persons and women of honour drink and sing bawdy songs?

HORNER. O, amongst friends, amongst friends. For your bigots in honour are just like those in religion; they fear the eye of the world more than the eye of Heaven and think there is no virtue but railing at vice and no sin but giving scandal. They rail at a poor, little, kept player and keep themselves some young, modest pulpit comedian to be privy to their sins in their closets, not to tell 'em of them in their chapels.

---

1 *fadges*: succeeds.
2 *projectors*: schemers, promoters of hare-brained and often fraudulent projects.
4 *domine*: master.
15 *pallats*: mattresses.
19 *squab*: short and plump.
29 *pulpit comedian*: chaplain.

QUACK. Nay, the truth on't is, priests among the women now have quite got the better of us lay confessors, physicians.

HORNER. And they are rather their patients, but –

Enter MY LADY FIDGET, *looking about her.*

Now we talk of women of honour, here comes one. Step behind the screen there and but observe if I have not particular privileges with the women of reputation already, doctor, already.

[QUACK *steps behind screen.*]

LADY FIDGET. Well, Horner, am not I a woman of honour? You see I'm as good as my word.

HORNER. And you shall see, madam, I'll not be behindhand with you in honour and I'll be as good as my word too, if you please but to withdraw into the next room.

LADY FIDGET. But first, my dear sir, you must promise to have a care of my dear honour.

HORNER. If you talk a word more of your honour, you'll make me incapable to wrong it. To talk of honour in the mysteries of love is like talking of heaven or the deity in an operation of witchcraft, just when you are employing the devil; it makes the charm impotent.

LADY FIDGET. Nay, fie, let us not be smooty. But you talk of mysteries and bewitching to me; I don't understand you.

HORNER. I tell you, madam, the word 'money' in a mistress's mouth, at such a nick of time, is not a more disheartening sound to a younger brother than that of 'honour' to an eager lover like myself.

LADY FIDGET. But you can't blame a lady of my reputation to be chary.

HORNER. Chary! I have been chary of it already, by the report I have caused of myself.

LADY FIDGET. Ay, but if you should ever let other women know that dear secret, it would come out. Nay, you must have a great care of your conduct, for my acquaintance are so censorious (oh, 'tis a

---

53 *smooty*: smutty.
56–8 younger brothers were traditionally impecunious.

wicked, censorious world, Mr Horner!), I say, are so censorious and detracting that perhaps they'll talk, to the prejudice of my honour, though you should not let them know the dear secret.

HORNER. Nay, madam, rather than they shall prejudice your honour, I'll prejudice theirs, and, to serve you, I'll lie with 'em all, make the secret their own, and then they'll keep it. I am a Machiavel in love, madam.

LADY FIDGET. Oh, no, sir, not that way.

HORNER. Nay, the devil take me if censorious women are to be silenced any other way.

LADY FIDGET. A secret is better kept, I hope, by a single person than a multitude; therefore pray do not trust anybody else with it, dear, dear Mr Horner. (*Embracing him*)

Enter SIR JASPAR FIDGET.

SIR JASPAR. How now!

LADY FIDGET. (*aside*) Oh, my husband – prevented – and what's almost as bad, found with my arms about another man – that will appear too much – what shall I say? – Sir Jaspar, come hither, I am trying if Mr Horner were ticklish, and he's as ticklish as can be; I love to torment the confounded toad. Let you and I tickle him.

SIR JASPAR. No, your ladyship will tickle him better without me, I suppose. But is this your buying china? I thought you had been at the china house.

HORNER. (*aside*) China house! That's my cue, I must take it. – A pox, can't you keep your impertinent wives at home? Some men are troubled with the husbands, but I with the wives. But I'd have you to know, since I cannot be your journeyman by night, I will not be your drudge by day, to squire your wife about and be your man of straw, or scarecrow, only to pies and jays, that would be nibbling at your forbidden fruit; I shall be shortly the hackney gentleman-usher of the town.

---

92 *china house*: place where china is exhibited and sold, notorious as places of assignation.

97 *journeyman*: one who labours for another.

99–100 *pies and jays*: fops.

101 *hackney*: hired.

SIR JASPAR. (*aside*) Heh, heh, he! Poor fellow, he's in the right on't, faith; to squire women about for other folks is as ungrateful an employment as to tell money for other folks. – Heh, he, he! Ben't angry, Horner –

LADY FIDGET. No, 'tis I have more reason to be angry, who am left by you to go abroad indecently alone; or, what is more indecent, to pin myself upon such ill-bred people of your acquaintance as this is.

SIR JASPAR. Nay, prithee, what has he done?

LADY FIDGET. Nay, he has done nothing.

SIR JASPAR. But what d'ye take ill, if he has done nothing?

LADY FIDGET. Hah, hah, hah! Faith, I can't but laugh, however; why d'ye think the unmannerly toad would not come down to me to the coach? I was fain to come up to fetch him, or go without him, which I was resolved not to do, for he knows china very well and has himself very good, but will not let me see it lest I should beg some. But I will find it out and have what I came for yet.

Exit LADY FIDGET *and locks the door, followed by* HORNER *to the door.*

HORNER. (*apart to* LADY FIDGET) Lock the door, madam. – So, she has got into my chamber, and locked me out. Oh, the impertinency of womankind! Well, Sir Jaspar, plain-dealing is a jewel; if ever you suffer your wife to trouble me again here, she shall carry you home a pair of horns, by my Lord Mayor she shall; though I cannot furnish you myself, you are sure, yet I'll find a way.

SIR JASPAR. (*aside*) Hah, ha, he! At my first coming in and finding her arms about him, tickling him it seems, I was half jealous, but now I see my folly. – Heh, he, he! Poor Horner.

HORNER. Nay, though you laugh now, 'twill be my turn ere long. Oh, women, more impertinent, more cunning and more mischievous than their monkeys, and to me almost as ugly! Now is she throwing my things about and rifling all I have, but I'll get into her the back way and so rifle her for it.

SIR JASPAR. Hah, ha, ha, poor angry Horner.

---

105 *tell*: count.

HORNER. Stay here a little; I'll ferret her out to you presently, I warrant. *Exit* HORNER *at t'other door.*

SIR JASPAR. Wife! My Lady Fidget! Wife! He is coming into you the back way.

SIR JASPAR *calls through the door to his wife; she answers from within.*

LADY FIDGET. Let him come, and welcome, which way he will.

SIR JASPAR. He'll catch you and use you roughly and be too strong for you.

LADY FIDGET. Don't you trouble yourself; let him if he can.

QUACK. (*behind*) This indeed I could not have believed from him, nor any but my own eyes.

Enter MRS SQUEAMISH.

SQUEAMISH. Where's this woman-hater, this toad, this ugly, greasy, dirty sloven?

SIR JASPAR. (*aside*) So, the women all will have him ugly; methinks he is a comely person, but his wants make his form contemptible to 'em and 'tis e'en as my wife said yesterday, talking of him, that a proper handsome eunuch was as ridiculous a thing as a gigantic coward.

SQUEAMISH. Sir Jaspar, your servant. Where is the odious beast?

SIR JASPAR. He's within in his chamber, with my wife; she's playing the wag with him.

SQUEAMISH. Is she so? And he's a clownish beast, he'll give her no quarter; he'll play the wag with her again, let me tell you. Come, let's go help her. – What, the door's locked?

SIR JASPAR. Ay, my wife locked it.

SQUEAMISH. Did she so? Let us break it open then.

SIR JASPAR. No, no, he'll do her no hurt.

SQUEAMISH. No. (*Aside*) But is there no other way to get in to 'em? Whither goes this? I will disturb 'em.

Exit SQUEAMISH *at another door.*

Enter OLD LADY SQUEAMISH.

OLD LADY SQUEAMISH. Where is this harlotry, this impudent baggage, this rambling tomrig? O Sir Jaspar, I'm glad to see you here. Did you not see my vild grandchild come in hither just now?

SIR JASPAR. Yes.

OLD LADY SQUEAMISH. Ay, but where is she then? Where is she? Lord, Sir Jaspar, I have e'en rattled myself to pieces in pursuit of her. But can you tell what she makes here? They say below, no woman lodges here.

SIR JASPAR. No.

OLD LADY SQUEAMISH. No! What does she here then? Say, if it be not a woman's lodging, what makes she here? But are you sure no woman lodges here?

SIR JASPAR. No, nor no man neither; this is Mr Horner's lodging.

OLD LADY SQUEAMISH. Is it so, are you sure?

SIR JASPAR. Yes, yes.

OLD LADY SQUEAMISH. So then there's no hurt in't, I hope. But where is he?

SIR JASPAR. He's in the next room with my wife.

OLD LADY SQUEAMISH. Nay, if you trust him with your wife, I may with my Biddy. They say he's a merry harmless man now, e'en as harmless a man as ever came out of Italy with a good voice, and as pretty harmless company for a lady as a snake without his teeth.

SIR JASPAR. Ay, ay, poor man.

Enter MRS SQUEAMISH.

SQUEAMISH. I can't find 'em. – Oh, are you here, Grandmother? I followed, you must know, my Lady Fidget hither; 'tis the prettiest lodging and I have been staring on the prettiest pictures.

Enter LADY FIDGET *with a piece of china in her hand, and* HORNER *following.*

---

176 *tomrig*: tomboy, strumpet.
177 *vild*: archaic form of *vile*.
197 *Biddy*: abbreviation of Bridget.
198–9 *a man . . . voice*: a castrato singer.

LADY FIDGET. And I have been toiling and moiling for the prettiest piece of china, my dear.

HORNER. Nay, she has been too hard for me, do what I could.

SQUEAMISH. O Lord, I'll have some china too. Good Mr Horner, don't think to give other people china and me none; come in with me too.

HORNER. Upon my honour, I have none left now.

SQUEAMISH. Nay, nay, I have known you deny your china before now, but you shan't put me off so. Come –

HORNER. This lady had the last there.

LADY FIDGET. Yes, indeed, madam, to my certain knowledge he has no more left.

SQUEAMISH. O, but it may be he may have some you could not find.

LADY FIDGET. What, d'ye think if he had had any left, I would not have had it too? For we women of quality never think we have china enough.

HORNER. Do not take it ill. I cannot make china for you all, but I will have a roll-wagon for you too, another time.

SQUEAMISH. Thank you, dear toad.

LADY FIDGET. (*to* HORNER *aside*) What do you mean by that promise?

HORNER. (*apart to* LADY FIDGET) Alas, she has an innocent, literal understanding.

OLD LADY SQUEAMISH. Poor Mr Horner, he has enough to do to please you all, I see.

HORNER. Ay, madam, you see how they use me.

OLD LADY SQUEAMISH. Poor gentleman, I pity you.

HORNER. I thank you, madam. I could never find pity but from such reverend ladies as you are; the young ones will never spare a man.

SQUEAMISH. Come, come, beast, and go dine with us, for we shall want a man at ombre after dinner.

HORNER. That's all their use of me, madam, you see.

---

207 *moiling*: labouring.

227 *roll-wagon*: 'the cylindrical-bodied vase of the type frequently found in Transitional and K'ang Hsi blue-and-white' (R.J. Charleston, writing in *Apollo*, vol. 65, 1957, p. 251; a picture accompanying the article shows the phallic shape that provides Horner's double meaning).

SQUEAMISH. Come, sloven, I'll lead you, to be sure of you. (*Pulls him by the cravat*)

OLD LADY SQUEAMISH. Alas, poor man, how she tugs him! Kiss, kiss her; that's the way to make such nice women quiet.

HORNER. No, madam, that remedy is worse than the torment; they know I dare suffer anything rather than do it.

OLD LADY SQUEAMISH. Prithee, kiss her and I'll give you her picture in little, that you admired so last night; prithee do.

HORNER. Well, nothing but that could bribe me; I love a woman only in effigy and good painting, as much as I hate them. I'll do't, for I could adore the devil well painted. (*Kisses* MRS SQUEAMISH)

SQUEAMISH. Foh, you filthy toad! Nay, now I've done jesting.

OLD LADY SQUEAMISH. Ha, ha, ha, I told you so.

SQUEAMISH. Foh, a kiss of his –

SIR JASPAR. Has no more hurt in't than one of my spaniel's.

SQUEAMISH. Nor no more good neither.

QUACK. (*behind*) I will now believe anything he tells me.

Enter MR PINCHWIFE.

LADY FIDGET. O Lord, here's a man! Sir Jaspar, my mask, my mask! I would not be seen here for the world.

SIR JASPAR. What, not when I am with you?

LADY FIDGET. No, no, my honour – let's be gone.

SQUEAMISH. Oh, Grandmother, let us be gone; make haste, make haste, I know not how he may censure us.

LADY FIDGET. Be found in the lodging of anything like a man! Away!

Exeunt SIR JASPAR, LADY FIDGET, OLD LADY SQUEAMISH, MRS SQUEAMISH.

QUACK. (*behind*) What's here? Another cuckold? He looks like one, and none else sure have any business with him.

HORNER. Well, what brings my dear friend hither?

---

247 *nice*: fastidious.
253 *picture in little*: miniature.

PINCHWIFE. Your impertinency.

HORNER. My impertinency! – Why, you gentlemen that have got handsome wives think you have a privilege of saying anything to your friends and are as brutish as if you were our creditors.

PINCHWIFE. No, sir, I'll ne'er trust you any way.

HORNER. But why not, dear Jack? Why diffide in me thou knowest so well?

PINCHWIFE. Because I do know you so well.

HORNER. Han't I been always thy friend, honest Jack, always ready to serve thee, in love or battle, before thou wert married, and am so still?

PINCHWIFE. I believe so; you would be my second now indeed.

HORNER. Well then, dear Jack, why so unkind, so grum, so strange to me? Come, prithee kiss me, dear rogue. Gad, I was always, I say, and am still as much thy servant as –

PINCHWIFE. As I am yours, sir. What, you would send a kiss to my wife, is that it?

HORNER. So, there 'tis – a man can't show his friendship to a married man but presently he talks of his wife to you. Prithee, let thy wife alone and let thee and I be all one, as we were wont. What, thou art as shy of my kindness as a Lombard Street alderman of a courtier's civility at Locket's.

PINCHWIFE. But you are overkind to me, as kind as if I were your cuckold already; yet I must confess you ought to be kind and civil to me, since I am so kind, so civil to you, as to bring you this. Look you there, sir. (*Delivers him a letter*)

HORNER. What is't?

PINCHWIFE. Only a love-letter, sir.

HORNER. From whom? – how! this is from your wife – hum – and hum – (*Reads*)

PINCHWIFE. Even from my wife, sir. Am I not wondrous kind and civil to you now too? (*Aside*) But you'll not think her so.

---

286 *diffide in*: distrust.
304 *Lombard Street*: famous for goldsmiths, hence *wealthy*.
305 *Locket's*: a fashionable restaurant in Charing Cross.
304–5 The moneylender suspects the gentleman is about to ask for a loan or to renege on the repayment of one.

HORNER. (*aside*) Ha, is this a trick of his or hers?

PINCHWIFE. The gentleman's surprised, I find. What, you expected a kinder letter?

HORNER. No, faith, not I, how could I?

PINCHWIFE. Yes, yes, I'm sure you did; a man so well made as you are must needs be disappointed if the women declare not their passion at first sight or opportunity.

HORNER. [*aside*] But what should this mean? Stay, the postscript. (*Reads aside*) 'Be sure you love me, whatsoever my husband says to the contrary, and let him not see this, lest he should come home and pinch me, or kill my squirrel.' (*Aside*) It seems he knows not what the letter contains.

PINCHWIFE. Come, ne'er wonder at it so much.

HORNER. Faith, I can't help it.

PINCHWIFE. Now, I think, I have deserved your infinite friendship and kindness and have showed myself sufficiently an obliging kind friend and husband; am I not so, to bring a letter from my wife to her gallant?

HORNER. Ay, the devil take me, art thou the most obliging, kind friend and husband in the world, ha, ha!

PINCHWIFE. Well, you may be merry, sir; but in short I must tell you, sir, my honour will suffer no jesting.

HORNER. What dost thou mean?

PINCHWIFE. Does the letter want a comment? Then know, sir, though I have been so civil a husband as to bring you a letter from my wife, to let you kiss and court her to my face, I will not be a cuckold, sir, I will not.

HORNER. Thou art mad with jealousy. I never saw thy wife in my life but at the play yesterday, and I know not if it were she or no. I court her, kiss her!

PINCHWIFE. I will not be a cuckold, I say; there will be danger in making me a cuckold.

HORNER. Why, wert thou not well cured of thy last clap?

PINCHWIFE. I wear a sword.

HORNER. It should be taken from thee lest thou shouldst do thyself a mischief with it; thou art mad, man.

PINCHWIFE. As mad as I am, and as merry as you are, I must have more reason from you ere we part. I say again, though you kissed and courted last night my wife in man's clothes, as she confesses in her letter –

HORNER. (*aside*) Ha!

PINCHWIFE. Both she and I say, you must not design it again, for you have mistaken your woman, as you have done your man.

HORNER. (*aside*) Oh – I understand something now. – Was that thy wife? Why wouldst thou not tell me 'twas she? Faith, my freedom with her was your fault, not mine.

PINCHWIFE. (*aside*) Faith, so 'twas.

HORNER. Fie, I'd never do't to a woman before her husband's face, sure.

PINCHWIFE. But I had rather you should do't to my wife before my face than behind my back, and that you shall never do.

HORNER. No – you will hinder me.

PINCHWIFE. If I would not hinder you, you see by her letter, she would.

HORNER. Well, I must e'en acquiesce then and be contented with what she writes.

PINCHWIFE. I'll assure you 'twas voluntarily writ; I had no hand in't, you may believe me.

HORNER. I do believe thee, faith.

PINCHWIFE. And believe her too, for she's an innocent creature, has no dissembling in her; and so fare you well, sir.

HORNER. Pray, however, present my humble service to her and tell her I will obey her letter to a tittle and fulfill her desires, be what they will, or with what difficulty soever I do't, and you shall be no more jealous of me, I warrant her and you.

PINCHWIFE. Well, then, fare you well, and play with any man's honour but mine, kiss any man's wife but mine, and welcome. *Exit* MR PINCHWIFE.

HORNER. Ha, ha, ha, doctor.

QUACK. It seems he has not heard the report of you, or does not believe it.

HORNER. Ha, ha! Now, doctor, what think you?

QUACK. Pray let's see the letter – hum – (*Reads the letter*) 'for – dear – love you – '

HORNER. I wonder how she could contrive it! What say'st thou to't? 'Tis an original.

QUACK. So are your cuckolds, too, originals, for they are like no other common cuckolds, and I will henceforth believe it not impossible for you to cuckold the Grand Signior amidst his guards of eunuchs, that I say.

HORNER. And I say for the letter, 'tis the first love-letter that ever was without flames, darts, fates, destinies, lying and dissembling in't.

Enter SPARKISH, *pulling in* MR PINCHWIFE.

SPARKISH. Come back, you are a pretty brother-in-law, neither go to church, nor to dinner with your sister bride!

PINCHWIFE. My sister denies her marriage and you see is gone away from you dissatisfied.

SPARKISH. Pshaw, upon a foolish scruple, that our parson was not in lawful orders and did not say all the Common Prayer; but 'tis her modesty only, I believe. But let women be never so modest the first day, they'll be sure to come to themselves by night, and I shall have enough of her then. In the meantime, Harry Horner, you must dine with me; I keep my wedding at my aunt's in the Piazza.

HORNER. Thy wedding! What stale maid has lived to despair of a husband, or what young one of a gallant?

SPARKISH. Oh, your servant, sir – this gentleman's sister then – no stale maid.

HORNER. I'm sorry for't.

PINCHWIFE. (*aside*) How comes he so concerned for her?

SPARKISH. You sorry for't? Why, do you know any ill by her?

HORNER. No, I know none but by thee; 'tis for her sake, not yours, and another man's sake that might have hoped, I thought.

SPARKISH. Another man, another man! What is his name?

HORNER. Nay, since 'tis past he shall be nameless. (*Aside*) Poor Harcourt, I am sorry thou hast missed her.

---

407 *Grand Signior*: the Sultan of Turkey.
423 *Piazza*: an open arcade on two sides of Covent Garden, designed by Inigo Jones; see Act V Scene iii.

PINCHWIFE. (*aside*) He seems to be much troubled at the match.

SPARKISH. Prithee tell me – nay, you shan't go, brother.

PINCHWIFE. I must of necessity, but I'll come to you to dinner. *Exit* PINCHWIFE.

SPARKISH. But, Harry, what, have I a rival in my wife already? But with all my heart, for he may be of use to me hereafter, for though my hunger is now my sauce and I can fall on heartily without, but the time will come when a rival will be as good sauce for a married man to a wife as an orange to veal.

HORNER. O thou damned rogue! Thou hast set my teeth on edge with thy orange.

SPARKISH. Then let's to dinner – there I was with you again. Come.

HORNER. But who dines with thee?

SPARKISH. My friends and relations, my brother Pinchwife, you see, of your acquaintance.

HORNER. And his wife?

SPARKISH. No, gad, he'll ne'er let her come amongst us good fellows. Your stingy country coxcomb keeps his wife from friends, as he does his little firkin of ale for his own drinking, and a gentleman can't get a smack on't; but his servants, when his back is turned, broach it at their pleasures and dust it away, ha, ha, ha! Gad, I am witty, I think, considering I was married today, by the world. But come –

HORNER. No, I will not dine with you, unless you can fetch her too.

SPARKISH. Pshaw, what pleasure canst thou have with women now, Harry?

HORNER. My eyes are not gone; I love a good prospect yet and will not dine with you unless she does too. Go fetch her, therefore, but do not tell her husband 'tis for my sake.

SPARKISH. Well, I'll try what I can do. In the meantime come away to my aunt's lodging; 'tis in the way to Pinchwife's.

---

462 *firkin*: cask.
463 *smack*: taste.
465 *dust it away*: polish it off.

HORNER. The poor woman has called for aid and stretched forth her hand, doctor; I cannot but help her over the pale out of the briars.

Exeunt SPARKISH, HORNER, QUACK.

SCENE IV

The scene changes to PINCHWIFE*'s house.*

MRS PINCHWIFE *alone, leaning on her elbow. A table, pen, ink and paper.*

MRS PINCHWIFE. Well, 'tis e'en so, I have got the London disease they call love; I am sick of my husband and for my gallant. I have heard this distemper called a fever, but methinks 'tis liker an ague, for when I think of my husband, I tremble and am in a cold sweat and have inclinations to vomit but when I think of my gallant, dear Mr Horner, my hot fit comes and I am all in a fever, indeed, and as in other fevers my own chamber is tedious to me and I would fain be removed to his and then methinks I should be well. Ah, poor Mr Horner! Well, I cannot, will not stay here; therefore I'd make an end of my letter to him, which shall be a finer letter than my last, because I have studied it like anything. O, sick, sick! (*Takes the pen and writes*)

Enter MR PINCHWIFE, *who, seeing her writing, steals softly behind her and, looking over her shoulder, snatches the paper from her.*

PINCHWIFE. What, writing more letters?

MRS PINCHWIFE. O Lord, bud, why d'ye fright me so?

She offers to run out; he stops her and reads.

PINCHWIFE. How's this! Nay, you shall not stir, madam. 'Dear, dear, dear Mr Horner' – very well – I have taught you to write letters to good purpose – but let's see't.

'First, I am to beg your pardon for my boldness in writing to you, which I'd have you to know I would not have done had not you said first you loved me so extremely, which if you do, you will never suffer me to lie in the arms of another man, whom I loathe, nauseate and detest.' – Now you can write these filthy words. But what follows? – 'Therefore I hope you will speedily find some way to free me from this unfortunate match, which was never, I assure you, of my choice, but I'm afraid 'tis already too far gone. However, if you love me, as I do you, you will try what you can do, but you must help me away before tomorrow, or else, alas, I shall be forever out of your reach, for I can defer no longer our – our' (*The letter concludes*) – What is to follow 'our'? – Speak, what? Our journey into the country, I suppose – Oh, woman, damned woman and love, damned love, their old tempter! For this is one of his miracles; in a moment he can make all those blind that could see and those see that were blind, those dumb that could speak and those prattle who were dumb before; nay, what is more than all, make these dough-baked, senseless, indocile animals, women, too hard for us, their politic lords and rulers, in a moment. But make an end of your letter and then I'll make an end of you thus, and all my plagues together. (*Draws his sword*)

MRS PINCHWIFE. O Lord, O Lord, you are such a passionate man, bud!

Enter SPARKISH.

SPARKISH. How now, what's here to do?

PINCHWIFE. This fool here now!

SPARKISH. What, drawn upon your wife? You should never do that but at night in the dark, when you can't hurt her. This is my sister-in-law, is it not? (*Pulls aside her handkerchief*) Ay, faith, e'en our country Margery; one may know her. Come, she and you must go dine with me; dinner's ready, come. But where's my wife? Is she not come home yet? Where is she?

PINCHWIFE. Making you a cuckold; 'tis that they all do, as soon as they can.

SPARKISH. What, the wedding day? No, a wife that designs to make a cully of her husband will be sure to

---

42 *dough-baked*: half-baked, foolish.
43 *indocile*: perhaps with the sense 'difficult to teach'.
61 *cully*: dupe, cuckold.

let him win the first stake of love, by the world. But come, they stay dinner for us. Come, I'll lead down our Margery.

PINCHWIFE. No – sir, go, we'll follow you.

SPARKISH. I will not wag without you.

PINCHWIFE. [*aside*] This coxcomb is a sensible torment to me amidst the greatest in the world.

SPARKISH. Come, come, Madam Margery.

PINCHWIFE. No, I'll lead her my way. What, would you treat your friends with mine, for want of your own wife? (*Leads her to t'other door and locks her in and returns. Aside*) I am contented my rage should take breath.

SPARKISH. [*aside*] I told Horner this.

PINCHWIFE. Come now.

SPARKISH. Lord, how shy you are of your wife! But let me tell you, brother, we men of wit have amongst us a saying that cuckolding, like the smallpox, comes with a fear, and you may keep your wife as much as you will out of danger of infection but if her constitution incline her to't, she'll have it sooner or later, by the world, say they.

PINCHWIFE. (*aside*) What a thing is a cuckold, that every fool can make him ridiculous! – Well, sir – but let me advise you, now you are come to be concerned, because you suspect the danger, not to neglect the means to prevent it, especially when the greatest share of the malady will light upon your own head, for –

Hows'e'er the kind wife's belly comes to swell,
The husband breeds for her and first is ill.

[*Exeunt* PINCHWIFE *and* SPARKISH.]

---

65 s.p. *Pinchwife*: Mrs Pinchwife Q1.
66 *wag*: stir.
67 *sensible*: acutely felt.
77 *shy*: suspicious.
92 *breeds for*: grows cuckold's horns on her behalf.

ACT V

SCENE I

Mr Pinchwife's house.

Enter MR PINCHWIFE *and* MRS PINCHWIFE. *A table and candle.*

PINCHWIFE. Come, take the pen and make an end of the letter, just as you intended; if you are false in a tittle, I shall soon perceive it and punish you with this as you deserve. (*Lays his hand on his sword*) Write what was to follow – let's see – 'You must make haste and help me away before tomorrow, or else I shall be forever out of your reach, for I can defer no longer our – ' What follows 'our'?

MRS PINCHWIFE. Must all out then, bud? (MRS PINCHWIFE *takes the pen and writes*) Look you there then.

PINCHWIFE. Let's see – 'For I can defer no longer our – wedding – Your slighted Alithea.' – What's the meaning of this? My sister's name to't. Speak, unriddle!

MRS PINCHWIFE. Yes, indeed, bud.

PINCHWIFE. But why her name to't? Speak – speak, I say!

MRS PINCHWIFE. Ay, but you'll tell her then again; if you would not tell her again –

PINCHWIFE. I will not – I am stunned, my head turns round. Speak.

MRS PINCHWIFE. Won't you tell her, indeed, and indeed?

PINCHWIFE. No, speak, I say.

MRS PINCHWIFE. She'll be angry with me, but I had rather she should be angry with me than you, bud; and to tell you the truth, 'twas she made me write the letter and taught me what I should write.

PINCHWIFE. (*aside*) Ha! I thought the style was some-

30 s.d. *aside*: not in Q1.

what better than her own. – But how could she come to you to teach you, since I had locked you up alone?

MRS PINCHWIFE. O, through the keyhole, bud.

PINCHWIFE. But why should she make you write a letter for her to him, since she can write herself?

MRS PINCHWIFE. Why, she said because – for I was unwilling to do it.

PINCHWIFE. Because what – because?

MRS PINCHWIFE. Because, lest Mr Horner should be cruel and refuse her or vain afterwards and show the letter, she might disown it, the hand not being hers.

PINCHWIFE. (*aside*) How's this? Ha! – then I think I shall come to myself again. This changeling could not invent this lie; but if she could, why should she? She might think I should soon discover it – stay – now I think on't too, Horner said he was sorry she had married Sparkish, and her disowning her marriage to me makes me think she has evaded it for Horner's sake. Yet why should she take this course? But men in love are fools; women may well be so. – But hark you, madam, your sister went out in the morning and I have not seen her within since.

MRS PINCHWIFE. Alackaday, she has been crying all day above, it seems, in a corner.

PINCHWIFE. Where is she? Let me speak with her.

MRS PINCHWIFE. (*aside*) O Lord, then he'll discover all! – Pray hold, bud. What, d'ye mean to discover me? She'll know I have told you then. Pray, bud, let me talk with her first.

PINCHWIFE. I must speak with her, to know whether Horner ever made her any promise and whether she be married to Sparkish or no.

MRS PINCHWIFE. Pray, dear bud, don't, till I have spoken with her and told her that I have told you all, for she'll kill me else.

PINCHWIFE. Go then, and bid her come out to me.

MRS PINCHWIFE. Yes, yes, bud.

PINCHWIFE. Let me see –

MRS PINCHWIFE. [*aside*] I'll go, but she is not within to come to him. I have just got time to know of Lucy her maid, who first set me on work, what lie I shall tell next, for I am e'en at my wit's end.

Exit MRS PINCHWIFE.

PINCHWIFE. Well, I resolve it; Horner shall have her. I'd

rather give him my sister than lend him my wife and such an alliance will prevent his pretensions to my wife, sure. I'll make him of kin to her and then he won't care for her.

MRS PINCHWIFE *returns.*

MRS PINCHWIFE. O Lord, bud, I told you what anger you would make me with my sister.

PINCHWIFE. Won't she come hither?

MRS PINCHWIFE. No, no, alackaday, she's ashamed to look you in the face, and she says, if you go in to her, she'll run away downstairs and shamefully go herself to Mr Horner, who has promised her marriage, she says, and she will have no other, so she won't –

PINCHWIFE. Did he so – promise her marriage – then she shall have no other. Go tell her so, and if she will come and discourse with me a little concerning the means, I will about it immediately. Go.

Exit MRS PINCHWIFE.

His estate is equal to Sparkish's, and his extraction as much better than his as his parts are; but my chief reason is, I'd rather be of kin to him by the name of brother-in-law than that of cuckold.

Enter MRS PINCHWIFE.

Well, what says she now?

MRS PINCHWIFE. Why, she says she would only have you lead her to Horner's lodging – with whom she first will discourse the matter before she talk with you, which yet she cannot do, for alack, poor creature, she says she can't so much as look you in the face, therefore she'll come to you in a mask, and you must excuse her if she make you no answer to any question of yours, till you have brought her to Mr Horner, and if you will not chide her, nor question her, she'll come out to you immediately.

PINCHWIFE. Let her come. I will not speak a word to her, nor require a word from her.

MRS PINCHWIFE. Oh, I forgot; besides, she says, she cannot look you in the face though through a mask, therefore would desire you to put out the candle.

PINCHWIFE. I agree to all; let her make haste – there, 'tis out. (*Puts out the candle*)

Exit MRS PINCHWIFE.

My case is something better. I'd rather fight with Horner for not lying with my sister than for lying with my wife, and of the two I had rather find my sister too forward than my wife; I expected no other from her free education, as she calls it, and her passion for the town. Well – wife and sister are names which make us expect love and duty, pleasure and comfort, but we find 'em plagues and torments, and are equally, though differently, troublesome to their keeper, for we have as much ado to get people to lie with our sisters as to keep 'em frm lying with our wives.

Enter MRS PINCHWIFE *masked and in hoods and scarves, and a nightgown and petticoat of* ALITHEA*'s, in the dark.*

What, are you come, sister? Let us go then – but first let me lock up my wife. – Mrs Margery, where are you?

MRS PINCHWIFE. Here, bud.

PINCHWIFE. Come hither, that I may lock you up; get you in. (*Locks the door*) Come, sister, where are you now?

MRS PINCHWIFE *gives him her hand but, when he lets her go, she steals softly on t'other side of him, and is led away by him for his sister* ALITHEA.

SCENE II

The scene changes to HORNER*'s lodging.*

QUACK, HORNER.

QUACK. What, all alone? Not so much as one of your cuckolds here, nor one of their wives! They use to take their turns with you, as if they were to watch you.

HORNER. Yes, it often happens that a cuckold is but his wife's spy and is more upon family duty when he is with her gallant abroad, hindering his pleasure, than when he is at home with her, playing the gallant. But

---

124 s.d. *nightgown*: a loose gown, usually but not necessarily worn at home.

the hardest duty a married woman imposes upon a lover is keeping her husband company always.

QUACK. And his fondness wearies you almost as soon as hers.

HORNER. A pox, keeping a cuckold company, after you have had his wife, is as tiresome as the company of a country squire to a witty fellow of the town, when he has got all his money.

QUACK. And as at first a man makes a friend of the husband to get the wife, so at last you are fain to fall out with the wife to be rid of the husband.

HORNER. Ay, most cuckold-makers are true courtiers; when once a poor man has cracked his credit for 'em, they can't abide to come near him.

QUACK. But at first, to draw him in, are so sweet, so kind, so dear, just as you are to Pinchwife. But what becomes of that intrigue with his wife?

HORNER. A pox, he's as surly as an alderman that has been bit and, since he's so coy, his wife's kindness is in vain, for she's a silly innocent.

QUACK. Did she not send you a letter by him?

HORNER. Yes, but that's a riddle I have not yet solved. Allow the poor creature to be willing, she is silly too, and he keeps her up so close –

QUACK. Yes, so close that he makes her but the more willing and adds but revenge to her love, which two, when met, seldom fail of satisfying each other one way or other.

HORNER. What, here's the man we are talking of, I think.

Enter MR PINCHWIFE, *leading in his wife masked, muffled and in her sister's gown.*

Pshaw!

QUACK. Bringing his wife to you is the next thing to bringing a love-letter from her.

HORNER. What means this?

PINCHWIFE. The last time, you know, sir, I brought you a love-letter; now, you see, a mistress. I think you'll say I am a civil man to you.

---

26 *bit*: tricked.

HORNER. Ay, the devil take me, will I say thou art the civilest man I ever met with, and I have known some! I fancy I understand thee now better than I did the letter. But hark thee, in thy ear –

PINCHWIFE. What?

HORNER. Nothing but the usual question, man: is she sound, on thy word?

PINCHWIFE. What, you take her for a wench and me for a pimp?

HORNER. Pshaw, wench and pimp, paw words. I know thou art an honest fellow and hast a great acquaintance among the ladies and perhaps hast made love for me rather than let me make love to thy wife –

PINCHWIFE. Come, sir, in short, I am for no fooling.

HORNER. Nor I neither; therefore, prithee, let's see her face presently. Make her show, man. Art thou sure I don't know her?

PINCHWIFE. I am sure you do know her.

HORNER. A pox, why dost thou bring her to me then?

PINCHWIFE. Because she's a relation of mine.

HORNER. Is she, faith, man? Then thou art still more civil and obliging, dear rogue.

PINCHWIFE. Who desired me to bring her to you.

HORNER. Then she is obliging, dear rogue.

PINCHWIFE. You'll make her welcome for my sake, I hope.

HORNER. I hope she is handsome enough to make herself welcome. Prithee, let her unmask.

PINCHWIFE. Do you speak to her; she would never be ruled by me.

HORNER. Madam –

MRS PINCHWIFE *whispers to* HORNER.

She says she must speak with me in private. Withdraw, prithee.

PINCHWIFE. (*aside*) She's unwilling, it seems, I should know all her undecent conduct in this business. – Well then, I'll leave you together and hope when I am gone you'll agree; if not, you and I shan't agree, sir.

HORNER. [*aside*] What means the fool? – If she and I agree, 'tis no matter what you and I do.

---

51 *sound*: free from the pox.
54 *paw*: naughty, improper.

Whispers to MRS PINCHWIFE, *who makes signs with her hand for him* [PINCHWIFE] *to be gone.*

PINCHWIFE. In the meantime, I'll fetch a parson and find out Sparkish and disabuse him. You would have me fetch a parson, would you not? Well then – now I think I am rid of her, and shall have no more trouble with her. Our sisters and daughters, like usurers' money, are safest when put out; but our wives, like their writings, never safe but in our closets under lock and key. *Exit* MR PINCHWIFE.

Enter BOY.

BOY. Sir Jaspar Fidget, sir, is coming up. [*Exit.*]

HORNER. Here's the trouble of a cuckold, now, we are talking of. A pox on him! Has he not enough to do to hinder his wife's sport but he must other women's too? – Step in here, madam.

Exit MRS PINCHWIFE.

Enter SIR JASPAR.

SIR JASPAR. My best and dearest friend.

HORNER. [*aside to* QUACK] The old style, doctor. – Well, be short, for I am busy. What would your impertinent wife have now?

SIR JASPAR. Well guessed, i'faith, for I do come from her.

HORNER. To invite me to supper. Tell her I can't come; go.

SIR JASPAR. Nay, now you are out, faith, for my lady and the whole knot of the virtuous gang, as they call themselves, are resolved upon a frolic of coming to you tonight in a masquerade and are all dressed already.

HORNER. I shan't be at home.

SIR JASPAR. [*aside*] Lord, how churlish he is to women! – Nay, prithee don't disappoint 'em; they'll think 'tis my fault. Prithee don't. I'll send in the banquet and the fiddles. But make no noise on't, for the poor virtuous rogues would not have it known for the world that they go a-masquerading, and they would come to no man's ball but yours.

---

90 *writings*: deeds, documents.

HORNER. Well, well – get you gone and tell 'em, if they come, 'twill be at the peril of their honour and yours.

SIR JASPAR. Heh, he, he! – we'll trust you for that; farewell. *Exit* SIR JASPAR.

HORNER. Doctor, anon you too shall be my guest,
But now I'm going to a private feast.

[*Exeunt.*]

SCENE III

The scene changes to the Piazza of Covent Garden.

SPARKISH, PINCHWIFE.

SPARKISH. (*with the letter in his hand*) But who would have thought a woman could have been false to me? By the world, I could not have thought it.

PINCHWIFE. You were for giving and taking liberty; she has taken it only, sir, now you find in that letter. You are a frank person and so is she you see there.

SPARKISH. Nay, if this be her hand – for I never saw it.

PINCHWIFE. 'Tis no matter whether that be her hand or no; I am sure this hand, at her desire, led her to Mr Horner, with whom I left her just now, to go fetch a parson to 'em, at their desire too, to deprive you of her forever, for it seems yours was but a mock marriage.

SPARKISH. Indeed, she would needs have it that 'twas Harcourt himself in a parson's habit that married us, but I'm sure he told me 'twas his brother Ned.

PINCHWIFE. Oh, there 'tis out, and you were deceived, not she, for you are such a frank person – but I must be gone. You'll find her at Mr Horner's; go and believe your eyes. *Exit* MR PINCHWIFE.

SPARKISH. Nay, I'll to her and call her as many crocodiles, sirens, harpies and other heathenish names as a poet would do a mistress who had refused to hear his suit, nay more, his verses on her. – But stay, is not

---

1 s.d. *letter*: the one written by Mrs Pinchwife as though from Alithea.

that she following a torch at t'other end of the Piazza? And from Horner's certainly – 'tis so.

Enter ALITHEA, *following a torch, and* LUCY *behind.*

You are well met, madam, though you don't think so. What, you have made a short visit to Mr Horner, but I suppose you'll return to him presently; by that time the parson can be with him.

ALITHEA. Mr Horner, and the parson, sir!

SPARKISH. Come, madam, no more dissembling, no more jilting, for I am no more a frank person.

ALITHEA. How's this?

LUCY. (*aside*) So, 'twill work, I see.

SPARKISH. Could you find out no easy country fool to abuse? None but me, a gentleman of wit and pleasure about the town? But it was your pride to be too hard for a man of parts, unworthy false woman, false as a friend that lends a man money to lose, false as dice who undo those that trust all they have to 'em.

LUCY. (*aside*) He has been a great bubble by his similes, as they say.

ALITHEA. You have been too merry, sir, at your wedding dinner, sure.

SPARKISH. What, d'ye mock me too?

ALITHEA. Or you have been deluded.

SPARKISH. By you.

ALITHEA. Let me understand you.

SPARKISH. Have you the confidence – I should call it something else, since you know your guilt – to stand my just reproaches? You did not write an impudent letter to Mr Horner, who I find now has clubbed with you in deluding me with his aversion for women, that I might not, forsooth, suspect him for my rival.

LUCY. (*aside*) D'ye think the gentleman can be jealous now, madam?

ALITHEA. I write a letter to Mr Horner!

SPARKISH. Nay, madam, do not deny it; your brother showed it me just now and told me likewise he left you at Horner's lodging to fetch a parson to marry

---

25 *torch*: a linkboy with a torch.

you to him, and I wish you joy, madam, joy, joy, and to him too, much joy, and to myself more joy for not marrying you.

ALITHEA. (*aside*) So, I find my brother would break off the match, and I can consent to't, since I see this gentleman can be made jealous. – O Lucy, by his rude usage and jealousy, he makes me almost afraid I am married to him. Art thou sure 'twas Harcourt himself and no parson that married us?

SPARKISH. No, madam, I thank you. I suppose that was a contrivance too of Mr Horner's and yours, to make Harcourt play the parson; but I would as little as you have him one now, no, not for the world, for shall I tell you another truth? I never had any passion for you till now, for now I hate you. 'Tis true I might have married your portion, as other men of parts of the town do sometimes, and so your servant, and to show my unconcernedness, I'll come to your wedding and resign you with as much joy as I would a stale wench to a new cully, nay, with as much joy as I would after the first night, if I had been married to you. There's for you, and so your servant, servant.

Exit SPARKISH.

ALITHEA. How was I deceived in a man!

LUCY. You'll believe, then, a fool may be made jealous now? For that easiness in him that suffers him to be led by a wife will likewise permit him to be persuaded against her by others.

ALITHEA. But marry Mr Horner! My brother does not intend it, sure; if I thought he did, I would take thy advice and Mr Harcourt for my husband. And now I wish that if there be any over-wise woman of the town who, like me, would marry a fool for fortune, liberty or title; first, that her husband may love play and be a cully to all the town but her and suffer none but fortune to be mistress of his purse; then, if for liberty, that he may send her into the country under the conduct of some housewifely mother-in-law, and, if for title, may the world give 'em none but that of cuckold.

LUCY. And for her greater curse, madam, may he not deserve it.

ALITHEA. Away, impertinent! – Is not this my old Lady Lanterlu's?

LUCY. Yes, madam. (*Aside*) And here I hope we shall find Mr Harcourt.

Exeunt ALITHEA, LUCY.

SCENE IV

The scene changes again to HORNER*'s lodging.*

HORNER, LADY FIDGET, MRS DAINTY FIDGET, MRS SQUEAMISH. *A table, banquet, and bottles.*

HORNER. (*aside*) A pox! They are come too soon – before I have sent back my new – mistress. All I have now to do is to lock her in, that they may not see her.

LADY FIDGET. That we may be sure of our welcome, we have brought our entertainment with us and are resolved to treat thee, dear toad.

DAINTY. And that we may be merry to purpose, have left Sir Jaspar and my old Lady Squeamish quarrelling at home at backgammon.

SQUEAMISH. Therefore let us make use of our time, lest they should chance to interrupt us.

LADY FIDGET. Let us sit then.

HORNER. First, that you may be private, let me lock this door and that, and I'll wait upon you presently.

LADY FIDGET. No, sir, shut 'em only and your lips forever, for we must trust you as much as our women.

HORNER. You know all vanity's killed in me; I have no occasion for talking.

LADY FIDGET. Now, ladies, supposing we had drank each of us our two bottles, let us speak the truth of our hearts.

DAINTY.
SQUEAMISH. } Agreed.

LADY FIDGET. By this brimmer, for truth is nowhere

---

104 *Lanterlu's*: the card game, lanterloo or loo.

23 *brimmer*: a full glass.

else to be found. (*Aside to* HORNER) Not in thy heart, false man!

HORNER. (*aside to* LADY FIDGET) You have found me a true man, I'm sure.

LADY FIDGET. (*aside to* HORNER) Not every way. – But let us sit and be merry. (LADY FIDGET *sings*)

1

Why should our damned tyrants oblige us to live
On the pittance of pleasure which they only give?
    We must not rejoice
    With wine and with noise.
In vain we must wake in a dull bed alone,
Whilst to our warm rival, the bottle, they're gone.
    They lay aside charms
    And take up these arms.* **The glasses.*

2

'Tis wine only gives 'em their courage and wit;
Because we live sober, to men we submit.
    If for beauties you'd pass,
    Take a lick of the glass;
'Twill mend your complexions and, when they are gone,
The best red we have is the red of the grape.
    Then, sisters, lay't on,
    And damn a good shape.

DAINTY. Dear brimmer! Well, in token of our openness and plain-dealing, let us throw our masks over our heads.

HORNER. So, 'twill come to the glasses anon.

SQUEAMISH. Lovely brimmer! Let me enjoy him first.

LADY FIDGET. No, I never part with a gallant till I've tried him. Dear brimmer, that mak'st our husbands shortsighted.

DAINTY. And our bashful gallants bold.

SQUEAMISH. And for want of a gallant, the butler lovely in our eyes. – Drink, eunuch.

LADY FIDGET. Drink, thou representative of a husband. Damn a husband!

DAINTY. And, as it were a husband, an old keeper.

SQUEAMISH. And an old grandmother.

HORNER. And an English bawd and a French chirurgeon.

---

62 The causes of Horner's 'state'; see I i 29–30.

LADY FIDGET. Ay, we have all reason to curse 'em.

HORNER. For my sake, ladies?

LADY FIDGET. No, for our own, for the first spoils all young gallants' industry.

DAINTY. And the other's art makes 'em bold only with common women.

SQUEAMISH. And rather run the hazard of the vile distemper amongst them than of a denial amongst us.

DAINTY. The filthy toads choose mistresses now as they do stuffs, for having been fancied and worn by others.

SQUEAMISH. For being common and cheap.

LADY FIDGET. Whilst women of quality, like the richest stuffs, lie untumbled and unasked for.

HORNER. Ay, neat and cheap and new often they think best.

DAINTY. No, sir, the beasts will be known by a mistress longer than by a suit.

SQUEAMISH. And 'tis not for cheapness neither.

LADY FIDGET. No, for the vain fops will take up druggets and embroider 'em. But I wonder at the depraved appetites of witty men; they use to be out of the common road and hate imitation. Pray tell me, beast, when you were a man, why you rather chose to club with a multitude in a common house for an entertainment than to be the only guest at a good table.

HORNER. Why, faith, ceremony and expectation are unsufferable to those that are sharp bent; people always eat with the best stomach at an ordinary, where every man is snatching for the best bit.

LADY FIDGET. Though he get a cut over the fingers. – But I have heard people eat most heartily of another man's meat, that is, what they do not pay for.

HORNER. When they are sure of their welcome and freedom, for ceremony in love and eating is as ridiculous as in fighting; falling on briskly is all should be done in those occasions.

LADY FIDGET. Well, then, let me tell you, sir, there is nowhere more freedom than in our houses and we

---

83 *druggets*: cheap woollen material.
87 *common house*: (*a*) an ordinary, a restaurant (*b*) a brothel.
91 *sharp bent*: hungry.

take freedom from a young person as a sign of good breeding, and a person may be as free as he pleases with us, as frolic, as gamesome, as wild as he will.

HORNER. Han't I heard you all declaim against wild men?

LADY FIDGET. Yes, but for all that, we think wildness in a man as desirable a quality as in a duck or rabbit; a tame man, foh!

HORNER. I know not, but your reputations frightened me, as much as your faces invited me.

LADY FIDGET. Our reputation! Lord, why should you not think that we women make use of our reputation, as you men of yours, only to deceive the world with less suspicion? Our virtue is like the statesman's religion, the Quaker's word, the gamester's oath and the great man's honour – but to cheat those that trust us.

SQUEAMISH. And that demureness, coyness and modesty that you see in our faces in the boxes at plays is as much a sign of a kind woman as a vizard-mask in the pit.

DAINTY. For, I assure you, women are least masked when they have the velvet vizard on.

LADY FIDGET. You would have found us modest women in our denials only.

SQUEAMISH. Our bashfulness is only the reflection of the men's.

DAINTY. We blush when they are shamefaced.

HORNER. I beg your pardon, ladies; I was deceived in you devilishly. But why that mighty pretence to honour?

LADY FIDGET. We have told you. But sometimes 'twas for the same reason you men pretend business often, to avoid ill company, to enjoy the better and more privately those you love.

HORNER. But why would you ne'er give a friend a wink then?

LADY FIDGET. Faith, your reputation frightened us as much as ours did you, you were so notoriously lewd.

HORNER. And you so seemingly honest.

LADY FIDGET. Was that all that deterred you?

HORNER. And so expensive – you allow freedom, you say –

LADY FIDGET. Ay, ay.

HORNER. That I was afraid of losing my little money, as well as my little time, both which my other pleasures required.

LADY FIDGET. Money, foh! You talk like a little fellow now; do such as we expect money?

HORNER. I beg your pardon, madam; I must confess, I have heard that great ladies, like great merchants, set but the higher prizes upon what they have, because they are not in necessity of taking the first offer.

DAINTY. Such as we make sale of our hearts?

SQUEAMISH. We bribed for our love? Foh!

HORNER. With your pardon, ladies, I know, like great men in offices, you seem to exact flattery and attendance only from your followers; but you have receivers about you and such fees to pay, a man is afraid to pass your grants. Besides, we must let you win at cards, or we lose your hearts, and if you make an assignation, 'tis at a goldsmith's, jeweller's or china house, where, for your honour you deposit to him, he must pawn his to the punctual cit, and so paying for what you take up, pays for what he takes up.

DAINTY. Would you not have us assured of our gallant's love?

SQUEAMISH. For love is better known by liberality than by jealousy.

LADY FIDGET. For one may be dissembled, the other not. (*Aside*) But my jealousy can be no longer dissembled, and they are telling ripe. – Come, here's to our gallants in waiting, whom we must name, and I'll begin. This is my false rogue. (*Claps him on the back*)

SQUEAMISH. How!

HORNER. So all will out now.

SQUEAMISH. (*aside to* HORNER) Did you not tell me, 'twas for my sake only you reported yourself no man?

---

154 *prizes*: prices.

160 *receivers*: servants to be bribed.

162 *pass your grants*: accept your favours.

165–7 *for your honour . . . he takes up*: for trusting your honour to your gallant, he must in turn pawn his to the citizen, who will be punctual about demanding repayment, and so, in paying for your purchases, your gallant pays for getting you.

174 *telling ripe*: ready to be told.

DAINTY. (*aside to* HORNER) Oh, wretch! Did you not swear to me, 'twas for my love and honour you passed for that thing you do?

HORNER. So, so.

LADY FIDGET. Come, speak, ladies; this is my false villain.

SQUEAMISH. And mine too.

DAINTY. And mine.

HORNER. Well then, you are all three my false rogues too, and there's an end on't.

LADY FIDGET. Well then, there's no remedy; sister sharers, let us not fall out, but have a care of our honour. Though we get no presents, no jewels of him, we are savers of our honour, the jewel of most value and use, which shines yet to the world unsuspected, though it be counterfeit.

HORNER. Nay, and is e'en as good as if it were true, provided the world think so, for honour, like beauty now, only depends on the opinion of others.

LADY FIDGET. Well, Harry Common, I hope you can be true to three. Swear – but 'tis to no purpose to require your oath, for you are as often forsworn as you swear to new women.

HORNER. Come, faith, madam, let us e'en pardon one another, for all the difference I find betwixt we men and you women, we forswear ourselves at the beginning of an amour, you as long as it lasts.

Enter SIR JASPAR FIDGET *and* OLD LADY SQUEAMISH.

SIR JASPAR. Oh, my Lady Fidget, was this your cunning, to come to Mr Horner without me? But you have been nowhere else, I hope.

LADY FIDGET. No, Sir Jaspar.

OLD LADY SQUEAMISH. And you came straight hither, Biddy?

SQUEAMISH. Yes, indeed, Lady Grandmother.

SIR JASPAR. 'Tis well, 'tis well; I knew when once they were thoroughly acquainted with poor Horner,

---

200 *Harry Common*: Harry Horner is shared by them all.

they'd ne'er be from him. You may let her masquerade it with my wife and Horner and I warrant her reputation safe.

Enter BOY.

BOY. Oh, sir, here's the gentleman come whom you bid me not suffer to come up without giving you notice, with a lady too, and other gentlemen –

HORNER. Do you all go in there, whilst I send 'em away, and, boy, do you desire 'em to stay below till I come, which shall be immediately.

Exeunt SIR JASPAR, [OLD] LADY SQUEAMISH, LADY FIDGET, MRS DAINTY, SQUEAMISH.

BOY. Yes, sir. *Exit.*

Exit HORNER *at t'other door and returns with* MRS PINCHWIFE.

HORNER. You would not take my advice to be gone home before your husband came back; he'll now discover all. Yet pray, my dearest, be persuaded to go home and leave the rest to my management. I'll let you down the back way.

MRS PINCHWIFE. I don't know the way home, so I don't.

HORNER. My man shall wait upon you.

MRS PINCHWIFE. No, don't you believe that I'll go at all. What, are you weary of me already?

HORNER. No, my life, 'tis that I may love you long, 'tis to secure my love, and your reputation with your husband; he'll never receive you again else.

MRS PINCHWIFE. What care I? D'ye think to frighten me with that? I don't intend to go to him again; you shall be my husband now.

HORNER. I cannot be your husband, dearest, since you are married to him.

MRS PINCHWIFE. Oh, would you make me believe that? Don't I see every day, at London here, women leave their first husbands and go and live with other men as their wives? Pish, pshaw, you'd make me angry, but that I love you so mainly.

HORNER. So, they are coming up – in again, in, I hear 'em.

---

249 *mainly*: strongly.

Exit MRS PINCHWIFE.

Well, a silly mistress is like a weak place, soon got, soon lost, a man has scarce time for plunder; she betrays her husband first to her gallant and then her gallant to her husband.

Enter PINCHWIFE, ALITHEA, HARCOURT, SPARKISH, LUCY *and a Parson.*

PINCHWIFE. Come, madam, 'tis not the sudden change of your dress, the confidence of your asseverations and your false witness there, shall persuade me I did not bring you hither just now; here's my witness, who cannot deny it, since you must be confronted. – Mr Horner, did not I bring this lady to you just now?

HORNER. (*aside*) Now must I wrong one woman for another's sake, but that's no new thing with me, for in these cases I am still on the criminal's side, against the innocent.

ALITHEA. Pray, speak, sir.

HORNER. (*aside*) It must be so – I must be impudent and try my luck; impudence uses to be too hard for truth.

PINCHWIFE. What, you are studying an evasion or excuse for her. Speak, sir.

HORNER. No, faith, I am something backward only to speak in women's affairs or disputes.

PINCHWIFE. She bids you speak.

ALITHEA. Ay, pray, sir, do; pray satisfy him.

HORNER. Then truly, you did bring that lady to me just now.

PINCHWIFE. O ho!

ALITHEA. How, sir!

HARCOURT. How, Horner!

ALITHEA. What mean you, sir? I always took you for a man of honour.

HORNER. (*aside*) Ay, so much a man of honour that I must save my mistress, I thank you, come what will on't.

SPARKISH. So, if I had had her, she'd have made me believe the moon had been made of a Christmas pie.

LUCY. (*aside*) Now could I speak, if I durst, and 'solve

---

288 *'solve*: dissolve.

the riddle, who am the author of it.

ALITHEA. O unfortunate woman! A combination against my honour, which most concerns me now, because you share in my disgrace, sir, and it is your censure, which I must now suffer, that troubles me, not theirs.

HARCOURT. Madam, then have no trouble, you shall now see 'tis possible for me to love too, without being jealous; I will not only believe your innocence myself, but make all the world believe it. (*Apart to* HORNER) Horner, I must now be concerned for this lady's honour.

HORNER. And I must be concerned for a lady's honour too.

HARCOURT. This lady has her honour and I will protect it.

HORNER. My lady has not her honour but has given it me to keep and I will preserve it.

HARCOURT. I understand you not.

HORNER. I would not have you.

MRS PINCHWIFE. (*peeping in behind*) What's the matter with 'em all?

PINCHWIFE. Come, come, Mr Horner, no more disputing. Here's the parson; I brought him not in vain.

HARCOURT. No, sir, I'll employ him, if this lady please.

PINCHWIFE. How! What d'ye mean?

SPARKISH. Ay, what does he mean?

HORNER. Why, I have resigned your sister to him; he has my consent.

PINCHWIFE. But he has not mine, sir; a woman's injured honour, no more than a man's, can be repaired or satisfied by any but him that first wronged it; and you shall marry her presently, or – (*Lays his hand on his sword*)

Enter to them MRS PINCHWIFE.

MRS PINCHWIFE. [*aside*] O Lord, they'll kill poor Mr Horner! Besides, he shan't marry her whilst I stand by and look on; I'll not lose my second husband so.

PINCHWIFE. What do I see?

---

313 s.p. *Harcourt*: Horner Q1.

ALITHEA. My sister in my clothes!

SPARKISH. Ha!

MRS PINCHWIFE. (*to* MR PINCHWIFE) Nay, pray now don't quarrel about finding work for the parson; he shall marry me to Mr Horner, for now, I believe, you have enough of me.

HORNER. Damned, damned, loving changeling!

MRS PINCHWIFE. Pray, sister, pardon me for telling so many lies of you.

HARCOURT. I suppose the riddle is plain now.

LUCY. No, that must be my work. Good sir, hear me.

Kneels to MR PINCHWIFE, *who stands doggedly, with his hat over his eyes.*

PINCHWIFE. I will never hear woman again, but make 'em all silent, thus – (*Offers to draw upon his wife*)

HORNER. No, that must not be.

PINCHWIFE. You then shall go first; 'tis all one to me.

Offers to draw on HORNER*; stopped by* HARCOURT.

HARCOURT. Hold!

Enter SIR JASPAR FIDGET, LADY FIDGET, [OLD] LADY SQUEAMISH, MRS DAINTY FIDGET, MRS SQUEAMISH.

SIR JASPAR. What's the matter, what's the matter, pray, what's the matter, sir? I beseech you communicate, sir.

PINCHWIFE. Why, my wife has communicated, sir, as your wife may have done too, sir, if she knows him, sir.

SIR JASPAR. Pshaw, with him? Ha, ha, he!

PINCHWIFE. D'ye mock me, sir? A cuckold is a kind of a wild beast; have a care, sir.

SIR JASPAR. No, sure, you mock me, sir – he cuckold you! It can't be, ha, ha, he! Why, I tell you, sir – (*Offers to whisper*)

PINCHWIFE. I tell you again, he has whored my wife, and yours too, if he knows her, and all the women he comes near; 'tis not his dissembling, his hypocrisy can wheedle me.

---

345 *communicated*: had sex.

SIR JASPAR. How! does he dissemble? Is he a hypocrite? Nay, then – how – wife – sister, is he an hypocrite?

OLD LADY SQUEAMISH. An hypocrite, a dissembler! Speak, young harlotry, speak, how?

SIR JASPAR. Nay, then – O, my head too! – O thou libidinous lady!

OLD LADY SQUEAMISH. O thou harloting harlotry! Hast thou done't then?

SIR JASPAR. Speak, good Horner, art thou a dissembler, a rogue? Hast thou –

HORNER. Soh –

LUCY. (*apart to* HORNER) I'll fetch you off, and her too, if she will but hold her tongue.

HORNER. (*apart to* LUCY) Canst thou? I'll give thee –

LUCY. (*to* MR PINCHWIFE) Pray have but patience to hear me, sir, who am the unfortunate cause of all this confusion. Your wife is innocent, I only culpable, for I put her upon telling you all these lies concerning my mistress, in order to the breaking off the match between Mr Sparkish and her, to make way for Mr Harcourt.

SPARKISH. Did you so, eternal rotten tooth? Then, it seems, my mistress was not false to me, I was only deceived by you. – Brother that should have been, now man of conduct, who is a frank person now? To bring your wife to her lover – ha!

LUCY. I assure you, sir, she came not to Mr Horner out of love, for she loves him no more –

MRS PINCHWIFE. Hold, I told lies for you, but you shall tell none for me, for I do love Mr Horner with all my soul, and nobody shall say me nay. Pray, don't you go to make poor Mr Horner believe to the contrary; 'tis spitefully done of you, I'm sure.

HORNER. (*aside to* MRS PINCHWIFE) Peace, dear idiot.

MRS PINCHWIFE. Nay, I will not peace.

PINCHWIFE. Not till I make you.

Enter DORILANT, QUACK.

---

362 *libidinous*: libinous Q1.
367 *Soh*: a sigh.

DORILANT. Horner, your servant; I am the doctor's guest, he must excuse our intrusion.

QUACK. But what's the matter, gentlemen? For heaven's sake, what's the matter?

HORNER. Oh, 'tis well you are come. 'Tis a censorious world we live in; you may have brought me a reprieve, or else I had died for a crime I never committed, and these innocent ladies had suffered with me. Therefore pray satisfy these worthy, honourable, jealous gentlemen – that – (*Whispers*)

QUACK. O, I understand you; is that all? (*Whispers to* SIR JASPAR) Sir Jaspar, by heavens and upon the word of a physician, sir –

SIR JASPAR. Nay, I do believe you truly. – Pardon me, my virtuous lady and dear of honour.

OLD LADY SQUEAMISH. What, then all's right again?

SIR JASPAR. Ay, ay, and now let us satisfy him too.

They whisper with MR PINCHWIFE.

PINCHWIFE. An eunuch! Pray, no fooling with me.

QUACK. I'll bring half the chirurgeons in town to swear it.

PINCHWIFE. They! – they'll swear a man that bled to death through his wounds died of an apoplexy.

QUACK. Pray hear me, sir – why, all the town has heard the report of him.

PINCHWIFE. But does all the town believe it?

QUACK. Pray inquire a little, and first of all these.

PINCHWIFE. I'm sure when I left the town he was the lewdest fellow in't.

QUACK. I tell you, sir, he has been in France since; pray, ask but these ladies and gentlemen, your friend Mr Dorilant. – Gentlemen and ladies, han't you all heard the late sad report of poor Mr Horner?

ALL THE LADIES. Ay, ay, ay.

DORILANT. Why, thou jealous fool, dost thou doubt it? He's an arrant French capon.

MRS PINCHWIFE. 'Tis false, sir, you shall not disparage poor Mr Horner, for to my certain knowledge –

LUCY. Oh, hold!

414–15 useful because duelling was illegal.

428 *capon*: castrated cock, hence an impotent person.

SQUEAMISH. (*aside to* LUCY) Stop her mouth!

LADY FIDGET. (*to* PINCHWIFE) Upon my honour, sir, 'tis as true –

DAINTY. D'ye think we would have been seen in his company?

SQUEAMISH. Trust our unspotted reputations with him!

LADY FIDGET. (*aside to* HORNER) This you get, and we too, by trusting your secret to a fool.

HORNER. Peace, madam. (*Aside to* QUACK) Well, doctor, is not this a good design, that carries a man on unsuspected and brings him off safe?

PINCHWIFE. (*aside*) Well, if this were true, but my wife –

DORILANT *whispers with* MRS PINCHWIFE.

ALITHEA. Come, brother, your wife is yet innocent, you see; but have a care of too strong an imagination, lest like an overconcerned, timorous gamester, by fancying an unlucky cast, it should come. Women and fortune are truest still to those that trust 'em.

LUCY. And any wild thing grows but the more fierce and hungry for being kept up and more dangerous to the keeper.

ALITHEA. There's doctrine for all husbands, Mr Harcourt.

HARCOURT. I edify, madam, so much that I am impatient till I am one.

DORILANT. And I edify so much by example I will never be one.

SPARKISH. And because I will not disparage my parts I'll ne'er be one.

HORNER. And I, alas, can't be one.

PINCHWIFE. But I must be one – against my will, to a country wife, with a country murrain to me.

MRS PINCHWIFE. (*aside*) And I must be a country wife still too, I find, for I can't, like a city one, be rid of my musty husband and do what I list.

HORNER. Now, sir, I must pronounce your wife innocent, though I blush whilst I do it, and I am the only man by her now exposed to shame, which I will straight

---

432, 438 s.p. *Lady Fidget*: Old Lady Fidget Q1.
458 s.p. *Sparkish*: Eew Q1 (inexplicably).
462 *murrain*: cattle plague.

drown in wine, as you shall your suspicion, and the ladies' troubles we'll divert with a ballet. – Doctor, where are your maskers?

LUCY. Indeed, she's innocent, sir, I am her witness; and her end of coming out was but to see her sister's wedding and what she has said to your face of her love to Mr Horner was but the usual innocent revenge on a husband's jealousy – was it not, madam? Speak.

MRS PINCHWIFE. (*aside to* LUCY *and* HORNER)
Since you'll have me tell more lies – Yes, indeed, bud.

PINCHWIFE. For my own sake fain I would all believe;
Cuckolds, like lovers, should themselves deceive.
But – (*Sighs*)
His honour is least safe, too late I find,
Who trusts it with a foolish wife or friend.

A dance of cuckolds.

HORNER. Vain fops but court and dress and keep a puther,
To pass for women's men with one another,
But he who aims by women to be priz'd,
First by the men, you see, must be despis'd.

---

473 *end of*: aim in.

482 s.d. *A dance of cuckolds*: the music must have made the point; presumably it was 'Cuckolds all a row' which Pepys saw the King dance on 31 December 1662 (see John Playford's *The Dancing Master*, published five times between 1652 and 1675).

483 *puther*: pother, turmoil.

EPILOGUE, *spoken by* MRS KNEP

Now, you the vigorous, who daily here
O'er vizard-mask in public domineer,
And what you'd do to her if in place where,
Nay, have the confidence to cry, 'Come out',
Yet when she says 'Lead on', you are not stout,
But to your well-dressed brother straight turn round
And cry, 'Pox on her, Ned, she can't be sound',
Then slink away, a fresh one to engage,
With so much seeming heat and loving rage,
You'd frighten listening actress on the stage,
Till she at last has seen you huffing come
And talk of keeping in the tiring-room,
Yet cannot be provok'd to lead her home.
Next, you Falstaffs of fifty, who beset
Your buckram maidenheads, which your friends get,
And whilst to them you of achievements boast,
They share the booty and laugh at your cost.
In fine, you essenced boys, both old and young,
Who would be thought so eager, brisk and strong,
Yet do the ladies, not their husbands, wrong,
Whose purses for your manhood make excuse,
And keep your Flanders mares for show, not use:
Encourag'd by our woman's man today,
A Horner's part may vainly think to play
And may intrigues so bashfully disown
That they may doubted be by few or none,
May kiss the cards at picquet, ombre, loo,
And so be thought to kiss the lady too;
But, gallants, have a care, faith, what you do.
The world, which to no man his due will give,
You by experience know you can deceive
And men may still believe you vigorous,
But then we women – there's no cozening us.

Mrs Knep: Mr Hart Q1 (but clearly spoken by a woman, corrected by Q2).

15 *buckram*: stiff but also, like Falstaff's buckram rogues (*1 Henry IV*, II iv), illusory.

22 *Flanders mares*: Flemish horses were primarily imported for breeding.

27 *picquet*: a card game, like ombre and loo.

THE

PLAIN-DEALER.

A

COMEDY.

As it is Acted at the

Theatre Royal.

Written by Mr WYCHERLEY.

HORAT.

—— *Ridiculum acre*
Fortius & melius magnas plerumque secat res.

Licensed *Jan.* 9. 1676.
ROGER L'ESTRANGE.

LONDON,

Printed by T. N. for *James Magnes* and *Rich. Bentley* in *Russel-street* in *Covent-garden* near the *Piazza's*.
M. DC. LXXVII.

Title-page of the 1677 Quarto of *The Plain-Dealer*, reproduced by permission of the Master and Fellows, Trinity College, Cambridge.

Motto

Horace, *Satires*, I x 14–15:

'Ridicule usually decides great matters more forcefully and better than severity'

INTRODUCTORY NOTE

Wycherley made use of more sources for *The Plain-Dealer* than for any of his other plays. Some are comparatively straightforward. Olivia's discussion with Eliza about the merits of Wycherley's previous play, *The Country Wife*, in Act II stems from Molière's *Critique de l'école des femmes* (1663). Manly's display of the way to get rid of importunate acquaintances at the end of Act III derives ultimately from the traditions of formal verse satire but may also owe something to Molière's *Les Fâcheux*. When Fidelia, disguised as a man, has her place taken in the assignation with Olivia by Manly, is surprised by Olivia's husband and nearly raped by him when her sex is discovered, Wycherley is making use of Marie-Catherine Desjardins's *Memoires de la vie de Henriette-Sylvie de Molière* (Paris, 1671) and the aftermath of the chaos, when Vernish cannot understand why Olivia should have run away and Olivia cannot understand why Vernish should have taken her lover for a woman, stems from the same source. Wycherley used Furetière's *Le Roman Bourgeois* (Paris, 1666, translated as *Scarron's City Romance* in 1671) as the source for Oldfox's argument with Widow Blackacre over who should read their papers (IV 255–98); he may also have taken a hint for his dedication from Mythophilacte's dedication of his work to the public executioner later in Furetière's work. It has been suggested that Manly was intended as a portrait of John Sheffield, Earl of Mulgrave, but the parallels are not convincing. Wycherley's father, Daniel, has traditionally been held to be the source for Widow Blackacre; they have only their litigiousness in common.

The other two sources are sources of an entirely different nature. Fidelia is a heroine derived from a long tradition of dramatic romance but the peculiar situation in which she finds herself is deliberately reminiscent of *Twelfth Night*; like Viola, she is ordered by the man she loves to woo Olivia (in both cases), who loves her. Wycherley wants his audience to recall Shakespeare's play, for it is Olivia, not the misanthropic Malvolio, who leaves the stage at the end. Even more complex is *The Plain-Dealer*'s relation to its most important source, Molière's *Le Misanthrope* (1666). Certain passages from Molière are imitated quite closely: Alceste's opening conversation with Philinte on friendship becomes Manly's with Plausible and Freeman (Act I); Olivia's gossiping with Novel (Act II) is patterned on the dissection of absent friends performed by Celimène and Acaste; the letters written by Olivia to Novel and Plausible parallel Celimène's to Clitandre and

Acaste. But Wycherley alters the structure of Molière's play in numerous ways: Alceste rushes off to the wilderness at the end of Molière's play while Manly returns from such an expedition at the beginning of Wycherley's; Philinte and Éliante agree to marry in Molière but Freeman and Eliza never speak to each other in Wycherley. The more Wycherley's audience knew *Le Misanthrope* the more they would have appreciated *The Plain-Dealer.*

The performance of *The Plain-Dealer* on 11 December 1676 at the Theatre Royal, Drury Lane, by the King's Company is probably the first. As John Dennis recorded in 1725, the audience were bemused and 'appeared doubtful what judgement to form of it' until a group including Rochester, Buckingham, Mulgrave and others 'by their loud approbation of it gave it both a sudden and a lasting reputation' (*The Critical Works*, vol. II, p. 277). The play was frequently performed until the end of the century, including the court performance in 1685 that helped Wycherley to be released from the Fleet prison. It was performed fairly frequently between 1715 and 1743 and there were occasional performances later in the century. In 1765 Isaac Bickerstaffe revised it in a version that was performed on odd occasions throughout the 1770s. In 1796 John Philip Kemble attempted to revive it in a new revised version but it was a flop. In this century it was performed by the Renaissance Theatre Company at the Scala Theatre in November 1925 but it still awaits a full-scale professional revival.

The play was first published in 1677 and there were numerous subsequent editions (1681, 1686, 1691, 1694, 1700 and 1709). Of modern editions, Leo Hughes edited the play for the Regents Restoration Drama Series in 1967 and James L. Smith for the New Mermaids in 1979. A facsimile of the first edition was published by Scolar Press in 1971.

TO MY LADY *B*–

Madam,

Though I never had the honour to receive a favour from you, nay, or be known to you, I take the confidence of an author to write to you a *billet doux* dedicatory; which is no new thing, for by most dedications it appears that authors, though they praise their patrons from top to toe and seem to turn 'em inside out, know 'em as little as sometimes their patrons their books, though they read 'em out; and if the poetical daubers did not write the name of the man or woman on top of the picture, 'twere impossible to guess whose it were. But you, madam, without the help of a poet, have made yourself known and famous in the world and, because you do not want it, are therefore most worthy of an epistle dedicatory. And this play claims naturally your protection, since it has lost its reputation with the ladies of stricter lives in the playhouse; and (you know) when men's endeavours are discountenanced and refused by the nice coy women of honour, they come to you, to you the great and noble patroness of rejected and bashful men, of which number I profess myself to be one, though a poet, a dedicating poet; to you, I say, madam, who have as discerning a judgement, in what's obscene or not, as any quick-sighted civil person of 'em all, and can make as much of a double-meaning saying as the best of 'em; yet would not, as some do, make nonsense of a poet's jest, rather than not make it bawdy; by which they show they as little value wit in a play as in a lover, provided they can bring t'other thing about. Their sense indeed lies all one way, and therefore are only for that in a poet which is moving, as they say. But what do they mean by that word 'moving'? Well, I must not put 'em to the blush, since I find I can do't. In short, madam, you would not be one of those who ravish a poet's innocent words and make 'em guilty of their own naughtiness (as 'tis termed) in spite of his teeth; nay, nothing is secure from the power of their imaginations, no, not their husbands, whom they cuckold with themselves by thinking of other men and so make the lawful matrimonial embraces adultery; wrong husbands and

---

1 *Lady B*–: Mother Bennet, a famous London bawd.

poets in thought and word, to keep their own reputations. But your ladyship's justice, I know, would think a woman's arraigning and damning a poet for her own obscenity, like her crying out a rape and hanging a man for giving her pleasure, only that she might be thought not to consent to't; and so, to vindicate her honour forfeits her modesty. But you, madam, have too much modesty to pretend to't, though you have as much to say for your modesty as many a nicer she, for you never were seen at this play, no, not the first day; and 'tis no matter what people's lives have been, they are unquestionably modest who frequent not this play. For, as Mr Bayes says of his, that it is the only touchstone of men's wit and understanding, mine is, it seems, the only touchstone of women's virtue and modesty. But hold, that touchstone is equivocal and by the strength of a lady's imagination may become something that is not civil; but your ladyship, I know, scorns to misapply a touchstone. And, madam, though you have not seen this play, I hope (like other nice ladies) you will the rather read it. Yet, lest the chambermaid or page should not be trusted and their indulgence could gain no further admittance for it than to their ladies' lobbies or outward rooms, take it into your care and protection, for, by your recommendation and procurement, it may have the honour to get into their closets; for what they renounce in public often entertains 'em there, with your help especially. In fine, madam, for these and many other reasons, you are the fittest patroness or judge of this play, for you show no partiality to this or that author. For from some many ladies will take a broad jest as cheerfully as from the watermen and sit at some downright filthy plays (as they call 'em) as well satisfied and

---

54 *Mr Bayes*: the name given by George Villiers, Duke of Buckingham, to his parody of Dryden in *The Rehearsal* (1671). Bayes comments in Act III, 'I know you have wit by the judgement you make of this play, for that's the measure I go by; my play is my touchstone.'

56 *touchstone*: (*a*) a stone to test gold, a criterion, a standard (*b*) a penis.

69 *In fine*: in short, to conclude.

73 *watermen*: the Thames boatmen, notorious for their inventive language of abuse.

as still as a poet could wish 'em elsewhere. Therefore it must be the doubtful obscenity of my plays alone they take exceptions at, because it is too bashful for 'em, and indeed most women hate men for attempting to halves on their chastity, and bawdy I find, like satire, should be home, not to have it taken notice of. But, now I mention satire, some there are who say, 'tis the plain-dealing of the play, not the obscenity, 'tis taking off the ladies' masks, not offering at their petticoats, which offends 'em. And generally they are not the handsomest, or most innocent, who are the most angry at being discovered:

– Nihil est audacius illis
Deprehensis; iram, atque animos a crimine sumunt.

Pardon, madam, the quotation, for a dedication can no more be without ends of Latin than flattery; and 'tis no matter for whom it is writ to, for an author can as easily (I hope) suppose people to have more understanding and languages than they have, as well as more virtues. But why the devil should any of the few modest and handsome be alarmed? (For some there are who as well as any deserve those attributes, yet refrain not from seeing this play, nor think it any addition to their virtue to set up for it in a playhouse, lest there it should look too much like acting.) But why, I say, should any at all of the truly virtuous be concerned, if those who are not so are distinguished from 'em? For by that mask of modesty which women wear promiscuously in public, they are all alike, and you can no more know a kept wench from a woman of honour by her looks than by her dress. For those who are of quality without honour (if any such there are), they have their quality to set off their false modesty, as well as their false jewels, and you must no more suspect their countenances for counterfeit than their pendants, though, as the Plain-dealer Montaigne

87–8 *Nihil . . . sumunt*: Juvenal, *Satires*, VI 284–5: 'Nothing is bolder than these when found out; they put on anger and passion from their guilt.'

says, *Elles envoyent leur conscience au bordel et tiennent leur contenance en règle*. But those who act as they look ought not to be scandalised at the reprehension of others' faults, lest they tax themselves with 'em and by too delicate and quick an apprehension not only make that obscene which I meant innocent but that satire on all which was intended only on those who deserved it. But, madam, I beg your pardon for this digression to civil women and ladies of honour, since you and I shall never be the better for 'em; for a comic poet and a lady of your profession make most of the other sort, and the stage and your houses, like our plantations, are propagated by the least nice women; and, as with the ministers of justice, the vices of the age are our best business. But, now I mention public persons, I can no longer defer doing you the justice of a dedication and telling you your own, who are, of all public-spirited people, the most necessary, most communicative, most generous and hospitable. Your house has been the house of the people, your sleep still disturbed for the public, and when you arose 'twas that others might lie down and you waked that others might rest. The good you have done is unspeakable. How many young unexperienced heirs have you kept from rash, foolish marriages and from being jilted for their lives by the worst sort of jilts, wives? How many bewitched widowers' children have you preserved from the tyranny of stepmothers? How many old dotards from cuckoldage and keeping other men's wenches and children? How many adulteries and unnatural sins have you prevented? In fine, you have been a constant scourge to the old lecher, and often a terror to the young. You have made concupiscence its own punishment and extinguished lust with lust, like blowing up of houses to stop the fire.

110–11 *Elles . . . règle*: Montaigne, *Essays*, Book III chapter 5: 'They send their conscience to the stews and keep their countenance in order' (Florio's translation, 1603).

110 *Elles envoyent*: Els envoy Q1.

110 *tiennent*: teinnent Q1.

122 *nice*: (*a*) fastidious (*b*) shy, unwilling.

134 *jilted*: deceived, cheated.

Nimirum propter continentiam, incontinentia
Necessaria est, incendium ignibus extinguitur.

There's Latin for you again, madam; I protest to you, as I am an author, I cannot help it. Nay, I can hardly keep myself from quoting Aristotle and Horace and talking to you of the rules of writing (like the French authors) to show you and my readers I understand 'em, in my epistle, lest neither of you should find it out by the play; and, according to the rules of dedication, 'tis no matter whether you understand or no what I quote or say to you of writing, for an author can as easily make anyone a judge or critic in an epistle as an hero in his play. But, madam, that this may prove to the end a true epistle dedicatory, I'd have you know 'tis not without a design upon you, which is in the behalf of the fraternity of Parnassus, that songs and sonnets may go at your houses and in your liberties for guineas and half guineas, and that wit, at least with you, as of old, may be the price of beauty; and so you will prove a true encourager of poetry, for love is a better help to it than wine and poets, like painters, draw better after the life than by fancy. Nay, in justice, madam, I think a poet ought to be as free of your houses as of the playhouses, since he contributes to the support of both and is as necessary to such as you as a ballad-singer to the pick-purse, in convening the cullies at the theatres, to be picked up and carried to supper and bed at your houses. And, madam, the reason of this motion of mine is because poor poets can get no favour in the tiring-rooms, for they are no keepers, you know; and folly and money,

---

144–5 *Nimirum . . . extinguitur*: Tertullian, *De Pudicitia*, I 16, quoted by Montaigne in the same essay: 'Belike we must be incontinent that we may be continent; burning is quenched by fire' (Florio's translation).

149–50 *French authors*: Corneille, for example, who prefaced his collected plays with *Discours* and *Examens*.

160 *liberties*: districts outside the city but under municipal control, as well as a pun on *freedoms*.

165–6 *a poet . . . playhouses*: playwrights were allowed free admission to the theatres.

169 *cullies*: dupes, often cuckolds.

172 *tiring-rooms*: dressing-rooms at the theatres.

173 *keepers*: men who maintain mistresses.

the old enemies of wit, are even too hard for it on its own dunghill. And for other ladies, a poet can least go to the price of them. Besides, his wit, which ought to recommend him to 'em, is as much an obstruction to his love as to his wealth or preferment, for most women nowadays apprehend wit in a lover as much as in a husband. They hate a man that knows 'em; they must have a blind, easy fool whom they can lead by the nose and, as the Scythian women of old, must baffle a man and put out his eyes ere they will lie with him, and then too, like thieves, when they have plundered and stripped a man, leave him. But if there should be one of an hundred of those ladies generous enough to give herself to a man that has more wit than money (all things considered) he would think it cheaper coming to you for a mistress though you made him pay his guinea, as a man in a journey (out of good husbandry) had better pay for what he has in an inn than lie on freecost at a gentleman's house.

In fine, madam, like a faithful dedicator I hope I have done myself right in the first place, then you and your profession, which in the wisest and most religious government of the world is honoured with the public allowance and in those that are thought the most uncivilised and barbarous is protected and supported by the ministers of justice. And of you, madam, I ought to say no more here, for your virtues deserve a poem rather than an epistle, or a volume entire to give the world your memoirs or life at large, and which (upon the word of an author that has a mind to make an end of his dedication) I promise to do, when I write the annals of our British love, which shall be dedicated to the ladies concerned, if they will not think them something too obscene too, when your life, compared with many that are thought innocent, I doubt not may vindicate you, and me, to the world for the confidence I have taken in this address to you, which then may be thought neither impertinent, nor immodest. And, whatsoever your amorous mis-

---

179 *apprehend*: fear.

182–3 *Scythian women . . . lie with him*: taken from Montaigne, *Essays*, Book III chapter 5.

182 *baffle*: humiliate.

fortunes have been, none can charge you with that heinous and worst of women's crimes, hypocrisy. Nay, in spite of misfortunes or age you are the same woman still, though most of your sex grow Magdalens at fifty and, as a solid French author has it,

Après le plaisir, vient la peine,
Après la peine la vertu.

But sure an old sinner's continency is much like a gamester's forswearing play when he has lost all his money; and modesty is a kind of a youthful dress, which as it makes a young woman more amiable makes an old one more nauseous. A bashful old woman is like an hopeful old man, and the affected chastity of antiquated beauties is rather a reproach than an honour to 'em, for it shows the men's virtue only, not theirs. But you, in fine, madam, are no more an hypocrite than I am when I praise you, therefore, I doubt not, will be thought (even by yours and the play's enemies, the nicest ladies) to be the fittest patroness for,

Madam,
Your ladyship's most obedient,
faithful, humble servant, and
The Plain-Dealer.

217–18 *Après . . . vertu*: 'After pleasure comes pain, after pain virtue' (source unknown).

PROLOGUE, *spoken by the Plain-Dealer*

I the Plain-Dealer am to act today
And my rough part begins before the play.
First, you who scribble, yet hate all that write,
And keep each other company in spite,
As rivals in your common mistress, fame,
And with faint praises one another damn;
'Tis a good play (we know) you can't forgive,
But grudge yourselves the pleasure you receive:
Our scribbler therefore bluntly bid me say,
He would not have the wits pleased here today.
Next, you, the fine, loud gentlemen o'th'pit,
Who damn all plays; yet if y'ave any wit,
'Tis but what here you sponge and daily get;
Poets, like friends to whom you are in debt,
You hate, and so rooks laugh, to see undone
Those pushing gamesters whom they live upon.
Well, you are sparks and still will be i'th'fashion;
Rail then at plays to hide your obligation.
Now, you shrewd judges who the boxes sway,
Leading the ladies' hearts and sense astray,
And, for their sakes, see all and hear no play,
Correct your cravats, foretops, lock behind,
The dress and breeding of the play ne'er mind;
Plain-dealing is, you'll say, quite out of fashion;
You'll hate it here, as in a dedication;
And your fair neighbours, in a limning poet,
No more than in a painter will allow it.
Pictures too like, the ladies will not please;
They must be drawn too here, like goddesses.
You, as at Lely's too, would truncheon wield,
And look like heroes in a painted field;
But the coarse dauber of the coming scenes
To follow life and nature only means,
Displays you as you are, makes his fine woman

---

13 *sponge*: by soaking up the poet's wit and using it as their own.
15 *rooks*: cheats, con-men.
17 *sparks*: fashionable and often foppish gallants.
22 *foretops*: a lock of hair ornamenting the forehead.
26 *limning poet*: a writer who draws portraits.
30 *Lely's*: Sir Peter Lely (1618–80), the fashionable portrait painter.
30 *truncheon*: officer's staff of authority.

A mercenary jilt, and true to no man;
His men of wit and pleasure of the age
Are as dull rogues as ever cumbered stage;
He draws a friend, only to custom just,
And makes him naturally break his trust.
I, only, act a part like none of you –
And yet, you'll say, it is a fool's part too –
An honest man, who, like you, never winks
At faults but, unlike you, speaks what he thinks,
The only fool who ne'er found patron yet,
For truth is now a fault, as well as wit.
And where else, but on stages, do we see
Truth pleasing or rewarded honesty?
Which our bold poet does this day in me.
If not to th'honest, be to th'prosperous kind;
Some friends at court let the Plain-Dealer find.

THE PERSONS

MANLY, of an honest, surly, nice humour, supposed first in the time of the Dutch War to have procured the command of a ship out of honour, not interest, and choosing a sea life only to avoid the world.	*Mr Hart*
FREEMAN, Manly's lieutenant, a gentleman well educated, but of a broken fortune, a complier with the age	*Mr Kynaston*
VERNISH, Manly's bosom and only friend	*Mr Griffin*
NOVEL, a pert, railing coxcomb and an admirer of novelties, makes love to Olivia	*Mr Clark*
MAJOR OLDFOX, an old impertinent fop, given to scribbling, makes love to the Widow Blackacre	*Mr Cartwright*
MY LORD PLAUSIBLE, a ceremonious, supple, commending coxcomb, in love with Olivia	*Mr Haines*
JERRY BLACKACRE, a true raw squire, under age and his mother's government, bred to the law	*Mr Charlton*
OLIVIA, Manly's mistress	*Mrs Marshall*
FIDELIA, in love with Manly and followed him to sea in man's clothes	*Mrs Boutell*
ELIZA, cousin to Olivia	*Mrs Knep*
LETTICE, Olivia's woman	*Mrs Knight*
THE WIDOW BLACKACRE, a petulant, litigious widow, always in law, and mother to Squire Jerry	*Mrs Corey*

LAWYERS, KNIGHTS OF THE POST, BAILIFFS, an ALDERMAN, a BOOKSELLER'S PRENTICE, a FOOT-BOY, SAILORS, WAITERS and attendants

The Scene: *London*

1–2 *nice humour*: punctilious disposition.

3 *Dutch War*: either the second war of 1664–7 or the third of 1672–4.

18 *Blackacre*: a legal phrase for a fictitious parcel of land.

30 *Knights of the Post*: professional perjurers and false witnesses.

THE PLAIN-DEALER

ACT I

SCENE I

Captain Manly's lodging.

Enter CAPTAIN MANLY, *surlily, and* MY LORD PLAUSIBLE *following him, and two* SAILORS *behind.*

MANLY. Tell not me, my good Lord Plausible, of your decorums, supercilious forms and slavish ceremonies, your little tricks, which you the spaniels of the world do daily over and over for and to one another, not out of love or duty, but your servile fear.

LORD PLAUSIBLE. Nay, i'faith, i'faith, you are too passionate, and I must humbly beg your pardon and leave to tell you, they are the arts, and rules, the prudent of the world walk by.

MANLY. Let 'em. But I'll have no leading-strings; I can walk alone. I hate a harness and will not tug on in a faction, kissing my leader behind, that another slave may do the like to me.

LORD PLAUSIBLE. What, will you be singular then, like nobody? Follow, love, and esteem nobody?

MANLY. Rather than be general, like you, follow everybody, court and kiss everybody, though perhaps at the same time you hate everybody.

LORD PLAUSIBLE. Why, seriously, with your pardon, my dear friend –

MANLY. With your pardon, my no friend, I will not, as you do, whisper my hatred or my scorn, call a man fool or knave by signs or mouths over his shoulder whilst you have him in your arms. For such as you, like common whores and pickpockets, are only dangerous to those you embrace.

LORD PLAUSIBLE. Such as I! Heavens defend me – upon my honour –

MANLY. Upon your title, my lord, if you'd have me believe you.

15 *follow, love*: follow Love Q1.

LORD PLAUSIBLE. Well then, as I am a person of honour, I never attempted to abuse or lessen any person in my life.

MANLY. What, you were afraid?

LORD PLAUSIBLE. No; but seriously, I hate to do a rude thing. No, faith, I speak well of all mankind.

MANLY. I thought so; but know that speaking well of all mankind is the worst kind of detraction, for it takes away the reputation of the few good men in the world by making all alike. Now I speak ill of most men, because they deserve it, I that can do a rude thing rather than an unjust thing.

LORD PLAUSIBLE. Well, tell not me, my dear friend, what people deserve; I ne'er mind that. I, like an author in a dedication, never speak well of a man for his sake but my own. I will not disparage any man to disparage myself, for to speak ill of people behind their backs is not like a person of honour, and truly to speak ill of 'em to their faces is not like a complaisant person. But if I did say or do an ill thing to anybody, it should be sure to be behind their backs out of pure good manners.

MANLY. Very well; but I, that am an unmannerly sea-fellow, if I ever speak well of people (which is very seldom indeed), it should be sure to be behind their backs, and if I would say or do ill to any, it should be to their faces. I would justle a proud, strutting, overlooking coxcomb at the head of his sycophants rather than put out my tongue at him when he were past me, would frown in the arrogant, big, dull face of an overgrown knave of business rather than vent my spleen against him when his back were turned, would give fawning slaves the lie whilst they embrace or commend me, cowards whilst they brag, call a rascal by no other title though his father had left him a duke's, laugh at fools aloud before their mistresses, and must desire people to leave me when their visits grow at last as troublesome as they were at first impertinent.

LORD PLAUSIBLE. I would not have my visits troublesome.

MANLY. The only way to be sure not to have 'em troublesome is to make 'em when people are not at home, for your visits, like other good turns, are most obliging when made or done to a man in his absence. A pox, why should anyone, because he has nothing to do, go and disturb another man's business?

LORD PLAUSIBLE. I beg your pardon, my dear friend. What, you have business?

MANLY. If you have any, I would not detain your lordship.

LORD PLAUSIBLE. Detain me, dear sir! I can never have enough of your company.

MANLY. I'm afraid I should be tiresome. I know not what you think.

LORD PLAUSIBLE. Well, dear sir, I see you would have me gone.

MANLY. (*aside*) But I see you won't.

LORD PLAUSIBLE. Your most faithful –

MANLY. God be w'ye, my lord.

LORD PLAUSIBLE. Your most humble –

MANLY. Farewell.

LORD PLAUSIBLE. And eternally –

MANLY. And eternally ceremony – (*Aside*) Then the devil take thee eternally.

LORD PLAUSIBLE. You shall use no ceremony, by my life.

MANLY. I do not intend it.

LORD PLAUSIBLE. Why do you stir then?

MANLY. Only to see you out of doors, that I may shut 'em against more welcomes.

LORD PLAUSIBLE. Nay, faith, that shan't pass upon your most faithful, humble servant.

MANLY. (*aside*) Nor this any more upon me.

LORD PLAUSIBLE. Well, you are too strong for me.

MANLY. (*aside*) I'd sooner be visited by the plague, for that only would keep a man from visits and his doors shut. *Exit, thrusting out* MY LORD PLAUSIBLE.

Manent SAILORS.

FIRST SAILOR. Here's a finical fellow, Jack! What a brave fair-weather captain of a ship he would make!

SECOND SAILOR. He a captain of a ship! It must be when she's in the dock then, for he looks like one of

---

109 *finical*: affectedly fastidious.

those that get the King's Commissions for Hulls to sell a king's ship, when a brave fellow has fought her almost to a longboat.

FIRST SAILOR. On my conscience then, Jack, that's the reason our bully tar sunk our ship: not only that the Dutch might not have her, but that the courtiers, who laugh at wooden legs, might not make her prize.

SECOND SAILOR. A pox of his sinking, Tom; we have made a base, broken, short voyage of it.

FIRST SAILOR. Ay, your brisk dealers in honour always make quick returns with their ship to the dock and their men to the hospitals. 'Tis, let me see, just a month since we set out of the river, and the wind was almost as cross to us as the Dutch.

SECOND SAILOR. Well, I forgive him sinking my own poor truck, if he would but have given me time and leave to have saved black Kate of Wapping's small venture.

FIRST SAILOR. Faith, I forgive him since, as the purser told me, he sunk the value of five or six thousand pound of his own with which he was to settle himself somewhere in the Indies, for our merry lieutenant was to succeed him in his commission for the ship back, for he was resolved never to return again for England.

SECOND SAILOR. So it seemed by his fighting.

FIRST SAILOR. No, but he was a-weary of this side of the world here, they say.

SECOND SAILOR. Ay, or else he would not have bid so fair for a passage into t'other.

FIRST SAILOR. Jack, thou think'st thyself in the forecastle, thou'rt so waggish; but I tell you then, he had a mind to go live and bask himself on the sunny side of the globe.

SECOND SAILOR. What, out of any discontent? For

113–14 the common practice of selling off out-of-commission ships.
115 *longboat*: the largest rowing-boat belonging to a sailing ship.
117 *bully*: fine fellow.
128 *truck*: odds and ends, goods of little value.
129 *Wapping*: a suburb of London beside the Thames, downriver from the Tower, frequented by sailors.
134 *Indies*: East Indies.

he's always as dogged as an old tarpaulin when hindered of a voyage by a young pantaloon captain.

FIRST SAILOR. 'Tis true, I never saw him pleased but in the fight, and then he looked like one of us coming from the pay-table, with a new lining to our hats under our arms.

SECOND SAILOR. A pox, he's like the Bay of Biscay, rough and angry, let the wind blow where 'twill.

FIRST SAILOR. Nay, there's no more dealing with him than with the land in a storm, no-near –

SECOND SAILOR. 'Tis a hurry-durry blade. Dost thou remember after we had tugged hard the old leaky longboat to save his life, when I welcomed him ashore, he gave me a box on the ear and called me fawning water-dog?

Enter MANLY *and* FREEMAN.

FIRST SAILOR. Hold thy peace, Jack, and stand by; the foul weather's coming.

MANLY. You rascals, dogs, how could this tame thing get through you?

FIRST SAILOR. Faith, to tell your honour the truth, we were at hob in the hall and, whilst my brother and I were quarrelling about a cast, he slunk by us.

SECOND SAILOR. He's a sneaking fellow I warrant for't.

MANLY. Have more care for the future, you slaves. Go and with drawn cutlasses stand at the stair foot and keep all that ask for me from coming up. Suppose you were guarding the scuttle to the powder room. Let none enter here at your and their peril.

FIRST SAILOR. No, for the danger would be the same; you would blow them and us up if we should.

148–9 the quarrel between the professional seamen and the gentlemen captains was long and acrimonious, especially in times of war.

148 *tarpaulin*: waterproof cloth, hence sailor, particularly a professional naval officer.

149 *pantaloon*: fashionable breeches.

157 *no-near*: a command to the helmsman to come no closer to the wind, hence to keep away from Manly's dangerous shores.

158 *hurry-durry*: rough weather (sailor's slang).

168 *hob*: a coin-tossing game.

174 *scuttle*: hatchway.

SECOND SAILOR. Must no one come to you, sir?

MANLY. No man, sir.

FIRST SAILOR. No man, sir, but a woman then, an't like your honour –

MANLY. No woman neither, you impertinent dog. Would you be pimping? A sea pimp is the strangest monster she has.

SECOND SAILOR. Indeed, an't like your honour, 'twill be hard for us to deny a woman anything since we are so newly come on shore.

FIRST SAILOR. We'll let no old woman come up, though it were our trusting landlady at Wapping.

MANLY. Would you be witty, you brandy casks you? You become a jest as ill as you do a horse. Be gone, you dogs, I hear a noise on the stairs.

Exeunt SAILORS.

FREEMAN. Faith, I am sorry you would let the fop go. I intended to have had some sport with him.

MANLY. Sport with him! A pox, then why did you not stay? You should have enjoyed your coxcomb and had him to yourself for me.

FREEMAN. No, I should not have cared for him without you neither, for the pleasure which fops afford is like that of drinking, only good when 'tis shared, and a fool, like a bottle, which would make you merry in company, will make you dull alone. But how the devil could you turn a man of his quality downstairs? You use a lord with very little ceremony, it seems.

MANLY. A lord! What, thou art one of those who esteem men only by the marks and value fortune has set upon 'em and never consider intrinsic worth. But counterfeit honour will not be current with me; I weigh the man, not his title. 'Tis not the king's stamp can make the metal better or heavier: your lord is a leaden shilling which you may bend every way, and debases the stamp he bears, instead of being raised by't. – Here again, you slaves?

Enter SAILORS.

FIRST SAILOR. Only to receive farther instructions, an't like your honour: what if a man should bring you money? Should we turn him back?

MANLY. All men, I say. Must I be pestered with you too? You dogs, away.

SECOND SAILOR. Nay, I know one man your honour would not have us hinder coming to you, I'm sure.

MANLY. Who's that? Speak quickly, slaves.

SECOND SAILOR. Why, a man that should bring you a challenge, for, though you refuse money, I'm sure you love fighting too well to refuse that.

MANLY. Rogue, rascal, dog.

Kicks the SAILORS *out.*

FREEMAN. Nay, let the poor rogues have their forecastle jests; they cannot help 'em in a fight, scarce when a ship's sinking.

MANLY. Damn their untimely jests. A servant's jest is more sauciness than his counsel.

FREEMAN. But what, will you see nobody? Not your friends?

MANLY. Friends – I have but one, and he, I hear, is not in town; nay, can have but one friend, for a true heart admits but of one friendship as of one love. But in having that friend I have a thousand, for he has the courage of men in despair, yet the diffidency and caution of cowards, the secrecy of the revengeful and the constancy of martyrs, one fit to advise, to keep a secret, to fight and die for his friend. Such I think him, for I have trusted him with my mistress in my absence, and the trust of beauty is sure the greatest we can show.

FREEMAN. Well, but all your good thoughts are not for him alone, I hope. Pray, what d'ye think of me for a friend?

MANLY. Of thee! Why, thou art a latitudinarian in friendship, that is, no friend; thou dost side with all mankind but will suffer for none. Thou art indeed like your Lord Plausible, the pink of courtesy, therefore hast no friendship, for ceremony and great professing renders friendship as much suspected as it does religion.

FREEMAN. And no professing, no ceremony at all in friendship were as unnatural and as undecent as in

---

247 *latitudinarian*: one who accepts as Christian anyone who accepts the Apostles' Creed, allowing many different concepts of God; Freeman has too many different friends for Manly.

religion; and there is hardly such a thing as an honest hypocrite, who professes himself to be worse than he is, unless it be yourself, for though I could never get you to say you were my friend, I know you'll prove so.

MANLY. I must confess I am so much your friend I would not deceive you, therefore must tell you, not only because my heart is taken up but according to your rules of friendship, I cannot be your friend.

FREEMAN. Why, pray?

MANLY. Because he that is, you'll say, a true friend to a man is a friend to all his friends. But you must pardon me, I cannot wish well to pimps, flatterers, detractors and cowards, stiff nodding knaves and supple, pliant, kissing fools. Now, all these I have seen you use like the dearest friends in the world.

FREEMAN. Hah, hah, hah – What, you observed me, I warrant, in the galleries at Whitehall doing the business of the place! Pshaw! Court professions, like court promises, go for nothing, man. But, faith, could you think I was a friend to all those I hugged, kissed, flattered, bowed to? Hah, ha –

MANLY. You told 'em so and swore it too; I heard you.

FREEMAN. Ay, but when their backs were turned did I not tell you they were rogues, villains, rascals whom I despised and hated?

MANLY. Very fine! But what reason had I to believe you spoke your heart to me since you professed deceiving so many?

FREEMAN. Why, don't you know, good captain, that telling truth is a quality as prejudicial to a man that would thrive in the world as square play to a cheat, or true love to a whore! Would you have a man speak truth to his ruin? You are severer than the law, which requires no man to swear against himself. You would have me speak truth against myself, I warrant, and tell my promising friend, the courtier, he has a bad memory?

MANLY. Yes.

---

272 *galleries at Whitehall*: the popular gathering-place in the king's residence, a place for gossip, rumour, seeking preferment.

276 *to*: too Q1.

FREEMAN. And so make him remember to forget my business. And I should tell the great lawyer too that he takes oftener fees to hold his tongue than to speak?

MANLY. No doubt on't.

FREEMAN. Ay, and have him hang or ruin me, when he should come to be a judge and I before him. And you would have me tell the new officer who bought his employment lately that he is a coward?

MANLY. Ay.

FREEMAN. And so get myself cashiered, not him, he having the better friends though I the better sword. And I should tell the scribbler of honour that heraldry were a prettier and fitter study for so fine a gentleman than poetry?

MANLY. Certainly.

FREEMAN. And so find myself mauled in his next hired lampoon. And you would have me tell the holy lady too she lies with her chaplain?

MANLY. No doubt on't.

FREEMAN. And so draw the clergy upon my back and want a good table to dine at sometimes. And by the same reason too, I should tell you that the world thinks you a madman, a brutal, and have you cut my throat, or worse, hate me! What other good success of all my plain-dealing could I have than what I've mentioned?

MANLY. Why, first your promising courtier would keep his word, out of fear of more reproaches or at least would give you no more vain hopes. Your lawyer would serve you more faithfully, for he, having no honour but his interest, is truest still to him he knows suspects him. The new officer would provoke thee to make him a coward and so be cashiered, that thou or some other honest fellow, who had more courage than money, might get his place. The noble sonneteer would trouble thee no more with his madrigals. The praying lady would leave off railing at wenching before thee and not turn away her chambermaid for her own known frailty with thee. And I, instead of hating thee, should love thee for thy plain-dealing

---

316 *brutal*: a short space after the word in Q1 may indicate that a word has dropped out.

and, in lieu of being mortified, am proud that the world and I think not well of one another.

FREEMAN. Well, doctors differ. You are for plain-dealing, I find; but against your particular notions I have the practice of the whole world. Observe but any morning what people do when they get together on the Exchange, in Westminster Hall, or the galleries in Whitehall.

MANLY. I must confess, there they seem to rehearse Bayes's grand dance: here you see a bishop bowing low to a gaudy atheist, a judge to a doorkeeper, a great lord to a fishmonger or a scrivener with a jack-chain about his neck, a lawyer to a sergeant-at-arms, a velvet physician to a threadbare chemist and a supple gentleman usher to a surly beefeater, and so tread round in a preposterous huddle of ceremony to each other, whilst they can hardly hold their solemn false countenances.

FREEMAN. Well, they understand the world.

MANLY. Which I do not, I confess.

FREEMAN. But, sir, pray believe the friendship I promise you real, whatsoever I have professed to others. Try me at least.

MANLY. Why, what would you do for me?

FREEMAN. I would fight for you.

MANLY. That you would do for your own honour. But what else?

FREEMAN. I would lend you money, if I had it.

MANLY. To borrow more of me another time. That were but putting your money to interest; a usurer would be as good a friend. But what other piece of friendship?

---

340 *Exchange*: either the New Exchange, the arcade of shops near the Strand, the location of Act III Scene ii of *The Country Wife*, or the Royal Exchange, the meeting-place of merchants and bankers.

340 *Westminster Hall*: part of the Palace of Westminster, site of the law-courts and also a number of shops; see Act III.

343 *Bayes's grand dance*: a ridiculous dance of the two Kings of Brentford in *The Rehearsal*, Act V.

345 *scrivener with a jack-chain*: a notary wearing his chain of office.

347 *chemist*: alchemist.

FREEMAN. I would speak well of you to your enemies.

MANLY. To encourage others to be your friends by a show of gratitude. But what else?

FREEMAN. Nay, I would not hear you ill spoken of behind your back by my friend.

MANLY. Nay, then thou'rt a friend indeed. But it were unreasonable to expect it from thee as the world goes now, when new friends, like new mistresses, are got by disparaging old ones.

Enter FIDELIA.

But here comes another will say as much at least. Dost not thou love me devilishly too, my little volunteer, as well as he or any man can?

FIDELIA. Better than any man can love you, my dear captain.

MANLY. Look you there. I told you so.

FIDELIA. As well as you do truth or honour, sir, as well.

MANLY. Nay, good young gentleman, enough, for shame. Thou hast been a page, by thy flattering and lying, to one of those praying ladies who love flattery so well they are jealous of it, and wert turned away for saying the same things to the old housekeeper for sweetmeats as you did to your lady; for thou flatterest everything and everybody alike.

FIDELIA. You, dear sir, should not suspect the truth of what I say of you, though to you. Fame, the old liar, is believed when she speaks wonders of you. You cannot be flattered, sir; your merit is unspeakable.

MANLY. Hold, hold, sir, or I shall suspect worse of you, that you have been a cushion-bearer to some state hypocrite and turned away by the chaplains for outflattering their probation sermons for a benefice.

FIDELIA. Suspect me for anything, sir, but the want of love, faith and duty to you, the bravest, worthiest of mankind. Believe me, I could die for you, sir.

MANLY. Nay, there you lie, sir. Did I not see thee more afraid in the fight than the chaplain of the ship or the purser that bought his place?

---

396 *probation sermons*: sermons preached by candidates for appointment to a living.

FIDELIA. Can he be said to be afraid that ventures to sea with you?

MANLY. Fie, fie, no more. I shall hate thy flattery worse than thy cowardice, nay, than thy bragging.

FIDELIA. Well, I own then I was afraid, mightily afraid; yet for you I would be afraid again, an hundred times afraid. Dying is ceasing to be afraid, and that I could do sure for you and you'll believe me one day. (*Weeps*)

FREEMAN. Poor youth! Believe his eyes if not his tongue; he seems to speak truth with them.

MANLY. What, does he cry? A pox on't, a maudlin flatterer is as nauseously troublesome as a maudlin drunkard. No more, you little milksop, do not cry. I'll never make thee afraid again, for of all men, if I had occasion, thou shouldst not be my second and, when I go to sea again, thou shalt venture thy life no more with me.

FIDELIA. Why, will you leave me behind then? (*Aside*) If you would preserve my life, I'm sure you should not.

MANLY. Leave thee behind! Ay, ay, thou art a hopeful youth for the shore only. Here thou wilt live to be cherished by fortune and the great ones, for thou may'st easily come to out-flatter a dull poet, out-lie a coffeehouse or gazette writer, out-swear a knight of the post, out-watch a pimp, out-fawn a rook, out-promise a lover, out-rail a wit and out-brag a sea-captain. All this thou canst do, because thou'rt a coward, a thing I hate; therefore thou'lt do better with the world than with me and these are the good courses you must take in the world. There's good advice, at least, at parting. Go and be happy with't.

FIDELIA. Parting, sir! O let me not hear that dismal word.

MANLY. If my words frighten thee, be gone the sooner, for, to be plain with thee, cowardice and I cannot dwell together.

FIDELIA. And cruelty and courage never dwelt together, sure, sir. Do not turn me off to shame and misery, for I am helpless and friendless.

MANLY. Friendless! There are half a score friends for thee then. (*Offers her gold*) I leave myself no more. They'll help thee a little. Be gone, go; I must be cruel to thee (if thou call'st it so) out of pity.

FIDELIA. If you would be cruelly pitiful, sir, let it be with your sword, not gold. *Exit.*

Enter FIRST SAILOR.

FIRST SAILOR. We have with much ado turned away two gentlemen who told us forty times over their names were Mr Novel and Major Oldfox.

MANLY. Well, to your post again.

Exit SAILOR.

But how come those puppies coupled always together?

FREEMAN. O, the coxcombs keep each other company to show each other, as Novel calls it, or, as Oldfox says, like two knives to whet one another.

MANLY. And set other people's teeth an edge.

Enter SECOND SAILOR.

SECOND SAILOR. Here is a woman, an't like your honour, scolds and bustles with us to come in, as much as a seaman's widow at the Navy Office. Her name is Mrs Blackacre.

MANLY. That fiend too!

FREEMAN. The Widow Blackacre, is it not? That litigious she-pettifogger, who is at law and difference with all the world; but I wish I could make her agree with me in the church. They say she has fifteen hundred pounds a year jointure and the care of her son, that is, the destruction of his estate.

MANLY. Her lawyers, attornies and solicitors have fifteen hundred pound a year whilst she is contented to be poor to make other people so, for she is as vexatious as her father was, the great attorney, nay, as a dozen Norfolk attornies, and as implacable an adversary as a wife suing for alimony or a parson for his tithes, and she loves an Easter term, or any term, not as other country ladies do, to come up to be fine, cuckold their husbands, and take their pleasure, for

---

460 *a seaman's widow . . . Office*: trying to collect her widow's pension.

464 *pettifogger*: a lawyer adept at chicanery.

467 *jointure*: the estate held by a wife or widow for the remainder of her life.

473 *Norfolk*: traditionally a litigious county.

475 *Easter term*: one of the four terms of the law-courts.

she has no pleasure but in vexing others and is usually clothed and daggled like a bawd in disguise, pursued through alleys by sergeants. When she is in town she lodges in one of the Inns of Chancery, where she breeds her son and is herself his tutoress in law-French, and for her country abode, though she has no estate there, she chooses Norfolk. But bid her come in, with a pox to her. She is Olivia's kinswoman and may make me amends for her visit by some discourse of that dear woman.

Exit SAILOR.

Enter WIDOW BLACKACRE *with a mantle and a green bag and several papers in the other hand,* JERRY BLACKACRE, *her son, in a gown, laden with green bags, following her.*

WIDOW. I never had so much to do with a judge's door-keeper, as with yours, but –

MANLY. But the incomparable Olivia, how does she since I went?

WIDOW. Since you went, my suit –

MANLY. Olivia, I say, is she well?

WIDOW. My suit, if you had not returned –

MANLY. Damn your suit. How does your cousin Olivia?

WIDOW. My suit, I say, had been quite lost, but now –

MANLY. But now, where is Olivia? In town? For –

WIDOW. For tomorrow we are to have a hearing.

MANLY. Would you'd let me have a hearing today.

WIDOW. But why won't you hear me?

MANLY. I am no judge and you talk of nothing but suits. But, pray tell me, when did you see Olivia?

WIDOW. I am no visitor but a woman of business, or if I ever visit 'tis only the Chancery Lane ladies, ladies towards the law and not any of your lazy, good-for-

---

479 *daggled*: muddy, bespattered.

481 *Inns of Chancery*: residences for law students in which they learnt the rudiments of law before being admitted to the Inns of Court.

482 *law-French*: the corrupted Norman French used in English law.

487 s.d. *green bags*: carried by barristers for documents and papers.

504 *Chancery Lane*: the street runs close to the Inns of Court in Holborn.

nothing flirts, who cannot read law-French, though a gallant writ it. But, as I was telling you, my suit –

MANLY. Damn these impertinent, vexatious people of business, of all sexes. They are still troubling the world with the tedious recitals of their lawsuits, and one can no more stop their mouths than a wit's when he talks of himself, or an intelligencer's when he talks of other people.

WIDOW. And a pox of all vexatious, impertinent lovers. They are still perplexing the world with the tedious narrations of their love-suits and discourses of their mistresses. You are as troublesome to a poor widow of business as a young coxcombly rithming lover.

MANLY. And thou art as troublesome to me as a rook to a losing gamester or a young putter of cases to his mistress and sempstress, who has love in her head for another.

WIDOW. Nay, since you talk of putting of cases and will not hear me speak, hear our Jerry a little. Let him put our case to you, for the trial's tomorrow and, since you are my chief witness, I would have your memory refreshed and your judgement informed, that you may not give your evidence improperly. Speak out, child.

JERRY. Yes, forsooth. Hemh! Hemh! John-a-Stiles –

MANLY. You may talk, young lawyer, but I shall no more mind you than a hungry judge does a cause after the clock has struck one.

FREEMAN. Nay, you'll find him as peevish too.

WIDOW. No matter. Jerry, go on. Do you observe it then, sir, for I think I have seen you in a gown once. Lord, I could hear our Jerry put cases all day long! Mark him, sir.

JERRY. John-a-Stiles – no – There are first Fitz, Pere and Ayle – No, no, Ayle, Pere and Fitz. Ayle is seised

---

512 *intelligencer*: newsmonger.

518 *rithming*: rhyming.

530 *John-a-Stiles*: a fictitious name for one of the parties in a legal action.

540 *Fitz, Pere and Ayle*: son, father and grandfather (Fr. *fils, père* and *aieul*), law-French equivalents to John-a-Stiles.

in fee of Blackacre; John-a-Stiles disseises Ayle; Ayle makes claim and the disseisor dies; then the Ayle – no, the Fitz.

WIDOW. No, the Pere, sirrah.

JERRY. O, the Pere. Ay, the Pere, sir, and the Fitz – no, the Ayle; no, the Pere and the Fitz, sir, and –

MANLY. Damn Pere, Mere and Fitz, sir.

WIDOW. No, you are out, child. Hear me, captain, then. There are Ayle, Pere and Fitz; Ayle is seised in fee of Blackacre and, being so seised, John-a-Stiles disseises the Ayle; Ayle makes claim and the disseisor dies. And then the Pere re-enters, (*to* JERRY) the Pere sirrah, the Pere – And the Fitz enters upon the Pere, and the Ayle brings his writ of disseisin in the *post*, and the Pere brings his writ of disseisin in the *per* and –

MANLY. Can'st thou hear this stuff, Freeman? I could as soon suffer a whole noise of flatterers at a great man's levy in a morning but thou hast servile complacency enough to listen to a quibbling statesman in disgrace, nay, and be beforehand with him in laughing at his dull no-jest. But I – (*Offering to go out*)

WIDOW. Nay, sir, hold. Where's the subpoena, Jerry? I must serve you, sir. You are required by this to give your testimony –

MANLY. I'll be forsworn to be revenged on thee.

Exit MANLY, *throwing away the subpoena.*

WIDOW. Get you gone for a lawless companion. Come, Jerry. I had almost forgot we were to meet at the Master's at three. Let us mind our business still, child.

JERRY. Ay, forsooth, e'en so let's.

FREEMAN. Nay, madam, now I would beg you to hear me a little, a little of my business.

WIDOW. I have business of my own calls me away, sir.

---

541 *Blackacre*: not the widow's lands but a legal phrase for a fictitious parcel of land.

548–56 See Additional Note.

555 *per*: Pere Q1.

562 s.d. *Offering*: Attempting.

569 *Master's*: either one of the twelve Masters in Ordinary of the Court of Chancery, assistants to the Lord Chancellor, or a member of the governing body of one of the Inns of Court.

FREEMAN. My business would prove yours too, dear madam.

WIDOW. Yours would be some sweet business, I warrant. What, 'tis no Westminster Hall business? Would you have my advice?

FREEMAN. No, faith, 'tis a little Westminster Abbey business: I would have your consent.

WIDOW. O fie, fie, sir, to me such discourse before my dear minor there!

JERRY. Ay, ay, mother, he would be taking livery and seisin of your jointure by digging the turf, but I'll watch your waters, bully, ifac. Come away, mother.

Exit JERRY, *haling away his mother.*

Manet FREEMAN. *Enter to him* FIDELIA.

FIDELIA. Dear sir, you have pity. Beget but some in our captain for me.

FREEMAN. Where is he?

FIDELIA. Within, swearing as much as he did in the great storm and cursing you and sometimes sinks into calms and sighs and talks of his Olivia.

FREEMAN. He would never trust me to see her. Is she handsome?

FIDELIA. No, if you'll take my word, but I am not a proper judge.

FREEMAN. What is she?

FIDELIA. A gentlewoman, I suppose, but of as mean a fortune as beauty, but her relations would not suffer her to go with him to the Indies, and his aversion to this side of the world, together with the late opportunity of commanding the convoy, would not let him stay here longer, though to enjoy her.

FREEMAN. He loves her mightily then.

FIDELIA. Yes, so well that the remainder of his fortune (I hear about five or six thousand pounds) he has left

---

583–4 *livery and seisin*: livery of seisin, delivery of possession of freehold estates by the handing over of a symbolic piece of turf, strictly by the widow to Freeman, though that would ruin Jerry's double meaning.

585 *watch your waters*: keep an eye on, derived from checking urine for diagnosis and hence associated with the kind of digging Freeman has in mind.

585 *ifac*: in faith.

her in case he had died by the way or before she could prevail with her friends to follow him, which he expected she should do, and has left behind him his great bosom friend to be her convoy to him.

FREEMAN. What charms has she for him if she be not handsome?

FIDELIA. He fancies her, I suppose, the only woman of truth and sincerity in the world.

FREEMAN. No common beauty I confess.

FIDELIA. Or else sure he would not have trusted her with so great a share of his fortune in his absence; I suppose (since his late loss) all he has.

FREEMAN. Why, has he left it in her own custody?

FIDELIA. I am told so.

FREEMAN. Then he has showed love to her indeed in leaving her, like an old husband that dies as soon as he has made his wife a good jointure. But I'll go in to him and speak for you and know more from him of his Olivia. *Exit.*

Manet FIDELIA *sola.*

FIDELIA. His Olivia indeed, his happy Olivia,
Yet she was left behind, when I was with him;
But she was ne'er out of his mind or heart.
She has told him she loved him; I have showed it
And durst not tell him so till I had done,
Under this habit, such convincing acts
Of loving friendship for him that through it
He first might find out both my sex and love,
And, when I'd had him from his fair Olivia
And this bright world of artful beauties here,
Might then have hoped he would have looked on me
Amongst the sooty Indians; and I could,
To choose, there live his wife, where wives are forced
To live no longer when their husbands die,
Nay, what's yet worse, to share them whil'st they live
With many rival wives. But here he comes,
And I must yet keep out of his sight, not
To lose it forever. *Exit.*

Enter MANLY *and* FREEMAN.

FREEMAN. But, pray, what strange charms has she that could make you love?

MANLY. Strange charms indeed! She has beauty enough to call in question her wit or virtue, and her form would make a starved hermit a ravisher; yet her virtue and conduct would preserve her from the subtle lust of a pampered prelate. She is so perfect a beauty that art could not better it nor affectation deform it; yet all this is nothing. Her tongue, as well as face, ne'er knew artifice; nor ever did her words or looks contradict her heart. She is all truth and hates the lying, masking, daubing world as I do, for which I love her and for which I think she dislikes not me. For she has often shut out of her conversation for mine the gaudy, fluttering parrots of the town, apes and echoes of men only, and refused their commonplace pert chat, flattery and submissions, to be entertained with my sullen bluntness and honest love. And, last of all, swore to me, since her parents would not suffer her to go with me, she would stay behind for no other man but follow me without their leave, if not to be obtained. Which oath –

FREEMAN. Did you think she would keep?

MANLY. Yes, for she is not (I tell you) like other women but can keep her promise, though she has sworn to keep it. But that she might the better keep it I left her the value of five or six thousand pound, for women's wants are generally their most importunate solicitors to love or marriage.

FREEMAN. And money summons lovers more than beauty, and augments but their importunity and their number, so makes it the harder for a woman to deny 'em. For my part, I am for the French maxim; if you would have your female subjects loyal, keep 'em poor. But, in short, that your mistress may not marry, you have given her a portion.

MANLY. She had given me her heart first and I am satisfied with the security; I can never doubt her truth and constancy.

FREEMAN. It seems you do since you are fain to bribe it with money. But how come you to be so diffident of the man that says he loves you and not doubt the woman that says it?

MANLY. I should, I confess, doubt the love of any other woman but her, as I do the friendship of any other man but him I have trusted, but I have such proofs of their faith as cannot deceive me.

FREEMAN. Cannot!

MANLY. Not but I know that generally no man can be a great enemy but under the name of friend; and if you are a cuckold, it is your friend only that makes you so, for your enemy is not admitted to your house; if you are cheated in your fortune, 'tis your friend that does it, for your enemy is not made your trustee; if your honour or good name be injured, 'tis your friend that does it still, because your enemy is not believed against you. Therefore I rather choose to go where honest, downright barbarity is professed, where men devour one another like generous hungry lions and tigers, not like crocodiles, where they think the devil white, of our complexion, and I am already so far an Indian. But if your weak faith doubts this miracle of a woman, come along with me and believe and thou wilt find her so handsome that thou, who art so much my friend, wilt have a mind to lie with her and so will not fail to discover what her faith and thine is to me.
When we're in love, the great adversity,
Our friends and mistresses at once we try.

ACT II

SCENE I

Olivia's lodging.

Enter OLIVIA, ELIZA, LETTICE.

OLIVIA. Ah, cousin, what a world 'tis we live in! I am so weary of it.

ELIZA. Truly, cousin, I can find no fault with it but that we cannot always live in't, for I can never be weary of it.

OLIVIA. O hideous! You cannot be in earnest, sure, when you say you like the filthy world.

ELIZA. You cannot be in earnest, sure, when you say you dislike it.

OLIVIA. You are a very censorious creature, I find.

ELIZA. I must confess I think we women as often discover where we love by railing, as men when they lie by their swearing, and the world is but a constant keeping gallant, whom we fail not to quarrel with when anything crosses us, yet cannot part with't for our hearts.

LETTICE. A gallant indeed, madam, whom ladies first make jealous and then quarrel with it for being so, for if, by her indiscretion, a lady be talked of for a man, she cries presently, ''Tis a censorious world'; if by her vanity the intrigue be found out, ''Tis a prying, malicious world'; if by her over-fondness the gallant proves unconstant, ''Tis a false world'; and if by her niggardliness the chambermaid tells, ''Tis a perfidious world' – but that, I'm sure, your ladyship cannot say of the world yet, as bad as 'tis.

OLIVIA. But I may say, ''Tis a very impertinent world.' Hold your peace. And, cousin, if the world be a gallant, 'tis such an one as is my aversion. Pray name it no more.

ELIZA. But is it possible the world, which has such variety of charms for other women, can have none for you? Let's see – first, what d'ye think of dressing and fine clothes?

OLIVIA. Dressing! Fie, fie, 'tis my aversion. But come hither, you dowdy, methinks you might have opened this toure better. O hideous! I cannot suffer it! D'ye see how't sits?

ELIZA. Well enough, cousin, if dressing be your aversion.

OLIVIA. 'Tis so, and for variety of rich clothes, they are more my aversion.

LETTICE. Ay, 'tis because your ladyship wears 'em too long, for indeed a gown, like a gallant, grows one's aversion by having too much of it.

OLIVIA. Insatiable creature! I'll be sworn I have had this not above three days, cousin, and within this month have made some six more.

ELIZA. Then your aversion to 'em is not altogether so great.

OLIVIA. Alas! 'Tis for my woman only I wear 'em, cousin.

---

36 *dowdy*: plain creature.
37 *toure*: usually *taure*, a forehead fringe of curls.

LETTICE. If it be for me only, madam, pray do not wear 'em.

ELIZA. But what d'ye think of visits – balls –

OLIVIA. O, I detest 'em.

ELIZA. Of plays?

OLIVIA. I abominate 'em: filthy, obscene, hideous things!

ELIZA. What say you to masquerading in the winter and Hyde Park in the summer?

OLIVIA. Insipid pleasures I taste not.

ELIZA. Nay, if you are for more solid pleasure, what think you of a rich, young husband?

OLIVIA. O horrid! Marriage! What a pleasure you have found out! I nauseate it of all things.

LETTICE. But what does your ladyship think then of a liberal, handsome young lover?

OLIVIA. A handsome young fellow, you impudent! Be gone, out of my sight. Name a handsome young fellow to me! Foh, a hideous, handsome young fellow I abominate. (*Spits*)

ELIZA. Indeed! But let's see – will nothing please you? What d'ye think of the court?

OLIVIA. How? The court! The court, cousin! My aversion, my aversion, my aversion of all aversions.

ELIZA. How? The court! Where –

OLIVIA. Where sincerity is a quality as out of fashion and as unprosperous as bashfulness. I could not laugh at a quibble, though it were a fat privy councillor's, nor praise a lord's ill verses, though I were myself the subject, nor an old lady's young looks, though I were her woman, nor sit to a vain young simile-maker, though he flattered me. In short, I could not gloat upon a man when he comes into a room and laugh at him when he goes out; I cannot rail at the absent to flatter the standers-by; I –

ELIZA. Well, but railing now is so common that 'tis no more malice but the fashion, and the absent think they are no more the worse for being railed at than the present think they are the better for being flattered. And for the court –

---

60 *Hyde Park*: a fashionable place for promenading.
83–4 *gloat upon*: feast my eyes on, admire.

OLIVIA. Nay, do not defend the court, for you'll make me rail at it, like a trusting citizen's widow.

ELIZA. Or like a Holborn lady, who could not get into the last ball or was out of countenance in the drawing-room the last Sunday of her appearance there; for none rail at the court but those who cannot get into it or else who are ridiculous when they are there, and I shall suspect you were laughed at when you were last there or would be a Maid of Honour.

OLIVIA. I a Maid of Honour! To be a Maid of Honour were yet of all things my aversion.

ELIZA. In what sense am I to understand you? But in fine by the word aversion I'm sure you dissemble, for I never knew woman yet that used it who did not. Come, our tongues belie our hearts more than our pocket-glasses do our faces; but methinks we ought to leave off dissembling, since 'tis grown of no use to us, for all wise observers understand us nowadays as they do dreams, almanacs and Dutch gazettes, by the contrary. And a man no more believes a woman when she says she has an aversion for him than when she says she'll cry out.

OLIVIA. O filthy, hideous! Peace, cousin, or your discourse will be my aversion, and you may believe me.

ELIZA. Yes, for if anything be a woman's aversion 'tis plain-dealing from another woman and perhaps that's your quarrel to the world, for that will talk, as your woman says.

OLIVIA. Talk not of me sure, for what men do I converse with? What visits do I admit?

Enter BOY.

BOY. Here's the gentleman to wait upon you, madam.

OLIVIA. On me! You little, unthinking fop, d'ye know what you say?

BOY. Yes, madam, 'tis the gentleman that comes every day to you, who –

---

94 *Holborn lady*: a citizen's wife. Holborn leads towards the city.

95–6 *drawing-room*: at Whitehall.

110 *Dutch gazettes*: the enemy's newspapers, of course, appeared to be inaccurate.

OLIVIA. Hold your peace, you heedless little animal, and get you gone. This country boy, cousin, takes my dancing-master, tailor or the spruce milliner for visitors.

Exit BOY.

LETTICE. No, madam, 'tis Mr Novel, I'm sure, by his talking so loud. I know his voice too, madam.

OLIVIA. You know nothing, you buffle-headed, stupid creature you. You would make my cousin believe I receive visits. But if it be Mr – what did you call him?

LETTICE. Mr Novel, madam, he that –

OLIVIA. Hold your peace, I'll hear no more of him. But if it be your Mr – (I can't think of his name again) I suppose he has followed my cousin hither.

ELIZA. No, cousin, I will not rob you of the honour of the visit; 'tis to you, cousin, for I know him not.

OLIVIA. Nor did I ever hear of him before, upon my honour, cousin. Besides, han't I told you that visits and the business of visits, flattery and detraction, are my aversion? D'ye think then I would admit such a coxcomb as he is, who rather than not rail will rail at the dead whom none speak ill of, and rather than not flatter will flatter the poets of the age, whom none will flatter, who affects novelty as much as the fashion and is as fantastical as changeable and as well known as the fashion, who likes nothing but what is new, nay, would choose to have his friend or his title a new one. In fine, he is my aversion.

ELIZA. I find you do know him, cousin, at least have heard of him.

OLIVIA. Yes, now I remember, I have heard of him.

ELIZA. Well, but since he is such a coxcomb, for heaven's sake let him not come up. Tell him, Mrs Lettice, your lady is not within.

OLIVIA. No, Lettice, tell him my cousin is here and that he may come up, for, notwithstanding I detest the sight of him, you may like his conversation and, though I would use him scurvily, I will not be rude to you in my own lodging. Since he has followed you hither, let him come up, I say.

---

133 *buffle-headed*: blockheaded, simpleton.

ELIZA. Very fine! Pray let him go to the devil, I say, for me. I know him not nor desire it. Send him away, Mrs Lettice.

OLIVIA. Upon my word, she shan't. I must disobey your commands, to comply with your desires. Call him up, Lettice.

ELIZA. Nay, I'll swear she shall not stir on that errand. (*Holds* LETTICE)

OLIVIA. Well then, I'll call him myself for you, since you will have it so. (*Calls out at the door*) Mr Novel, sir, sir.

Enter NOVEL.

NOVEL. Madam, I beg your pardon; perhaps you were busy. I did not think you had company with you.

ELIZA. (*aside*) Yet he comes to me, cousin!

OLIVIA. – Chairs there.

They sit. [*Exit* LETTICE.]

NOVEL. Well, but, madam, d'ye know whence I come now?

OLIVIA. From some melancholy place I warrant, sir, since they have lost your good company.

ELIZA. So.

NOVEL. From a place where they have treated me, at dinner, with so much civility and kindness, a pox on 'em, that I could hardly get away to you, dear madam.

OLIVIA. You have a way with you so new and obliging, sir.

ELIZA. (*apart to* OLIVIA) You hate flattery, cousin!

NOVEL. Nay, faith, madam, d'ye think my way new? Then you are obliging, madam. I must confess I hate imitation, to do anything like other people; all that know me do me the honour to say I am an original, faith. But, as I was saying, madam, I have been treated today with all the ceremony and kindness imaginable at my Lady Autum's, but the nauseous old woman at the upper end of her table –

OLIVIA. Revives the old Grecian custom of serving in a death's head with their banquets.

199–200 Weales suggests that Olivia is misremembering Herodotus's comments on Egyptian feasts.

NOVEL. Hah, ha! Fine, just, i'faith, nay, and new. 'Tis like eating with the ghost in *The Libertine*; she would frighten a man from her dinner with her hollow invitations and spoil one's stomach –

OLIVIA. To meat or women. I detest her hollow cherry cheeks; she looks like an old coach new painted, affecting an unseemly smugness whilst she is ready to drop in pieces.

ELIZA. (*apart to* OLIVIA) You hate detraction I see, cousin!

NOVEL. But the silly old fury, whilst she affects to look like a woman of this age, talks –

OLIVIA. Like one of the last, and as passionately as an old courtier who has outlived his office.

NOVEL. Yes, madam, but pray let me give you her character. Then, she never counts her age by the years but –

OLIVIA. By the masques she has lived to see.

NOVEL. Nay then, madam, I see you think a little harmless railing too great a pleasure for any but yourself and therefore I've done.

OLIVIA. Nay, faith, you shall tell me who you had there at dinner.

NOVEL. If you would hear me, madam.

OLIVIA. Most patiently. Speak, sir.

NOVEL. Then, we had her daughter –

OLIVIA. Ay, her daughter, the very disgrace to good clothes, which she always wears but to heighten her deformity, not mend it, for she is still most splendidly, gallantly ugly and looks like an ill piece of daubing in a rich frame.

NOVEL. So! But have you done with her, madam? And can you spare her to me a little now?

OLIVIA. Ay, ay, sir.

NOVEL. Then, she is like –

OLIVIA. She is, you'd say, like a city bride, the greater fortune but not the greater beauty for her dress.

NOVEL. Well, yet have you done, madam? Then, she –

OLIVIA. Then she bestows as unfortunately on her face all the graces in fashion, as the languishing eye, the

---

202 *The Libertine*: Shadwell's play on the Don Juan theme (1675).

hanging or pouting lip; but as the fool is never more provoking than when he aims at wit, the ill-favoured of our sex are never more nauseous than when they would be beauties, adding to their natural deformity the artificial ugliness of affectation.

ELIZA. So, cousin, I find one may have a collection of all one's acquaintances' pictures as well at your house as at Mr Lely's. Only the difference is, there we find 'em much handsomer than they are and like; here, much uglier and like. And you are the first of the profession of picture-drawing I ever knew without flattery.

OLIVIA. I draw after the life, do nobody wrong, cousin.

ELIZA. No, you hate flattery and detraction!

OLIVIA. But, Mr Novel, who had you besides at dinner?

NOVEL. Nay, the devil take me if I tell you, unless you will allow me the privilege of railing in my turn; but, now I think on't, the women ought to be your province, as the men are mine. And you must know, we had him whom –

OLIVIA. Him whom –

NOVEL. What? Invading me already? And giving the character before you know the man?

ELIZA. No, that is not fair, though it be usual.

OLIVIA. I beg your pardon, Mr Novel. Pray, go on.

NOVEL. Then, I say, we had that familiar coxcomb, who is at home wheresoe'er he comes.

OLIVIA. Ay, that fool –

NOVEL. Nay then, madam, your servant. I'm gone. Taking a fool out of one's mouth is worse than taking the bread out of one's mouth.

OLIVIA. I've done. Your pardon, Mr Novel, pray proceed.

NOVEL. I say, the rogue, that he may be the only wit in the company, will let nobody else talk and –

OLIVIA. Ay, those fops who love to talk all themselves are of all things my aversion.

NOVEL. Then you'll let me speak, madam, sure. The rogue, I say, will force his jest upon you, and I hate a jest that's forced upon a man as much as a glass.

ELIZA. Why, I hope, sir, he does not expect a man of your temperance in jesting should do him reason?

---

281 *do him reason*: do him justice, keep up with his jesting.

NOVEL. What, interruption from this side too! I must then –

Offers to rise; OLIVIA *holds him.*

OLIVIA. No, sir – You must know, cousin, that fop he means, though he talks only to be commended, will not give you leave to do't.

NOVEL. But, madam –

OLIVIA. He a wit! Hang him, he's only an adopter of straggling jests and fatherless lampoons, by the credit of which he eats at good tables and so, like the barren beggar-woman, lives by borrowed children.

NOVEL. Madam –

OLIVIA. And never was author of anything but his news, but that is still all his own.

NOVEL. Madam, pray –

OLIVIA. An eternal babbler, and makes no more use of his ears than a man that sits at a play by his mistress or in fop-corner. He's, in fine, a base, detracting fellow, and is my aversion. But who else prithee, Mr Novel, was there with you? Nay, you shan't stir.

NOVEL. I beg your pardon, madam, I cannot stay in any place where I'm not allowed a little Christian liberty of railing.

OLIVIA. Nay, prithee, Mr Novel, stay, and, though you should rail at me, I would hear you with patience. Prithee, who else was there with you?

NOVEL. Your servant, madam.

OLIVIA. Nay, prithee tell us, Mr Novel, prithee do.

NOVEL. We had nobody else.

OLIVIA. Nay, faith I know you had. Come, my Lord Plausible was there too, who is, cousin, a –

ELIZA. You need not tell me what he is, cousin, for I know him to be a civil, good-natured, harmless gentleman, that speaks well of all the world and is always in good humour and –

OLIVIA. Hold, cousin, hold. I hate detraction, but I must tell you, cousin, his civility is cowardice, his good nature want of wit, and has neither courage or sense to rail. And for his being always in humour, 'tis because he is never dissatisfied with himself. In fine,

---

298 *fop-corner*: the part of the playhouse favoured by self-styled wits.

he is my aversion, and I never admit his visits beyond my hall.

NOVEL. No, he visit you! Damn him, cringing, grinning rogue. If I should see him coming up to you, I would make bold to kick him down again. Ha! –

Enter MY LORD PLAUSIBLE

My dear lord, your most humble servant. (*Rises and salutes* PLAUSIBLE *and kisses him*)

ELIZA. (*aside*) So! I find kissing and railing succeed each other with the angry men as well as with the angry women, and their quarrels are like love-quarrels, since absence is the only cause of them, for, as soon as the man appears again, they are over.

LORD PLAUSIBLE. Your most faithful, humble servant, generous Mr Novel, and, madam, I am your eternal slave and kiss your fair hands, which I had done sooner, according to your commands, but –

OLIVIA. No excuses, my lord.

ELIZA. (*apart*) What, you sent for him then, cousin?

NOVEL. (*aside*) Ha! Invited!

OLIVIA. I know you must divide yourself, for your good company is too general a good to be engrossed by any particular friend.

LORD PLAUSIBLE. O Lord, madam, my company! Your most obliged, faithful, humble servant, but I could have brought you good company indeed, for I parted at your door with two of the worthiest, bravest men –

OLIVIA. Who were they, my lord?

NOVEL. Who do you call the worthiest, bravest men, pray?

LORD PLAUSIBLE. O the wisest, bravest gentlemen! Men of such honour and virtue! Of such good qualities! Ah –

ELIZA. (*aside*) This is a coxcomb that speaks ill of all people a different way and libels everybody with dull praise and commonly in the wrong place, so makes his panegyrics abusive lampoons.

OLIVIA. But pray let me know who they were.

LORD PLAUSIBLE. Ah! Such patterns of heroic virtue! Such –

NOVEL. Well, but who the devil were they?

LORD PLAUSIBLE. The honour of our nation, the glory of our age. Ah! I could dwell a twelvemonth on their praise, which indeed I might spare by telling their names: Sir John Current and Sir Richard Court-Title.

NOVEL. Court-Title! Hah, ha.

OLIVIA. And Sir John Current! Why will you keep such a wretch company, my lord?

LORD PLAUSIBLE. Oh, madam, seriously you are a little too severe, for he is a man of unquestioned reputation in everything.

OLIVIA. Yes, because he endeavours only with the women to pass for a man of courage and with the bullies for a wit, with the wits for a man of business and with the men of business for a favourite at court and at court for good city security.

NOVEL. And for Sir Richard, he –

LORD PLAUSIBLE. He loves your choice, picked company, persons that –

OLIVIA. He loves a lord indeed, but –

NOVEL. Pray, dear madam, let me have but a bold stroke or two at his picture. He loves a lord, as you say, though –

OLIVIA. Though he borrowed his money and ne'er paid him again.

NOVEL. And would bespeak a place three days before at the back end of a lord's coach to Hyde Park.

LORD PLAUSIBLE. Nay, i'faith, i'faith, you are both too severe.

OLIVIA. Then, to show yet more his passion for quality, he makes love to that fulsome coach-load of honour, my Lady Goodly, for he is always at her lodging.

LORD PLAUSIBLE. Because it is the conventicle-gallant, the meetinghouse of all the fair ladies and glorious, superfine beauties of the town.

NOVEL. Very fine ladies! There's first –

OLIVIA. Her honour, as fat as an hostess.

LORD PLAUSIBLE. She is something plump indeed, a goodly, comely, graceful person.

---

393 *conventicle-gallant*: meeting-place *à la mode.*

NOVEL. Then there's my Lady Frances What-d'ye-call-'er? As ugly –

OLIVIA. As a citizen's lawfully begotten daughter.

LORD PLAUSIBLE. She has wit in abundance and the handsomest heel, elbow and tip of an ear you ever saw.

NOVEL. Heel and elbow! Hah, ha! And there's my Lady Betty you know –

OLIVIA. As sluttish and slatternly as an Irishwoman bred in France.

LORD PLAUSIBLE. Ah, all she has hangs with a loose air indeed and becoming negligence.

ELIZA. You see all faults with lover's eyes, I find, my lord.

LORD PLAUSIBLE. Ah, madam, your most obliged, faithful, humble servant to command! But you can say nothing sure against the superfine mistress –

OLIVIA. I know who you mean. She is as censorious and detracting a jade as a superannuated sinner.

LORD PLAUSIBLE. She has a smart way of raillery, 'tis confessed.

NOVEL. And then, for Mrs Grideline.

LORD PLAUSIBLE. She I'm sure is –

OLIVIA. One that never spoke ill of anybody, 'tis confessed, for she is as silent in conversation as a country lover and no better company than a clock or a weather-glass, for if she sounds 'tis but once an hour to put you in mind of the time of day or to tell you 'twill be cold or hot, rain or snow.

LORD PLAUSIBLE. Ah, poor creature! She's extremely good and modest.

NOVEL. And for Mrs Bridlechin, she's –

OLIVIA. As proud as a churchman's wife.

LORD PLAUSIBLE. She's a woman of great spirit and honour and will not make herself cheap, 'tis true.

NOVEL. Then Mrs Hoyden, that calls all people by their surnames and is –

OLIVIA. As familiar a duck –

NOVEL. As an actress in the tiring-room. There I was once beforehand with you, madam.

---

421 *Grideline*: *gris de lin*, flax-grey, pale purple.

LORD PLAUSIBLE. Mrs Hoyden! A poor, affable, good-natured soul! But the divine Mrs Trifle comes thither too; sure her beauty, virtue and conduct you can say nothing to.

OLIVIA. No!

NOVEL. No! – Pray let me speak, madam.

OLIVIA. First, can anyone be called beautiful that squints?

LORD PLAUSIBLE. Her eyes languish a little, I own.

NOVEL. Languish! Hah, ha.

OLIVIA. Languish! Then for her conduct she was seen at *The Country Wife* after the first day. There's for you, my lord.

LORD PLAUSIBLE. But, madam, she was not seen to use her fan all the play long, turn aside her head, or by a conscious blush discover more guilt than modesty.

OLIVIA. Very fine! Then you think a woman modest that sees the hideous *Country Wife* without blushing or publishing her detestation of it? D'ye hear him, cousin?

ELIZA. Yes, and am, I must confess, something of his opinion and think that as an over-conscious fool at a play, by endeavouring to show the author's want of wit, exposes his own to more censure, so may a lady call her modesty in question by publicly cavilling with the poets, for all those grimaces of honour and artificial modesty disparage a woman's real virtue as much as the use of white and red does the natural complexion, and you must use very, very little if you would have it thought your own.

OLIVIA. Then you would have a woman of honour with passive looks, ears and tongue undergo all the hideous obscenity she hears at nasty plays?

ELIZA. Truly, I think a woman betrays her want of modesty by showing it publicly in a playhouse as much as a man does his want of courage by a quarrel there, for the truly modest and stout say least and are least exceptious, especially in public.

---

443 *to*: too Q1.
451 *after the first day*: after the first performance, when she had no excuse for not knowing what kind of play it was.
477 *stout*: brave.

OLIVIA. O hideous! Cousin, this cannot be your opinion, but you are one of those who have the confidence to pardon the filthy play.

ELIZA. Why, what is there of ill in't, say you?

OLIVIA. O fie, fie, fie, would you put me to the blush anew? Call all the blood into my face again? But to satisfy you then, first, the clandestine obscenity in the very name of Horner.

ELIZA. Truly, 'tis so hidden I cannot find it out, I confess.

OLIVIA. O horrid! Does it not give you the rank conception or image of a goat, a town-bull or a satyr? Nay, what is yet a filthier image than all the rest, that of an eunuch?

ELIZA. What then? I can think of a goat, a bull or satyr without any hurt.

OLIVIA. Ay, but, cousin, one cannot stop there.

ELIZA. I can, cousin.

OLIVIA. O no, for when you have those filthy creatures in your head once, the next thing you think is what they do, as their defiling of honest men's beds and couches, rapes upon sleeping and waking country virgins under hedges and on haycocks. Nay, farther –

ELIZA. Nay, no farther, cousin. We have enough of your comment on the play, which will make me more ashamed than the play itself.

OLIVIA. O, believe me, 'tis a filthy play, and you may take my word for a filthy play as soon as another's, but the filthiest thing in that play, or any other play, is –

ELIZA. Pray keep it to yourself, if it be so.

OLIVIA. No, faith, you shall know it. I'm resolved to make you out of love with the play. I say, the lewdest, filthiest thing is his china; nay, I will never forgive the beastly author his china. He has quite taken away the reputation of poor china itself and sullied the most innocent and pretty furniture of a lady's chamber,

---

490 *town-bull*: a bull for the use of the town, hence a rake.
492 *an eunuch*: Horner's disguise in *The Country Wife*.
501 *haycocks*: conical haystacks.
512 *china*: see *The Country Wife*, Act IV Scene iii.

insomuch that I was fain to break all my defiled vessels. You see I have none left; nor you, I hope.

ELIZA. You'll pardon me, I cannot think the worse of my china for that of the playhouse.

OLIVIA. Why, you will not keep any now sure! 'Tis now as unfit an ornament for a lady's chamber as the pictures that come from Italy and other hot countries, as appears by their nudities, which I always cover or scratch out, wheresoe'er I find 'em. But china! Out upon't, filthy china, nasty, debauched china!

ELIZA. All this will not put me out of conceit with china nor the play, which is acted today or another of the same beastly author's, as you call him, which I'll go see.

OLIVIA. You will not, sure! Nay, you sha'not venture your reputation by going and mine by leaving me alone with two men here. Nay, you'll disoblige me for ever, if – (*Pulls her back*)

ELIZA. I stay! – your servant. *Exit* ELIZA.

OLIVIA. Well – but my lord, though you justify everybody, you cannot in earnest uphold so beastly a writer, whose ink is so smutty, as one may say.

LORD PLAUSIBLE. Faith, I dare swear the poor man did not think to disoblige the ladies by any amorous, soft, passionate, luscious saying in his play.

OLIVIA. Foy, my lord, but what think you, Mr Novel, of the play? Though I know you are a friend to all that are new.

NOVEL. Faith, madam, I must confess the new plays would not be the worse for my advice but I could never get the silly rogues, the poets, to mind what I say; but I'll tell you what counsel I gave the surly fool you speak of.

OLIVIA. What was't?

NOVEL. Faith, to put his play into rithme, for rithme, you know, often makes mystical nonsense pass with the critics for wit and a double-meaning saying with the ladies for soft, tender and moving passion. But, now I talk of passion, I saw your old lover this morning – Captain – (*Whispers*)

---

541 *Foy*: *ma foi*, faith.

Enter CAPTAIN MANLY, FREEMAN *and* FIDELIA *standing behind.*

OLIVIA. Whom? – Nay, you need not whisper.

MANLY. We are luckily got hither unobserved. – How! In a close conversation with these supple rascals, the outcasts of sempstresses' shops?

FREEMAN. Faith, pardon her, captain, that, since she could no longer be entertained with your manly bluntness and honest love, she takes up with the pert chat and commonplace flattery of these fluttering parrots of the town, apes and echoes of men only.

MANLY. Do not you, sir, play the echo too, mock me, dally with my own words and show yourself as impertinent as they are.

FREEMAN. Nay, captain –

FIDELIA. Nay, lieutenant, do not excuse her. Methinks she looks very kindly upon 'em both and seems to be pleased with what that fool there says to her.

MANLY. You lie, sir, and hold your peace that I may not be provoked to give you a worse reply.

OLIVIA. Manly returned, d'ye say! And is he safe?

NOVEL. My lord saw him too. (*Whispers to* PLAUSIBLE) Hark you, my lord.

MANLY. (*aside*) She yet seems concerned for my safety and perhaps they are admitted now here but for their news of me, for intelligence indeed is the common passport of nauseous fools when they go their round of good tables and houses.

OLIVIA. I heard of his fighting only, without particulars, and confess I always loved his brutal courage because it made me hope it might rid me of his more brutal love.

MANLY. (*apart*) What's that?

OLIVIA. But is he at last returned, d'ye say, unhurt?

NOVEL. Ay faith, without doing his business, for the rogue has been these two years pretending to a wooden leg, which he would take from fortune as kindly as the staff of a marshal of France and rather read his name in a gazette –

---

579 *intelligence*: news.
592 *gazette*: war report.

OLIVIA. Than in the entail of a good estate.

MANLY. (*aside*) So! –

NOVEL. I have an ambition, I must confess, of losing my heart before such a fair enemy as yourself, madam, but that silly rogues should be ambitious of losing their arms and –

OLIVIA. Looking like a pair of compasses.

NOVEL. But he has no use of his arms but to set them on kimbow, for he never pulls off his hat, at least not to me, I'm sure, for you must know, madam, he has a fanatical hatred to good company: he can't abide me.

LORD PLAUSIBLE. O, be not so severe to him as to say he hates good company, for I assure you he has a great respect, esteem and kindness for me.

MANLY. [*aside*] That kind, civil rogue has spoken yet ten thousand times worse of me than t'other.

OLIVIA. Well, if he be returned, Mr Novel, then shall I be pestered again with his boisterous sea love, have my alcove smell like a cabin, my chamber perfumed with his tarpaulin Brandenburgh, and hear vollies of brandy sighs, enough to make a fog in one's room. Foh! I hate a lover that smells like Thames Street!

MANLY. (*aside*) I can bear no longer and need hear no more. – But, since you have these two pulvillio boxes, these essence bottles, this pair of musk-cats here, I hope I may venture to come yet nearer you.

OLIVIA. Overheard us then?

NOVEL. (*aside*) I hope he heard me not.

LORD PLAUSIBLE. Most noble and heroic captain, your most obliged, faithful, humble servant.

NOVEL. Dear tar, thy humble servant.

MANLY. Away – madam. (*Thrusts* NOVEL *and* PLAUSIBLE *on each side*)

OLIVIA. Nay, I think I have fitted you for listening.

---

593 *entail*: the prescribed and often highly restrictive rules under which future ownership of an estate is determined.
601 *on kimbow*: akimbo.
612 *Brandenburgh*: morning gown.
614 *Thames Street*: a notoriously smelly street along the north bank of the river.
616 *pulvillio*: scented powder.
617 *essence*: perfume.
624 s.d. After line 625 in Q1.

MANLY. You have fitted me for believing you could not be fickle though you were young, could not dissemble love though 'twas your interest, nor be vain though you were handsome, nor break your promise though to a parting lover, nor abuse your best friend though you had wit. But I take not your contempt of me worse than your esteem or civility for these things here though you know 'em.

NOVEL. Things!

LORD PLAUSIBLE. Let the captain rally a little.

MANLY. Yes, things. Can'st thou be angry, thou thing? (*Coming up to* NOVEL)

NOVEL. No, since my lord says you speak in raillery, for, though your sea-raillery be something rough, yet I confess we use one another to as bad every day at Locket's and never quarrel for the matter.

LORD PLAUSIBLE. Nay, noble captain, be not angry with him. A word with you, I beseech you – (*Whispers to* MANLY)

OLIVIA. (*aside*) Well, we women, like the rest of the cheats of the world, when our cullies or creditors have found us out and will or can trust no longer, pay debts and satisfy obligations with a quarrel, the kindest present a man can make to his mistress when he can make no more presents, for oftentimes in love as at cards we are forced to play foul, only to give over the game, and use our lovers, like the cards, when we can get no more by 'em, throw 'em up in a pet upon the first dispute.

MANLY. My lord, all that you have made me know by your whispering, which I knew not before, is that you have a stinking breath: there's a secret for your secret.

LORD PLAUSIBLE. Pshaw! Pshaw!

MANLY. But, madam, tell me, pray, what was't about this spark could take you? Was it the merit of his fashionable impudence, the briskness of his noise, the wit of his laugh, his judgement or fancy in his garniture? Or was it a well-trimmed glove or the scent of it that charmed you?

---

628 *vain*: in vain Q1.

640 *Locket's*: famous restaurant in Charing Cross.

NOVEL. Very well, sir. Gad, these sea-captains make nothing of dressing. But let me tell you, sir, a man by his dress, as much as by anything, shows his wit and judgement, nay, and his courage too.

FREEMAN. How his courage, Mr Novel?

NOVEL. Why, for example, by red breeches, tucked-up hair or peruke, a greasy broad belt and nowadays a short sword.

MANLY. Thy courage will appear more by thy belt than thy sword, I dare swear. Then, madam, for this gentle piece of courtesy, this man of tame honour, what could you find in him? Was it his languishing affected tone? His mannerly look? His secondhand flattery, the refuse of the playhouse tiring-rooms? Or his slavish obsequiousness in watching at the door of your box at the playhouse for your hand to your chair? Or his janty way of playing with your fan? Or was it the gunpowder spot on his hand or the jewel in his ear that purchased your heart?

OLIVIA. Good jealous captain, no more of your –

LORD PLAUSIBLE. No, let him go on, madam, for perhaps he may make you laugh, and I would contribute to your pleasure any way.

MANLY. Gentle rogue!

OLIVIA. No, noble captain, you cannot sure think anything could take me more than that heroic title of yours, captain, for you know we women love honour inordinately.

NOVEL. Hah, ha, faith, she is with thee, bully, for thy raillery.

MANLY. (*aside to* NOVEL) Faith, so shall I be with you, no bully, for your grinning.

OLIVIA. Then, that noble lion-like mien of yours, that soldier-like, weather-beaten complexion and that manly rougliness of your voice, how can they otherwise than charm us women who hate effeminacy!

NOVEL. Hah, ha! Faith, I can't hold from laughing.

669–71 Novel describes military dress as usually worn, there being no prescribed uniform.

680 *janty*: genteel (Fr. *gentil*).

681 *gunpowder spot*: a beauty spot made by using gunpowder.

MANLY. (*aside to* NOVEL) Nor shall I from kicking anon.

OLIVIA. And then, that captain-like carelessness in your dress, but especially your scarf; 'twas just such another, only a little higher tied, made me in love with my tailor as he passed by my window the last training day, for we women adore a martial man, and you have nothing wanting to make you more one, or more agreeable, but a wooden leg.

LORD PLAUSIBLE. Nay, i'faith there your ladyship was a wag, and it was fine, just and well rallied.

NOVEL. Ay, ay, madam, with you ladies too, martial men must needs be very killing.

MANLY. Peace, you Bartholomew-Fair buffoons, and be not you vain that these laugh on your side, for they will laugh at their own dull jests. But no more of 'em, for I will only suffer now this lady to be witty and merry.

OLIVIA. You would not have your panegyric interrupted. I go on then to your humour. Is there anything more agreeable than the pretty sullenness of that? Than the greatness of your courage? – which most of all appears in your spirit of contradiction, for you dare give all mankind the lie and your opinion is your only mistress, for you renounce that too when it becomes another man's.

NOVEL. Hah, ha! I cannot hold. I must laugh at thee, tar, faith!

LORD PLAUSIBLE. And i'faith, dear captain, I beg your pardon and leave to laugh at you too, though I protest I mean you no hurt, but when a lady rallies, a stander-by must be complaisant and do her reason in laughing. Hah, ha.

MANLY. Why, you impudent, pitiful wretches, you presume sure upon your effeminacy to urge me, for you are in all things so like women that you may think it in me a kind of cowardice to beat you.

---

706 *tailor*: tailors were notoriously cowardly.

706–7 *training day*: for the train-bands, the citizen militia.

714 *Bartholomew-Fair*: the very popular fair held in Smithfield at the end of August, famous for its drolls, puppets and other such entertainments.

OLIVIA. No hectoring, good captain.

MANLY. Or perhaps you think this lady's presence secures you. But have a care, she has talked herself out of all the respect I had for her, and by using me ill before you has given me a privilege of using you so before her. But if you would preserve your respect to her and not be beaten before her, go, be gone immediately.

NOVEL. Be gone! What?

LORD PLAUSIBLE. Nay, worthy, noble, generous captain.

MANLY. Be gone, I say.

NOVEL. Be gone again! To us be gone!

MANLY. No chattering, baboons, instantly be gone. Or –

MANLY *puts 'em out of the room:* NOVEL *struts,* PLAUSIBLE *cringes.*

NOVEL. Well, madam, we'll go make the cards ready in your bedchamber. Sure you will not stay long with him.

Exeunt PLAUSIBLE, NOVEL.

OLIVIA. Turn hither your rage, good Captain Swaggerhuff, and be saucy with your mistress, like a true captain; but be civil to your rivals and betters and do not threaten anything but me here, no, not so much as my windows, nor do not think yourself in the lodgings of one of your suburb mistresses beyond the Tower.

MANLY. Do not give me cause to think so, for those less infamous women part with their lovers, just as you did from me, with unforced vows of constancy and floods of willing tears, but the same winds bear away their lovers and their vows; and for their grief, if the credulous, unexpected fools return, they find new comforters, fresh cullies, such as I found here. The mercenary love of those women too suffers shipwrack with their gallants' fortunes. Now you have heard chance has used me scurvily, therefore you do too. Well, persevere in your ingratitude, falsehood and disdain; have constancy in something and I promise you to be as just to your real scorn as I was to your feigned love and henceforward will despise, contemn, hate loathe and detest you, most faithfully.

Enter LETTICE.

OLIVIA. Get the ombre cards ready in the next room, Lettice, and –

Whispers to LETTICE [*who goes out*].

FREEMAN. Bravely resolved, captain.

FIDELIA. And you'll be sure to keep your word, I hope, sir.

MANLY. I hope so too.

FIDELIA. Do you but hope it, sir? If you are not as good as your word, 'twill be the first time you ever bragged, sure.

MANLY. She has restored my reason with my heart.

FREEMAN. But, now you talk of restoring, captain, there are other things which, next to one's heart, one would not part with: I mean your jewels and money, which it seems she has, sir.

MANLY. What's that to you, sir?

FREEMAN. Pardon me, whatsoever is yours, I have a share in't, I'm sure, which I will not lose for asking, though you may be too generous, or too angry now to do't yourself.

FIDELIA. Nay, then I'll make bold to make my claim too.

Both going towards OLIVIA.

MANLY. Hold, you impertinent, officious fops! (*Aside*) How have I been deceived!

FREEMAN. Madam, there are certain appurtenances to a lover's heart, called jewels, which always go along with it.

FIDELIA. And which, with lovers, have no value in themselves but from the heart they come with; our captain's, madam, it seems you scorn to keep and much more will those worthless things without it, I am confident.

OLIVIA. A gentleman so well made as you are may be confident – us easy women could not deny you anything you ask, if'twere for yourself; but, since 'tis for another, I beg your leave to give him my answer. (*Aside*) An agreeable young fellow this! – And would not be my aversion! (*Aside to* MANLY) Captain, your young friend here has a very persuading face, I con-

777 *ombre*: a card game.

fess; yet you might have asked me yourself for those trifles you left with me, which (hark you a little, for I dare trust you with the secret; you are a man of so much honour, I'm sure), I say then, not expecting your return, or hoping ever to see you again, I have delivered your jewels to –

MANLY. Whom?

OLIVIA. My husband.

MANLY. Your husband!

OLIVIA. Ay, my husband, for, since you could leave me, I am lately and privately married to one who is a man of so much honour and experience in the world that I dare not ask him for your jewels again to restore 'em to you, lest he should conclude you never would have parted with 'em to me, on any other score but the exchange of my honour, which rather than you'd let me lose, you'd lose, I'm sure, yourself those trifles of yours.

MANLY. Triumphant impudence! But married too!

OLIVIA. O, speak not so loud; my servants know it not. I am married; there's no resisting one's destiny, or love, you know.

MANLY. Why, did you love him too?

OLIVIA. Most passionately, nay, love him now, though I have married him, and he me; which mutual love, I hope, you are too good, too generous a man to disturb by any future claim or visits to me. 'Tis true he is now absent in the country but returns shortly. Therefore, I beg of you, for your own ease and quiet, and my honour, you will never see me more.

MANLY. I wish I never had seen you.

OLIVIA. But if you should ever have anything to say to me hereafter, let that young gentleman there be your messenger.

MANLY. You would be kinder to him; I find he should be welcome.

OLIVIA. Alas, his youth would keep my husband from suspicions and his visits from scandal, for we women may have pity for such as he but no love. And I already think you do not well to spirit him away to sea, and the sea is already but too rich with the spoils of the shore.

MANLY. (*aside*) True perfect woman! If I could say anything more injurious to her now, I would, for I could out-rail a bilked whore or a kicked coward, but, now I think on't, that were rather to discover my love than hatred, and I must not talk, for something I must do.

OLIVIA. (*aside*) I think I have given him enough of me now never to be troubled with him again.

Enter LETTICE.

Well, Lettice, are the cards and all ready within? I come then. Captain, I beg your pardon; you will not make one at ombre?

MANLY. No, madam, but I'll wish you a little good luck before you go.

OLIVIA. No, if you would have me thrive, curse me, for that you'll do heartily, I suppose.

MANLY. Then, if you will have it so, may all the curses light upon you women ought to fear and you deserve: first, may the curse of loving play attend your sordid covetousness and fortune cheat you by trusting to her as you have cheated me; the curse of pride or a good reputation fall on your lust; the curse of affectation on your beauty; the curse of your husband's company on your pleasures; and the curse of your gallant's disappointments in his absence; and the curse of scorn, jealousy or despair on your love – and then the curse of loving on.

OLIVIA. And, to requite all your curses, I will only return you your last. May the curse of loving me still fall upon your proud, hard heart that could be so cruel to me in these horrid curses, but heaven forgive you. *Exit* OLIVIA.

MANLY. Hell and the devil reward thee.

FREEMAN. Well, you see now mistresses, like friends, are lost by letting 'em handle your money, and most women are such kind of witches, who can have no power over a man unless you give 'em money; but when once they have got any from you, they never leave you, till they have all; therefore I never dare give a woman a farthing.

MANLY. Well, there is yet this comfort by losing one's money with one's mistress: a man is out of danger of

---

859 *bilked*: cheated out of payment.

getting another, of being made prize again by love, who, like a pirate, takes you by spreading false colours, but when once you have run your ship aground, the treacherous picaroon loofs, so by your ruin you save yourself from slavery at least.

Enter BOY.

BOY. Mrs Lettice, here's Madam Blackacre come to wait upon her honour.

[*Exeunt* BOY *and* LETTICE.]

MANLY. D'ye hear that? Let us be gone before she comes, for henceforward I'll avoid the whole damned sex forever and woman as a sinking ship.

Exeunt MANLY *and* FIDELIA.

FREEMAN. And I'll stay to revenge on her your quarrel to the sex, for out of love to her jointure and hatred to business I would marry her, to make an end of her thousand suits and my thousand engagements, to the comfort of two unfortunate sorts of people: my plaintiffs and her defendants, my creditors and her adversaries.

Enter WIDOW BLACKACRE *led in by* MAJOR OLDFOX, *and* JERRY BLACKACRE *following, laden with green bags.*

WIDOW. 'Tis an arrant sea-ruffian, but I am glad I met with him at last to serve him again, major, for the last service was not good in law. Boy, duck, Jerry, where is my paper of memorandums? Give me, child. So. Where is my cousin Olivia now, my kind relation?

FREEMAN. Here is one that would be your kind relation, madam.

WIDOW. What mean you, sir?

FREEMAN. Why, faith (to be short) to marry you, widow.

WIDOW. Is not this the wild, rude person we saw at Captain Manly's?

JERRY. Ay, forsooth, an't please.

899–900 *spreading false colours*: flying false flags.
901 *picaroon*: pirate.
901 *loofs*: luffs, changes course nearer the wind.
917 *service*: delivery of the subpoena.

WIDOW. What would you? What are you? Marry me!

FREEMAN. Ay, faith, for I am a younger brother and you are a widow.

WIDOW. You are an impertinent person, and go about your business.

FREEMAN. I have none but to marry thee, widow.

WIDOW. But I have other business, I'd have you to know.

FREEMAN. But you have no business anights, widow, and I'll make you pleasanter business than any you have; for anights, I assure you, I am a man of great business, for the business –

WIDOW. Go, I'm sure you're an idle fellow.

FREEMAN. Try me but, widow, and employ me as you find my abilities and industry.

OLDFOX. Pray be civil to the lady, Mr –. She's a person of quality, a person that is no person –

FREEMAN. Yes, but she's a person that is a widow. Be you mannerly to her because you are to pretend only to be her squire, to arm her to her lawyer's chambers; but I will be impudent and bawdy, for she must love and marry me.

WIDOW. Marry come up, you saucy familiar Jack! You think with us widows, 'tis no more than up and ride. Gad forgive me, nowadays every idle, young, hectoring, roaring companion with a pair of turned red breeches and a broad back thinks to carry away any widow of the best degree, but I'd have you to know, sir, all widows are not got, like places at court, by impudence and importunity only.

OLDFOX. No, no, soft, soft. You are a young man and not fit –

FREEMAN. For a widow? Yes, sure, old man, the fitter.

OLDFOX. Go to, go to, if others had not laid in their claims before you –

FREEMAN. Not you, I hope.

OLDFOX. Why not I, sir? Sure, I am a much more proportionable match for her than you, sir, I, who am an elder brother, of a comfortable fortune and of equal years with her.

---

952 *roaring*: roistering.

952–3 *turned red breeches*: unclear, either 'well-cut' or 'military trousers dyed' or 're-used'.

WIDOW. How's that? You unmannerly person, I'd have you to know, I was born but in *ann' undec' Caroli prim'*.

OLDFOX. Your pardon, lady, your pardon. Be not offended with your very servant. – But I say, sir, you are a beggarly younger brother, twenty years younger than her, without any land or stock but your great stock of impudence. Therefore what pretension can you have to her?

FREEMAN. You have made it for me; first, because I am a younger brother.

WIDOW. Why, is that a sufficient plea to a relict? How appears it, sir? By what foolish custom?

FREEMAN. By custom time out of mind only. Then, sir, because I have nothing to keep me after her death, I am the likelier to take care of her life. And, for my being twenty years younger than her and having a sufficient stock of impudence, I leave it to her whether they will be valid exceptions to me in her widow's law or equity.

OLDFOX. Well, she has been so long in Chancery that I'll stand to her equity and decree between us. Come, lady, pray snap up this young snap at first or we shall be troubled with him. Give him a city widow's answer (*aside to the* WIDOW) that is, with all the ill breeding imaginable. – Come, madam.

WIDOW. Well then, to make an end of this foolish wooing, for nothing interrupts business more. First, for you, major –

OLDFOX. You declare in my favour then?

FREEMAN. What, direct the court? (*To* JERRY) Come, young lawyer, thou shalt be a counsel for me.

JERRY. Gad, I shall betray your cause then as well as an older lawyer, never stir.

969–70 *ann' undec' Caroli prim'*: the eleventh year of Charles I's reign, 1636; the form of dating used in law.

978 *relict*: widow.

986 *equity*: the parallel system of law to common law and having authority over it to correct defects, based on general principles of law and justice; equity was administered by the Courts of Chancery in particular.

989 *snap up . . . snap*: shut up this young rogue.

WIDOW. First, I say, for you, major, my walking hospital of an ancient foundation, thou bag of mummy that wouldst fall asunder if 'twere not for thy cerecloths –

OLDFOX. How, lady?

FREEMAN. Hah, ha –

JERRY. Hey, brave mother! Use all suitors thus, for my sake.

WIDOW. Thou withered, hobbling, distorted cripple; nay, thou art a cripple all over. Wouldst thou make me the staff of thy age, the crutch of thy decrepitness? Me –

FREEMAN. Well said, widow! Faith, thou wouldst make a man love thee now without dissembling.

WIDOW. Thou senseless, impertinent, quibbling, drivelling, feeble, paralytic, impotent, fumbling, frigid nincompoop.

JERRY. Hey, brave mother for calling of names, ifac!

WIDOW. Wouldst thou make a caudlemaker, a nurse of me? Can't you be bedrid without a bedfellow? Won't your swanskins, furs, flannels and the scorched trencher keep you warm there? Would you have me your Scotch warming-pan, with a pox to you? Me! –

OLDFOX. O heavens!

FREEMAN. I told you I should be thought the fitter man, major.

JERRY. Ay, you old fobus, and you would have been my guardian, would you? To have taken care of my estate, that half of't should never come to me, by letting long leases at peppercorn rents.

WIDOW. If I would have married an old man, 'tis well known I might have married an earl, nay, what's more, a judge and been covered the winter nights with the lambskins which I prefer to the ermines of nobles. And dost thou think I would wrong my poor minor there for you?

1003 *cerecloths*: winding-sheets for a corpse.
1017 *caudlemaker*: maker of drinks for invalids.
1020 *trencher*: platter, here used to heat the bed.
1021 *Scotch warming-pan*: a woman to take to bed.
1025 *fobus*: fool, perhaps from 'to fob', to trick.
1028 *peppercorn rents*: nominal, token payments of rent.
1032 *lambskins*: used in judges' robes.

FREEMAN. Your minor is a chopping minor, God bless him. (*Strokes* JERRY *on the head*)

OLDFOX. Your minor may be a major of horse or foot for his bigness, and it seems you will have the cheating of your minor to yourself.

WIDOW. Pray, sir, bear witness. Cheat my minor! I'll bring my action of the case for the slander.

FREEMAN. Nay, I would bear false witness for thee now, widow, since you have done me justice and have thought me the fitter man for you.

WIDOW. Fair and softly, sir. 'Tis my minor's case more than my own, and I must do him justice now on you.

FREEMAN. How?

OLDFOX. So then.

WIDOW. You are first, I warrant, some renegado from the Inns of Court and the law, and thou'lt come to suffer for't by the law, that is, be hanged.

JERRY. Not about your neck, forsooth, I hope.

FREEMAN. But, madam –

OLDFOX. Hear the court.

WIDOW. Thou art some debauched, drunken, lewd, hectoring, gaming companion and want'st some widow's old gold to nick upon; but, I thank you sir, that's for my lawyers.

FREEMAN. Faith, we should ne'er quarrel about that, for guineas would serve my turn. But, widow –

WIDOW. Thou art a foul-mouthed boaster of thy lust, a mere braggadocio of thy strength for wine and women and wilt belie thyself more than thou dost women and art every way a base deceiver of women; and would deceive me too, would you?

FREEMAN. Nay, faith, widow, this is judging without seeing the evidence.

WIDOW. I say, you are a worn-out whoremaster at five

1035 *chopping*: strapping.

1041 *action of the case*: usually 'action on the case', a common-law claim for damages for loss or injury resulting only indirectly from the act complained of.

1057 *nick upon*: gamble with.

1060 *guineas*: first minted in 1663 and therefore newer than the 'old gold' of line 1057.

1062 *braggadocio*: braggart.

1068 *whoremaster*: one experienced in whoring.

and twenty both in body and fortune, and cannot be trusted by the common wenches of the town, lest you should not pay 'em, nor by the wives of the town, lest you should pay 'em; so you want women and would have me your bawd, to procure 'em for you.

FREEMAN. Faith, if you had any good acquaintance, widow, 'twould be civilly done of thee, for I am just come from sea.

WIDOW. I mean, you would have me keep you that you might turn keeper, for poor widows are only used like bawds by you; you go to church with us but to get other women to lie with. In fine, you are a cheating, chousing spendthrift and, having sold your own annuity, would waste my jointure.

JERRY. And make havoc of our estate personal and all our old gilt plate. I should soon be picking up all our mortgaged apostle-spoons, bowls and beakers out of most of the alehouses betwixt Hercules' Pillars and the Boatswain in Wapping; nay, and you'd be scouring amongst my trees and make 'em knock down one another, like routed, reeling watchmen at midnight. Would you so, bully?

FREEMAN. Nay, prithee, widow, hear me.

WIDOW. No, sir. I'd have you to know, thou pitiful, paltry, lath-backed fellow, if I would have married a young man, 'tis well known I could have had any young heir in Norfolk, nay, the hopefullest young man this day at the King's Bench Bar, I that am a relict and executrix of known plentiful assets and

---

1071–2 *lest you should pay 'em*: presumably by passing on venereal disease.

1081 *chousing*: cheating.

1085 *apostle-spoons*: silver spoons with figures of the apostles on the handles.

1086–7 *Hercules' Pillars . . . Wapping*: Hercules' Pillars was an inn in Fleet Street, close to the Inns of Court; the Boatswain is not known but Wapping was at the opposite end of the city.

1096 *King's Bench Bar*: the highest of the three common-law courts at Westminster Hall, originally dealing with cases involving the Crown. The other two were Common Pleas (for cases of subject against subject) and Exchequer (for revenue cases). In practice, the jurisdiction of each court was not clearly defined.

parts, who understand myself and the law. And would you have me under covert baron again? No, sir, no covert baron for me.

FREEMAN. But, dear widow, hear me. I value you only, not your jointure.

WIDOW. Nay, sir, hold there. I know your love to a widow is covetousness of her jointure. And a widow a little stricken in years with a good jointure is like an old mansion house in a good purchase, never valued, but take one, take t'other. And perhaps when you are in possession you'd neglect it, let it drop to the ground for want of necessary repairs or expenses upon't.

FREEMAN. No, widow, one would be sure to keep all tight when one is to forfeit one's lease by dilapidation.

WIDOW. Fie, fie, I neglect my business with this foolish discourse of love. Jerry, child, let me see the list of the jury; I'm sure my cousin Olivia has some relations amongst 'em. But where is she?

FREEMAN. Nay, widow, but hear me one word only.

WIDOW. Nay, sir, no more, pray. I will no more hearken again to your foolish love motions than to offers of arbitration.

Exeunt WIDOW *and* JERRY.

FREEMAN. Well, I'll follow thee yet, for he that has a pretension at court or to a widow must never give over for a little ill usage.

OLDFOX. Therefore I'll get her by assiduity, patience and long-sufferings, which you will not undergo, for you idle young fellows leave off love when it comes to be business, and industry gets more women, than love.

FREEMAN. Ay, industry, the fool's and old man's merit; but I'll be industrious too and make a business on't and get her by law, wrangling and contests and not by sufferings. And, because you are no dangerous rival, I'll give thee counsel, major:
If you litigious widow e'er would gain,
Sigh not to her but by the law complain;
To her, as to a bawd, defendant sue
With statutes and make justice pimp for you.

Exeunt.

1099 *covert baron*: under a husband's protection.

ACT III

SCENE I

Westminster Hall.

Enter MANLY *and* FREEMAN, *two* SAILORS *behind.*

MANLY. I hate this place, worse than a man that has inherited a chancery suit. I wish I were well out on't again.

FREEMAN. Why, you need not be afraid of this place, for a man without money needs no more fear a crowd of lawyers than a crowd of pickpockets.

MANLY. This, the reverend of the law would have thought the palace or residence of justice; but, if it be, she lives here with the state of a Turkish Emperor, rarely seen, and beseiged, rather than defended, by her numerous black guard here.

FREEMAN. Methinks 'tis like one of their own halls in Christmas time, whither from all parts fools bring their money to try by the dice – not the worst judges – whether it shall be their own or no. But after a tedious fretting and wrangling they drop away all their money on both sides and, finding neither the better, at last go emptily and lovingly away together to the tavern, joining their curses against the young lawyers' box, that sweeps all like the old ones.

MANLY. Spoken like a revelling Christmas lawyer.

FREEMAN. Yes, I was one, I confess, but was fain to leave the law out of conscience and fall to making

1–2 the delays in Chancery were notorious even then.
7 *the reverend*: (= *reverent*) those who revere.
11 *black*: the colour of lawyers' gowns.
12–15 gambling was permitted in the Inns of Court at Christmas.
19–20 *the young lawyers' . . . the old ones*: the box which takes the house's cut during the gambling takes all the money, just as the old lawyers' cash-box does in litigation.

false musters, rather chose to cheat the king than his subjects, plunder rather than take fees.

MANLY. Well, a plague and a purse famine light on the law, and that female limb of it who dragged me hither today. But prithee go see if in that crowd of daggled gowns there thou canst find her. (*Pointing to a crowd of lawyers at the end of the stage*)

Exit FREEMAN.
Manet MANLY.

How hard it is to be an hypocrite!
At least to me, who am but newly so.
I thought it once a kind of knavery,
Nay, cowardice, to hide one's faults; but now
The common frailty, love, becomes my shame.
He must not know I love th'ungrateful still,
Lest he contemn me more than she, for I,
It seems, can undergo a woman's scorn
But not a man's –

Enter to him FIDELIA.

FIDELIA. Sir, good sir, generous captain.

MANLY. Prithee, kind impertinence, leave me. Why shouldst thou follow me, flatter my generosity now, since thou know'st I have no money left? If I had it, I'd give it thee, to buy my quiet.

FIDELIA. I never followed yet, sir, reward or fame but you alone, nor do I now beg anything but leave to share your miseries. You should not be a niggard of 'em, since methinks you have enough to spare. Let me follow you now because you hate me, as you have often said.

MANLY. I ever hated a coward's company, I must confess.

FIDELIA. Let me follow you till I am none then, for you, I'm sure, will through such worlds of dangers that I shall be inured to 'em; nay, I shall be afraid of your anger more than danger and so turn valiant out of fear. Dear captain, do not cast me off till you have

---

24 *false musters*: by claiming to have more soldiers than they had, officers could claim subsistence money for the non-existent troops.

tried me once more. Do not, do not go to sea again without me.

MANLY. Thou to sea! To court, thou fool. Remember the advice I gave thee: thou art a handsome spaniel and canst fawn naturally. Go, busk about and run thyself into the next great man's lobby; first fawn upon the slaves without and then run into the lady's bedchamber; thou may'st be admitted at last to tumble her bed. Go seek, I say, and lose me, for I am not able to keep thee; I have not bread for myself.

FIDELIA. Therefore I will not go, because then I may help and serve you.

MANLY. Thou!

FIDELIA. I warrant you, sir, for at worst I could beg or steal for you.

MANLY. Nay, more bragging! Dost thou not know there's venturing your life in stealing? Go, prithee, away. Thou art as hard to shake off as that flattering effeminating mischief, love.

FIDELIA. Love, did you name? Why, you are not so miserable as to be yet in love, sure!

MANLY. No, no, prithee away, be gone, on – (*Aside*) I had almost discovered my love and shame. Well, if I had? That thing could not think the worse of me – or if he did? – No – yes, he shall know it – he shall – but then I must never leave him, for they are such secrets that make parasites and pimps lords of their masters, for any slavery or tyranny is easier than love's. – Come hither. Since thou art so forward to serve me, hast thou but resolution enough to endure the torture of a secret? For such to some is insupportable.

FIDELIA. I would keep it as safe as if your dear precious life depended on't.

MANLY. Damn your dearness. It concerns more than my life, my honour.

FIDELIA. Doubt it not, sir.

MANLY. And do not discover it by too much fear of discovering it, but have a great care you let not Freeman find it out.

---

61 *busk about*: change course.

FIDELIA. I warrant you, sir. I am already all joy with the hopes of your commands and shall be all wings in the execution of 'em. Speak quickly, sir.

MANLY. You said you would beg for me.

FIDELIA. I did, sir.

MANLY. Then you shall beg for me.

FIDELIA. With all my heart, sir.

MANLY. That is, pimp for me.

FIDELIA. How, sir?

MANLY. D'ye start! Thinkst thou thou couldst do me any other service? Come, no dissembling honour. I know you can do it handsomely; thou wert made for't. You have lost your time with me at sea; you must recover it.

FIDELIA. Do not, sir, beget yourself more reasons for your aversion to me and make my obedience to you a fault. I am the unfittest in the world to do you such a service.

MANLY. Your cunning arguing against it shows but how fit you are for it. No more dissembling. Here, I say, you must go use it for me to Olivia.

FIDELIA. To her, sir?

MANLY. Go flatter, lie, kneel, promise, anything to get her for me. I cannot live unless I have her. Didst thou not say thou wouldst do anything to save my life? And she said you had a persuading face.

FIDELIA. But did not you say, sir, your honour was dearer to you than your life? And would you have me contribute to the loss of that and carry love from you to the most infamous, most false and –

MANLY. And most beautiful! (*Sighs aside*)

FIDELIA. Most ungrateful woman that ever lived, for sure she must be so that could desert you so soon, use you so basely, and so lately too. Do not, do not forget it, sir, and think –

MANLY. No, I will not forget it but think of revenge. I will lie with her, out of revenge. Go, be gone, and prevail for me or never see me more.

FIDELIA. You scorned her last night.

MANLY. I know not what I did last night. I dissembled last night.

FIDELIA. Heavens!

MANLY. Be gone, I say, and bring me love or compliance

back, or hopes at least, or I'll never see thy face again. By –

FIDELIA. O do not swear, sir. First hear me.

MANLY. I am impatient. Away. You'll find me here till twelve. (*Turns away*)

FIDELIA. Sir –

MANLY. Not one word, no insinuating argument more or soothing persuasion; you'll have need of all your rhetoric with her. Go, strive to alter her, not me. Be gone. *Exit* MANLY *at the end of the stage.*

Manet FIDELIA.

FIDELIA. Should I discover to him now my sex
And lay before him his strange cruelty,
'Twould but incense it more. – No, 'tis not time.
For his love, must I then betray my own?
Were ever love or chance, till now, severe?
Or shifting woman posed with such a task?
Forced to beg that which kills her if obtained
And give away her lover not to lose him.

Exit FIDELIA.

Enter WIDOW BLACKACRE *in the middle of half a dozen lawyers, whispered to by a fellow in black,* JERRY BLACKACRE *following the crowd.*

WIDOW. Offer me a reference, you saucy companion you! D'ye know who you speak to? Art thou a solicitor in Chancery and offer a reference? A pretty fellow! Mr Serjeant Ploddon, here's a fellow has the impudence to offer me a reference.

SERJEANT PLODDON. Who's that has the impudence to offer a reference within these walls?

WIDOW. Nay, for a splitter of causes to do't!

SERJEANT PLODDON. No, madam, to a lady learned in the law as you are the offer of a reference were to impose upon you.

---

158 *reference*: submitting a matter to be decided by the Masters in Ordinary of the Court of Chancery, a kind of arbitration to speed up litigation and hence unacceptable to Widow Blackacre.

161 *Serjeant*: officer of the court.

165 *splitter of causes*: lawyer.

WIDOW. No, no, never fear me for a reference, Mr Serjeant. But, come, have you not forgot your brief? Are you sure you shan't make the mistake of – hark you – (*Whispers*) Go then, go to your Court of Common Pleas and say one thing over and over again. You do it so naturally, you'll never be suspected for protracting time.

SERJEANT PLODDON. Come, I know the course of the court, and your business.

Exit SERJEANT PLODDON.

WIDOW. Let's see, Jerry, where are my minutes? Come, Mr Quaint, pray, go talk a great deal for me in Chancery. Let your words be easy and your sense hard; my cause requires it. Branch it bravely and deck my cause with flowers that the snake may lie hidden. Go, go, and be sure you remember the decree of my Lord Chancellor *tricesimo quart'* of the Queen.

QUAINT. I will, as I see cause, extenuate or examplify matter of fact, baffle truth with impudence, answer exceptions with questions, though never so impertinent, for reasons give 'em words, for law and equity, tropes and figures; and so relax and enervate the sinews of their argument with the oil of my eloquence. But when my lungs can reason no longer, and not being able to say anything more for our cause, say everything of our adversary, whose reputation, though never so clear and evident in the eye of the world, yet with sharp invectives –

WIDOW. (Alias Billingsgate.)

QUAINT. With poignant and sour invectives, I say, I will deface, wipe out and obliterate his fair reputation, even as a record with the juice of lemons, and tell such a story – for the truth on't is, all that we can do for our client in Chancery is telling a story – a fine story, a long story, such a story –

WIDOW. Go, save thy breath for the cause; talk at the bar, Mr Quaint. You are so copiously fluent you can weary anyone's ears sooner than your own tongue.

---

181 *branch*: embroider.

184 *tricesimo quart' of the Queen*: the thirty-fourth year of Elizabeth's reign, 1592.

196 *Billingsgate*: the London fish market's famous style of abuse.

Go, weary our adversary's counsel and the court. Go, thou art a fine-spoken person. Adad, I shall make thy wife jealous of me if you can but court the court into a decree for us. Go, get you gone, and remember – (*Whispers*)

Exit QUAINT.

Come, Mr Blunder, pray bawl soundly for me at the King's Bench, bluster, sputter, question, cavil, but be sure your argument be intricate enough to confound the court, and then you do my business. Talk what you will but be sure your tongue never stand still, for your own noise will secure your sense from censure – 'tis like coughing or hemming when one has got the bellyache, which stifles the unmannerly noise. Go, dear rogue, and succeed and I'll invite thee, ere it be long, to more soused venison.

BLUNDER. I'll warrant you, after your verdict your judgement shall not be arrested upon ifs and ands.

[*Exit* BLUNDER.]

WIDOW. Come, Mr Petulant, let me give you some new instructions for our cause in the Exchequer. Are the barons sat?

PETULANT. Yes, no. May be they are, may be they are not. What know I? What care I?

WIDOW. Hey-day! I wish you would but snap up the counsel on t'other side anon, at the bar, as much and have a little more patience with me that I might instruct you a little better.

PETULANT. You instruct me! What is my brief for, mistress?

WIDOW. Ay, but you seldom read your brief but at the bar, if you do it then.

PETULANT. Perhaps I do, perhaps I don't, and perhaps 'tis time enough. Pray hold yourself contented, mistress.

WIDOW. Nay, if you go there too, I will not be contented, sir. Though you, I see, will lose my cause for want of speaking, I won't. You shall hear me and shall be instructed. Let's see your brief.

---

219 *soused*: pickled.
224 *barons*: the judges in the Court of Exchequer.

PETULANT. Send your solicitor to me. Instructed by a woman! I'd have you to know, I do not wear a bar-gown –

WIDOW. By a woman! And I'd have you to know, I am no common woman but a woman conversant in the laws of the land, as well as yourself, though I have no bar-gown.

PETULANT. Go to, go to, mistress. You are impertinent, and there's your brief for you. Instruct me! (*Flings her breviate at her*)

WIDOW. Impertinent to me, you saucy Jack you! You return my breviate but where's my fee? You'll be sure to keep that and scan that so well that if there chance to be but a brass halfcrown in't, one's sure to hear on't again. Would you would but look on your breviate half so narrowly. But pray give me my fee too as well as my brief.

PETULANT. Mistress, that's without precedent. When did a counsel ever return his fee, pray? And you are impertinent, and ignorant, to demand it.

WIDOW. Impertinent again and ignorant to me! Gadsbodikins, you puny upstart in the law, to use me so, you green bag carrier, you murderer of unfortunate causes. The clerk's ink is scarce off of your fingers, you that newly come from lamp-blacking the judge's shoes and are not fit to wipe mine. You call me impertinent and ignorant! I would give thee a cuff on the ear, sitting the courts, if I were ignorant. Marry gep, if it had not been for me, thou hadst been yet but a hearing counsel at the bar.

Exit PETULANT.

Enter MR BUTTONGOWN *crossing the stage in haste.*

Mr Buttongown, Mr Buttongown, whither so fast? What, won't you stay till we are heard?

---

265 *lamp-blacking*: smearing with lamp-soot, polishing.

268 *sitting the courts*: the penalty for assault in Westminster Hall while the courts were in session was life imprisonment and confiscation of one's goods.

268–9 *Marry gep*: a corruption of 'By Mary Gipsey', i.e. 'By St Mary of Egypt'.

270 *hearing counsel*: a barrister without a case.

BUTTONGOWN. I cannot, Mrs Blackacre, I must be at the Council; my lord's cause stays there for me.

WIDOW. And mine suffers here.

BUTTONGOWN. I cannot help it.

WIDOW. I'm undone.

BUTTONGOWN. What's that to me?

WIDOW. Consider the five pound fee if not my cause – that was something to you.

BUTTONGOWN. Away, away, pray be not so troublesome, mistress. I must be gone.

WIDOW. Nay, but consider a little. I am your old client, my lord but a new one; or, let him be what he will, he will hardly be a better client to you than myself. I hope you believe I shall be in law as long as I live, therefore am no despicable client. Well, but go to your lord. I know you expect he should make you a judge one day; but I hope his promise to you will prove a true lord's promise. But that he might be sure to fail you I wish you had his bond for't.

BUTTONGOWN. But, what, will you yet be thus impertinent, mistress?

WIDOW. Nay, I beseech you, sir, stay, if it be but to tell me my lord's case. Come, in short.

BUTTONGOWN. Nay then – *Exit* BUTTONGOWN.

WIDOW. Well, Jerry, observe, child, and lay it up for hereafter: these are those lawyers who by being in all causes are in none; therefore if you would have 'em for you, let your adversary fee 'em, for he may chance to depend upon 'em, and so in being against thee they'll be for thee.

JERRY. Ay, mother, they put me in mind of the unconscionable wooers of widows, who undertake briskly their matrimonial business for their money, but when they have got it once, let who's will drudge for them; therefore have a care of 'em, forsooth. There's advice for your advice.

WIDOW. Well said, boy. Come, Mr Splitcause, pray go see when my cause in Chancery comes on; and go speak with Mr Quillet in the King's Bench and Mr Quirk in the Common Pleas and see how our matters go there.

Enter MAJOR OLDFOX.

OLDFOX. Lady, a good and propitious morning to you, and may all your causes go as well as if I myself were judge of 'em.

WIDOW. Sir, excuse me, I am busy and cannot answer compliments in Westminster Hall. Go, Mr Splitcause, and come to me again to that bookseller's – there I'll stay for you that you may be sure to find me.

OLDFOX. No, sir, come to the other bookseller's, I'll attend your ladyship thither.

Exit SPLITCAUSE.

WIDOW. Why to the other?

OLDFOX. Because he is my bookseller, lady.

WIDOW. What, to sell you lozenges for your catarrh? Or medicines for your corns? What else can a major deal with a bookseller for?

OLDFOX. Lady, he prints for me.

WIDOW. Why, are you an author?

OLDFOX. Of some few essays. Deign you, lady, to peruse 'em. (*Aside*) She is a woman of parts and I must win her by showing mine.

BOOKSELLER'S BOY. Will you see Culpepper, mistress? Aristotle's *Problems*? *The Compleat Midwife*?

WIDOW. No, let's see Dalton, Hughes, Shepherd, Wingate.

BOY. We have no lawbooks.

WIDOW. No? You are a pretty bookseller then.

OLDFOX. Come, have you e'er a one of my essays left?

BOY. Yes, sir, we have enough, and shall always have 'em.

OLDFOX. How so?

333–4 *Culpepper . . . Midwife*: Nicholas Culpepper was a medical writer, best known for *The English Physician* (1652 and many later editions); *The Problems of Aristotle* (1595, editions in 1666 and 1670), 'wherein are contained divers questions, with their answers, touching the estate of man's body', not by Aristotle at all; *The Compleat Midwifes Practice* (1656) probably by Thomas Chamberlayne.

335 *Dalton . . . Wingate*: all lawbooks: Michael Dalton, *The Country Justice* (1618, editions in 1661, 1666); William Hughes wrote many lawbooks, e.g. *The Parson's Law* (1641, third edition 1673); William Sheppard was highly prolific – the most frequently reprinted of his works was *The Court-Keeper's Guide* (1649, sixth edition 1676); Edmund Wingate, *The Body of the Common Law* (1655, third edition 1670). Both Hughes and Sheppard had published new works in 1675.

BOY. Why, they are good, steady, lasting ware.

OLDFOX. Nay, I hope they will live. Let's see. Be pleased, madam, to peruse the poor endeavours of my pen, for I have a pen, though I say it, that – (*Gives her a book*)

JERRY. Pray let me see *St George for Christendom* or *The Seven Champions of England.*

WIDOW. No, no, give him *The Young Clerk's Guide.* What, we shall have you read yourself into a humour of rambling and fighting and studying military discipline and wearing red breeches!

OLDFOX. Nay, if you talk of military discipline, show him my treatise of *The Art Military.*

WIDOW. Hold, I would as willingly he should read a play.

JERRY. O pray, forsooth, mother, let me have a play.

WIDOW. No, sirrah, there are young students of the law enough spoiled already by plays; they would make you in love with your laundress or, what's worse, some queen of the stage that was a laundress, and so turn keeper before you are of age.

Several crossing the stage.

But stay, Jerry, is not that Mr What-d'y'call-him that goes there, he that offered to sell me a suit in Chancery for five hundred pound, for a hundred down and only paying the clerks' fees?

JERRY. Ay, forsooth, 'tis he.

WIDOW. Then stay here and have a care of the bags whilst I follow him. Have a care of the bags, I say.

JERRY. And do you have a care, forsooth, of the statute against champerty, I say.

Exit WIDOW.

Enter FREEMAN *to them.*

345–6 *St George . . . England*: probably Richard Johnson's extraordinarily popular *The Most Famous History of the Seven Champions of Christendom* (1596, editions in 1660, 1670 and 1675).

347 *The Young Clerk's Guide*: by Sir Richard Hutton (1649, fourteenth edition 1673).

368 *champerty*: an illegal agreement for someone not involved in a case to receive part of the lands or money in dispute in exchange for payment of the costs.

FREEMAN. (*aside*) So, there's a limb of my widow which was wont to be inseparable from her. She can't be far. – How now, my pretty son-in-law that shall be, where's my widow?

JERRY. My mother, but not your widow, will be forthcoming presently.

FREEMAN. Your servant, major. What, are you buying furniture for a little sleeping closet which you miscall a study? For you do only by your books as by your wenches, bind 'em up neatly and make 'em fine, for other people to use 'em; and your bookseller is properly your upholster, for he furnishes your room rather than your head.

OLDFOX. Well, well, good sea-lieutenant, study you your compass – that's more than your head can deal with. (*Aside*) I will go find out the widow to keep her out of his sight, or he'll board her whilst I am treating a peace. *Exit* OLDFOX.

Manent FREEMAN, JERRY.

JERRY. Nay, prithee, friend, now let me have but the *Seven Champions*. You shall trust me no longer than till my mother's Mr Splitcause comes, for I hope he'll lend me wherewithal to pay for't.

FREEMAN. Lend thee! Here, I'll pay him. Do you want money, squire? I'm sorry a man of your estate should want money.

JERRY. Nay, my mother will ne'er let me be at age. And till then she says –

FREEMAN. At age! Why, you are at age already to have spent an estate, man; there are younger than you have kept their women these three years, have had half a dozen claps, and lost as many thousand pounds at play.

JERRY. Ay, they are happy sparks! Nay, I know some of my schoolfellows who when we were at school were two years younger than me but now, I know not how, are grown men before me and go where they will and look to themselves, but my curmudgeonly mother won't allow me wherewithal to be a man of myself with.

FREEMAN. Why, there 'tis. I knew your mother was in

---

371 *son-in-law*: stepson.
399 *claps*: doses of syphilis.

the fault. Ask but your schoolfellows what they did to be men of themselves.

JERRY. Why, I know they went to law with their mothers, for they say there's no good to be done upon a widow-mother till one goes to law with her, but mine is as plaguey a lawyer as any's of our Inn. Then would she marry too and cut down my trees. Now I should hate, man, to have my father's wife kissed and slapped and t'other thing too (you know what I mean) by another man, and our trees are the purest, tall, even, shady twigs, by my fa –

FREEMAN. Come, squire, let your mother and your trees fall as she pleases rather than wear this gown and carry green bags all thy life and be pointed at for a tony. But you shall be able to deal with her yet the common way; thou shalt make false love to some lawyer's daughter, whose father, upon the hopes of thy marrying her, shall lend the money, and law, to preserve thy estate and trees, and thy mother is so ugly nobody will have her if she cannot cut down thy trees.

JERRY. Nay, if I had but anybody to stand by me, I am as stomachful as another.

FREEMAN. That will I. I'll not see any hopeful young gentleman abused.

BOY. (*aside*) By any but yourself.

JERRY. The truth on't is, mine's as arrant a widow-mother to her poor child as any's in England: she won't so much as let one have sixpence in one's pocket to see a motion or the dancing of the ropes or –

FREEMAN. Come, you shan't want money. There's gold for you.

JERRY. O Lurd, sir, two guineas! D'ye lend me this? Is there no trick in't? Well, sir, I'll give you my bond for security.

FREEMAN. No, no, thou hast given me thy face for security. Anybody would swear thou dost not look like a cheat. You shall have what you will of me and,

---

418 *purest*: finest.
422 *tony*: simpleton.
430 *stomachful*: brave.
437 *motion*: puppet-play.

if your mother will not be kinder to you, come to me, who will.

JERRY. (*aside*) By my fa – he's a curious fine gentleman! – But, will you stand by one?

FREEMAN. If you can be resolute.

JERRY. Can be resolved! Gad, if she gives me but a cross word, I'll leave her tonight and come to you. But now I have got money I'll go to Jack of All Trades, at t'other end of the Hall, and buy the neatest, purest things –

FREEMAN. [*aside*] And I'll follow the great boy and my blow at his mother. Steal away the calf and the cow will follow you.

Exit JERRY, *followed by* FREEMAN.

Enter, on the other side, MANLY, WIDOW BLACKACRE *and* OLDFOX.

MANLY. Damn your cause; can't you lose it without me? Which you are like enough to do if it be, as you say, an honest one. I will suffer no longer for't.

WIDOW. Nay, captain, I tell you, you are my prime witness and the cause is just now coming on, Mr Splitcause tells me. Lord, methinks you should take a pleasure in walking here as half you see now do, for they have no business here, I assure you.

MANLY. Yes, but I'll assure you then, their business is to persecute me. But d'ye think I'll stay any longer, to have a rogue, because he knows my name, pluck me aside and whisper a newsbook-secret to me with a stinking breath? A second come piping angry from the court and sputter in my face his tedious complaints against it? A third law-coxcomb, because he saw me once at a Reader's dinner, come and put me a long lawcase, to make discovery of his indefatigable dullness and my wearied patience? A fourth, a most barbarous civil rogue, who will keep a man half an hour in the crowd with a bowed body and a hat off,

---

470 *newsbook-secret*: no secret because already published in the newspapers.

474 *Reader's dinner*: feast given at the end of his term by one of the two lecturers appointed annually at the Inns.

acting the reformed sign of the Salutation Tavern, to hear his bountiful professions of service and friendship, whilst he cares not if I were damned and I am wishing him hanged out of my way? I'd as soon run the gauntlet as walk t'other turn.

Enter to them JERRY BLACKACRE *without his bags but laden with trinkets, which he endeavours to hide from his mother, and followed at a distance by* FREEMAN.

WIDOW. O, are you come, sir? But where have you been, you ass? And how come you thus laden?

JERRY. Look here, forsooth mother, now here's a duck, here's a boar-cat and here's an owl. (*Making a noise with catcalls and other suchlike instruments*)

WIDOW. Yes, there is an owl, sir.

OLDFOX. He's an ungracious bird, indeed.

WIDOW. But go, thou trangame, and carry back those trangames which thou hast stolen or purloined, for nobody would trust a minor in Westminster Hall, sure.

JERRY. Hold yourself contented, forsooth. I have these commodities by a fair bargain and sale, and there stands my witness and creditor.

WIDOW. How's that! What, sir, d'ye think to get the mother by giving the child a rattle? But where are my bags, my writings, you rascal?

JERRY. (*aside*) O law! Where are they indeed?

WIDOW. How, sirrah? Speak, come –

MANLY. (*apart to him*) You can tell her, Freeman, I suppose?

FREEMAN. (*apart to him*) 'Tis true, I made one of your salt-water sharks steal 'em, whilst he was eagerly choosing his commodities, as he calls 'em, in order to my design upon his mother.

WIDOW. Won't you speak? Where were you, I say, you son of a – an unfortunate woman? O major, I'm undone. They are all that concern my estate, my

---

479 *reformed . . . Tavern*: the sign which originally showed the Annunciation by the Angel Gabriel to Mary was changed to two men bowing. There were a number of Salutation Taverns in London.

487 s.d. *catcalls*: squeaking whistles.

490 *trangame*: trinket, toy; originally a fictitious law term.

jointure, my husband's deed of gift, my evidences for all my suits now depending! What will become of them?

FREEMAN. (*aside*) I'm glad to hear this. – They'll be safe, I warrant you, madam.

WIDOW. O where? Where? Come, you villain, along with me and show me where.

Exeunt WIDOW, JERRY, OLDFOX.
Manent MANLY, FREEMAN.

MANLY. Thou hast taken the right way to get a widow, by making her great boy rebel, for when nothing will make a widow marry she'll do't to cross her children. But canst thou in earnest marry this harpy, this volume of shrivelled, blurred parchments and law, this attorney's desk?

FREEMAN. Ay, ay, I'll marry and live honestly, that is, give my creditors, not her, due benevolence, pay my debts.

MANLY. Thy creditors, you see, are not so barbarous as to put thee in prison; and wilt thou commit thyself to a noisome dungeon for thy life, which is the only satisfaction thou canst give thy creditors by this match?

FREEMAN. Why, is not she rich?

MANLY. Ay, but he that marries a widow for her money will find himself as much mistaken as the widow that marries a young fellow for due benevolence, as you call it.

FREEMAN. Why, d'ye think I shan't deserve wages? I'll drudge faithfully.

MANLY. I tell thee again, he that is the slave in the mine has the least propriety in the ore. You may dig and dig, but if thou wouldst have her money rather get to be her trustee than her husband, for a true widow will make over her estate to anybody and cheat herself rather than be cheated by her children or a second husband.

Enter to them JERRY, *running in a fright.*

JERRY. O law! I'm undone, I'm undone, My mother will kill me. You said you'd stand by one.

FREEMAN. So I will, my brave squire, I warrant thee.

JERRY. Ay, but I dare not stay till she comes, for she's

as furious, now she has lost her writings, as a bitch when she has lost her puppies.

MANLY. The comparison's handsome!

JERRY. O, she's here!

Enter WIDOW BLACKACRE *and* OLDFOX.

FREEMAN. (*to the* SAILOR) Take him, Jack, and make haste with him to your master's lodging; and be sure you keep him up till I come.

Exeunt JERRY *and* SAILOR.

WIDOW. O my dear writings! Where's this heathen rogue, my minor?

FREEMAN. Gone to drown or hang himself.

WIDOW. No, I know him too well, he'll ne'er be *felo de se* that way; but he may go and choose a guardian of his own head and so be *felo de ses biens*: for he has not yet chosen one.

FREEMAN. (*aside*) Say you so? And he shan't want one.

WIDOW. But, now I think on't, 'tis you, sir, have put this cheat upon me; for there is a saying, 'Take hold of a maid by her smock and a widow by her writings and they cannot get from you.' But I'll play fast and loose with you yet, if there be law; and my minor and writings are not forthcoming, I'll bring my action of detinue or trover. But first I'll try to find out this guardianless, graceless villain. Will you jog, major?

MANLY. If you have lost your evidence, I hope your causes cannot go on and I may be gone?

WIDOW. O no, stay but a making-water while, as one may say, and I'll be with you again.

Exeunt WIDOW *and* OLDFOX.

Manent MANLY, FREEMAN.

---

555 *keep him up*: keep him locked in.

555 s.d. *Exeunt*: *Exit* Q1. There is no entrance for the sailor in Q1 and I have deliberately not added one for him. He was presumably one of the crowd passing to and fro throughout this act.

559–60 *felo de se*: suicide, in which case the goods were forfeit to the state.

561 *felo de ses biens*: murderer of his goods.

570 *detinue or trover*: action to recover property lawfully obtained but unlawfully detained or action to recover the value of such property when used by the detainor.

FREEMAN. Well, sure I am the first man that ever began a love intrigue in Westminster Hall.

MANLY. No, sure, for the love to a widow generally begins here. And as the widow's cause goes against the heir or executors, the jointure rivals commence their suit to the widow.

FREEMAN. Well, but how, pray, have you passed your time here since I was forced to leave you alone? You have had a great deal of patience.

MANLY. Is this a place to be alone or have patience in? But I have had patience indeed, for I have drawn upon me, since I came, but three quarrels and two lawsuits.

FREEMAN. Nay, faith, you are too cursed to be let loose in the world; you should be tied up again in your sea-kennel called a ship. But how could you quarrel here?

MANLY. How could I refrain? A lawyer talked peremptorily and saucily to me and as good as gave me the lie.

FREEMAN. They do it so often to one another at the bar that they make no bones on't elsewhere.

MANLY. However, I gave him a cuff on the ear; whereupon he jogs two men, whose backs were turned to us, for they were reading at a bookseller's, to witness I struck him, sitting the courts, which office they so readily promised that I called 'em rascals and knights of the post. One of 'em presently calls two other absent witnesses who were coming towards us at a distance, whilst the other with a whisper desires to know my name that he might have satisfaction by way of challenge as t'other by way of writ; but if it were not rather to direct his brother's writ than his own challenge. There you see is one of my quarrels and two of my lawsuits.

FREEMAN. So – and the other two?

MANLY. For advising a poet to leave off writing and turn lawyer because he is dull and impudent and says or writes nothing now but by precedent.

FREEMAN. And the third quarrel?

MANLY. For giving more sincere advice to a handsome, well-dressed young fellow (who asked it too) not to marry a wench that he loved and I had lain with.

FREEMAN. Nay, if you will be giving your sincere advice to lovers and poets you will not fail of quarrels.

MANLY. Or if I stay in this place, for I see more quarrels crowding upon me. Let's be gone and avoid 'em.

Enter NOVEL, *at a distance, coming towards them.*

A plague on him, that sneer is ominous to us; he is coming upon us and we shall not be rid of him.

NOVEL. Dear bully, don't look so grum upon me; you told me just now you had forgiven me a little harmless raillery upon wooden legs last night.

MANLY. Yes, yes, pray be gone. I am talking of business.

NOVEL. Can't I hear it? I love thee and will be faithful and always –

MANLY. Impertinent! 'Tis business that concerns Freeman only.

NOVEL. Well, I love Freeman too and would not divulge his secret. Prithee speak, prithee, I must –

MANLY. Prithee, let me be rid of thee. I must be rid of thee.

NOVEL. Faith, thou canst hardly, I love thee so. Come, I must know the business.

MANLY. (*aside*) So, I have it now. – Why, if you needs will know it, he has a quarrel and his adversary bids him bring two friends with him. Now, I am one and we are thinking who we shall have for a third.

Several crossing the stage.

NOVEL. A pox, there goes a fellow owes me an hundred pound and goes out of town tomorrow. I'll speak with him and come to you presently. *Exit* NOVEL.

MANLY. No but you won't.

FREEMAN. You are dextrously rid of him.

Enter OLDFOX.

MANLY. To what purpose, since here comes another as impertinent? I know by his grin he is bound hither.

OLDFOX. Your servant, worthy, noble captain. Well, I have left the widow because she carried me from your

625 *grum*: sullen.

company, for, faith, captain, I must needs tell thee thou art the only officer in England who was not an Edgehill officer that I care for.

MANLY. I'm sorry for't.

OLDFOX. Why, wouldst thou have me love them?

MANLY. Anybody rather than me.

OLDFOX. What, you are modest, I see! Therefore too I love thee.

MANLY. No, I am not modest but love to brag myself and can't patiently hear you fight over the last civil war; therefore go look out the fellow I saw just now here, that walks with his stockings and his sword out at heels, and let him tell you the history of that scar on his cheek, to give you occasion to show yours, got in the field at Bloomsbury, not that of Edgehill. Go to him, poor fellow. He is fasting and has not yet the happiness this morning to stink of brandy and tobacco; go, give him some to hear you. I am busy.

OLDFOX. Well, ygad, I love thee now, boy, for thy surliness. Thou art no tame captain, I see, that will suffer –

MANLY. An old fox.

OLDFOX. All that shan't make me angry. I consider thou art peevish and fretting at some ill success at law. Prithee tell me what ill luck you have met with here.

MANLY. You.

OLDFOX. Do I look like the picture of ill luck? Gadsnouns, I love thee more and more; and shall I tell thee what made me love thee first?

MANLY. Do, that I may be rid of that damned quality and thee.

OLDFOX. 'Twas thy wearing that broad sword there.

MANLY. Here, Freeman, let's change. I'll never wear it more.

OLDFOX. How! You won't sure. Prithee don't look like

---

654 *Edgehill*: the first major battle of the Civil War, October 1642; it seems from line 699 that Oldfox was for Parliament, not the King.

666 *Bloomsbury*: probably the fields behind Southampton House in London, popular for duels.

678–9 *Gadsnouns*: by God's wounds.

one of our holiday captains nowadays, with a bodkin by your side, your Martinet rogues.

MANLY. (*aside*) O, then there's hopes. – What, d'ye find faults with Martinet? Let me tell you, sir, 'tis the best exercise in the world, the most ready, most easy, most graceful exercise that ever was used and the most –

OLDFOX. Nay, nay, sir, no more, sir, your servant. If you praise Martinet once, I have done with you, sir. Martinet! Martinet! *Exit* OLDFOX.

FREEMAN. Nay, you have made him leave you as willingly as ever he did an enemy, for he was truly for the king and parliament: for the parliament in their list and for the king in cheating 'em of their pay and never hurting the king's party in the field.

Enter a LAWYER *towards them.*

MANLY. A pox! This way; here's a lawyer I know threatening us with another greeting.

LAWYER. Sir, sir, your very servant. I was afraid you had forgotten me.

MANLY. I was not afraid you had forgotten me.

LAWYER. No, sir, we lawyers have pretty good memories.

MANLY. You ought to have, by your wits.

LAWYER. O, you are a merry gentleman, sir. I remember you were merry when I was last in your company.

MANLY. I was never merry in your company, Mr Lawyer, sure.

LAWYER. Why, I'm sure you joked upon me and shammed me all night long.

MANLY. Shammed! Prithee, what barbarous law-term is that?

LAWYER. Shamming! Why, don't you know that? 'Tis all our way of wit, sir.

MANLY. I am glad I do not know it then. Shamming! What does he mean by't, Freeman?

FREEMAN. Shamming is telling you an insipid, dull lie, with a dull face, which the sly wag the author only

---

688 *Martinet*: the system of drill developed by Lt.-Col. Jean Martinet and an integral part of the modernisation of the French army in the 1660s.

laughs at himself, and making himself believe 'tis a good jest, puts the sham only upon himself.

MANLY. So, your lawyer's jest, I find, like his practice, has more knavery than wit in't. I should make the worst shammer in England. I must always deal ingeniously, as I will with you, Mr Lawyer, and advise you to be seen rather with attornies and solicitors then such fellows as I am; they will credit your practice more.

LAWYER. No, sir, your company's an honour to me.

MANLY. No, faith, go this way, there goes an attorney; leave me for him. Let it be never said a lawyer's civility did him hurt.

LAWYER. No, worthy, honoured sir, I'll not leave you for any attorney, sure.

MANLY. Unless he had a fee in his hand.

LAWYER. Have you any business here, sir? Try me. I'd serve you sooner than any attorney breathing.

MANLY. Business! (*Aside*) So, I have thought of a sure way. – Yes, faith, I have a little business.

LAWYER. Have you so, sir? In what court, sir? What is't, sir? Tell me but how I may serve you and I'll do't, sir, and take it for as great an honour –

MANLY. Faith, 'tis for a poor orphan of a sea-officer of mine that has no money; but if it could be followed *in forma pauperis*, and when the legacy's recovered –

LAWYER. *Forma pauperis*, sir!

MANLY. Ay, sir.

Several crossing the stage.

LAWYER. Mr Bumblecase, Mr Bumblecase, a word with you. – Sir, I beg your pardon at present, I have a little business –

MANLY. Which is not *in forma pauperis*.

Exit LAWYER.

FREEMAN. So, you have now found a way to be rid of people without quarrelling.

Enter ALDERMAN.

---

729 *ingeniously*: ingenuously.
749 *in forma pauperis*: free of court costs and legal fees, for a pauper.

MANLY. But here's a city rogue will stick as hard upon us as if I owed him money.

ALDERMAN. Captain, noble sir, I am yours heartily, d'ye see. Why should you avoid your old friends?

MANLY. And why should you follow me? I owe you nothing.

ALDERMAN. Out of my hearty respects to you, for there is not a man in England –

MANLY. Thou wouldst save from hanging with the expense of a shilling only.

ALDERMAN. Nay, nay, but captain, you are like enough to tell me –

MANLY. Truth, which you won't care to hear; therefore you had better go talk with somebody else.

ALDERMAN. No, I know nobody can inform me better of some young wit or spendthrift that has a good dipped seat and estate in Middlesex, Hertfordshire, Essex or Kent – any of these would serve my turn. Now, if you knew of such an one and would but help –

MANLY. You to finish his ruin.

ALDERMAN. I'faith, you should have a snip –

MANLY. Of your nose. You thirty in the hundred rascal, would you make me your squire setter, your bawd for manors? (*Takes him by the nose*)

ALDERMAN. Oh!

FREEMAN. Hold or here will be your third lawsuit.

ALDERMAN. Gad's precious, you hectoring person you, are you wild? I meant you no hurt, sir. I begin to think, as things go, land security best and have, for a convenient mortgage, some ten, fifteen or twenty thousand pound by me.

MANLY. Then go lay it out upon an hospital and take a mortgage of heaven according to your city custom, for you think by laying out a little money to hook in that too hereafter. Do, I say, and keep the poor you've made by taking forfeitures that heaven may not take yours.

---

774 *dipped seat*: mortgaged country estate.
778 *snip*: share.
779 *thirty in the hundred*: charging 30% interest on loans; the highest leval rate was 6%.
780 *setter*: pimp.

ALDERMAN. No, to keep the cripples you make this war; this war spoils our trade.

MANLY. Damn your trade; 'tis the better for't.

ALDERMAN. What, will you speak against our trade?

MANLY. And dare you speak against the war, our trade?

ALDERMAN. (*aside*) Well, he may be a convoy of ships I am concerned in. – Come, captain, I will have a fair correspondency with you, say what you will.

MANLY. Then prithee be gone.

ALDERMAN. No, faith, prithee, captain, let's go drink a dish of laced coffee and talk of the times. Come, I'll treat you. Nay, you shall go, for I have no business here.

MANLY. But I have.

ALDERMAN. To pick up a man to give thee a dinner? Come, I'll do thy business for thee.

MANLY. Faith, now I think on't, so you may, as well as any man, for 'tis to pick up a man to be bound with me to one who expects city security, for –

ALDERMAN. Nay, then your servant, captain. Business must be done.

MANLY. Ay, if it can, but hark you, alderman, without you –

ALDERMAN. Business, sir, I say, must be done, and there's an officer of the Treasury I have an affair with –

Several crossing the stage. Exit ALDERMAN.

MANLY. You see now what the mighty friendship of the world is, what all ceremony, embraces and plentiful professions come to. You are no more to believe a professing friend than a threatening enemy and, as no man hurts you that tells you he'll do you a mischief, no man, you see, is your servant who says he is so. Why the devil, then, should a man be troubled with the flattery of knaves, if he be not a fool or cully, or with the fondness of fools, if he be not a knave or cheat?

FREEMAN. Only for his pleasure, for there is some in laughing at fools and disappointing knaves.

MANLY. That's a pleasure, I think, would cost you too dear, as well as marrying your widow to disappoint

---

806 *laced*: with brandy.

her; but, for my part, I have no pleasure by 'em, but in despising 'em, wheresoe'er I meet 'em, and then the pleasure of hoping so to be rid of 'em. But now my comfort is, I am not worth a shilling in the world, which all the world shall know; and then I'm sure I shall have none of 'em come near me.

FREEMAN. A very pretty comfort, which I think you pay too dear for. But is the twenty pound gone since the morning?

MANLY. To my boat's crew. Would you have the poor, honest, brave fellows want?

FREEMAN. Rather than you or I.

MANLY. Why, art thou without money? Thou who art a friend to everybody?

FREEMAN. I ventured my last stake upon the squire, to nick him of his mother and cannot help you to a dinner, unless you will go dine with my lord –

MANLY. No, no, the ordinary is too dear for me, where flattery must pay for my dinner; I am no herald, or poet.

FREEMAN. We'll go then to the bishop's –

MANLY. There you must flatter the old philosophy. I cannot renounce my reason for a dinner.

FREEMAN. Why, then let's go to your alderman's.

MANLY. Hang him, rogue! That were not to dine, for he makes you drunk with lees of sack before dinner to take away your stomach and there you must call usury and extortion, God's blessings or the honest turning of the penny; hear him brag of the leather breeches in which he trotted first to town, and make a greater noise with his money in his parlour than his cashiers do in his counting-house, without hopes of borrowing a shilling.

FREEMAN. Ay, a pox on't, 'tis like dining with the great gamesters and, when they fall to their common dessert, see the heaps of gold drawn on all hands, without going to twelve. Let us go to my Lady Goodly's.

---

850 *nick*: cheat, defraud.
852 *ordinary*: eating-house.
860 *lees of sack*: dregs of sherry.
871 *without going to twelve*: gambler's slang whose meaning is lost; here it seems to mean 'without joining the game'.

MANLY. There to flatter her looks you must mistake her grandchildren for her own, praise her cook that she may rail at him and feed her dogs, not yourself.

FREEMAN. What d'ye think of eating with your lawyer then?

MANLY. Eat with him! Damn him, to hear him employ his barbarous eloquence in a reading upon the two and thirty good bits in a shoulder of veal and be forced yourself to praise the cold bribe pie that stinks and drink law-French wine as rough and harsh as his law-French. A pox on him, I'd rather dine in the Temple Rounds or Walks, with the knights without noses, or the knights of the post, who are honester fellows and better company. But let us home and try our fortune, for I'll stay no longer here for your damned widow.

FREEMAN. Well, let us go home then, for I must go for my damned widow and look after my new damned charge. Three or four hundred year ago a man might have dined in this hall.

MANLY. But now, the lawyer only here is fed
And, bullylike, by quarrels gets his bread.

Exeunt.

ACT IV

SCENE I

Manly's lodging.

Enter MANLY *and* FIDELIA.

MANLY. Well, there's success in thy face. Hast thou prevailed? Say.

879–80 *two and thirty good bits*: a garbled version of the saying: there are thirty bits but only two good ones.

889–90 *knights without noses*: decayed statues of the Knights Templar in the Round Church belonging to the Middle and Inner Temples, two of the Inns of Court.

891–2 Westminster Hall had been a royal banqueting-hall.

FIDELIA. As I could wish, sir.

MANLY. So, I told thee what thou wert fit for and thou wouldst not believe me. Come, thank me for bringing thee acquainted with thy genius. Well, thou hast mollified her heart for me?

FIDELIA. No, sir, not so, but what's better.

MANLY. How? What's better!

FIDELIA. I shall harden your heart against her.

MANLY. Have a care, sir. My heart is too much in earnest to be fooled with and my desire at heighth and needs no delays to incite it. What, you are too good a pimp already and know how to endear pleasure by withholding it? But leave off your page's bawdyhouse tricks, sir, and tell me; will she be kind?

FIDELIA. Kinder than you could wish, sir.

MANLY. So then. Well, prithee what said she?

FIDELIA. She said –

MANLY. What? Thou'rt so tedious. Speak comfort to me. What?

FIDELIA. That, of all things, you were her aversion.

MANLY. How?

FIDELIA. That she would sooner take a bedfellow out of an hospital and diseases into her arms than you.

MANLY. What?

FIDELIA. That she would rather trust her honour with a dissolute, debauched hector, nay worse, with a finical, baffled coward, all over loathsome with affectation of the fine gentleman.

MANLY. What's all this you say?

FIDELIA. Nay, that my offers of your love to her were more offensive than when parents woo their virgin daughters to the enjoyment of riches only and that you were in all circumstances as nauseous to her as a husband on compulsion.

MANLY. Hold, I understand you not.

FIDELIA. (*aside*) So, 'twill work, I see.

MANLY. Did not you tell me –

FIDELIA. She called you ten thousand ruffians.

MANLY. Hold, I say.

FIDELIA. Brutes –

MANLY. Hold.

---

29 *baffled*: disgraced.

FIDELIA. Sea-monsters –

MANLY. Damn your intelligence. Hear me a little now.

FIDELIA. Nay, surly coward she called you too.

MANLY. Won't you hold yet? Hold, or –

FIDELIA. Nay, sir, pardon me. I could not but tell you she had the baseness, the injustice, to call you coward, sir, coward, coward, sir.

MANLY. Not yet?

FIDELIA. I've done. Coward, sir.

MANLY. Did not you say she was kinder than I could wish her?

FIDELIA. Yes sir.

MANLY. How then? – O – I understand you now. At first she appeared in rage and disdain, the truest sign of a coming woman, but at last you prevailed, it seems; did you not?

FIDELIA. Yes, sir.

MANLY. So then, let's know that only. Come, prithee, without delays. I'll kiss thee for that news beforehand.

FIDELIA. (*aside*) So, the kiss, I'm sure, is welcome to me, whatsoe'er the news will be to you.

MANLY. Come, speak, my dear volunteer.

FIDELIA. (*aside*) How welcome were that kind word too, if it were not for another woman's sake!

MANLY. What, won't you speak? You prevailed for me at last, you say?

FIDELIA. No, sir.

MANLY. No more of your fooling, sir; it will not agree with my impatience or temper.

FIDELIA. Then, not to fool you, sir, I spoke to her for you but prevailed for myself. She would not hear me when I spoke in your behalf but bid me say what I would in my own – though she gave me no occasion, she was so coming – and so was kinder, sir, than you could wish, which I was only afraid to let you know without some warning.

MANLY. How's this? Young man, you are of a lying age, but I must hear you out, and if –

FIDELIA. I would not abuse you and cannot wrong her by any report of her, she is so wicked.

---

77 *coming*: eager, willing.

MANLY. How, wicked! Had she the impudence, at the second sight of you only –

FIDELIA. Impudence, sir! O, she has impudence enough to put a court out of countenance and debauch a stews.

MANLY. Why, what said she?

FIDELIA. Her tongue, I confess, was silent, but her speaking eyes gloated such things, more immodest and lascivious than ravishers can act or women under a confinement think.

MANLY. I know there are whose eyes reflect more obscenity than the glasses in alcoves, but there are others too who use a little art with their looks to make 'em seem more beautiful, not more loving, which vain young fellows like you are apt to interpret in their own favour and to the lady's wrong.

FIDELIA. Seldom, sir. Pray have you a care of gloating eyes, for he that loves to gaze upon 'em will find at last a thousand fools and cuckolds in 'em, instead of cupids.

MANLY. Very well, sir. But, what, you had only eye-kindness from Olivia?

FIDELIA. I tell you again, sir, no woman sticks there. Eye-promises of love they only keep; nay, they are contracts which make you sure of 'em. In short, sir, she, seeing me with shame and amazement dumb, unactive and resistless, threw her twisting arms about my neck and smothered me with a thousand tasteless kisses – believe me, sir, they were so to me.

MANLY. Why did you not avoid 'em then?

FIDELIA. I fenced with her eager arms as you did with the grapples of the enemy's fireship and nothing but cutting 'em off could have freed me.

MANLY. Damned, damned woman, that could be so false and infamous! And damned, damned heart of mine, that cannot yet be false, though so infamous! What easy, tame, suffering, trampled things does that little god of talking cowards make of us! But –

FIDELIA. (*aside*) So! It works I find as I expected.

---

88 *stews*: brothel.
115 *fireship*: Fidelia puns on the meaning 'whore'.

MANLY. But she was false to me before. She told me so herself, and yet I could not quite believe it. But she was, so that her second falseness is a favour to me, not an injury, in revenging me upon the man that wronged me first of her love. Her love! – A whore's, a witch's love! – But, what, did she not kiss well, sir? I'm sure I thought her lips – but I must not think of 'em more – but yet they are such I could still kiss – grow to – and then tear off with my teeth, grind 'em into mammocks and spit 'em into her cuckold's face.

FIDELIA. (*aside*) Poor man, how uneasy he is! I have hardly the heart to give him so much pain, though withal I give him a cure and to myself new life.

MANLY. But, what, her kisses sure could not but warm you into desire at last or a compliance with hers at least?

FIDELIA. Nay, more, I confess –

MANLY. What more? Speak.

FIDELIA. All you could fear had passed between us, if I could have been made to wrong you, sir, in that nature.

MANLY. Could have been made! You lie, you did.

FIDELIA. Indeed, sir, 'twas impossible for me; besides, we were interrupted by a visit. But, I confess, she would not let me stir till I promised to return to her again within this hour, as soon as it should be dark, by which time she would dispose of her visit and her servants and herself for my reception, which I was fain to promise to get from her.

MANLY. Ha!

FIDELIA. But if ever I go near her again, may you, sir, think me as false to you as she is, hate and renounce me, as you ought to do her and I hope will do now.

MANLY. Well, but now I think on't, you shall keep your word with your lady. What, a young fellow and fail the first, nay, so tempting an assignation!

FIDELIA. How, sir?

MANLY. I say you shall go to her when 'tis dark and shall not disappoint her.

FIDELIA. I, sir! I should disappoint her more by going, for –

---

132 *mammocks*: shreds.

MANLY. How so?

FIDELIA. Her impudence and injustice to you will make me disappoint her love, loathe her.

MANLY. Come, you have my leave and, if you disgust her, I'll go with you and act love whilst you shall talk it only.

FIDELIA. You, sir! Nay, then I'll never go near her. You act love, sir! You must but act it indeed after all I have said to you. Think of your honour, sir. Love –

MANLY. Well, call it revenge and that is honourable. I'll be revenged on her and thou shalt be my second.

FIDELIA. Not in a base action, sir, when you are your own enemy. O, go not near her, sir, for heaven's sake, for your own, think not of it.

MANLY. How concerned you are! I thought I should catch you. What, you are my rival at last and are in love with her yourself and have spoken ill of her out of your love to her, not me, and therefore would not have me go to her!

FIDELIA. Heaven witness for me, 'tis because I love you only I would not have you go to her.

MANLY. Come, come, the more I think on't, the more I'm satisfied you do love her. Those kisses, young man, I knew were irresistible; 'tis certain.

FIDELIA. There is nothing certain in the world, sir, but my truth and your courage.

MANLY. Your servant, sir. Besides, false and ungrateful as she has been to me, and though I may believe her hatred to me as great as you report it, yet I cannot think you are so soon and at that rate beloved by her, though you may endeavour it.

FIDELIA. Nay, if that be all and you doubt it still, sir, I will conduct you to her and, unseen, your ears shall judge of her falseness and my truth to you, if that will satisfy you.

MANLY. Yes, there is some satisfaction in being quite out of doubt: because 'tis that alone withholds us from the pleasure of revenge.

FIDELIA. Revenge! What revenge can you have, sir? Disdain is best revenged by scorn, and faithless love

166 *disgust*: dislike.

by loving another and making her happy with the other's losings, which, if I might advise –

Enter FREEMAN.

MANLY. Not a word more.

FREEMAN. What, are you talking of love yet, captain? I thought you had done with't.

MANLY. Why, what did you hear me say?

FREEMAN. Something imperfectly of love, I think.

MANLY. I was only wondering why fools, rascals and desertless wretches should still have the better of men of merit with all women, as much as with their own common mistress, Fortune!

FREEMAN. Because most women, like Fortune, are blind, seem to do all things in jest and take pleasure in extravagant actions. Their love deserves neither thanks or blame, for they cannot help it; 'tis all sympathy. Therefore the noisy, the finical, the talkative, the cowardly and effeminate have the better of the brave, the reasonable and man of honour, for they have no more reason in their love or kindness than Fortune herself.

MANLY. Yes, they have their reason. First, honour in a man they fear too much to love and sense in a lover upbraids their want of it and they hate anything that disturbs their admiration of themselves; but they are of that vain number who had rather show their false generosity in giving away profusely to worthless flatterers than in paying just debts. And, in short, all women, like Fortune, as you say, and rewards, are lost by too much meriting.

FIDELIA. All women, sir! Sure, there are some who have no other quarrel to a lover's merit but that it begets their despair of him.

MANLY. Thou art young enough to be credulous, but we –

Enter FIRST SAILOR.

FIRST SAILOR. Here are now below the scolding, daggled gentlewoman and that Major Old – old – Fop, I think you call him.

FREEMAN. Oldfox. Prithee, bid 'em come up, with your leave, captain, for now I can talk with her upon the square, if I shall not disturb you.

MANLY. No, for I'll be gone. Come, volunteer.

FREEMAN. Nay, pray stay. The scene between us will not be so tedious to you as you think. Besides, you shall see how I have rigged my squire out with the remains of my shipwracked wardrobe. He is under your sea *valet de chambre*'s hands and by this time dressed and will be worth your seeing. Stay and I'll fetch my fool.

MANLY. No, you know I cannot easily laugh; besides, my volunteer and I have business abroad.

Exeunt MANLY, FIDELIA, *on one side,* FREEMAN *on t'other.*

Enter MAJOR OLDFOX *and* WIDOW BLACKACRE.

WIDOW. What, nobody here! Did not the fellow say he was within?

OLDFOX. Yes, lady, and he may be perhaps a little busy at present, but if you think the time long till he comes, (*unfolding papers*) I'll read you here some of the fruits of my leisure, the overflowings of my fancy and pen. (*Aside*) To value me right, she must know my parts. – Come –

WIDOW. No, no, I have reading work enough of my own in my bag, I thank you.

OLDFOX. Ay, law, madam, but here is a poem in blank verse which I think a handsome declaration of one's passion.

WIDOW. O! If you talk of declarations, I'll show you one of the prettiest penned things which I mended too myself you must know.

OLDFOX. Nay, lady, if you have used yourself so much to the reading of harsh law that you hate smooth poetry, here is a character for you of –

WIDOW. A character! Nay, then I'll show you my bill in Chancery here that gives you such a character of my adversary, makes him as black –

OLDFOX. Pshaw, away, away, lady. But if you think the character too long, here is an epigram not above

---

271 *character*: a short, often satirical prose sketch of a person or type, developed from those by Theophrastus.

twenty lines, upon a cruel lady who decreed her servant should hang himself to demonstrate his passion.

WIDOW. Decreed! If you talk of decreeing, I have such a decree here, drawn by the finest clerk –

OLDFOX. O lady, lady, all interruption and no sense between us, as if we were lawyers at the bar! But I had forgot, Apollo and Littleton never lodge in a head together. If you hate verses, I'll give you a cast of my politics in prose: 'tis a letter to a friend in the country, which is now the way of all such sober, solid persons as myself, when they have a mind to publish their disgust to the times, though perhaps, between you and I, they have no friend in the country. And, sure, a politic, serious person may as well have a feigned friend in the country to write to as well as an idle poet a feigned mistress to write to. And so here is my letter to a friend, or no friend, in the country concerning the late conjuncture of affairs in relation to coffeehouses, or the Coffeeman's Case.

WIDOW. Nay, if your letter have a case in't, 'tis something, but first I'll read you a letter of mine to a friend in the country, called a letter of attorney.

Enter to them FREEMAN *and* JERRY BLACKACRE *in a gaudy suit and red breeches of Freeman's.*

OLDFOX. (*aside*) What, interruption still? O the plague of interruption, worse to an author than the plague of critics!

WIDOW. What's this I see, Jerry Blackacre, my minor, in red breeches! What, hast thou left the modest, seemly garb of gown and cap for this? And have I lost all my good Inns of Chancery breeding upon thee then? And thou wilt go a-breeding thyself, from our Inn of Chancery and Westminster Hall, at coffeehouses and ordinaries, playhouses, tennis courts and bawdyhouses.

---

283 *Apollo and Littleton*: art and the law; Sir Thomas Littleton (1422–81) was a jurist famous for his treatise on tenure.

294–5 *the late . . . coffeehouses*: in an attempt to suppress seditious talk, a royal proclamation, never enforced, announced the closure of the coffeehouses in January 1676.

298 *letter of attorney*: a document empowering a person to act on another's behalf.

JERRY. Ay, ay, what then? Perhaps I will. But what's that to you? Here's my guardian and tutor now, forsooth, that I am out of your huckster's hands.

WIDOW. How? Thou hast not chosen him for thy guardian yet?

JERRY. No, but he has chosen me for his charge and that's all one; and I'll do anything he'll have me and go all the world over with him, to ordinaries and bawdyhouses, or anywhere else.

WIDOW. To ordinaries and bawdyhouses! Have a care, minor. Thou wilt infeeble there thy estate and body. Do not go to ordinaries and bawdyhouses, good Jerry.

JERRY. Why, how come you to know any ill by bawdyhouses? You never had any hurt by 'em, had you, forsooth? Pray hold yourself contented. If I do go where money and wenches are to be had, you may thank yourself, for you used me so unnaturally, you would never let me have a penny to go abroad with nor so much as come near the garret where your maidens lay; nay, you would not so much as let me play at hotcockles with 'em nor have any recreation with 'em, though one should have kissed you behind, you were so unnatural a mother, so you were.

FREEMAN. Ay, a very unnatural mother, faith, squire.

WIDOW. But Jerry, consider thou art yet but a minor. However, if thou wilt go home with me again and be a good child, thou shalt see –

FREEMAN. Madam, I must have a better care of my heir under age than so. I would sooner trust him alone with a stale waiting-woman and a parson than with his widow-mother and her lover or lawyer.

WIDOW. Why, thou villain, part mother and minor! Rob me of my child and my writings! But thou shalt find there's law, and as in the case of ravishment of guard – Westminster the second.

---

311 *huckster's*: mercenary.

330 *hotcockles*: (*a*) an innocent game of blindfolding (*b*) a less innocent game of sex-play.

343–4 *ravishment . . . the second*: the statute known as Westminster 2, 1285, includes sections covering the abduction of wards and minors.

OLDFOX. Young gentleman, squire, pray be ruled by your mother and your friends.

JERRY. Yes, I'll be ruled by my friends, therefore not by my mother, so I won't. I'll choose him for my guardian till I am of age, nay, maybe for as long as I live.

WIDOW. Wilt thou so, thou wretch? And when thou'rt of age, thou wilt sign, seal and deliver too, wilt thou?

JERRY. Yes, marry will I, if you go there too.

WIDOW. O do not squeeze wax, son. Rather go to ordinaries and bawdyhouses than squeeze wax. If thou dost that, farewell the goodly manor of Blackacre with all its woods, underwoods and appurtenances whatever. Oh, Oh! (*Weeps*)

FREEMAN. Come, madam, in short, you see I am resolved to have a share in the estate, yours or your son's: if I cannot get you, I'll keep him, who is less coy you find; but if you would have your son again, you must take me too. Peace or war? Love or law? You see my hostage is in my hand. I'm in possession.

WIDOW. Nay, if one of us must be ruined, e'en let it be him. By my body, a good one! Did you ever know yet a widow marry or not marry for the sake of her child? I'd have you to know, sir, I shall be hard enough for you both yet without marrying you, if Jerry won't be ruled by me. What say you, booby, will you be ruled? Speak.

JERRY. Let one alone, can't you?

WIDOW. Wilt thou choose him for guardian whom I refuse for husband?

JERRY. Ay, to choose, I thank you.

WIDOW. And are all my hopes frustrated? Shall I never hear thee put cases again to John the butler or our vicar? Never see thee amble the circuit with the judges and hear thee in our town hall louder than the crier?

JERRY. No, for I have taken my leave of lawyering and pettifogging.

WIDOW. Pettifogging! Thou profane villain, hast thou so? Pettifogging! – Then you shall take your leave of me and your estate too. Thou shalt be an alien to me and it forever. Pettifogging!

JERRY. O, but if you go there too, mother, we have the

deeds and settlements, I thank you. Would you cheat me of my estate, ifac?

WIDOW. No, no, I will not cheat your little brother Bob, for thou wert not born in wedlock.

FREEMAN. How's that?

JERRY. How? What quirk has she got in her head now?

WIDOW. I say thou canst not, shalt not inherit the Blackacres' estate.

JERRY. Why? Why, forsooth? What d'ye mean, if you go there too?

WIDOW. Thou art but my base child and according to the law canst not inherit it; nay, thou art not so much as bastard eigne.

JERRY. What, what? Am I then the son of a whore, mother?

WIDOW. The law says –

FREEMAN. Madam, we know what the law says, but have a care what you say. Do not let your passion to ruin your son ruin your reputation.

WIDOW. Hang reputation, sir. Am not I a widow? Have no husband nor intend to have any? Nor would you, I suppose, now have me for a wife. So I think now I'm revenged on my son and you, without marrying, as I told you.

FREEMAN. But consider, madam.

JERRY. What, have you no shame left in you, mother?

WIDOW. (*aside to* OLDFOX) Wonder not at it, major. 'Tis often the poor pressed widow's case, to give up her honour to save her jointure and seem to be a light woman rather than marry, as some young men, they say, pretend to have the filthy disease and lose their credit with most women to avoid the importunities of some.

FREEMAN. But one word with you, madam.

WIDOW. No, no, sir. Come, major, let us make haste now to the Prerogative Court.

OLDFOX. But, lady, if what you say be true, will you stigmatise your reputation on record? And, if it be not true, how will you prove it?

---

400 *bastard eigne*: the elder of two bastards (eigne = Fr. *aîné*).
423 *Prerogative Court*: the archbishop's court for probate of wills and cases caused by wills.

WIDOW. Pshaw! I can prove anything and, for my reputation, know, major, a wise woman will no more value her reputation in disinheriting a rebellious son of a good estate than she would in getting him to inherit an estate.

Exeunt WIDOW *and* OLDFOX.

FREEMAN. Madam – We must not let her go so, squire.

JERRY. Nay, the devil can't stop her though if she has a mind to't. But come, bully guardian, we'll go and advise with three attornies, two proctors, two solicitors and a shrewd man of Whitefriars, neither attorney, proctor or solicitor but as pure a pimp to the law as any of 'em; and, sure, all they will be hard enough for her, for I fear, bully guardian, you are too good a joker to have any law in your head.

FREEMAN. Thou'rt in the right on't, squire; I understand no law, especially that against bastards, since I'm sure the custom is against that law, and more people get estates by being so than lose 'em.

Exeunt.

SCENE II

The scene changes to Olivia's lodgings.

Enter LORD PLAUSIBLE *and* BOY *with a candle.*

LORD PLAUSIBLE. Little gentleman, your most obedient, faithful, humble servant; where, I beseech you, is that divine person, your noble lady?

BOY. Gone out, my lord, but commanded me to give you this letter. (*Gives him a letter*)

Enter to him NOVEL.

LORD PLAUSIBLE. (*aside*) Which he must not observe. (*Puts it up*)

NOVEL. Hey, boy, where is thy lady?

---

436 *Whitefriars*: an area of the East End which was a sanctuary for debtors and other criminals.

6 s.d. *Puts it up*: set as part of speech Q1.

BOY. Gone out, sir, but I must beg a word with you.

Gives him a letter and exit.

NOVEL. For me? So. (*Puts up the letter*) Servant, servant, my lord. You see the lady knew of your coming, for she is gone out.

LORD PLAUSIBLE. Sir, I humbly beseech you not to censure the lady's good breeding. She has reason to use more liberty with me than with any other man.

NOVEL. How, viscount, how?

LORD PLAUSIBLE. Nay, I humbly beseech you, be not in choler. Where there is most love there may be most freedom.

NOVEL. Nay, then 'tis time to come to an éclaircissement with you and to tell you you must think no more of this lady's love.

LORD PLAUSIBLE. Why, under correction, dear sir?

NOVEL. There are reasons, reasons, viscount.

LORD PLAUSIBLE. What, I beseech you, noble sir?

NOVEL. Prithee, prithee, be not impertinent, my lord. Some of you lords are such conceited, well-assured, impertinent rogues.

LORD PLAUSIBLE. And you noble wits are so full of shamming and drolling one knows not where to have you, seriously.

NOVEL. Well, you shall find me in bed with this lady one of these days.

LORD PLAUSIBLE. Nay, I beseech you, spare the lady's honour, for hers and mine will be all one shortly.

NOVEL. Prithee, my lord, be not an ass. Dost thou think to get her from me? I have had such encouragements –

LORD PLAUSIBLE. I have not been thought unworthy of 'em.

NOVEL. What, not like mine! Come to an éclaircissement, as I said.

LORD PLAUSIBLE. Why, seriously then, she has told me viscountess sounded prettily.

NOVEL. And me that Novel was a name she would sooner change hers for than for any title in England.

19–20 *éclaircissement*: clarification.

LORD PLAUSIBLE. She has commended the softness and respectfulness of my behaviour.

NOVEL. She has praised the briskness of my raillery of all things, man.

LORD PLAUSIBLE. The sleepiness of my eyes she liked.

NOVEL. Sleepiness! Dullness, dullness. But the fierceness of mine she adored.

LORD PLAUSIBLE. The brightness of my hair she liked.

NOVEL. The brightness! No, the greasiness, I warrant. But the blackness and lustre of mine she admires.

LORD PLAUSIBLE. The gentleness of my smile.

NOVEL. The subtlety of my leer.

LORD PLAUSIBLE. The clearness of my complexion.

NOVEL. The redness of my lips.

LORD PLAUSIBLE. The whiteness of my teeth.

NOVEL. My janty way of picking them.

LORD PLAUSIBLE. The sweetness of my breath.

NOVEL. Hah, ha! – Nay then she abused you, 'tis plain, for you know what Manly said; the sweetness of your pulvillio she might mean, but for your breath! Ha, ha, ha. Your breath is such, man, that nothing but tobacco can perfume, and your complexion nothing could mend but the smallpox.

LORD PLAUSIBLE. Well, sir, you may please to be merry, but, to put you out of all doubt, sir, she has received some jewels from me of value.

NOVEL. And presents from me, besides what I presented her jantily by way of ombre, of three or four hundred pound value, which, I'm sure, are the earnest pence for our love bargain.

LORD PLAUSIBLE. Nay then, sir, with your favour and to make an end of all your hopes, look you there, sir, she has writ to me. –

NOVEL. How! How! Well, well, and so she has to me: look you there. –

Deliver to each other their letters.

LORD PLAUSIBLE. What's here!

NOVEL. How's this? (*Reads out*)

My Dear Lord,

You'll excuse me for breaking my word with you since 'twas to oblige, not to offend you, for I am only

81 s.d. after line 79 Q1.

gone abroad but to disappoint Novel and meet you in the drawing-room, where I expect you with as much impatience as when I used to suffer Novel's visits, the most impertinent fop that ever affected the name of a wit, therefore not capable, I hope, to give you jealousy, for, for your sake alone, you saw, I renounced an old lover and will do all the world. Burn the letter but lay up the kindness of it in your heart, with your

Olivia

Very fine! But pray let's see mine.

LORD PLAUSIBLE. I understand it not but, sure, she cannot think so of me.

NOVEL. (*reads the other letter*) Humh! – Ha! – meet – for your sake – umh – quitted an old lover – world – burn – in your heart, with your

Olivia

Just the same, the names only altered.

LORD PLAUSIBLE. Surely there must be some mistake, or somebody has abused her, and us.

NOVEL. Yes, you are abused, no doubt on't, my lord, but I'll to Whitehall and see.

LORD PLAUSIBLE. And I, where I shall find you are abused.

NOVEL. Where, if it be so, for our comfort we cannot fail of meeting with fellow-sufferers enough, for, as Freeman said of another, she stands in the drawing-room like the glass, ready for all comers to set their gallantry by her, and, like the glass too, lets no man go from her unsatisfied with himself.

Exeunt ambo.

Enter OLIVIA *and* BOY.

OLIVIA. Both here and just gone?

BOY. Yes, madam.

OLIVIA. But are you sure neither saw you deliver the other a letter?

BOY. Yes, yes, madam, I am very sure.

OLIVIA. Go then to the Old Exchange, to Westminster, Holborn and all the other places I told you of; I

---

88 *drawing-room*: at the palace at Whitehall.

121–2 *Old Exchange . . . Holborn*: widely spread all over London.

shall not need you these two hours. Be gone and take the candle with you and be sure you leave word again below, I am gone out to all that ask.

BOY. Yes, madam. *Exit.*

OLIVIA. And my new lover will not ask I'm sure. He has his lesson and cannot miss me here, though in the dark, which I have purposely designed as a remedy against my blushing gallant's modesty, for young lovers like gamecocks are made bolder by being kept without light.

Enter her husband VERNISH *as from a journey.*

VERNISH. (*softly*) Where is she? Darkness everywhere!

OLIVIA. What, come before your time? My soul! My life! Your haste has augmented your kindness and let me thank you for it thus and thus – (*Embracing and kissing him*) And though, my soul, the little time since you left me has seemed an age to my impatience, sure it is yet but seven –

VERNISH. How! Who's that you expected after seven?

OLIVIA. [*aside*] Ha! My husband returned! And have I been throwing away so many kind kisses on my husband and wronged my lover already?

VERNISH. Speak, I say, who was't you expected after seven?

OLIVIA. (*aside*) What shall I say? – O – Why, 'tis but seven days, is it, dearest, since you went out of town? And I expected you not so soon.

VERNISH. No, sure, 'tis but five days since I left you.

OLIVIA. Pardon my impatience, dearest, I thought 'em seven at least.

VERNISH. Nay then –

OLIVIA. But, my life, you shall never stay half so long from me again, you shan't, indeed, by this kiss, you shan't.

VERNISH. No, no, but why alone in the dark?

OLIVIA. Blame not my melancholy in your absence – But, my soul, since you went, I have strange news to tell you: Manly is returned.

VERNISH. Manly returned! Fortune forbid.

OLIVIA. Met with the Dutch in the Channel, fought, sunk his ship and all he carried with him. He was here with me yesterday.

VERNISH. And did you own our marriage to him?

OLIVIA. I told him I was married, to put an end to his love and my trouble, but to whom is yet a secret kept from him and all the world. And I have used him so scurvily his great spirit will ne'er return to reason it farther with me. I have sent him to sea again, I warrant.

VERNISH. 'Twas bravely done. And sure he will now hate the shore more than ever after so great a disappointment. Be you sure only to keep awhile our great secret till he be gone. In the meantime I'll lead the easy, honest fool by the nose as I used to do and, whilst he stays, rail with him at thee and, when he's gone, laugh with thee at him. But have you his cabinet of jewels safe? Part not with a seed pearl to him to keep him from starving.

OLIVIA. Nor from hanging.

VERNISH. He cannot recover 'em and, I think, will scorn to beg 'em again.

OLIVIA. But, my life, have you taken the thousand guineas he left in my name out of the goldsmith's hands?

VERNISH. Ay, ay, they are removed to another goldsmith's.

OLIVIA. Ay but, my soul, you had best have a care he find not where the money is, for his present wants, as I'm informed, are such as will make him inquisitive enough.

VERNISH. You say true and he knows the man too, but I'll remove it tomorrow.

OLIVIA. Tomorrow! O do not stay till tomorrow. Go tonight, immediately.

VERNISH. Now I think on't, you advise well and I will go presently.

OLIVIA. Presently! Instantly! I will not let you stay a jot.

VERNISH. I will then, though I return not home till twelve.

OLIVIA. Nay, though not till morning with all my heart. Go, dearest, I am impatient till you are gone –

Thrusts him out.

So, I have at once now brought about those two grateful businesses which all prudent women do together, secured money and pleasure, and now all interruptions of the last are removed. Go husband

and come up friend, just the buckets in the well: the absence of one brings the other but I hope, like them too, they will not meet in the way, justle and clash together.

Enter FIDELIA, *and* MANLY *treading softly and staying behind at some distance.*

So, are you come? (But not the husband-bucket, I hope, again.) Who's there? My dearest? (*Softly*)

FIDELIA. My life –

OLIVIA. Right, right. Where are thy lips? Here, take the dumb and best welcomes, kisses and embraces; 'tis not a time for idle words. In a duel of love, as in others, parleying shows basely. Come, we are alone, and now the word is only satisfaction and defend not thyself.

MANLY. (*aside*) How's this? Wuh, she makes love like a devil in a play and, in this darkness, which conceals her angel's face, if I were apt to be afraid I should think her a devil.

OLIVIA. What, you traverse ground, young gentleman.

FIDELIA *avoiding her.*

FIDELIA. I take breath only.

MANLY. (*aside*) Good heavens! How was I deceived!

OLIVIA. Nay, you are a coward. What, are you afraid of the fierceness of my love?

FIDELIA. Yes, madam, lest its violence might presage its change and I must needs be afraid you would leave me quickly who could desert so brave a gentleman as Manly.

OLIVIA. O! Name not his name, for in a time of stolen joys, as this is, the filthy name of husband were not a more allaying sound.

MANLY. (*aside*) There's some comfort yet.

FIDELIA. But did you not love him?

OLIVIA. Never. How could you think it?

FIDELIA. Because he thought it, who is a man of that sense, nice discerning and diffidency that I should think it hard to deceive him.

OLIVIA. No, he that distrusts most the world trusts

---

225 *traverse ground*: move from side to side (fencing term).

most to himself and is but the more easily deceived because he thinks he can't be deceived. His cunning is like the coward's sword by which he is oftener worsted than defended.

FIDELIA. Yet, sure, you used no common art to deceive him.

OLIVIA. I knew he loved his own singular moroseness so well as to dote upon any copy of it; wherefore I feigned an hatred to the world too that he might love me in earnest. But if it had been hard to deceive him I'm sure 'twere much harder to love him. A dogged, ill-mannered –

FIDELIA. (*aside to* MANLY) D'ye hear her, sir? Pray hear her.

OLIVIA. Surly, untractable, snarling brute! He! A masty dog were as fit a thing to make a gallant of.

MANLY. (*aside*) Ay, a goat or monkey were fitter for thee.

FIDELIA. I must confess for my part, though my rival, I cannot but say he has a manly handsomeness in's face and mien.

OLIVIA. So has a Saracen in the sign.

FIDELIA. Is proper and well made.

OLIVIA. As a drayman.

FIDELIA. Has wit.

OLIVIA. He rails at all mankind.

FIDELIA. And undoubted courage.

OLIVIA. Like the hangman's, can murder a man when his hands are tied. He has cruelty indeed, which is no more courage than his railing is wit.

MANLY. (*aside*) Thus women, and men like women, are too hard for us when they think we do not hear 'em and reputation, like other mistresses, is never true to a man in his absence.

FIDELIA. He is –

OLIVIA. Prithee no more of him. I thought I had satisfied you enough before that he could never be a rival for you to apprehend; and you need not be more assured of my aversion to him but by the last testi-

---

258 *masty*: mastiff.

265 *Saracen in the sign*: the large and ugly face of a Saracen used on street signs.

mony of my love to you which I am ready to give you. Come, my soul, this way – (*Pulls* FIDELIA)

FIDELIA. But, madam, what could make you dissemble love to him, when 'twas so hard a thing for you, and flatter his love to you?

OLIVIA. That which makes all the world flatter and dissemble; 'twas his money – I had a real passion for that. Yet I loved not that so well as for it to take him, for as soon as I had his money I hastened his departure like a wife who, when she has made the most of a dying husband's breath, pulls away the pillow.

MANLY. [*aside*] Damned money! Its master's potent rival still and like a saucy pimp corrupts itself the mistress it procures for us.

OLIVIA. But I did not think with you, my life, to pass my time in talking. Come hither, come. Yet stay till I have locked a door in the other room that might chance to let us in some interruption, which reciting poets or losing gamesters fear not more than I at this time do. *Exit* OLIVIA.

FIDELIA. Well, I hope you are now satisfied, sir, and will be gone to think of your revenge.

MANLY. No, I am not satisfied and must stay to be revenged.

FIDELIA. How, sir? You'll use no violence to her, I hope, and forfeit your own life to take away hers? That were no revenge.

MANLY. No, no, you need not fear; my revenge shall only be upon her honour, not her life.

FIDELIA. How, sir? Her honour? O heavens! Consider, sir, she has no honour. D'ye call that revenge? Can you think of such a thing? But reflect, sir, how she hates and loathes you.

MANLY. Yes, so much she hates me that it would be a revenge sufficient to make her accessory to my pleasure and then let her know it.

FIDELIA. No, sir, no, to be revenged on her now were to disappoint her. Pray, sir, let us be gone. (*Pulls* MANLY)

MANLY. Hold off. What, you are my rival then and therefore you shall stay and keep the door for me whilst I go in for you. But when I'm gone, if you dare to stir off from this very board or breathe the least murmuring accent, I'll cut her throat first and if you love her you will not venture her life; nay, then I'll cut your throat too and I know you love your own life at least.

FIDELIA. But, sir, good sir.

MANLY. Not a word more, lest I begin my revenge on her by killing you.

FIDELIA. But are you sure 'tis revenge that makes you do this? How can it be?

MANLY. Whist.

FIDELIA. 'Tis a strange revenge indeed.

MANLY. If you make me stay, I shall keep my word and begin with you. No more.

Exit MANLY *at the same door* OLIVIA *went.* *Manet* FIDELIA.

FIDELIA. O heavens! Is there not punishment enough
In loving well, if you will have't a crime,
But you must add fresh torments daily to't
And punish us like peevish rivals still,
Because we fain would find a heaven here?
But did there never any love like me,
That, untried tortures, you must find me out?
Others, at worst, you force to kill themselves,
But I must be self-murderess of my love,
Yet will not grant me power to end my life,
My cruel life, for, when a lover's hopes
Are dead and gone, life is unmerciful. (*Sits down and weeps*)

Enter MANLY *to her.*

MANLY. I have thought better on't; I must not discover myself now; I am without witnesses, for if I barely should publish it, she would deny it with as much impudence as she would act it again with this young fellow here. Where are you?

FIDELIA. Here – oh – now I suppose we may be gone.

MANLY. I will, but not you; you must stay and act the second part of a lover, that is, talk kindness to her.

FIDELIA. Not I, sir.

MANLY. No disputing, sir, you must; 'tis necessary to my design of coming again tomorrow night.

---

341 *peevish*: spiteful.

FIDELIA. What, can you come again then hither?

MANLY. Yes, and you must make the appointment and an apology for your leaving her so soon, for I have said not a word to her but have kept your counsel, as I expect you should do mine. Do this faithfully and I promise you here you shall run my fortune still and we will never part as long as we live, but if you do not do it expect not to live.

FIDELIA. 'Tis hard, sir, but such a consideration will make it easier. You won't forget your promise, sir?

MANLY. No, by heavens. But I hear her coming. *Exit.*

Enter OLIVIA *to* FIDELIA.

OLIVIA. Where is my life? Run from me already! You do not love me, dearest; nay, you are angry with me, for you would not so much as speak a kind word to me within. What was the reason?

FIDELIA. I was transported too much.

OLIVIA. That's kind; but come, my soul, what make you here? Let us go in again. We may be surprised in this room, 'tis so near the stairs.

FIDELIA. No, we shall hear the better here if anybody should come up.

OLIVIA. Nay, I assure you, we shall be secure enough within. Come, come –

FIDELIA. I am sick and, troubled with a sudden dizziness, cannot stir yet.

OLIVIA. Come, I have spirits within.

FIDELIA. Oh! – don't you hear a noise madam?

OLIVIA. No, no, there is none. Come, come. (*Pulls her*)

FIDELIA. Indeed there is, and I love you so much I must have a care of your honour, if you won't, and go, but to come to you tomorrow night if you please.

OLIVIA. With all my soul, but you must not go yet. Come, prithee.

FIDELIA. Oh! – I am now sicker and am afraid of one of my fits.

OLIVIA. My fits?

FIDELIA. Of the falling sickness, and I lie generally an hour in a trance; therefore pray consider your honour

---

397 *falling sickness*: epilepsy.

for the sake of my love and let me go that I may return to you often.

OLIVIA. But you will be sure then to come tomorrow night?

FIDELIA. Yes.

OLIVIA. Swear.

FIDELIA. By our past kindness.

OLIVIA. Well, go your ways then, if you will, you naughty creature you.

Exit FIDELIA.

These young lovers with their fears and modesty make themselves as bad as old ones to us and I apprehend their bashfulness more than their tattling.

FIDELIA *returns.*

FIDELIA. O, madam, we're undone! There was a gentleman upon the stairs, coming up, with a candle, which made me retire. Look you, here he comes!

Enter VERNISH *and his man with a light.*

OLIVIA. How! My husband! Oh, undone indeed! This way. *Exit.*

VERNISH. Ha! You shall not scape me so, sir. (*Stops* FIDELIA)

FIDELIA. (*aside*) O heavens! More fears, plagues and torments yet in store!

VERNISH. Come, sir, I guess what your business was here, but this must be your business now. Draw. (*Draws*)

FIDELIA. Sir –

VERNISH. No expostulations. I shall not care to hear of't. Draw.

FIDELIA. Good sir. –

VERNISH. How, you rascal! Not courage to draw yet durst do me the greatest injury in the world? Thy cowardice shall not save thy life. (*Offers to run at* FIDELIA)

FIDELIA. O hold, sir, and send but your servant down and I'll satisfy you, sir, I could not injure you as you imagine.

---

410 *tattling*: telling the secret.

VERNISH. Leave the light and be gone.

Exit SERVANT.

Now quickly, sir, what you've to say, or –

FIDELIA. I am a woman, sir, a very unfortunate woman.

VERNISH. How! A very handsome woman, I'm sure, then. Here are witnesses of't too, I confess – (*Pulls off her peruke and feels her breasts. Aside*) Well, I'm glad to find the tables turned, my wife in more danger of cuckolding than I was.

FIDELIA. Now, sir, I hope you are so much a man of honour as to let me go now I have satisfied you, sir.

VERNISH. When you have satisfied me, madam, I will.

FIDELIA. I hope, sir, you are too much a gentleman to urge those secrets from a woman which concern her honour. You may guess my misfortune to be love by my disguise; but a pair of breeches could not wrong you, sir.

VERNISH. I may believe love has changed your outside, which could not wrong me, but why did my wife run away?

FIDELIA. I know not, sir. Perhaps because she would not be forced to discover me to you or to guide me from your suspicions that you might not discover me yourself, which ungentlemanlike curiosity I hope you will cease to have and let me go.

VERNISH. Well, madam, if I must not know who you are, 'twill suffice for me only to know certainly what you are, which you must not deny me. Come, there is a bed within, the proper rack for lovers, and if you are a woman, there you can keep no secrets; you'll tell me there all unasked. Come. (*Pulls her*)

FIDELIA. Oh! What d'ye mean? Help, oh –

VERNISH. I'll show you, but 'tis in vain to cry out. No one dares help you, for I am lord here.

FIDELIA. Tyrant here. But if you are master of this house, which I have taken for a sanctuary, do not violate it yourself.

VERNISH. No, I'll preserve you here and nothing shall hurt you and will be as true to you as your disguise, but you must trust me then. Come, come.

FIDELIA. Oh, oh! Rather than you shall drag me to a death so horrid and so shameful I'll die here a thousand deaths; but you do not look like a ravisher, sir.

VERNISH. Nor you like one would put me to't but if you will –

FIDELIA. Oh! Oh! Help, help –

Enter SERVANT.

VERNISH. You saucy rascal, how durst you come in when you heard a woman squeak? That should have been your cue to shut the door.

SERVANT. I come, sir, to let you know the alderman, coming home immediately after you were at his house, has sent his cashier with the money, according to your note.

VERNISH. Damn his money! Money never came to any, sure, unseasonably till now. Bid him stay.

SERVANT. He says he cannot a moment.

VERNISH. Receive it you then.

SERVANT. He says he must have your receipt for it. He is in haste, for I hear him coming up, sir.

VERNISH. Damn him. Help me in here then with this dishonourer of my family.

FIDELIA. Oh! Oh!

SERVANT. You say she is a woman, sir.

VERNISH. No matter, sir. Must you prate?

FIDELIA. O heavens! Is there –

They thrust her in and lock the door.

VERNISH. Stay there, my prisoner. You have a short reprieve.

I'll fetch the gold and that she can't resist,
For with a full hand 'tis we ravish best.

Exeunt.

ACT V

SCENE I

Eliza's lodging.

Enter OLIVIA *and* ELIZA.

OLIVIA. Ah, cousin, nothing troubles me but that I have

given the malicious world its revenge and reason now to talk as freely of me as I used to do of it.

ELIZA. Faith, then, let not that trouble you, for, to be plain, cousin, the world cannot talk worse of you than it did before.

OLIVIA. How, cousin? I'd have you to know, before this faux pas, this trip of mine, the world could not talk of me.

ELIZA. Only that you mind other people's actions so much that you take no care of your own but to hide 'em, that, like a thief, because you know yourself most guilty you impeach your fellow criminals first to clear yourself.

OLIVIA. O wicked world!

ELIZA. That you pretend an aversion to all mankind in public only that their wives and mistresses may not be jealous and hinder you of their conversation in private.

OLIVIA. Base world!

ELIZA. That abroad you fasten quarrels upon innocent men for talking of you, only to bring 'em to ask you pardon at home and to become dear friends with 'em who were hardly your acquaintance before.

OLIVIA. Abominable world!

ELIZA. That you condemn the obscenity of modern plays only that you may not be censured for never missing the most obscene of the old ones.

OLIVIA. Damned world!

ELIZA. That you deface the nudities of pictures and little statues only because they are not real.

OLIVIA. O fie, fie, fie. Hideous, hideous, cousin! The obscenity of their censures makes me blush.

ELIZA. The truth of 'em, the naughty world would say now.

Enter LETTICE *hastily*.

LETTICE. O! Madam, here is that gentleman coming up who now you say is my master.

OLIVIA. O! Cousin, whither shall I run? Protect me, or – (OLIVIA *runs away and stands at a distance*)

Enter VERNISH.

VERNISH. Nay, nay, come –

OLIVIA. O, sir, forgive me.

VERNISH. Yes, yes, I can forgive you being alone in the dark with a woman in man's clothes, but have a care of a man in woman's clothes.

OLIVIA. (*aside*) What does he mean? He dissembles only to get me into his power. Or has my dear friend made him believe he was a woman? My husband may be deceived by him but I'm sure I was not.

VERNISH. Come, come, you need not have lain out of your house for this, but perhaps you were afraid, when I was warm with suspicions, you must have discovered who she was; and prithee may I not know it?

OLIVIA. She was – (*Aside*) I hope he has been deceived, and since my lover has played the card I must not renounce.

VERNISH. Come, what's the matter with thee? If I must not know who she is, I'm satisfied without. Come hither.

OLIVIA. Sure you do know her. She has told you herself, I suppose.

VERNISH. No, I might have known her better but that I was interrupted by the goldsmith, you know, and was forced to lock her into your chamber to keep her from his sight but when I returned I found she was got away by tying the window-curtains to the balcony, by which she slid down into the street, for, you must know, I jested with her and made her believe I'd ravish her, which she apprehended, it seems, in earnest.

OLIVIA. Then she got from you?

VERNISH. Yes.

OLIVIA. And is quite gone?

VERNISH. Yes.

OLIVIA. I'm glad on't – otherwise you had ravished her, sir? But how dar'st you go so far as to make her believe you would ravish her? Let me understand that, sir. What! There's guilt in your face; you blush too – nay, then you did ravish her, you did, you base fellow. What, ravish a woman in the first month of our

50 *discovered*: revealed.

54 *renounce*: fail to follow suit though an appropriate card is held, revoke.

marriage! 'Tis a double injury to me, thou base ungrateful man. Wrong my bed already, villain! I could tear out those false eyes, barbarous, unworthy wretch.

ELIZA. So, so! –

VERNISH. Prithee hear, my dear.

OLIVIA. I will never hear you, my plague, my torment.

VERNISH. I swear – prithee hear me.

OLIVIA. I have heard already too many of your false oaths and vows, especially your last in the church. O wicked man! And wretched woman that I was! I wish I had then sunk down into a grave rather than to have given you my hand to be led to your loathsome bed. Oh – oh – (*Seems to weep*)

VERNISH. So, very fine! Just a marriage quarrel! Which, though it generally begins by the wife's fault, yet in the conclusion it becomes the husband's and, whosoever offends at first, he only is sure to ask pardon at last. My dear –

OLIVIA. My devil –

VERNISH. Come, prithee be appeased and go home. I have bespoken our supper betimes, for I could not eat till I found you. Go, I'll give you all kind of satisfactions and one which uses to be a reconciling one, two hundred of those guineas I received last night, to do what you will with.

OLIVIA. What, would you pay me for being your bawd?

VERNISH. Nay, prithee no more. Go, and I'll thoroughly satisfy you when I come home, and then too we will have a fit of laughter at Manly, whom I am going to find at the Cock in Bow Street, where, I hear, he dined. Go, dearest, go home.

ELIZA. (*aside*) A very pretty turn indeed, this!

VERNISH. Now, cousin, since by my wife I have that honour and privilege of calling you so, I have something to beg of you too, which is not to take notice of our marriage, to any whatever, yet awhile for some reasons very important to me; and next, that you will do my wife the honour to go home with her

---

108 *Cock . . . Street*: a famous tavern where events like those of the next scene were not unexpected.

and me the favour to use that power you have with her in our reconcilement.

ELIZA. That, I dare promise, sir, will be no hard matter. Your servant.

Exit VERNISH.

Well, cousin, this I confess was reasonable hypocrisy. You were the better for't.

OLIVIA. What hypocrisy?

ELIZA. Why, this last deceit of your husband was lawful since in your own defence.

OLIVIA. What deceit? I'd have you to know I never deceived my husband.

ELIZA. You do not understand me, sure. I say, this was an honest come-off and a good one. But 'twas a sign your gallant had had enough of your conversation since he could so dextrously cheat your husband in passing for a woman!

OLIVIA. What d'ye mean, once more, with 'my gallant' and 'passing for a woman'?

ELIZA. What do you mean? You see your husband took him for a woman.

OLIVIA. Whom?

ELIZA. Hey-day! Why, the man he found you with, for whom last night you were so much afraid and who you told me –

OLIVIA. Lord, you rave sure!

ELIZA. Why, did not you tell me last night –

OLIVIA. I know not what I might tell you last night, in a fright.

ELIZA. Ay, what was that fright for? For a woman? Besides, were you not afraid to see your husband just now? I warrant, only for having been found with a woman! Nay, did you not just now too own your false step, or trip, as you called it? Which was with a woman too! Fie, this fooling is so insipid, 'tis offensive.

OLIVIA. And fooling with my honour will be more offensive. Did you not hear my husband say he found me with a woman in man's clothes? And d'ye think he does not know a man from a woman?

ELIZA. Not so well, I'm sure, as you do; therefore I'd rather take your word.

OLIVIA. What, you grow scurrilous and are, I find, more censorious than the world! I must have a care of you, I see.

ELIZA. No, you need not fear yet; I'll keep your secret.

OLIVIA. My secret! I'd have you to know I have no need of confidants, though you value yourself upon being a good one.

ELIZA. O admirable confidence! You show more in denying your wickedness than other people in glorying in't.

OLIVIA. Confidence, to me! To me such language! Nay, then I'll never see your face again. (*Aside*) I'll quarrel with her that people may never believe I was in her power but take for malice all the truth she may speak against me. – Lettice, where are you? Let us be gone from this censorious, ill woman.

ELIZA. (*aside*) Nay, thou shalt stay a little to damn thyself quite. – One word first, pray, madam. Can you swear that whom your husband found you with –

OLIVIA. Swear! Ay, that whosoever 'twas that stole up, unknown, into my room when 'twas dark, I know not whether man or woman, by heavens, by all that's good or may I never more have joys here or in the other world; nay, may I eternally –

ELIZA. Be damned. So, so, you are damned enough already by your oaths, and I enough confirmed, and now you may please to be gone. Yet take this advice with you, in this plain-dealing age, to leave off forswearing yourself; for, when people hardly think the better of a woman for her real modesty, why should you put that great constraint upon yourself to feign it?

OLIVIA. O hideous! Hideous advice! Let us go out of the hearing of it. She will spoil us, Lettice.

Exeunt OLIVIA *and* LETTICE *at one door,* ELIZA *at t'other.*

SCENE II

The scene changes to the Cock in Bow Street. A table and bottles.

MANLY *and* FIDELIA.

MANLY. How! Saved her honour by making her husband believe you were a woman! 'Twas well, but hard enough to do sure.

FIDELIA. We were interrupted before he could contradict me.

MANLY. But can't you tell me, d'ye say, what kind of man he was?

FIDELIA. I was so frightened, I confess, I can give no other account of him but that he was pretty tall, round-faced and one I'm sure I ne'er had seen before.

MANLY. But she, you say, made you swear to return tonight?

FIDELIA. But I have since sworn never to go near her again, for the husband would murder me, or worse, if he caught me again.

MANLY. No, I'll go with you and defend you tonight and then I'll swear too never to go near her again.

FIDELIA. Nay, indeed sir, I will not go to be accessory to your death too. Besides, what should you go again, sir, for?

MANLY. No disputing or advice, sir. You have reason to know I am unalterable. Go therefore presently and write her a note to inquire if her assignation with you holds and, if not to be at her own house, where else. And be importunate to gain admittance to her tonight. Let your messenger, ere he deliver your letter, inquire first if her husband be gone out. Go, 'tis now almost six of the clock. I expect you back here before seven with leave to see her again. Go, do this dextrously and expect the performance of my last night's promise, never to part with you.

FIDELIA. Ay, sir, but will you be sure to remember that?

MANLY. Did I ever break my word? Go, no more replies or doubts.

Exit FIDELIA.

Enter FREEMAN *to* MANLY.

Where hast thou been?

FREEMAN. In the next room with my Lord Plausible and Novel.

MANLY. Ay, we came hither because 'twas a private house, but with thee indeed no house can be private, for thou hast that pretty quality of the familiar fops of the town who in an eating-house always keep company with all people in't but those they came with.

FREEMAN. I went into their room but to keep them and my own fool the squire out of your room; but you shall be peevish now because you have no money. But why the devil won't you write to those we were speaking of? Since your modesty or your spirit will not suffer you to speak to 'em to lend you money, why won't you try 'em at last that way?

MANLY. Because I know 'em already and can bear want better than denials, nay, than obligations.

FREEMAN. Deny you! They cannot. All of 'em have been your intimate friends.

MANLY. No, they have been people only I have obliged particularly.

FREEMAN. Very well, therefore you ought to go to 'em the rather, sure.

MANLY. No, no. Those you have obliged most, most certainly avoid you when you can oblige 'em no longer and they take your visits like so many duns. Friends, like mistresses, are avoided for obligations past.

FREEMAN. Pshaw! But most of 'em are your relations, men of great fortune and honour.

MANLY. Yes, but relations have so much honour as to think poverty taints the blood and disown their wanting kindred, believing, I suppose, that, as riches at first makes a gentleman, the want of 'em degrades him. But, damn 'em, now I'm poor I'll anticipate their contempt and disown them.

FREEMAN. But you have many a female acquaintance whom you have been liberal to who may have a heart to refund to you a little if you would ask it. They are not all Olivias.

MANLY. Damn thee! How couldst thou think of such a thing? I would as soon rob my footman of his wages. Besides, 'twere in vain too, for a wench is like a box in an ordinary, receives all people's money easily but there's no getting, nay, shaking any out again and he that fills it is sure never to keep the key.

78–9 *box in an ordinary*: the box which receives the house share in gambling; ordinaries were often gambling houses as well as eating-houses.

FREEMAN. Well, but noble captain, would you make me believe that you who know half the town, have so many friends and have obliged so many can't borrow fifty or an hundred pound?

MANLY. Why, noble lieutenant, you who know all the town and call all you know friends methinks should not wonder at it, since you find ingratitude too; for how many lords' families (though descended from blacksmiths or tinkers) hast thou called great and illustrious? How many ill tables called good eating? How many noisy coxcombs wits? How many pert, cocking cowards stout? How many tawdry, affected rogues well-dressed? How many perukes admired? And how many ill verses applauded? And yet canst not borrow a shilling. Dost thou expect I, who always spoke truth, should?

FREEMAN. Nay, now you think you have paid me; but hark you, captain, I have heard of a thing called grinning honour but never of starving honour.

MANLY. Well, but it has been the fate of some brave men; and if they won't give me a ship again I can go starve anywhere with a musket on my shoulder.

FREEMAN. Give you a ship! Why, you will not solicit it?

MANLY. If I have not solicited it by my services, I know no other way.

FREEMAN. Your servant, sir. Nay, then I'm satisfied I must solicit my widow the closer and run the desperate fortune of matrimony on shore. *Exit.*

Enter, to MANLY, VERNISH.

MANLY. How! – Nay, here is a friend indeed, and he that has him in his arms can know no wants. (*Embraces* VERNISH)

VERNISH. Dear sir! And he that is in your arms is secure from all fears whatever. Nay, our nation is secure by your defeat at sea and the Dutch that fought against you have proved enemies to themselves only, in bringing you back to us.

MANLY. Fie, fie! This from a friend? And yet from any

---

91 *called good*: call good Q1.
93 *cocking*: coaching Q1 (some copies only).

other 'twere unsufferable. I thought I should never have taken anything ill from you.

VERNISH. A friend's privilege is to speak his mind though it be taken ill.

MANLY. But your tongue need not tell me you think too well of me. I have found it from your heart, which spoke in actions, your unalterable heart. But Olivia is false, my friend, which I suppose is no news to you.

VERNISH. (*aside*) He's in the right on't.

MANLY. But couldst thou not keep her true to me?

VERNISH. Not for my heart, sir.

MANLY. But could you not perceive it at all before I went? Could she so deceive us both?

VERNISH. I must confess, the first time I knew it was three days after your departure when she received the money you had left in Lombard Street in her name, and her tears did not hinder her it seems from counting that. You would trust her with all, like a true, generous lover!

MANLY. And she, like a mean jilting –

VERNISH. Traitorous –

MANLY. Base –

VERNISH. Damned –

MANLY. Covetous –

VERNISH. Mercenary whore – (*Aside*) I can hardly hold from laughing.

MANLY. Ay, a mercenary whore indeed, for she made me pay her before I lay with her.

VERNISH. How! – Why, have you lain with her?

MANLY. Ay, ay.

VERNISH. Nay, she deserves you should report it at least, though you have not.

MANLY. Report it! By heaven, 'tis true.

VERNISH. How! Sure not.

MANLY. I do not use to lie, nor you to doubt me.

VERNISH. When?

MANLY. Last night about seven or eight of the clock.

VERNISH. (*aside*) Ha! – Now I remember, I thought

---

134 *Lombard Street*: street in the city known for its bankers and goldsmiths.

she spake as if she expected some other rather than me. A confounded whore indeed!

MANLY. But, what, thou wonderest at it! Nay, you seem to be angry too.

VERNISH. I cannot but be enraged against her for her usage of you, damned, infamous, common jade.

MANLY. Nay, her cuckold, who first cuckolded me in my money, shall not laugh all himself. We will do him reason, shan't we?

VERNISH. Ay, ay.

MANLY. But thou dost not, for so great a friend, take pleasure enough in your friend's revenge, methinks.

VERNISH. Yes, yes, I'm glad to know it since you have lain with her.

MANLY. Thou canst not tell me who that rascal, her cuckold, is?

VERNISH. No.

MANLY. She would keep it from you, I suppose.

VERNISH. Yes, yes –

MANLY. Thou wouldst laugh if thou knewest but all the circumstances of my having her. Come, I'll tell thee.

VERNISH. Damn her. I care not to hear any more of her.

MANLY. Faith, thou shalt. You must know –

Enter FREEMAN, *backwards, endeavouring to keep out* NOVEL, LORD PLAUSIBLE, JERRY *and* OLDFOX, *who all press in upon him.*

FREEMAN. I tell you he has a wench with him and would be private.

MANLY. Damn 'em! A man can't open a bottle in these eating-houses but presently you have these impudent, intruding, buzzing flies and insects in your glass. – Well, I'll tell thee all anon. In the meantime, prithee go to her, but not from me, and try if you can get her to lend me but an hundred pound of my money to supply my present wants, for I suppose there is no recovering any of it by law.

VERNISH. Not any. Think not of it, nor by this way neither.

MANLY. Go, try, at least.

VERNISH. I'll go, but I can satisfy you beforehand, 'twill be to no purpose. You'll no more find a refunding wench –

MANLY. Than a refunding lawyer; indeed their fees alike scarce ever return. However, try her, put it to her.

VERNISH. Ay, ay, I'll try her, put it to her home, with a vengeance. *Exit* VERNISH.

Manent caeteri.

NOVEL. Nay, you shall be our judge, Manly. Come, major, I'll speak it to your teeth. If people provoke me to say bitter things to their faces, they must take what follows, though, like my Lord Plausible, I'd rather do't civilly behind their backs.

MANLY. Nay, thou art a dangerous rogue, I've heard, behind a man's back.

LORD PLAUSIBLE. You wrong him sure, noble captain. He would do a man no more harm behind his back than to his face.

FREEMAN. I am of my lord's mind.

MANLY. Yes, a fool, like a coward, is the more to be feared behind a man's back, more than a witty man, for as a coward is more bloody than a brave man a fool is more malicious than a man of wit.

NOVEL. A fool, tar – a fool! Nay, thou art a brave sea-judge of wit! A fool! Prithee, when did you ever find me want something to say, as you do often?

MANLY. Nay, I confess, thou art always talking, roaring or making a noise; that I'll say for thee.

NOVEL. Well, and is talking a sign of a fool?

MANLY. Yes, always talking, especially too if it be loud and fast, is the sign of a fool.

NOVEL. Pshaw! Talking is like fencing, the quicker the better; run 'em down, run 'em down, no matter for parrying, push on still, sa, sa, sa. No matter whether you argue in form, push in guard or no.

MANLY. Or hit or no. I think thou always talkest without thinking, Novel.

NOVEL. Ay, ay, studied play's the worse, to follow the allegory, as the old pedant says.

OLDFOX. A young fop!

MANLY. I ever thought the man of most wit had been like him of most money, who has no vanity in show-

---

199 s.d. *manent caeteri*: the others remain.
225 *sa, sa, sa*: fencing cry when delivering a thrust (Fr. *ça*).
226 *push in guard*: thrust inside the defence.

ing it everywhere, whilst the beggarly pusher of his fortune has all he has about him still, only to show.

NOVEL. Well, sir, and makes a very pretty show in the world, let me tell you, nay, a better than your close hunks. A pox, give me ready money in play. What care I for a man's reputation? What are we the better for your substantial, thrifty curmudgeon in wit, sir?

OLDFOX. Thou art a profuse young rogue indeed.

NOVEL. So much for talking, which I think I have proved a mark of wit, and so is railing, roaring and making a noise, for railing is satire, you know, and roaring and making a noise, humour.

Enter to them FIDELIA, *taking* MANLY *aside and showing him a paper.*

FIDELIA. The hour is betwixt seven and eight exactly. 'Tis now half an hour after six.

MANLY. Well, go then to the Piazza and wait for me; as soon as it is quite dark I'll be with you. I must stay here yet awhile for my friend. But is railing satire, Novel?

Exit FIDELIA.

FREEMAN. And roaring and making a noise humour?

NOVEL. What, won't you confess there's humour in roaring and making a noise?

FREEMAN. No.

NOVEL. Nor in cutting napkins and hangings?

MANLY. No, sure.

NOVEL. Dull fops!

OLDFOX. O rogue, rogue, insipid rogue! Nay, gentlemen, allow him those things for wit, for his parts lie only that way.

NOVEL. Peace, old fool, I wonder not at thee, but that young fellows should be so dull as to say there's no humour in making a noise and breaking windows! I tell you, there's wit and humour too in both. And a wit is as well known by his frolic as by his simile.

OLDFOX. Pure rogue! There's your modern wit for you!

---

238 *hunks*: miser.

248 *Piazza*: arcade on two sides of Covent Garden, scene of Act V Scene iii of *The Country Wife*.

Wit and humour in breaking of windows! There's mischief if you will but no wit or humour.

NOVEL. Prithee, prithee peace, old fool. I tell you, where there is mischief there's wit. Don't we esteem the monkey a wit amongst beasts only because he's mischievous? And let me tell you, as good nature is a sign of a fool, being mischievous is a sign of wit.

OLDFOX. O rogue, rogue! Pretend to be a wit by doing mischief and railing!

NOVEL. Why, thou, old fool, hast no other pretence to the name of a wit but by railing at new plays.

OLDFOX. Thou by railing at that facetious, noble way of wit, quibbling.

NOVEL. Thou call'st thy dullness, gravity and thy dozing, thinking.

OLDFOX. You, sir, your dullness, spleen. And you talk much and say nothing.

NOVEL. Thou readest much and understand'st nothing, sir.

OLDFOX. You laugh loud and break no jest.

NOVEL. You rail and nobody hangs himself. And thou hast nothing of the satyr but in thy face.

OLDFOX. And you have no jest but your face, sir.

NOVEL. Thou art an illiterate pedant.

OLDFOX. Thou art a fool with a bad memory.

MANLY. Come, a pox on you both. You have done like wits now, for you wits, when you quarrel, never give over till you prove one another fools.

NOVEL. And you fools have never any occasion of laughing at us wits but when we quarrel; therefore let us be friends, Oldfox.

MANLY. They are such wits as thou art who make the name of a wit as scandalous as that of a bully and signify a loud-laughing, talking, incorrigible coxcomb, as bully a roaring, hardened coward.

FREEMAN. And would have his noise and laughter pass for wit, as t'other his huffing and blustering for courage.

Enter VERNISH.

---

289 *satyr*: (*a*) satire (*b*) the half-man, half-goat figure of Greek mythology, lustful, drunken companions of Bacchus.

MANLY. Gentlemen, with your leave, here is one I would speak with and I have nothing to say to you.

Pulls 'em out of the room. Manent MANLY, VERNISH.

VERNISH. I told you 'twas in vain to think of getting money out of her. She says, if a shilling would do't, she would not save you from starving or hanging or what you would think worse, begging or flattering, and rails so at you one would not think you had lain with her.

MANLY. O friend, never trust for that matter a woman's railing, for she is no less a dissembler in her hatred than her love. And as her fondness of her husband is a sign he's a cuckold, her railing at another man is a sign she lies with him.

VERNISH. (*aside*) He's in the right on't. I know not what to trust to.

MANLY. But you did not take any notice of it to her, I hope?

VERNISH. (*aside*) So! Sure he is afraid I should have disproved him, by an inquiry of her. All may be well yet.

MANLY. What hast thou in thy head that makes thee seem so unquiet?

VERNISH. Only this base, impudent woman's falseness; I cannot put her out of my head.

MANLY. O my dear friend, be not you too sensible of my wrongs, for then I shall feel 'em too, with more pain, and think 'em unsufferable. Damn her, her money and that ill-natured whore, too, Fortune herself; but if thou wouldst ease a little my present trouble prithee go borrow me somewhere else some money. I can trouble thee.

VERNISH. You trouble me indeed, most sensibly, when you command me anything I cannot do. I have lately lost a great deal of money at play, more than I can yet pay, so that not only my money but my credit too is gone and I know not where to borrow; but could rob a church for you. (*Aside*) Yet would rather end your wants, by cutting your throat.

MANLY. Nay, then I doubly feel my poverty since I'm incapable of supplying thee. (*Embraces* VERNISH)

---

338 *at play*: gambling.

VERNISH. But methinks she that granted you the last favour (as they call it) should not deny you anything.

NOVEL. Hey, tarpaulin, have you done?

NOVEL looks in and retires again.

VERNISH. I understand not that point of kindness, I confess.

MANLY. No, thou dost not understand it and I have not time to let you know all now, for these fools, you see, will interrupt us; but anon, at supper, we'll laugh at leisure together at Olivia's cuckold, who took a young fellow that goes between his wife and me for a woman.

VERNISH. Ha!

MANLY. Senseless, easy rascal! 'Twas no wonder she chose him for a husband, but she thought him, I thank her, fitter than me for that blind, bearing office.

VERNISH. (*aside*) I could not be deceived in that long woman's hair tied up behind nor those infallible proofs, her pouting, swelling breasts; I have handled too many sure not to know 'em.

MANLY. What, you wonder the fellow could be such a blind coxcomb!

VERNISH. Yes, yes –

NOVEL. Nay, prithee come to us, Manly. Gad, all the fine things one says in their company are lost without thee.

NOVEL looks in again and retires.

MANLY. Away, fop, I'm busy yet. – You see we cannot talk here at our ease; besides, I must be gone immediately in order to meeting with Olivia again tonight.

VERNISH. Tonight! It cannot be, sure –

MANLY. I had an appointment just now from her.

VERNISH. For what time?

MANLY. At half an hour after seven precisely.

VERNISH. Don't you apprehend the husband?

MANLY. He! Snivelling gull! He a thing to be feared! A husband, the tamest of creatures!

VERNISH. (*aside*) Very fine!

MANLY. But, prithee, in the meantime go try to get me some money. Though thou art too modest to borrow for thyself, thou canst do anything for me, I know. Go, for I must be gone to Olivia. Go and meet me here anon. – Freeman, where are you? *Exit* MANLY.

Manet VERNISH.

VERNISH. Ay, I'll meet with you, I warrant, but it shall

be at Olivia's. Sure it cannot be. She denies it so calmly and with that honest, modest assurance, it can't be true – and he does not use to lie – but belying a woman when she won't be kind is the only lie a brave man will least scruple. But then the woman in man's clothes, whom he calls a man! Well but by her breasts I know her to be a woman. – But then again his appointment from her to meet with him tonight! I am distracted more with doubt than jealousy. Well, I have no way to disabuse or revenge myself but by going home immediately, putting on a riding suit, and pretending to my wife the same business which carried me out of town last requires me again to go post to Oxford tonight. Then, if the appointment he boasts of be true, it's sure to hold and I shall have an opportunity either of clearing her or revenging myself on both. Perhaps she is his wench of an old date and I am his cully whilst I think him mine and he has seemed to make his wench rich only that I might take her off of his hands; or if he has but lately lain with her, he must needs discover, by her, my treachery to him, which I'm sure he will revenge with my death and which I must prevent with his, if it were only but for fear of his too just reproaches, for, I must confess, I never had till now any excuse but that of interest for doing ill to him. *Exit* VERNISH.

Re-enter MANLY *and* FREEMAN.

MANLY. Come hither, only I say be sure you mistake not the time. You know the house exactly where Olivia lodges; 'tis just hard by.

FREEMAN. Yes, yes.

MANLY. Well then, bring 'em all, I say, thither, and all you know that may be then in the house, for the more witnesses I have of her infamy the greater will be my revenge. And be sure you come straight up to her chamber without more ado. Here, take the watch. You see 'tis above a quarter past seven. Be there in half an hour exactly.

FREEMAN. You need not doubt my diligence or dexterity. I am an old scourer and can naturally beat up a

424 *scourer*: late night roisterer.

wench's quarters that won't be civil. Shan't we break her windows too?

MANLY. No, no. Be punctual only.

Exeunt ambo.

Enter WIDOW BLACKACRE *and two* KNIGHTS OF THE POST; *a* WAITER *with wine.*

WIDOW. Sweetheart, are you sure the door was shut close, that none of those roisters saw us come in?

WAITER. Yes, mistress, and you shall have a privater room above instantly. *Exit* WAITER.

WIDOW. You are safe enough, gentlemen, for I have been private in this house ere now upon other occasions when I was something younger. Come, gentlemen, in short, I leave my business to your care and fidelity and so, here's to you.

FIRST KNIGHT. We were ungrateful rogues if we should not be honest to you, for we have had a great deal of your money.

WIDOW. And you have done me many a good job for't, and so, here's to you again.

SECOND KNIGHT. Why, we have been perjured but six times for you.

FIRST KNIGHT. Forged but four deeds with your husband's last deed of gift.

SECOND KNIGHT. And but three wills.

FIRST KNIGHT. And counterfeited hands and seals to some six bonds. I think that's all, brother.

WIDOW. Ay, that's all, gentlemen, and so, here's to you again.

SECOND KNIGHT. Nay, 'twould do one's heart good to be forsworn for you. You have a conscience in your ways and pay us well.

FIRST KNIGHT. You are in the right on't, brother; one would be damned for her with all one's heart.

SECOND KNIGHT. But there are rogues who make us forsworn for 'em and when we come to be paid they'll be forsworn too and not pay us our wages which they promised with oaths sufficient.

FIRST KNIGHT. Ay, a great lawyer, that shall be nameless, bilked me too.

WIDOW. That was hard, methinks, that a lawyer should use gentlemen witnesses no better.

SECOND KNIGHT. A lawyer! D'ye wonder a lawyer should do't? I was bilked by a reverend divine that preaches twice on Sundays and prays half an hour still before dinner.

WIDOW. How? A conscientious divine and not pay people for damning themselves! Sure then, for all his talking he does not believe damnation. But come, to our business. Pray be sure to imitate exactly the flourish at the end of this name. (*Pulls out a deed or two*)

FIRST KNIGHT. O he's the best in England at untangling a flourish, madam.

WIDOW. And let not the seal be a jot bigger. Observe well the dash too at the end of this name.

SECOND KNIGHT. I warrant you, madam.

WIDOW. Well, these and many other shifts poor widows are put to sometimes, for everybody would be riding a widow, as they say, and breaking into her jointure. They think marrying a widow an easy business, like leaping the hedge where another has gone over before; a widow is a mere gap, a gap with them.

Enter to them MAJOR OLDFOX *with two waiters. The* KNIGHTS OF THE POST *huddle up the writings.*

What, he here! Go then, go, my hearts, you have your instructions.

Exeunt KNIGHTS OF THE POST.

OLDFOX. Come, madam, to be plain with you, I'll be fobbed off no longer. (*Aside*) I'll bind her and gag her but she shall hear me. – Look you, friends, there's the money I promised you and now do you what you promised me. Here are my garters and here's a gag. You shall be acquainted with my parts, lady, you shall.

WIDOW. Acquainted with your parts! A rape, a rape – What, will you ravish me?

The waiters tie her to the chair and gag her and exeunt.

OLDFOX. Yes, lady, I will ravish you, but it shall be through the ear, lady, the ear only, with my well-penned acrostics.

---

496 *acrostics*: a short poem in which the initial letters of the lines spell out a word, often a name.

Enter to them FREEMAN, JERRY BLACKACRE, *three* BAILIFFS, *a constable and his assistants, with the two* KNIGHTS OF THE POST.

What, shall I never read my things undisturbed again?

JERRY. O law! My mother bound hand and foot and gaping as if she rose before her time today!

FREEMAN. What means this, Oldfox? But I'll release you from him. You shall be no man's prisoner but mine. Bailiffs, execute your writ. (FREEMAN *unties her*)

OLDFOX. Nay, then I'll be gone for fear of being bail and paying her debts without being her husband.

Exit OLDFOX.

FIRST BAILIFF. We arrest you, in the King's name at the suit of Mr Freeman, guardian to Jeremiah Blackacre, Esquire, in an action of ten thousand pounds.

WIDOW. How! How! In a choke-bail action! What, and the pen-and-ink gentlemen taken too! Have you confessed, you rogues?

FIRST KNIGHT. We needed not to confess, for the bailiffs dogged us hither to the very door and overheard all that you and we said.

WIDOW. Undone, undone then! No man was ever too hard for me till now. O, Jerry, child, wilt thou vex again the womb that bore thee?

JERRY. Ay, for bearing me before wedlock, as you say. But I'll teach you to call a Blackacre a bastard, though you were never so much my mother.

WIDOW. (*aside*) Well, I'm undone. not one trick left? No law-meush imaginable? – Cruel sir, a word with you I pray.

FREEMAN. In vain, madam, for you have no other way to release yourself but by the bonds of matrimony.

WIDOW. How, sir, how! That were but to sue out an *habeas corpus* for a removal from one prison to another. Matrimony!

---

508 *choke-bail action*: a suit in which bail is not allowed.
521 *law-meush*: legal loophole.
526 *habeas corpus*: a writ requiring an individual under restraint to be brought before a judge in order to establish the legality of the restraint.

FREEMAN. Well, bailiffs, away with her.

WIDOW. O stay, sir, can you be so cruel as to bring me under covert baron again and put it out of my power to sue in my own name? Matrimony, to a woman, is worse than excommunication in depriving her of the benefit of the law and I would rather be deprived of life. But hark you, sir, I am contented you should hold and enjoy my person by lease or patent but not by the spiritual patent called a licence, that is, to have the privileges of a husband without the dominion, that is, *durante beneplacito*; in consideration of which I will, out of my jointure, secure you an annuity of three hundred pounds a year and pay your debts, and that's all you younger brothers desire to marry a widow for, I'm sure.

FREEMAN. Well, widow, if –

JERRY. What, I hope, bully guardian, you are not making agreements without me?

FREEMAN. No, no. First, widow, you must say no more that he is the son of a whore; have a care of that. And then he must have a settled exhibition of forty pounds a year and a nag of assizes, kept by you, but not upon the common, and have free ingress, egress and regress to and from your maids' garret.

WIDOW. Well, I can grant all that too.

JERRY. Ay, ay, fair words butter no cabbage; but, guardian, make her sign, sign and seal, for otherwise, if you knew her as well as I, you would not trust her word for a farthing.

FREEMAN. I warrant thee, squire. Well, widow, since thou art so generous, I will be generous too, and if you'll secure me four hundred pound a year but during your life and pay my debts, not above a thousand pound, I'll bate you your person to dispose of as you please.

---

531 *is*: Q1 omits.

538 *durante beneplacito*: so long as one is satisfactory (term used of tenure of judges).

548 *exhibition*: gift for maintenance.

549 *nag of assizes*: a horse of good quality, as prescribed by the ordinances governing weights and measures.

WIDOW. Have a care, sir, a settlement without a consideration is void in law. You must do something for't.

FREEMAN. Prithee then, let the settlement on me be called alimony and the consideration our separation. Come, my lawyer, with writings ready drawn, is within and in haste. Come.

WIDOW. But, what, no other kind of consideration, Mr Freeman? Well, a widow, I see, is a kind of a *sine cure*, by custom of which the unconscionable incumbent enjoys the profits without any duty but does that still elsewhere.

Exeunt omnes.

SCENE III

The scene changes to Olivia's lodging.

Enter OLIVIA *with a candle in her hand.*

OLIVIA. So, I am now prepared once more for my timorous young lover's reception; my husband is gone and go thou out too, thou next interrupter of love. (*Puts out the candle*) Kind darkness that frees us lovers from scandal and bashfulness, from the censure of our gallants and the world. So, are you there?

Enter to OLIVIA, FIDELIA, *followed softly by* MANLY.

Come, my dear punctual lover, there is not such another in the world; thou hast beauty and youth to please a wife, address and wit to amuse and fool a husband; nay, thou hast all things to be wished in a lover but your fits. I hope, my dear, you won't have one tonight and, that you may not, I'll lock the door though there be no need of it but to lock out your fits, for my husband is just gone out of town again. Come, where are you? (*Goes to the door and locks it*)

MANLY. (*aside*) Well, thou hast impudence enough to

563–4 *consideration*: an action undertaken by the one who is to gain by the settlement and for which settlement is made.

give me fits too and make revenge itself impotent, hinder me from making thee yet more infamous, if it can be.

OLIVIA. Come, come, my soul, come.

FIDELIA. Presently, my dear. We have time enough sure.

OLIVIA. How! Time enough! True lovers can no more think they ever have time enough than love enough. You shall stay with me all night, but that is but a lover's moment. Come.

FIDELIA. But won't you let me give you and myself the satisfaction of telling you how I abused your husband last night?

OLIVIA. Not when you can give me and yourself too the satisfaction of abusing him again tonight. Come.

FIDELIA. Let me but tell you how your husband –

OLIVIA. O name not his or Manly's more loathsome name, if you love me. I forbid 'em last night, and you know I mentioned my husband but once and he came. No talking, pray; 'twas ominous to us. You make me fancy a noise at the door already, but I'm resolved not to be interrupted.

A noise at the door.

Where are you? Come, for rather than lose my dear expectation now, though my husband were at the door and the bloody ruffian Manly here in the room with all his awful insolence, I would give myself to this dear hand, to be led away to heavens of joy which none but thou canst give. But what's this noise at the door? So, I told you what talking would come to.

The noise at the door increases.

Ha! – O heavens, my husband's voice! – (OLIVIA *listens at the door*)

MANLY. (*aside*) Freeman is come too soon.

OLIVIA. O 'tis he! – Then here is the happiest minute lost that ever bashful boy or trifling woman fooled away! I'm undone! My husband's reconcilement too was false, as my joy, all delusion. But, come this way. Here's a back door. (*Exit and returns*) The officious jade has locked us in instead of locking others out; but let us then escape your way, by the balcony, and, whilst you pull down the curtains, I'll fetch from my closet what next will best secure our escape. I have left my key in the door and 'twill not suddenly be broke open. *Exit.*

A noise as it were people forcing the door.

MANLY. Stir not, yet fear nothing.

FIDELIA. Nothing but your life, sir.

MANLY. We shall now know this happy man she calls husband.

OLIVIA *re-enters.*

OLIVIA. O, where are you? What, idle with fear? Come, I'll tie the curtains if you will hold. Here, take this cabinet and purse, for it is thine if we escape.

MANLY *takes from her the cabinet and purse.*

Therefore let us make haste. *Exit* OLIVIA.

MANLY. 'Tis mine indeed now again and it shall never escape more from me, to you at least.

The door broken open, enter VERNISH *alone with a dark lanthorn and a sword, running at* MANLY, *who draws, puts by the thrust and defends himself, whilst* FIDELIA *runs at* VERNISH *behind.*

VERNISH. (*with a low voice*) So, there I'm right, sure –

MANLY. (*softly*) Sword and dark lanthorn, villain, are some odds, but –

VERNISH. (*with a low voice*) Odds! I'm sure I find more odds than I expected. What, has my insatiable two seconds at once? But –

Whilst they fight, OLIVIA *re-enters, tying two curtains together.*

OLIVIA. Where are you now? – What, is he entered then and are they fighting? O do not kill one that can make no defence.

MANLY *throws* VERNISH *down and disarms him.*

How! But I think he has the better on't. Here's his scarf; 'tis he. So keep him down still. I hope thou hast no hurt, my dearest? (*Embraces* MANLY)

---

69 s.d. *lanthorn*: lantern.

Enter to them FREEMAN, LORD PLAUSIBLE, NOVEL, JERRY BLACKACRE *and the* WIDOW BLACKACRE, *lighted in by the two* SAILORS *with torches.*

Ha! – What? – Manly! And have I been thus concerned for him, embracing him? And has he his jewels again too? What means this? O 'tis too sure, as well as my shame, which I'll go hide for ever!

Offers to go out; MANLY *stops her.*

MANLY. No, my dearest, after so much kindness as has passed between us, I cannot part with you yet. Freeman, let nobody stir out of the room, for, notwithstanding your lights, we are yet in the dark till this gentleman please to turn his face. – (*Pulls* VERNISH *by the sleeve*) How! Vernish! Art thou the happy man then? Thou! Thou! Speak, I say. But thy guilty silence tells me all. – Well, I shall not upbraid thee, for my wonder is striking me as dumb as thy shame has made thee. But, what? My little volunteer hurt and fainting!

FIDELIA. My wound, sir, is but a slight one, in my arm. 'Tis only my fear of your danger, sir, not yet well over.

MANLY. (*observing* FIDELIA*'s hair untied behind and without a peruke, which she lost in the scuffle*) But what's here? More strange things! What means this long woman's hair? And face, now all of it appears, too beautiful for a man? Which I still thought womanish indeed! What, you have not deceived me too, my little volunteer?

OLIVIA. (*aside*) Me she has I'm sure.

MANLY. Speak.

Enter ELIZA *and* LETTICE.

ELIZA. What, cousin, I am brought hither by your woman, I suppose, to be a witness of the second vindication of your honour?

OLIVIA. Insulting is not generous. You might spare me; I have you.

ELIZA. Have a care, cousin. You'll confess anon too much and I would not have your secrets.

MANLY. (*to* FIDELIA) Come, your blushes answer me sufficiently and you have been my volunteer in love.

FIDELIA. I must confess I needed no compulsion to follow you all the world over, which I attempted in this habit, partly out of shame to own my love to you and fear of a greater shame, your refusal of it, for I knew of your engagement to this lady and the constancy of your nature, which nothing could have altered but herself.

MANLY. Dear madam, I desired you to bring me out of confusion and you have given me more. I know not what to speak to you or how to look upon you. The sense of my rough, hard and ill usage of you, though chiefly your own fault, gives me more pain now 'tis over than you had when you suffered it; and if my heart, the refusal of such a woman (*pointing to* OLIVIA), were not a sacrifice to profane your love and a greater wrong to you than ever yet I did you, I would beg of you to receive it, though you used it as she had done, for though it deserved not from her the treatment she gave it, it does from you.

FIDELIA. Then it has had punishment sufficient from her already and needs no more from me, and, I must confess, I would not be the only cause of making you break your last night's oath to me of never parting with me, if you do not forget or repent it.

MANLY. Then, take forever my heart and this with it (*gives her the cabinet*), for 'twas given to you before and my heart was before your due. I only beg leave to dispose of these few – Here, madam, I never yet left my wench unpaid.

Takes some of the jewels and offers 'em to OLIVIA. *She strikes 'em down.*
PLAUSIBLE *and* NOVEL *take 'em up.*

OLIVIA. So it seems, by giving her the cabinet.

LORD PLAUSIBLE. These pendants appertain to your most faithful, humble servant.

NOVEL. And this locket is mine, my earnest for love, which she never paid, therefore my own again.

WIDOW. By what law, sir, pray? Cousin Olivia, a word. What, do they make a seizure on your goods and chattels, *vi et armis*? Make your demand, I say, and

---

152 *vi et armis*: by force of arms.

bring your trover, bring your trover. I'll follow the law for you.

OLIVIA. And I my revenge. *Exit* OLIVIA.

MANLY. (*to* VERNISH) But 'tis, my friend, in your consideration most that I would have returned part of your wife's portion, for 'twere hard to take all from thee, since thou hast paid so dear for't in being such a rascal. Yet thy wife is a fortune without a portion and thou art a man of that extraordinary merit in villainy, the world and fortune can never desert thee, though I do; therefore be not melancholy. Fare you well, sir.

Exit VERNISH *doggedly.*

Now, madam, I beg your pardon (*turning to* FIDELIA), for lessening the present I made you, but my heart can never be lessened. This, I confess, was too small for you before, for you deserve the Indian world and I would now go thither out of covetousness for your sake only.

FIDELIA. Your heart, sir, is a present of that value I can never make any return to't. (*Pulling* MANLY *from the company*) But I can give you back such a present as this, which I got by the loss of my father, a gentleman of the North, of no mean extraction, whose only child I was, therefore left me in the present possession of two thousand pounds a year, which I left, with multitudes of pretenders, to follow you, sir, having in several public places seen you and observed your actions throughly, with admiration, when you were too much in love to take notice of mine, which yet was but too visible. The name of my family is Grey, my other Fidelia. The rest of my story you shall know when I have fewer auditors.

MANLY. Nay, now, madam, you have taken from me all power of making you any compliment on my part, for I was going to tell you that for your sake only I would quit the unknown pleasure of a retirement and stay in this ill world of ours still, though odious to me, than give you more frights again at sea and make again too great a venture there in you alone. But if I

---

164 s.d. *doggedly*: sullenly.

should tell you now all this and that your virtue (since greater than I thought any was in this world) had now reconciled me to't, my friend here would say, 'tis your estate that has made me friends with the world.

FREEMAN. I must confess I should, for I think most of our quarrels to the world are just such as we have to a handsome woman, only because we cannot enjoy her as we would do.

MANLY. Nay, if thou art a plain-dealer too, give me thy hand, for now I'll say I am thy friend indeed. And, for your two sakes, though I have been so lately deceived in friends of both sexes,
I will believe there are now in the world
Good-natured friends who are not prostitutes,
And handsome women worthy to be friends.
Yet for my sake let no one e'er confide
In tears or oaths, in love or friend untried.

Exeunt omnes.

EPILOGUE, *spoken by the* WIDOW BLACKACRE

To you, the judges learned in stage laws,
Our poet now, by me, submits his cause,
For with young judges, such as most of you,
The men by women best their business do;
And, truth on't is, if you did not sit here,
To keep for us a term throughout the year,
We could not live by'r tongues; nay, but for you,
Our chamber-practice would be little too.
And 'tis not only the stage practiser
Who, by your meeting, gets her living here,
For, as in Hall of Westminster,
Sleek sempstress vents, amidst the courts, her ware,
So, while we bawl, and you in judgement sit,
The visor-mask sells linen too i'th'pit.
O many of your friends, besides us here,
Do live by putting off their several ware.
Here's daily done the great affair o'th'nation;

14 *visor-mask sells linen*: prostitute solicits customers.

Let love, and us then, ne'er have long vacation.
But hold; like other pleaders, I have done
Not my poor client's business, but my own.
Spare me a word then, now, for him. First know,
Squires of the long robe, he does humbly show
He has a just right in abusing you
Because he is a brother Templar too,
For, at the bar, you rally one another,
And fool, and knave, is swallowed from a brother;
If not the poet here, the Templar spare;
And maul him, when you catch him at the bar.
From you, our common modish censurers,
Your favour, not your judgement, 'tis he fears;
Of all love begs you then to rail, find fault,
For plays, like women, by the world are thought
(When you speak kindly of 'em) very naught.

---

22 *Squires . . . robe*: law students at the Inns of Court.
24 *brother Templar*: fellow member of Middle or Inner Temple.

NOTES

TEXTUAL NOTE

The Gentleman Dancing-Master

For every editor of Wycherley the greatest nightmare is Monsieur's French. It is difficult to tell how many of the disasters are Monsieur's, Wycherley's or the compositor's. As it stands, the first quarto scatters grave accents over everything with gay profusion. I have tried to modernise consistently in order to reflect what was actually heard on stage and what a modern actor would speak. Monsieur learnt his French from hearing it spoken, not from reading it, and then exaggerated it. I have therefore eliminated 's' where it is printed but not voiced in the 1670s (e.g. *teste* becomes *tête*), but I have conserved spellings that may reflect Monsieur's pronunciation (*foy* rather than *foi*). Monsieur plainly sounded all final 'e' forms and the grave accents frequently indicate that; I suspect this was over-emphasised in French and English words (*cousine*, *ventre* but also *drunke*, *speake*, etc.) but I have not put in an accent, leaving it instead for the reader to put in the sound, in a suitably ridiculous tone. The compositor's grave accents are used in one peculiar way that I have changed, that is, to indicate a genuine acute accent: *disobligeè* changes to *disobligé*. Monsieur's French is, of course, comic; I hope my modernisation has not obscured any of Wycherley's jokes.

ADDITIONAL NOTES

Love in A Wood

Dedication. John Dennis describes Wycherley's encounter with Barbara Villiers as follows: 'Upon the writing of his first play . . . he became acquainted with several of the most celebrated wits both of the court and town. The writing of that play was likewise the occasion of his becoming acquainted with one of King Charles's mistresses after a very particular manner. As Mr Wycherley was going through Pall Mall towards St James's in his chariot he met the foresaid lady in hers, who, thrusting half her body out of the chariot, cried aloud to him 'You, Wycherley, you are a son of a whore', at the same time laughing aloud and heartily. Perhaps, sir, if you never heard of this passage before, you may be surprised at so strange a greeting from one of the most beautiful and best bred ladies in the world. Mr Wycherley was certainly very much surprised at it, yet not so much but he soon apprehended it was spoke with allusion to the latter end of a song in the forementioned play.

When parents are slaves
Their brats cannot be any other.
Great wits and great braves
Have always a punk to their mother.

As, during Mr Wycherley's surprise, the chariots drove different ways, they were soon at a considerable distance from each other when Mr Wycherley, recovering from his surprise, ordered his coachman to drive back and to overtake the lady. As soon as he got over against her he said to her 'Madam, you have been pleased to bestow a title on me which generally belongs to the fortunate. Will your ladyship be at the play tonight?' 'Well', she replied, 'What if I am there?' 'Why, then I will be there to wait on your ladyship, though I disappoint a very fine woman who has made me an assignation.' 'So', said she, 'you are sure to disappoint a woman who has favoured you for one who has not.' 'Yes', he replied, 'if she who has not favoured me is the finer woman of the two. But he who will be constant to your ladyship till he can find a finer woman is sure to die your captive.' The lady blushed and bade her coachman drive away. As she was then in all her bloom and the most celebrated beauty that was then in England or perhaps that has been in England since, she was touched with the gallantry of that compliment. In short, she was that night in the first row of the King's Box in Drury Lane and Mr Wycherley in the pit under her, where he entertained her during the whole play. And this, sir, was the beginning of a correspondence between these two persons, which afterwards made a great noise in the town' (*The Critical Works*, II 409–10).

The Gentleman Dancing-Master

II i s.d. Antoine de Brunel in *A Journey into Spain* (1670) offers this description of Spanish costume: 'The Spaniards wear a cassock with deep skirts which sits very close to the body from the neck to the haunches, a black leather girdle which buckles on the breast or towards the navel; their breeches are so straight that for more easy putting them on and off they are buttoned at the sides towards the bottom; their shoes are shaped exactly to their feet, with narrow soles, and a little foot and large calf of the leg are in such request that gallants bind their feet about with riband, to their no small torment, whilst by quilted stockings they put themselves perfectly in the mode. Their silk stockings are knit very open, almost like net-work, which they stretch very straight upon white that is seen through them' (p. 57)

III i 52–4. John Downes describes Nokes's acting a French fop in a famous story: 'Our company were commanded to Dover in May, 1670, the King with ali his court meeting his sister, the Duchess of Orleans, there . . . The French court wearing then excessive short laced coats, some scarlet, some blue, with broad waist belts, Mr Nokes having at that time one shorter than the French fashion to act Sir Arthur Addle in [in John Caryll's *Sir Salomon*], the Duke of Monmouth gave Mr Nokes his sword and belt from his side and buckled it on himself on purpose to ape the French, that Mr Nokes looked more like a dressed-up ape than a Sir Arthur, which, upon his first entrance on the stage, put the King and court to an excess-ive laughter, at which the French looked very shaggrin to see them-selves aped by such a buffoon as Sir Arthur. Mr Nokes kept the Duke's sword to his dying day' (*Roscius Anglicanus* (1708), p. 29).

III i 289. Ned Ward's comments are irresistible: 'We were got amongst a parcel of lank-haired formalists, in flat-crowned hats and short cloaks, walking with as much state and gravity as a snail o'er the leaf of a cabbage, with a box of tobacco dust in one hand, the other employed in charging their nostrils, from whence it drops into their mustachoes which were always as full of snuff as a beau's wig is full of powder . . . These, my friend told me, were Spaniards' (*The London Spy*, quoted by Weales, p. 246).

The Country Wife

I i 29–30. Commentators have been unsure of the nationality of both whore and surgeon. Since Horner has been in France we could expect the whore to be French and the English–French disaster to be Horner's making love to her. But at V iv 62 Horner blames 'an English Bawd' and therefore the whore may well have been English with a French disease. As to the doctor, the 'English–French chiruregon' becomes 'a French chirurgeon' at V iv 62; however, I think the latter means an English doctor specialising in syphilis (cf. 'horse-doctor') – though in that case it is not clear why Horner has been in France at all!

I i 364. Most editors follow Q2 and later editions and read 'Go to him again', assuming that Harcourt is telling Sparkish to go back to his earl. But Q1 could mean that Harcourt is speaking to Dorilant, encouraging him to tease Sparkish further.

The Plain-Dealer

I i 548–56. Once Widow Blackacre straightens out Jerry's mistake, the case does make sense. For those who worry about such things, it concerns suit and countersuit over dispossession: 'Ayle owns Black-acre as a freeholder. John-a-Stiles dispossesses and evicts Ayle. Ayle files a claim for repossession and John-a-Stiles dies. Pere takes possession of the land and Fitz dispossesses Pere. Ayle brings an action for recovery in the *post* (because the current holder is distant from the original dispossessor) and Pere brings an action for recovery in the *per* (against the heir to the dispossessor).' Either Pere, Widow Blackacre or Wycherley is at this point making a mistake. Some editors have further confused matters by mistaking post-disseisin and entry in the *post*, which has not helped their explanations.